MEMOIRS
MUSEUM OF ANTHROPOLOGY, UNIVERSITY OF MICHIGAN
NO. 26

Temples for Cahokia Lords

Preston Holder's 1955–1956 Excavations of Kunnemann Mound

by
Timothy R. Pauketat

with contributions by
John R. Bozell
Sandra L. Dunavan

and a foreword by
John O'Shea

ANN ARBOR, MICHIGAN
1993

Printed in the United States of America
ISBN 0-915703-33-5
Cover design by Katherine Clahassey

The University of Michigan Museum of Anthropology currently publishes three monograph series: Anthropological Papers, Memoirs, and Technical Reports. We have over seventy titles in print. For a complete catalog, write to Museum of Anthropology Publications, 4009 Museums Bldg., Ann Arbor, MI 48109-1079, or call (313) 764-0485.

Library of Congress Cataloging-in-Publication Data

Pauketat, Timothy.
Temples for Cahokia Lords : Preston Holder's 1955-1956 excavations of Kunnemann Mound / by Timothy R. Pauketat ; with contributions by John R. Bozell, Sandra L. Dunavan ; and a foreword by John O'Shea.
p. cm.—(Memoirs, Museum of Anthropology, University of Michigan ; no. 26)
Includes bibliographical references.
ISBN 0-915703-33-5 (pbk. : acid-free paper)
1. Kunneman Mounds (Cahokia Site, East Saint Louis, Ill.). 2. Mississippian culture—Illinois. 3. Indians of North America—Illinois—Kings and rulers. 4. Indians of North America—Illinois—Architecture. 5. Holder, Preston, 1907- —Diaries. 6. American Bottom—antiquities. I. Bozell, John R. II. Dunavan, Sandra L. III. Title. IV. Series: Memoirs of the Museum of Anthropology, University of Michigan ; no. 26.
GN2.M52 no. 26
[E99.M6815]
306 s—dc20 93-13529
[977.3'89] CIP

The paper used in this publication meets the requirements of the ANSI Standard Z39.48-1984 (Permanence of Paper)

CONTENTS

List of Tables	*vii*
List of Figures	*ix*
List of Plates	*xi*
Foreword, *by John O'Shea*	*xiii*
Preface: Preston Holder (1907–1980)	*xv*
Acknowledgments	*xxi*
Chapter 1 INTRODUCTION	*1*
Problem Orientation	*3*
Elite Residences, Sacred Temples, and Mounds in Southeast	*3*
A Monument in Diachronic Perspective	*4*
Late Prehistoric Chronology and Settlement Patterns	*5*
Summary	*6*
Chapter 2 HISTORICAL BACKGROUND	*7*
The Kunnemann Tract Excavations of Gerard Fowke	*11*
The Mound 10/11 Tumulus in the Twentieth Century	*12*
The Mound 11 Excavations of Warren K. Moorehead	*12*
Two Episodes of Mound Borrowing	*14*
The 1955–1956 Excavations	*16*
Archaeology since 1956 in the American Bottom	*17*
Chapter 3 THE EXCAVATIONS	*21*
Features	*21*
The Moorehead Profile	*24*
Exploration Areas 1, 2, and 3	*26*
Exploration Area 1	*27*
Exploration Area 2	*31*
Exploration Area 3	*33*
The Borrow Pit Area	*36*
Feature 40 and the Amorphous Pits	*36*
The Burned Structure (Feature 3–5)	*37*
The South Mound and Prepared Surface Feature 72	*43*
Mound Fill Features 75 and 77, Prepared Surface(s) Feature 73	*49*
Mound Fill Features 79, 130, 131, 132 and Prepared Surface Feature 74	*49*
Mound Fill Features 81, 87, 114, and 129	*55*
Upper Mound Strata	*55*
Summary and Discussion	*56*
Chapter 4 CERAMICS	*71*
Method of Analysis	*71*

Kunnemann Mound Ceramics 72
Mound Fill Sherds 75
Lohmann Phase Vessels 75
Early Stirling Phase Vessels: Submound and Early Mound 77
Stirling Phase Prepared Surface Feature 72 Ceramics 79
Stirling Phase Prepared Surface Feature 73 Ceramics 80
Stirling Phase Prepared Surface Feature 74 Ceramics 81
Stirling Phase Prepared Surface Feature 93 Ceramics 81
Late Stirling Phase Vessels in EA1 82
Discussion 82
Temporal Trends 82
Possible Sacred-Elite Wares 85
Conclusions 86

Chapter 5 LITHICS 89
Expedient-Tool Industry 89
Microlithic Industry 89
Formal Chert Tools 92
Sandstone Artifacts 92
Saws and Chisels 92
Abraders 93
Miscellaneous Artifacts 95
Discussion 96

Chapter 6 MOLLUSC SHELL ARTIFACTS 99
Marine Shell Ornaments and Manufacturing Debris 99
Mussel Shell Artifacts 104
Small Snail Shells 106
Discussion 106

Chapter 7 VERTEBRATE FAUNAL REMAINS, *by John R. Bozell* 107
Introduction and Background 107
Method of Analysis 108
Unmodified Remains 108
Modified Remains 114
Discussion 119

Chapter 8 PLANT REMAINS, *by Sandra L. Dunavan* 125
Methods 125
Results 125
Wood 125
Nutshell, Seeds, Maize, and Other Botanical Remains 130
Interpretations 131

Chapter 9 WOVEN MATERIAL 135
The Feature 5 Fabric 135
The Feature 74 Impressions 135

Chapter 10 SACRED RHYTHMS AND MONUMENTAL CHANGES: INTERPRETING CRAFT, TEMPLE, AND MOUND 137
The Kunnemann Tract Residential Occupation and Craft Production 137
Human Remains 138
Craft Production 138
The F3–5 Household 140

The Kunnemann Mound Temples *140*
The Formal Qualities of Kunnemann Mound Temples *140*
Architectural Form and Function *141*
The Rhythm of Mound Construction *142*
Mound Comparisons *143*
Mound Structure and Function *144*
The Meanings of Mounds *146*
The Potential Implications of Gumbo Caps *146*
Conclusion: The Hands of Time *147*

References Cited *149*

APPENDIX I Feature Inventory *158*
APPENDIX II Ceramic Jar Attributes *161*
APPENDIX III Ceramic Beaker and Bowl Attributes *163*
APPENDIX IV Other Ceramic Vessel Attributes *164*
APPENDIX V Vessel Body Sherds *165*
APPENDIX VI Decorated Vessel Body Sherds and Miscellaneous Ceramic Artifacts *166*

TABLES

3.1 Kunnemann Mound structure attributes *23*
3.2 Kunnemann Mound hearth attributes *24*
3.3 Pit and post pit attributes *25*
4.1 Vessel orifice diameter summary data *72*
4.2 Reconstructed ceramic vessel assemblages *81*
4.3 Ceramic jar rim and lip shape indices *83*
5.1 Burlington chert artifacts *90*
5.2 Other chert artifacts *90*
5.3 Miscellaneous tools *93*
5.4 Sandstone artifacts *94*
5.5 Microlith assemblage comparison *98*
6.1 Mollusc shell artifacts *100*
6.2 Mollusc shell bead metric attributes *105*
7.1 Frequency and weight data for unmodified fauna *109*
7.2 Frequency and weight data, by analytical unit *109*
7.3 Summary of identified unmodified vertebrates *110*
7.4 Identified unmodified vertebrate remains, by analytic unit *110*
7.5 Inventory of unmodified identified vertebrate remains *111*
7.6 Frequency of modified bone and antler, by analytic unit *115*
7.7 Modified antler (cat. no. 55192) data *119*
8.1 Plant remains from Kunnemann Mound *126*
8.2 Kunnemann Mound wood *130*
8.3 Kunnemann Mound non-wood materials identified *130*
8.4 Kunnemann Mound botanical remains in the ISM collections *131*
8.5 Maize kernels from Kunnemann Mound *133*

FIGURES

1.1	Location of the Cahokia site in the American Bottom	*2*
2.1	The Cahokia site	*8*
2.2	The Kunnemann Tract Mounds 8 through 11	*10*
2.3	Moorehead's 1921 profile of the Kunnemann Mound	*13*
2.4	Leighton's 1921 profile of the Kunnemann Mound	*14*
3.1	The 1955–1956 Kunnemann Mound excavation areas	*22*
3.2	Map key	*26*
3.3	The 1955 Moorehead profile strata (view to south)	*27*
3.4	The 1955 Moorehead profile strata (view to west)	*28*
3.5	The lower section of the 1955 Moorehead profile	*29*
3.6	Exploration Area 1 composite plan	*30*
3.7	Exploration Area 1 profile at A66, B7–15	*31*
3.8	Exploration Area 1 profile at A67, B7–15	*32*
3.9	Exploration Area 1 profile at B11, A67–69.5	*33*
3.10	Exploration Area 1 profile at A69.5, B7–11	*34*
3.11	Exploration Area 3, trench 1 profile	*35*
3.12	Exploration Area 3, trench 2 profile	*37*
3.13	Borrow pit area profile of Feature 3–5	*38*
3.14	Borrow pit area submound features	*39*
3.15	Borrow pit area profile at A3, B28–39	*40*
3.16	Borrow pit area profile at A4, B28–31	*41*
3.17	Borrow pit area profile at A7, B15–19 and A6, B16–24.5	*42*
3.18	Borrow pit area profile at A9, B16–24.5 and A8, B25–37	*42*
3.19	Plan of Feature 3–5 with *in situ* artifacts and debris	*44*
3.20	Borrow pit area profile at A0, B37–42	*45*
3.21	Plan of structures associated with the south mound	*46*
3.22	Plan of the Feature 72 structure	*47*
3.23	Kunnemann Mound hearth profiles	*48*
3.24	Plan of Feature 73 structures	*50*
3.25	Borrow pit area profile at A4.5, B35–37	*51*
3.26	Borrow pit area profile at B37, A3–8	*52*
3.27	Borrow pit area profile at B40, A1–6	*53*
3.28	Plan of the Feature 74 circular structure and adjacent features	*54*
3.29	Borrow pit area profile at A8, B28–31	*56*
3.30	Plan of Feature 74 structures north of the rotunda	*57*
3.31	Borrow pit area profile (MP2) at B25, A5–19	*58*
3.32	Plan of Features 100 and 101	*59*
3.33	Reconstruction of primary Mound 11 building stages	*59*
4.1	Vessel orifice diameters	*73*
4.2	Rim profiles of jars from basal mound stages	*73*
4.3	Rim profiles of jars from upper basal mound stage Feature 87	*74*
4.4	Rim profiles of bowls and beakers	*74*

4.5 Rim profiles of bowls, beakers, and their handles *75*
4.6 Rim profiles of constricted bowls and pans *75*
4.7 Rim profiles of decorated bowls and beakers *76*
4.8 Other decorated sherds *76*
4.9 Rim profiles of Lohmann phase jars *78*
4.10 Rim profiles of seed jars *78*
4.11 Rim profiles of jugs *79*
4.12 Rim profiles of early Stirling phase jars from Feature 3–5 *79*
4.13 Rim profiles of early Stirling phase jars from Features 86 and 89 *80*
4.14 Rim profiles of ceramic funnels *80*
4.15 Rim profiles of jars from Features 9, 73, and 95 *81*
4.16 Rim profiles of late Stirling phase and miscellaneous jars *84*
4.17 Rim profiles of jars in late Stirling phase Feature 48 *84*
4.18 Temporal trends in jar rim and lip shape *86*
4.19 Vessel assemblages *87*
7.1 Polished bone or antler projectile point from borrow pit area *115*
7.2 Habitats represented by MNI of vertebrates recovered from the early Stirling phase component *120*
7.3 Deer skeletal portions represented from the early Stirling phase component *120*
7.4 Modified General Utility Indices (MGUI) values for deer remains recovered from the early Stirling phase component *121*
7.5 Comparison of identified unmodified vertebrates from select early Stirling phase components *122*
9.1 Sketch of the Feature 74 mat impressions *136*

Plates

Preston Holder and Bell Cole in the borrow pit *xvi*

2.1 The Kunnemann Mound in 1955 and 1956 *9*
2.2 Mound 11 in 1955 showing possible prehistoric dimensions *15*
2.3 Excavations in Exploration Area 1 in 1955 *18*
2.4 Borrow pit area excavations in 1956 *19*
2.5 The 1956 excavations of Mound 11 *20*
3.1 The 1955 Moorehead profile and Preston Holder *61*
3.2 Exploration Area 1 in its early stages *61*
3.3 Features 48 and 60 in Exploration Area 1 *62*
3.4 Borrow pit area submound features *63*
3.5 Submound structure Feature 3-5 during excavation *64*
3.6 Lower mound fill elements in the borrow pit area profile *64*
3.7 Feature 123 hearth and square groove *65*
3.8 Feature 74 circular structure *66*
3.9 Feature 74 hearths and wall trenches *67*
3.10 The borrow pit area profile, view to northeast *68*
3.11 The eastern extension of the Borrow Pit Area excavations *69*
4.1 Late Stirling phase Ramey Incised jar *85*
5.1 Microlithic artifacts *91*
5.2 Mill Creek chert hoe blade from Feature 3-5 *93*
5.3 Sandstone saws and chisels *95*
5.4 Type 1 sandstone abrader from Feature 46 *96*
5.5 Igneous rock celts from Feature 40 *97*
6.1 Marine shell artifacts *102*
6.2 Mollusc shell beads *103*
6.3 Mollusc shell ornaments from Feature 3-5 *104*
6.4 Mollusc shell pendants and bead blanks *105*
7.1 Bone awls *116*
7.2 Modified animal bone *117*
7.3 Cut elk or deer antler *118*
8.1 Maize cobs from early Stirling phase Feature 3-5 or Feature 89 *132*
9.1 The charred fabric on the Feature 3-5 floor *136*

FOREWORD

John O'Shea
University of Michigan

As an undergraduate at the University of Nebraska in the still new days of the New Archaeology, we were all required to read Walter Taylor's classic *A Study of Archaeology*. We often wondered among ourselves why "P. Holder" had been singled out in this landmark essay as one of the small number of coming archaeologists that had gotten it right. Holder to us was simply a somewhat eccentric anthro professor with a single tweed suit and a ponytail. Having read this monograph, I now know why his name appeared, and I know that Taylor was correct in his assessment.

The production of this monograph became a possibility in 1988 when Dr. Joyce Wike, Holder's wife, decided that the records from Kunnemann should be reunited with the archaeological collections at the University of Michigan Museum of Anthropology. John Ludwickson and Rob Bozell of the Nebraska State Historical Society acted as intermediaries in Lincoln and received the boxes of notes, photographs, drawings and scattered artifacts that Holder had maintained. These materials were then transferred to their place of permanent curation in the North American Range of the Museum of Anthropology in Ann Arbor. Tim Pauketat, then an advanced graduate student working on social and political transformations at Cahokia, accepted the challenge of bringing this manuscript into being. He did this despite the already heavy demands of completing his doctoral dissertation. I am delighted that the we are able to bring Holder's important work at Kunnemann Mound to the wider archaeological audience through this memoir.

There can be no doubt of the significance of Holder's pioneering work at Kunnemann. The careful stratigraphic and feature-oriented approach he applied to the investigation of Kunnemann Mound still stands, thirty-five years later, as one of the best documented major excavations in the Cahokia region. Equally, there can be no doubt of the importance Holder attached to his work at Kunnemann. From the time he left St. Louis, through his retirement, and up to the time of his death, he actively worked to complete a final report on the site. It is indicative of the importance Holder attached to the project that he continued, and in fact intensified, his efforts on the manuscript even after his hospitalization.

Yet, the manuscript was never completed. Many plans and drawings were produced, as was an outline for the projected manuscript and various rough fragments of chapters, but nothing that could have, even with editing, been transformed into a real report. Perhaps he, like Taylor, found making the archaeological report live up to his lofty anthropological expectations, an impossible goal. In any event, it should be clear that the present monograph is not Preston Holder's. It is based on Holder's work and records and it draws inspiration from the anthropological perspective that Holder maintained, yet, it is not the report that Holder intended to write. There are two major differences.

First, the present volume reflects the massive research and theoretical developments that have emerged since 1957 concerning the nature of Cahokia as an archaeological phenomenon and as a civil polity. Many of the core issues Holder felt obliged to defend, such as the need to view archaeological materials in an anthropological light, have been accepted. Indeed most current issues in North American archaeology, from the study of the evolution of complex societies to the applicability of theories of social action or world systems, are predicated on the assumption that archaeology can provide the basis for an anthropological understanding of the past. The present volume places Holder's Kunnemann work into this broader context of contemporary research.

The second major difference is in the description and analysis of the material culture recovered from the excavations. While Holder was the archaeologist's archaeologist when it came to stratigraphy and the recognition of cultural features, he was much more the anthropologist in his lesser concern for the material remains recovered from the excavations. The "junk" from the excavations, which was sent to Griffin's Ceramic Repository, is actually an outstanding group of well provenienced ceramic, lithic, shell, preserved textiles, floral and faunal collections. That these materials were collected at all and that they were curated with precise provenience data is again a credit to Holder's approach to field archaeology. Nevertheless, in his "Overall Design of Report," dated May 24, 1966 (papers on file, UMMA), the only mention of artifacts is in the second of two appendices, titled "Detailed List and Description of Artifacts." This perspective is similarly reflected in the final paragraph of Holder's draft Preface.

> Furthermore as one of the more active local enthusiasts said: "I don't see why you're digging that site. You're not finding anything worth taking home. I can show you a lot of sites around here where you can really find good things and get something out of all the work you're doing." True enough we found very few artifacts, and those were amazingly uniform and plain. But the structural complexities which we uncovered will give some idea of some basic patterns of thinking that went on among the people who built the site.

I think it will be clear after reading this volume that the material remains were perhaps not quite so plain or uniform as Holder maintained. Yet, despite the differences, I believe Holder would be hard pressed to find much fault with the perspectives or conclusions that appear in this volume. Albeit in somewhat different words, it represents a major step toward Holder's goal of understanding the Cahokians' "basic pattern of thinking."

Finally, this report highlights the value and potential of museum collections for the contemporary study of American archaeology. Although the excavations were conducted more than thirty years ago, the results, when appraised with a contemporary eye and current theory, yield as much, or even more, insight than would new excavations today. There simply are no more Kunnemann mounds left to excavate, and if there were, financial and political considerations might well preclude their investigation. While the potential of old collections is often overlooked by researchers and funding sources alike, the careful analysis of important and well-documented site collections, such as those from Kunnemann, may yet hold the key to many of the unresolved issues in North American archaeology.

PREFACE

*Preston Holder**
1907–1980

Preston Holder was a colorful iconoclast, a man who had little patience with accepted conventions, in both his personal and professional life. His approach to life and archaeology was exuberant and unorthodox, and he frequently exasperated his friends and colleagues. Unconventional though he was, however, his work was careful and meticulous. Kunnemann Mound, partially excavated by Holder in 1955–56, is one of the few earthen mounds at the great Mississippian center of Cahokia ever to be excavated under well-controlled conditions. Holder was solely responsible for the quality of the work done there. In fact, the information obtained from his 1955–56 excavation is of a quality that exceeds even the work of some more recent explorations at Cahokia. This book is a tribute to Preston Holder, the archaeologist. His contribution to Mississippian archaeology is an important one. Here in this preface I'd like to give a little background on Preston Holder, the man.

Preston Holder was born and raised in his mother's hometown of Wabash, Indiana, and began his undergraduate years at the University of Nebraska at Lincoln. In 1932, he went to Berkeley to complete his undergraduate degree at the University of California, and immediately fell in with an artistic, bohemian crowd. While at Berkeley, he dabbled in poetry and knew photographer Edward Weston. His strongly held political and social convictions, which would deeply influence his work, were also formed during these years. It is not known whether he actually joined the Communist Party, but his openly expressed leftwing views were reason enough for the University of California to deny him honors upon graduation in 1935, in spite of his academic brilliance.

During his Berkeley years, he developed an interest in archaeology working in Kern County, California, under William Duncan Strong, the prominent culture historian and Plains archaeologist. From California, Holder traveled to the southeastern United States. He spent a short time in Florida, then in 1936 went to Georgia to work on the WPA Federal Relief Projects. There he was instrumental in establishing the regional archaeological chronology (Williams 1968:6, 29, 101ff.). These were important formative years for him philosophically. Still a young man, and not even a graduate student, he was already developing a concern for the sociological interpretation of excavation data that would guide his Kunnemann Mound excavations years later.

*This preface was compiled based on information obtained from Leonard Blake, John Bozell, James B. Griffin, June Helm, Richard Krause, Frank Livingstone, John Ludwickson, John O'Shea, George Quimby, Elman Service, Thomas Riley, and Joyce Wike, and from the field notes, correspondence, and manuscripts of Holder and his University of Michigan contemporaries on file at the Museum of Anthropology in Ann Arbor.

Preston Holder (left) and Bell Cole in the borrow pit area of the Kunnemann Mound excavations, 1956.

Holder's graduate career began at Columbia University, where he had followed William Duncan Strong in 1938. While completing coursework, he did ethnographic research among the Arikara Indians of North Dakota. He participated in William Duncan Strong's graduate seminars that also influenced Holder's contemporaries at Columbia: Elman Service in 1950, Joyce Wike in 1951, Eleanor Leacock in 1952 (Vincent 1990:232). Already a person with a strong socialist outlook, influenced by the Marxism and functionalism of the 1930s and 1940s (he openly proclaimed himself a Marxist), Holder was also influenced by Strong's concern for ethnohistory in the anthropological study of politics (Vincent 1990:232–39). He had strong ties to the American Cultural Historical school. He spoke especially highly of Ruth Benedict.

Holder's theoretical orientation at this point in his career is revealed in an article he coauthored with Antonio J. Waring, entitled "A Prehistoric Ceremonial Complex in the Southeastern United States" (*American Anthropologist*, n.s. vol. 47). This classic piece of American archaeological literature was published in 1945, but Stephen Williams suggests that the ideas in this landmark paper had largely been formulated by 1937 (Williams 1968:6).

The year 1939 found Holder in Louisiana doing fieldwork, but this came to a sudden halt when he clashed with the law. It seems that Holder was arrested peeking into the shutters of a house in New Orlean's French Quarter. Holder maintained that he had merely been trying to listen to some classical music coming from within, but this explanation did not convince the authorities, who charged and jailed him. This may have blown over with little repercussion had not his then-wife and mother-in-law, knowing nothing of the situation, arrived for a visit. George Quimby, preeminent Eastern U.S. archaeologist who had recently arrived in New Orleans to replace Gordon R. Willey as the State Supervisor of the Louisiana State University WPA project, thought fast and told them Holder was "in the field and would be back in a few days." Quimby then raised the necessary funds and hustled them all off to Arkansas.

A brief stint in Virginia followed, excavating the Appotomax Court House in Virgina, as an archaeologist with the National Park Service. With the entrance of the United States into World War II, however, he was called into active duty for the USNR.

Though he later claimed that he and the Navy were incompatible, he also told a story about himself that showed him at least once carrying out his duties with enthusiasm—though in a characteristically unorthodox and creative way. Attaining the rank of Lieutenant Commander, he was assigned by the Office of Naval Intelligence to conduct "ethnographic field research" on the South Pacific Island of Espiritú Santo. Holder not only accomplished the ethnographic research, but found an application for it. He busied himself trying to undo the work of former missionaries, encouraging the native ex-head hunters to resume their head-hunting, pointing them in particular toward the Japanese troops occupying Espiritú Santo. When American troops later invaded the island, there was little resistance from the desparate and demoralized Japanese.

After the war, Holder's life began to drift into, what were for him, calmer, more conventional waters. He directed an American Museum of Natural History expedition to Colombia and Venezuela to study the Motilones, inhabitants of the tropical rain forest. In 1947, he became an assistant professor of Anthropology at the University of Buffalo in New York and was awarded a Ph.D. in 1950. His dissertation was entitled *The Role of Caddoan Horticulturalists in Culture History on the Great Plains*, a heavily revised version of which was published in 1970 by the University of Nebraska Press as *The Hoe and the Horse on the Plains* (see Vincent 1990:233). In 1952, Holder accepted a position as an assistant professor at Washington University in St. Louis.

It was this Washington University position that permitted Holder to embark on a series of archaeological field projects at and around the Cahokia site. While in St. Louis, he witnessed the destruction of archaeological sites by expanding urban development, and took action to mitigate some of these post World War II impacts. From 1952 to 1957, he provided the energy and leadership behind a series of salvage archaeological projects in the greater St. Louis region. These salvage projects were conducted with little or no external funding. Holder was seldom able to obtain support from the Department of Sociology/Anthropology at Washington University because most of the attention and resources of the St. Louis community were directed toward classical archaeology in the Mediterranean. A typed draft of a presentation to an unknown audience (edited only slightly for clarity), gives a little of the flavor of these projects:

> My work at the Cahokia complex was entirely that of crash-program salvage work to rescue what could be got out from under various commercial and public construction activities which were carried out with no regard to the scientific value of the materials being destroyed. The work was mainly done on weekends as time from my duties as a teacher at Washington University allowed. The University evinced little interest in the work and the delay in the publication of results not to mention the failure to follow up these important leads is directly due to this apathy. I was helped by many willing and able volunteers. The funds expended were primarily my own. But the American Philosophical Society furnished a grant of two thousand dollars which, with further grants from the University, allowed two fairly uninterrupted summer field seasons, 1955 and 1956, spent at Kunnemann Mound. Materials recovered from all of these activities [at Kunnemann Mound] were given to the Illinois State Museum—the intact and flashy pieces—and the run of the mill sherds and debris were sent to the Ceramic Repository at the University of Michigan.

With little besides personal funds to rely upon, Holder exhibited expedient creativity when confronted with salvage excavation problems in his St. Louis area projects. In the 1966 CSAS meeting paper, Holder revealed his feelings about salvage archaeology.

> The value of salvage archaeology is frequently questioned on the basis that it is difficult to design research problems under salvage conditions. I do not wholeheartedly share this attitude. Problems bring themselves to the front in any carefully executed archaeological research. They frequently turn subsequent research in a direction unanticipated by the most Olympian of planners.

Preston Holder's Kunnemann Mound excavations clearly demonstrate his concern for detail and its rewards. However, he avoided 5-×-5 foot test pits and the telephone-booth excavation mentality, better suited for the taxonomic-stratigraphic problems of an earlier era. Instead, he favored the areally extensive exposure of structural remains and living areas. To this end, Holder used mechanical excavation strategies where they proved necessary. Holder used heavy machinery (a paddlewheel) to strip off the plow-zone overburden at the Dreckshage site in St. Charles County, Missouri, during 1953. Perhaps this mechanically aided exposure of a large area was inspired by his familiarity with the methods of WPA archaeology in the Southeast during the 1930s. He was one of the first, if not the first, archaeologist in the region to employ heavy machinery in order to strip away the plow-zone overburden of a site in order to obtain the kind of spatial information valuable to studies of social organization – a practice now integral to large-scale mitigation efforts in the region (Bareis and Porter 1984).

In a paper on the Kunnemann Mound delivered in a Cahokia symposium at the Central States Anthropological Society in 1966, Holder, following a familiar Walter-Taylorian diatribe, reveals his archaeological philosophy:

> [A]rchaeology has been particularly misused over the past generation in efforts to reconstruct the culture history of the Mississippi Valley. It has been forced . . . to act as the handmaiden, on the one hand of a rather simple minded sort of taxonomy, and on the other of a falsely precise brand of Early Middle Middle Middle Late Middle Paradiddle chronology. The real point of course is to reconstruct the way of life of the indigenous peoples of this part of the world. . . . In this context it seems to me that even a bare description of our work at the Kunnemann Mound #11 remnant will be useful. [Holder 1966:2]

In an unpublished proposal concerning the Kunnemann Mound project written in 1955, Holder notes his desire to

> determine not only the formal ceramic sequences of the central valley in an effort to obtain a chronological key but perhaps even more importantly, we must get data on the larger gestalts involved: we need a wealth of knowledge regarding settlement patterns, status relations, technological traditions and patterns of labor expenditure. [Holder 1955:3]

This archaeological philosophy necessitates large-scale excavations which, while commonplace today, were not so prevalent in the 1950s. To wit, Gene Kozlovich and Frank Livingstone, University of Michigan students working at the Dreckshage site under James B. Griffin's Central Mississippi Valley Archaeological Survey, complained:

> Holder thinks he sees a house floor outline in our [test unit] profile and wants to go wild with it. I think I've spent enough time at this [Dreckshage] site, but will sort of work along with him on it. Every time we put in a sq. [square] he wants to make a major production out of it and he keeps saying "I know you don't have the time to do archaeology, but God! I'd love to dig this site!!" [letter from Kozlovich to Griffin, July 8, 1953, UMMA files]

Under Holder's direction, an entire structure featuring multiple wall trenches and burned *in situ* structural elements was eventually exposed in the area of the former test unit using the heavy machinery.

Holder personally directed the salvage excavation of at least six locations at and around the Cahokia site in the greater St. Louis vicinity from 1952 to 1956 (see Holder and Stewart 1958; Milner 1984c:480–81) and assisted in a number of others (Leonard Blake, pers.

comm.; Tarr 1955). The final project, his largest and perhaps finest undertaking in the region, was the Kunnemann Mound excavation (Holder 1957, 1966, 1980). His Cahokia research, however, was cut short when in 1957 he suddenly left Washington University and took an assignment with the Bureau of Indian Affairs in Washington state, working on an Indian reservation. Later in 1958 he accepted a position at the University of Nebraska, where he served as Chair of the Department of Anthropology and administered archaeological projects in Kansas, Nebraska and South Dakota. He remained at the University of Nebraska until his retirement in 1973.

This volume presents but one of Holder's important research projects, one which he guarded over the years and was actively engaged in preparing for publication at the time of his death. The notes upon which this volume are based were transmitted to the Museum of Anthropology at the University of Michigan by his widow, Joyce Wike, in 1988. Here they were reunited with the Kunnemann Mound materials, most of which Holder had sent to Dr. James B. Griffin in 1957 when he left his position at Washington University.* The lure of these data was irresistible, and I accepted the task of seeing the project to published fruition. With the support of the Great Lakes Division of the Museum of Anthropology and its curator John O'Shea, this volume was compiled.

The credit for the quality of the information contained within this volume is due entirely to Preston Holder's professional dedication, archaeological expertise, and energetic pursuit of what is today called "anthropological archaeology." He was one of a special breed of archaeologists who performed field research in both archaeology and ethnology.

He had been a poet, a philosopher, and remained a political activist from his undergraduate years at Berkeley during the Great Depression of the 1930s to the Vietnam War years at the University of Nebraska. As an archaeologist, his unconventional attitudes and behaviors proved bothersome to some coworkers. Kozlovich complained: "Holder got us up at *4:00 A.M.* to go out and dig this damn spot—The guy's crazy!" (letter from Kozlovich to Griffin regarding the Booker T. Washington site, July 8, 1953, UMMA files). At Cahokia, he clashed with the local artifact collectors who had more conservative and rigid political and sexual standards.

The flip side of his controversial, iconoclastic personality was his "uncanny ability to attract people of all classes and conditions and to obtain their cooperation" (Leonard Blake, pers. comm.). Most of his field research in the St. Louis area was performed with the aid of volunteer excavators. At Dreckshage, for instance, he recruited two nuns and their students from a nearby Catholic girl's school to excavate an extended human burial. He later persuaded an engineer associated with nearby ongoing highway construction to allow a dozer operator to "cut the area . . . in thin layers" in order to expose the floor plan of that late prehistoric structure mentioned earlier (UMMA 1953). During the excavation of the Kunnemann Mound, two boys, eleven and twelve, showed up and wanted to work: "OK" he noted in his daily journal.

Indeed, Preston Holder was genuinely concerned with people and with social phenomena. There were, and are, few individuals like him. His contribution to American Anthropology was multi-dimensional. His mark has been left, in indelible ink. It is a mark of sweat, devotion, and poetry.

Timothy R. Pauketat
January 1993

*At the University of Michigan, this collection was organized by then graduate students Dan F. Morse and Phyllis Morse. This collection served as Dan Morse's inspiration in defining the Cahokia microlithic industry (later published by Mason and Perino 1961; see Perino 1960) and the Big Lake microlithic industry in Arkansas (Morse 1974).

ACKNOWLEDGEMENTS

Preston Holder was working on a Kunnemann Mound manuscript at the time of his death in 1980 and, unfortunately, it is not now possible to acknowledge the individuals that he would have wished to credit in the report. Among these individuals no doubt would have been fellow anthropologists, friends, students, volunteers during the 1955–1956 field work, and his wife, Joyce Wike. In the absence of Preston's own acknowledgements, a sadly incomplete account of the individuals and institutions which contributed to the completion of the present manuscript is offered here.

Foremost among those individuals to be noted here is Joyce Wike, who passed along the torch of Preston's original field records to the University of Michigan Museum of Anthropology (UMMA) in Ann Arbor. John O'Shea at the Museum of Anthropology is to be credited with actually reuniting these archives with the artifactual materials in Ann Arbor. John has carried much of the burden of bringing this volume to fruition. He has served tirelessly as negotiator, planner, and manager, seeing the analyses and volume preparation through from this volume's inception in 1987 to its present published form. John Ludwickson of the Nebraska State Historical Society proved an invaluable aid in the transfer and initial organization of the Kunnemann Mound archives.

The Museum of Anthropology and the Department of Anthropology at the University of Michigan provided direct and indirect financial support for this project, all of which is greatly appreciated. At the Museum of Anthropology, Kay Clahassey prepared nearly all of the maps, diagrams, rim profiles, and photographs contained in this volume; her skills and diligence are really quite remarkable. Sally Horvath provided the patient guidance which marks a truly professional editor. The advice of and discussions with Henry T. Wright and Richard I. Ford concerning the Kunnemann Mound and other related topics have had a positive influence on me and on the content of this volume. In addition, John Kelly and Thomas Emerson provided valuable comments on an earlier draft of this manuscript.

I'd like to express gratitude to Terrance Martin and the Illinois State Museum (ISM) for permitting access to the collections curated there. Likewise, I thank William Iseminger of the Cahokia Mounds Interpretive Center for providing information on the Kunnemann and Wilson Mound artifacts on display there. David Kennedy organized and cared for the photographic and paper archives of Preston Holder at the UMMA, a task which archaeologists still too often take for granted or ignore altogether.

The contributors to this volume, Sandra L. Dunavan of the Museum of Anthropology at the University of Michigan, and John R. Bozell of the Nebraska State Historical Society, performed their tasks for the sake of knowledge itself. Holder undoubtedly would have thanked both graciously. In the same vein, he probably would have recognized the debt owed to our families for their continued emotional support and failure to admonish our zealotry as we blissfully engage other worlds, sometimes oblivious to our own. Thanks Stephanie.

Chapter 1

Introduction

Sedentary or semi-sedentary communities of Native American horticulturalists had existed in the Mississippi River floodplain for centuries prior to the end of the first millennium A.D. However, between about A.D. 800 and 1000, community life in the central Mississippi valley underwent significant changes. In one portion of the Mississippi River floodplain, called the American Bottom (Fig. 1.1), these "Emergent Mississippian" communities seem to have been made up of hierarchically ranked social groups farming both native cultigens and the newly adopted maize crop (Kelly 1990a). Large multihousehold communities and smaller single-family farmsteads were scattered across the bottom. In the largest communities probably resided the local chiefly officials (see Emerson and Jackson 1984; Kelly 1980, 1990a; Kelly et al. 1984, 1990; McElrath and Finney 1987; Milner 1984b, 1990; Stahl 1985).

From this traditional base, an even more dramatic social transformation occurred subsequent to A.D. 1000. At that time, the largest and perhaps most complex of all the so called Mississippian polities is evident in the archaeological record of the American Bottom (Pauketat 1991). This polity was centered at the site of Cahokia, the seat of regional political authority for much of the period between A.D. 1000 and 1300. Cultural and political ripples eminated from Cahokia and altered in some ways the lifestyles of many native groups in the American midcontinent (see Emerson and Lewis 1991).

The site itself was immense, perhaps covering up to 15 km^2. It contained large residential areas and elaborate special-purpose facilities, including around 100 earthen mounds (Fowler 1975, 1977, 1989; Kelly 1990b; Milner 1990; Pauketat 1991). The magnitude of the Cahokia site and its earthen monuments astounded an early nineteenth-century traveler through the Illinois country, Henry Brackenridge. He wrote:

> When I reached the foot of the principal mound, I was struck with a degree of astonishment. . . . What a stupendous pile of earth! . . . I every where observed a great number of small elevations of earth, to the height of a few feet, at regular distances from each other, and which appeared to observe some order; near them I also observed pieces of flint, and fragments of earthen vessels. I concluded, that a very populous town had once existed here, similar to those of Mexico. . . . [Brackenridge 1814:187–88]

The reasons for the prehistoric development of a "populous town" in the Mississippi Valley have remained a topic of concern to researchers since Brackenridge wrote these lines. Archaeologists have solid leads concerning the gross developmental trajectory of the social and political phenomenon of the American Bottom during late prehistory (see Emerson 1991; Kelly 1990a; Milner 1990; Pauketat 1991), but the cultural and chronological relationships of the archaeological features at Cahokia itself and the details of the development remain poorly understood.

When and how, for instance, the monumental architecture was constructed, who occupied or maintained the resulting monument, and the relationship of those in charge of the monument with the surrounding community are basic bits of information largely lacking in American Bottom archaeology. There is no lack of excavated data from Cahokia. Extensive excavations were conducted at Cahokia in the 1960s, and other significant investigations were conducted in the decades prior to and after the 1960s. These investigations, however, have, for the most part, remained unreported and, thus, the groundwork necessary for guiding advanced research programs for the most part remains unlaid.

This volume presents an analysis of the extant records and materials from Preston Holder's 1955–1956 excavation of one of these archaeological features, the Kunnemann Mound, number 10 and 11 of the Cahokia group (Fowler 1989:70–72). The Kunnemann Mound is one of the few Cahokia tumuli for which an adequate understanding of its temporal affiliation and political-religious significance can be established. As the analysis of the Kunnemann Mound will demonstrate, there is more to an earthen Mississippian mound than meets the eye. This tumulus, and others at Cahokia and in the larger American Bottom region, con-

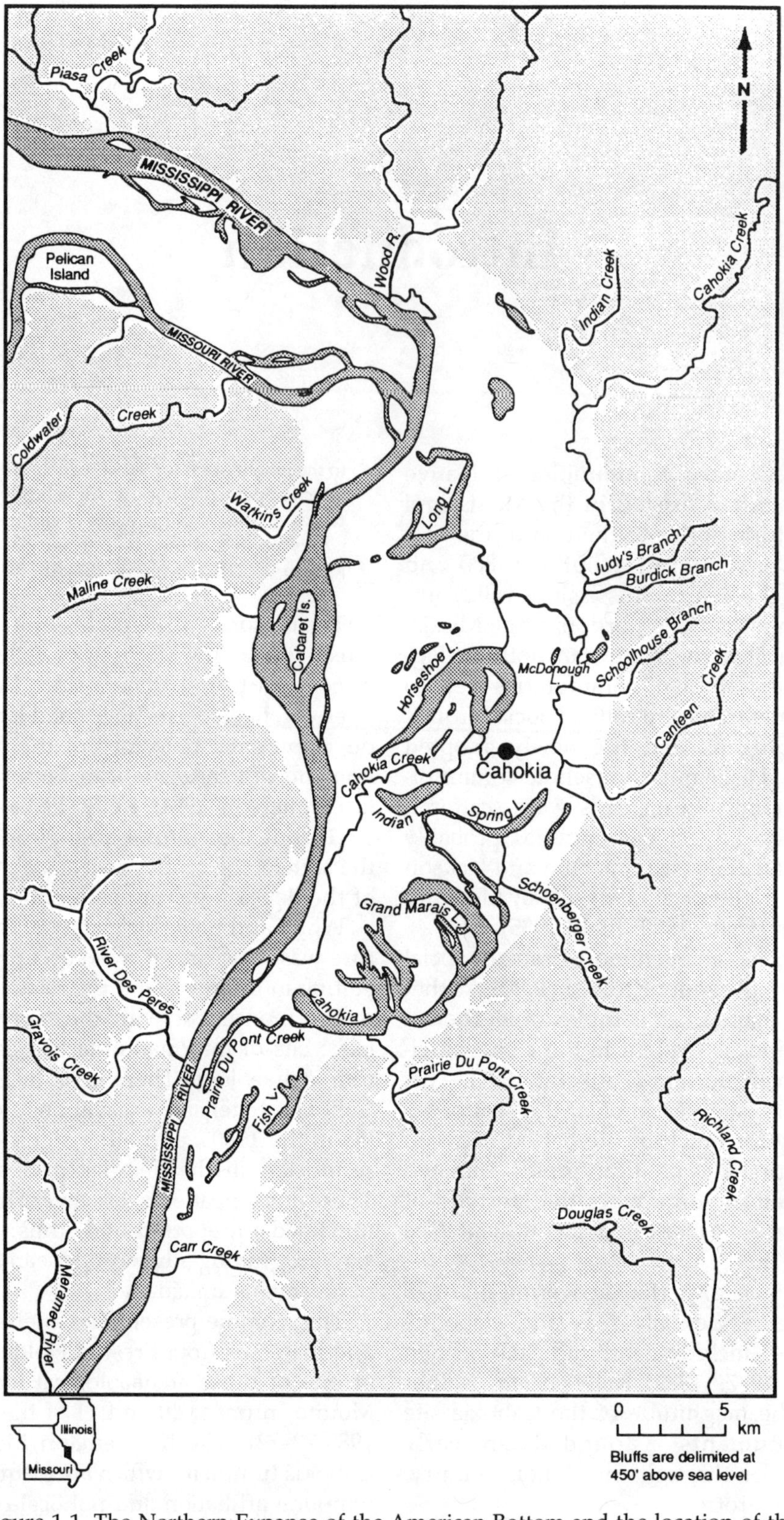

Figure 1.1. The Northern Expanse of the American Bottom and the location of the Cahokia site.

tains unique archaeological information of unreproducible sociological importance.

Problem Orientation

The sociological implications of the Cahokia mounds were the subject of conjecture as early as Brackenridge's observations.

> The mounds were sites of temples, or monuments to the great men. . . . Amongst a numerous population, the power of the chief must necessarily be more absolute, and where there are no laws, degenerates into despotism [Brackenridge 1814:188]

The relationship of these earthen monuments to the surrounding Cahokia community appears to have been at the fore of Preston Holder's thoughts when he outlined the following problem orientation for his work with the Kunnemann Mound:

> They built tumuli, mainly as the foundation for ceremonial buildings. . . . [B]ut except for the occasional study . . . there has been little effort to delineate just what is meant by ceremonial. . . . [T]he structural complexities which we uncovered will give some idea of some basic patterns of thinking that went on among the people who built the site [of Cahokia]. [Holder 1980]

Ethnohistorical and archaeological studies have warranted the logical bridge that the "basic patterns of thinking" of Holder's Cahokians—the essence of "what is meant by ceremonial"—intimately involved the social elite (Holder 1968:77; e.g., Brown 1976, 1985; DePratter 1983; Knight 1986; papers in Barker and Pauketat 1992; Galloway 1989). The elite and the ceremonial in fact were inseparable. The main focus of this volume is the elucidation of this elite-sacred relationship. This focus guides us first to examine the composition of the mound and the configuration of buildings and temples on its summit. Second, it becomes necessary to probe for the cultural meanings of mound and mound-top usage. A consequence of such examination and interpretation is a step toward obtaining "some idea" of the Cahokians' basic patterns of thinking.

Elite Residences, Sacred Temples, and Mounds in the North American Southeast

Numerous accounts of early European explorers of the Southeast describe in detail the important residences and community buildings of Native American towns (see Black 1967:493–514; DePratter 1983:111–53; Swanton 1911:158–74; 1979 [1946]:388–420, 613–19). DePratter (1983:128) has summarized a number of salient features of Southeastern temples. The temple, through elite mediators,

> functioned in ceremonies relating to the preparation for war, the negotiation of peace, the display of war trophies, the blessing of seeds, the blessing of first fruits, and the making of rain. [DePratter 1983:143]

The temple and its contents, it seems, were symbols of the political-religious authority of the native lords, an authority embedded within a sense of community and venerated through the close association with elite ancestors and powerful symbols of the cosmos (Brown 1975; DePratter 1983:142; Knight 1989; Schnell, Knight and Schnell 1981: 143–45; Waring 1968:58–62; Willoughby 1932).

Temples contained the bones of the elite dead and, in many cases, a wealth of other material objects. Ornaments (made from pearls, marine shell, or feathers), animal pelts, weaponry, and other sumptuary regalia were common features of this mortuary temple complex as were wooden "giants" or stone and wooden statues thought to be images of the dead ancestors (Brown 1985:104–6; DePratter 1983:134–35; Knight 1986:679; Swanton 1911; Willoughby 1932:27–33). The sacred fire, a central point of articulation between the powers of earth and sky, burned inside the temple (DePratter 1983:134; Waring 1968). This fire, along with the temple and the mound, was closely guarded, kept pure, and maintained without interruption. Annual renewal of these features ritually reaffirmed their purity and sanctity (see Waring 1968:57; Knight 1986:678–79, 1989:285).

The domiciles of chiefly title-holders, community houses, and sacred temples maintained by elite individuals often stood atop earthen platforms. For instance, in the chronicles of the De Soto expedition, we read passages like the following:

> From a distance the habitations of the lord appeared because they were situated in the highest place, and they revealed themselves to be his by a size and construction superior to the others. [Varner and Varner 1988:314]
>
> [I]t is the custom of the Caciques to have near their houses a high hill, made by hand, some having the houses placed thereon . . . [Bourne 1904, Vol. II:27–28]
>
> [T]his house of worship was on a high mound and much revered. The *caney*, or house of the chief, was very large, high and broad, all decorated above and below with very fine handsome mats, arranged so skilfully [*sic*] that all these mats appeared to be a single one . . . [Bourne 1904, Vol. II:101–2]
>
> The Chief's house stood near the beach, upon a very high mount made by hand for defence [sic]; at the other end of the town was a temple [Bourne 1904, Vol. I:23]

These high places were constructed "with the strength of their arms, piling up very large quantities of earth and stamping on it . . ." (Varner and Varner 1988:170–71). As noted by Garcilaso de la Vega (Varner and Varner 1988), the buildings atop these mounds were "superior to" ordinary domiciles. They included elite residential structures, town houses, and mortuary temples, these three forms not necessarily being mutually exclusive (Schnell, Knight and Schnell 1981:135–45; Waring 1968:55–56).

Because of the diversity of architecture and activities which are found on tops of Mississippian flat-topped mounds, Knight (1989:285) contends that "the symbolism of mound-building ritual and of the mound as an icon may be viewed as analytically independent of the wide variety of summit uses, whether sacred or secular. . . ." Waring (1968:57–58) and Knight (1986, 1989) understand the construction of mounds as an aspect of annual communal purification rites. Adding mantles of earth to extant mounds was a part of restoring the order and balance of the world, just as the sacred hearth would have been cleaned out or the temples swept and repainted (e.g., Adair 1775:100–101). By means of an examination of historic Southeastern mythical and lexical elements, Knight proposes that the mound itself "may be interpreted as an expression of a broad-based communal cult type, oriented to earth, fertility, and purification" (Knight 1989:287). It symbolized the "world" or, more specifically, the center or navel of the world possessing "symbolic associations with autochthony, the underworld, birth, fertility, death, burial, the placation of spirits, emergence, purification, and supernatural protection" (Knight 1989:283). He continues:

> The "earth island" as a cosmological entity among the southeastern Indians was normally conceived as flat-surfaced and as manifesting four world directions. A Muskogee source conceives of the earth as both flat and square, dropping off on four sides. The quadrilaterality and flat-topped configuration of most Mississippian mounds may express this image concretely in an appropriate medium, earth. [Knight 1989:287]

A Monument in Diachronic Perspective

The descriptions of elite domiciles and temples atop earthen platforms among the chiefdoms of the Southeast provide a jumping off point for the problems which may be addressed from an archaeological investigation of the Kunnemann Mound. An archaeological sequence of mound construction, along with the evidence of the maintenance and reconstruction of mound-related architectural facilities, provides the critical temporal dimension necessary for understanding the general sacred-temple theme of the Native American Southeast (sensu DePratter 1983) in the context of a dynamic political economy–namely that of Cahokia within the period of A.D. 1000–1300.

The late-prehistoric political economy of the American Bottom undoubtedly revolved around the means by which the elite legitimized and reproduced (and in the process transformed) their own social positions (Pauketat 1991). As social hierarchy and authority are symbolic structures of dominance, the means by which legitimacy was conferred would have involved the control of symbols (see Kertzer 1988). All things distant–both geographically and temporally–would have had powerful meanings because these require explanation in nonsocial, cosmogonic or cosmographic terms (Helms 1988, 1992). The sanctity of the temple would have derived from the consolidation of the temporally distant power of the ancestors with the geographically distant power of exotic objects and knowledge not available to the masses. Even the chiefly aristocracies of the Southeast, as social classes distinct from the nonelite masses, were considered sacred.

However, what was sacred to a commoner was competition to another aristocrat (see Earle 1987; Wright 1984). Elites competed to control the symbols of authority and thereby perpetuate the symbolic hegemony that was integral to Mississippian culture (see Pauketat 1991). Material items of legitimation, prestigious objects, exotic goods, or other symbols of contacts beyond the community were sources of political power by virtue of their symbolic meanings and utility in social display and transactions (Brown et al. 1990; Helms 1979, 1991).

> The production, display, and distribution of wealth are politically important activities because they are the means by which rulers define their own social statuses and the statuses of others, with all the rights and obligations adhering thereto. [Brumfiel and Earle 1987:4]

> [T]here are . . . a great many societies in which the control over certain kinds of valuables is in itself a source of prestige and power. . . . [C]ontrol over 'elite' goods that circulate over wide areas is the basis of political-economic power because such goods are necessary for the marriage and other obligatory payments of all groups. In this way the prestige goods accumulated through long distance contacts are converted directly into control over labour. [Friedman and Rowlands 1978:214]

> [L]uxury and ceremonial items . . . reinforce ritual superiority since the enormous royal accumulation of wealth is proof of the supernatural effectiveness of the ruler. [Friedman and Rowlands 1978:222]

The local production of craft goods would have provided a chiefly title-holder with the prestige goods necessary for social exchanges. This is especially true where control could have been exercized over production. That is, the centralization of craft production, the attachment of craft producers to chiefly patrons, and the sanctification of the craft itself are logical concomitants of the legitimation of chiefly office (Brumfiel and Earle 1987:7–9; Friedman and Rowlands 1978:219).

Craft production, mound building, temple maintenance, and the ceremonies surrounding the monument all were symbolic acts involving the "basic patterns of thinking" to which Holder referred. Delineating the internal structure of the Kunnemann Mound–the size, configuration, and constitution of its accretionary components–and the architectural facilities which the mound supported provides a means of broaching these basic patterns of thinking. The Kunnemann Mound data provide a glimpse of the architecture and artifacts of the living Cahokia elite, rather than merely their mortuary facilities (cf. Fowler 1991; Fowler and Anderson 1975; Milner 1984c; Kelly n.d.). Here, archaeologically transformed, are the residues of living. These residues include the facilities and materials of the elite occupants or caretakers of the mounds, the houses or temples beside and atop the platform, and the very structure of the mound itself.

The examination of residential features below or adjacent to the Kunnemann platform will contribute significant information on the problem of craft production at Cahokia. The degree of production centralization at Cahokia remains an open question (cf. Muller 1984, 1986, 1987:17; Yerkes 1983, 1986, 1989, 1991). Either in living debris or in the residual elements of temple ornamentation, we might expect to begin to solve the mystery of the relationship of the craft, the artisan, and the elite. Likewise, these same residential features will provide information on the diet of the Kunnemann Tract inhabitants. What these people ate may well be related to their craft, as this is suspected to be a function of their elite status or affiliation with or attachment to elite patrons.

The temporal series of artifacts and features located on the mound allow us not simply to affirm an ethnohistoric pattern of elite residences or sacred temples but to explore the unique qualities of a Cahokia monument. We need not adhere strictly to Southeastern analogs, but they do provide a standard to begin investigating the "basic patterns of thinking" as represented in the Kunnemann Mound. Moreover, the sequence of mound-top features as well as the strata themselves provide a guide of potential significance to the intrapolity changes in these basic Cahokia-Mississippian patterns of thinking. That is, changes in the manner in which the mound was constructed or, as Holder would have said, the "rhythm" of construction may be of significance for understanding region-wide political-religious changes in the late prehistoric American Bottom. With this in mind, it is useful to place the Kunnemann Mound within a regional developmental framework.

Late Prehistoric Chronology and Settlement Patterns

Our present concern with the Kunnemann Mound means that we work within a relatively brief span of, at most, two centuries. As it happens, this span—about A.D. 1000 to 1200—conforms to that portion of the Mississippi Period during which the American Bottom political centers appear to have exerted maximum control over the surrounding Native American population, if present measures of site size and distribution are at all reliable (see Esarey and Pauketat 1992; Fowler and Hall 1978; Milner 1990). The Mississippi Period in the American Bottom has been dated to the period A.D. 1000 to 1400 (Milner et al. 1984; cf. Smith 1986; Steponaitis 1986), although recent archaeological field work has made it increasingly likely that the last century of this span also witnessed the beginning of a Bold Counselor Oneota occupation, which in subsequent Oneota guises lasted into the protohistoric period (Jackson 1992).

Gross changes in vessel morphology, ceramic paste, and vessel surface treatment have served as the basis of the regional Mississippian chronology since A.R. Kelly (1933), Titterington (1938), and Griffin (1941, 1949) defined a bipartite Mississippian sequence at Cahokia. The ceramic chronology was refined by Vogel (1975), Hall (1966), and O'Brien (1972) leading up to the Cahokia Ceramic Conference (Fowler and Hall 1975). Recent revisions to the cultural sequence have been made by Kelly (1980) and by the FAI-270 highway mitigation project (Kelly et al. 1984; Milner et al. 1984). This project, coordinated by the University of Illinois, involved the excavation of a number of late prehistoric sites in the American Bottom and has greatly expanded the archaeological data base of the region (Bareis and Porter 1984).

Within the American Bottom in the vicinity of the Cahokia site (Fig. 1.1), the Mississippi Period has been subdivided into four principal phases. The Lohmann phase (A.D. 1000–1050) originally was part of the "Fairmount" phase prior to Kelly's (1980) initial revision of the 1972 Cahokia Ceramic Conference chronology (see Fowler and Hall 1975). The Lohmann site, a Mississippian center just to the south of Cahokia (Esarey and Pauketat 1992), provided the basis for the definition of this phase (Milner et al. 1984). Since then, a Lindhorst variant of the Lohmann phase, in the vicinity of the Lunsford-Pulcher site (Kelly 1990a, 1991b), has been recognized.

Most Lohmann phase sites outside of Cahokia and smaller religious-administrative centers appear to have been homesteads where one to a few households obtained a livelihood (see Emerson 1992; Mehrer 1988:108–13; Milner 1986; Milner et al. 1984; Pauketat 1989). At the Cahokia site, the Lohmann phase residential occupation appears to have been the most dense of the Mississippi Period (Collins 1990; Pauketat 1991).

> There is a strong indication that in its layout the . . . Lohmann community conforms to a generally linear north-south pattern. . . . It is difficult to escape the conclusion that the development of the Cahokia site during the Lohmann phase, including residential development, was planned by a central authority. [Collins 1990:230]

The subsequent Stirling phase (A.D. 1050–1150) conforms to the classic "pure Village" (A.R. Kelly 1933) or "Old Village" (Griffin 1941, 1949; Titterington 1938) complex which was so readily apparent based even on the relatively meager samples of material culture available to these pioneer Cahokia researchers. The Stirling phase is recognized region-wide; its outstanding material components are found throughout the midcontinent (Kelly 1991a, 1991b). Like the rural Lohmann phase settlement pattern,

> Stirling phase features were scattered along the slopes and crests of the bottomland ridges in spatially discrete groups consisting of one, or occasionally more, structures with their internal and external features, mostly pits, situated nearby. [Milner et al. 1984:173]

The structures in the largest of these feature groups probably included rectangular domiciles, storage houses, and circular sweat lodges. Paired rectangular structures often seem apparent. These domiciles may have been used seasonally.

In the rural American Bottom immediately surrounding the Mississippian centers, the mode of farming and living appears to have changed little from the Lohmann phase, although there are certain trends in the degree of land reuse and "neighborhood" development which have been identified (cf. Emerson 1992; Mehrer 1988). At Cahokia, elite architecture and constructions seem literally to have reached monumental proportions during the Stirling phase (Pauketat 1991, 1992). Of the residential occupation, Collins (1990: 230) notes:

> After its initial establishment, the Early Stirling community was characterized by considerable spatial continuity. . . . Stirling feature clusters appear to be oriented around . . . [a] plaza area. . . . During the Late Stirling sub-phase . . . the distribution and orientation of feature clusters appears to have been related to the development of a local mound/plaza complex. . . .

By the Moorehead phase (A.D. 1150–1250), the region seems to have witnessed a political-economic contraction (Collins 1990:230; Milner 1990:30–31; Pauketat 1991:242–47). Residential occupation returns to portions of Cahokia which previously had been put to elite nonresidential uses. Population levels appear to have declined both at the site of Cahokia and in the hinterlands (see Collins 1990; Mehrer 1988; Mehrer and Collins 1989; Milner 1986, 1990; Pauketat 1991). Craft items or sumptuary goods that in decades past were probably reserved for elite personages appear, by the Moorehead phase, to have been accessible to nonelites. The ceramic tradition also is suspected to reflect broad-scale changes in the basal organizational units of American Bottom society.

Not much archaeological evidence is available from the final Mississippian Sand Prairie phase (A.D. 1250–1400). What does exist supports the interpretation of the virtual disappearance of the formal political hierarchy of the earlier Mississippian world and the continued depopulation of the region (see Fowler 1975:100; Fowler and Hall 1978:566; Milner 1984c:485, 1986:234, 1990:30–31).

Summary

The regional consolidation of chiefly authority in the American Bottom seems to have resulted in the aggrandizement of Cahokia, one aspect of which was the construction and maintenance of monuments. Earthen mounds were the "sites of temples" (Brackenridge 1814:188), foundations for "ceremonial buildings" (Holder 1980) and elite domiciles. The mounds and the buildings on their summits possessed sacred qualities and were the domain of the elite.

What occurred on and around the mounds, then, and the manner in which the earthen monument took form over a period of time may be used to address diachronic issues surrounding political, economic, and religious developments at Cahokia. Specifically, the issues of craft production centralization and subsidization, and change in the basic Cahokia-Mississippian patterns of thinking—the meanings of monuments—may inform us about order and authority in this late prehistoric Native American context.

CHAPTER 2

Historical Background

The Kunnemann Mound (nos. 10 and 11) is one of a group of six mounds (nos. 6 through 12) arranged along a linear, east-west trending ridge (126 meters a.s.l) which delimit the northern edge of the Cahokia site. This ridge upon which the mound rests was formed as a point bar along the southern inner bank of an ancient oxbow of the Mississippi River, locally called the Edelhardt meander. During the Mississippian occupation of the Cahokia site, the ridge demarcated the northern border of the oxbow floodplain of the meandering channel of Cahokia Creek (Fig. 2.1).

These six mounds and the surrounding ridge at Cahokia have been referred to as the "Kunnemann Tract" (Fowler 1989:68–72; Woods and Holley 1989:229). It is this Kunnemann Tract which has been recognized as a possible shell bead-making workshop at Cahokia, providing the tantalizing hints of craft specialization at Cahokia (Yerkes 1983, 1991). Further hint of craft production in this area is suggested by the cache of unfinished "megalithic" celts reportedly recovered from Mound 12 (Fowler 1989:72; see Esarey and Pauketat 1992).

> There is a low mound on Mr. Merrell's land some 300 yds. due west from Kunnemann's sites. At the present time this is not over one or two ft. in elevation. Mr. Seever informs me that large numbers of unfinished celts, many of them of considerable size, were here discovered and that he secured and distributed something like 100 of these objects the past twenty-five years. [Moorehead 1922:31]

In his 1923 report, Moorehead adds that "Mr. Seever obtained a number of these for the Missouri Historical Society collection years ago" (Moorehead 1923:45). Titterington (1938:7) says of the same cache:

> There is a small mound about 1/4 of a mile north of Monks Mound from which a large number of unfinished celts were taken about 30 or 40 years ago. All were pecked out into a fairly good shape except for some on which the bit had not been formed. The largest weighted about 25 pounds.

Without a doubt, the artifact assemblage from the Kunnemann Tract stands out even at the Cahokia site. Interestingly, however, the lithic and shell artifacts—possible craft-good residues—found scattered across the surface of Mounds 6 through 12 have received little attention. This no doubt is due to the uncertainty in the past of the relationship between the Kunnemann Tract artifactual refuse and the mounds themselves. However, including the celt cache from Mound 12, information directly relevant to this empirical uncertainty does exist from four of the seven Kunnemann Tract mounds.

The present focus, of course, is on the principal mound, a single massive tumulus having a lower terrace labeled Mound 10 and an upper circular terrace or conical peak called Mound 11 (Plate 2.1). It is of interest that Fowler suggests (1989:68–70), based primarily on the plan map of the Cahokia site produced by John J. R. Patrick around 1876, that the four smaller mounds to the east of Mound 10/11 may have been arranged in a paired configuration similar to Mound 10/11.

> Mound 6 is associated with Mound 7, to its west. Patrick's map indicates that Mound 6 was conical in shape, whereas Mound 7 is apparently a rectangular platform mound. [Fowler 1989:68]

> On the Patrick Map, Mound 8 is indicated as a large, oval mound with a flat top. It is very close to Mound 7, but it seems to be connected by a small platform to Mound 9, thus bearing the same relationship to Mound 9 that Mound 7 bears to Mound 6. [Fowler 1989:70]

It remains possible that Patrick mistook the natural point-bar feature underlying the mounds as artificial connecting platforms (Fowler 1989:70). However, if Patrick's map of Mounds 6–9 is accurate, then the Kunnemann Tract mounds may represent a unique set of features distinct as a set from other mound groups at the Cahokia site. Preston Holder's topographic map of Mounds 7–11, made in 1955, is presented in Figure 2.2.

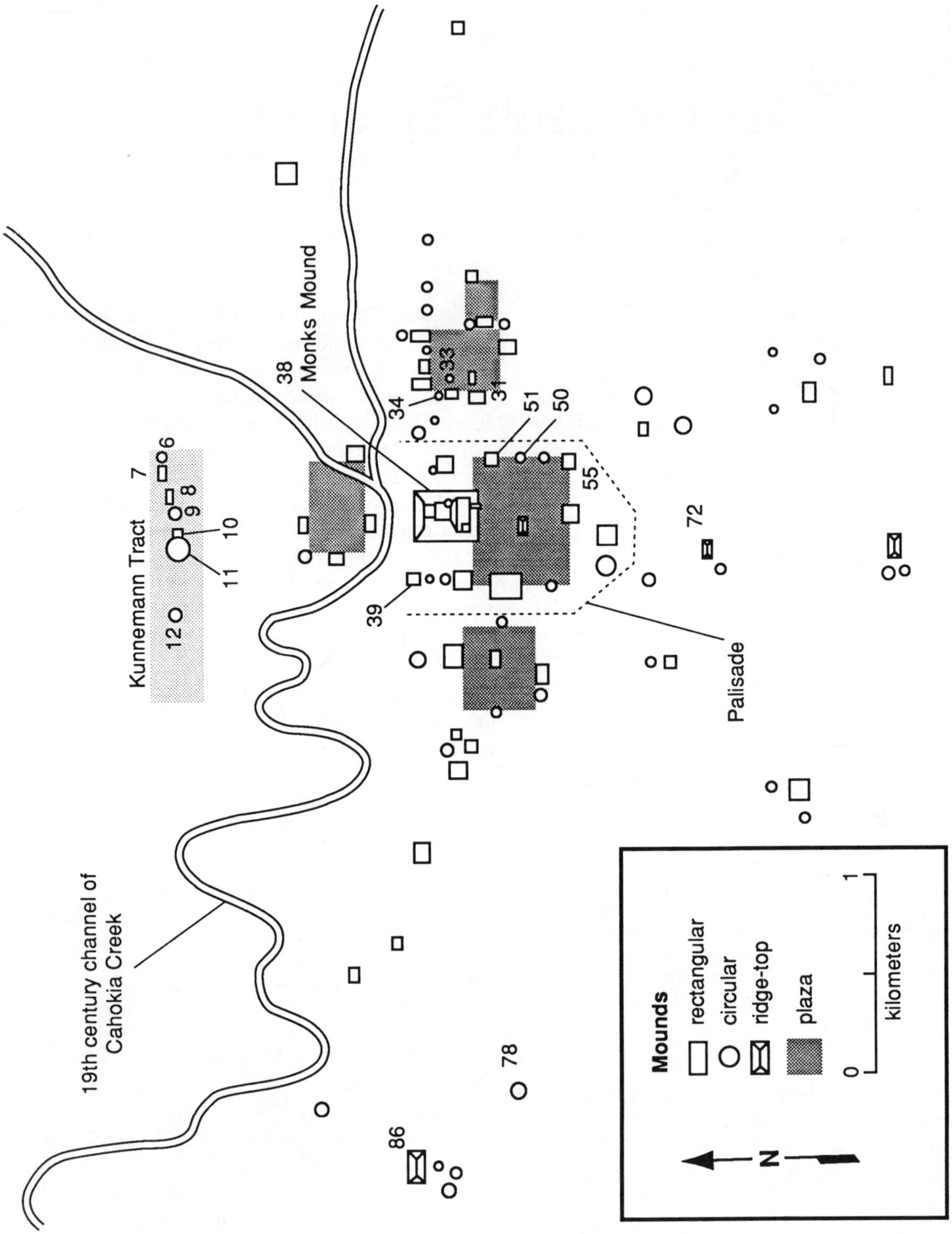

Figure 2.1. The Cahokia site (adapted from Fowler 1975; J. Kelly 1991b; Smith 1992).

Plate 2.1. The Kunnemann Mound in 1955 and 1956: *top*, view to west with Mound 10 terrace in the foreground; *bottom*, view to south, Mound 10 to left and Mound 11 remnant to right.

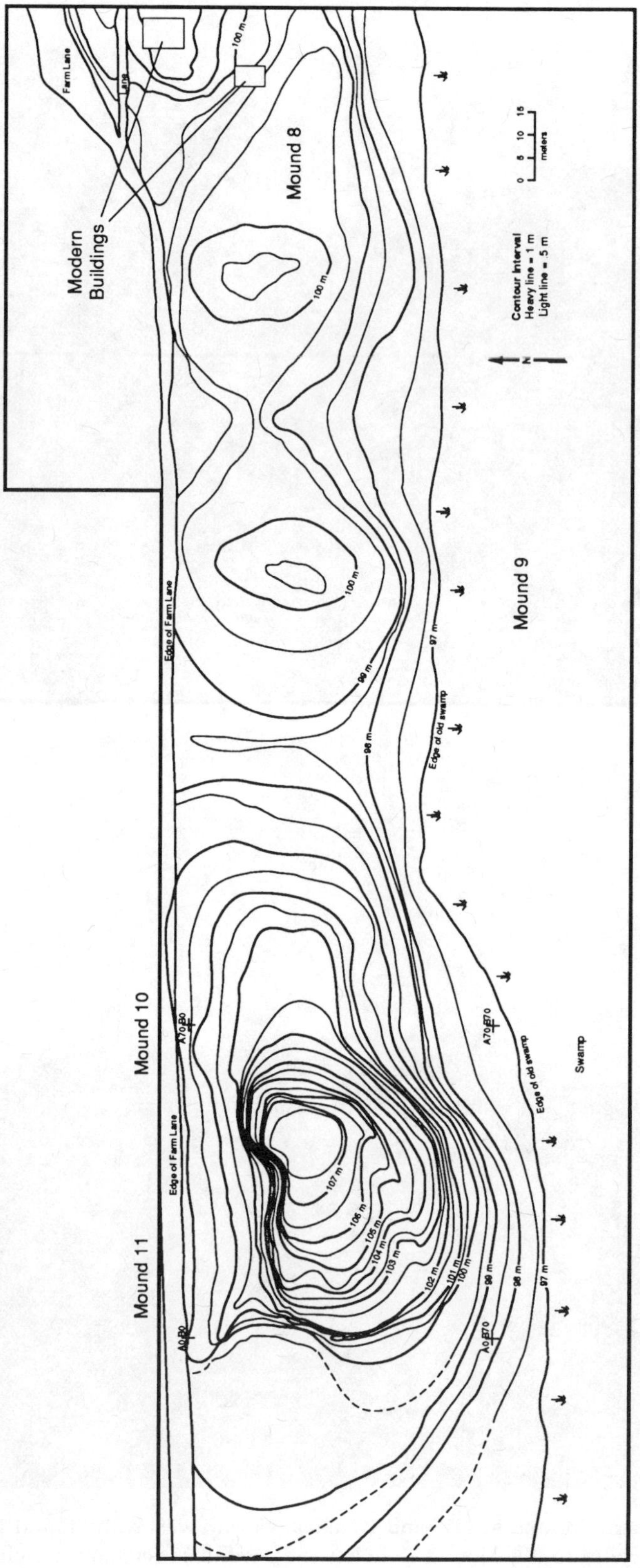

Figure 2.2. The Kunnemann Tract Mounds 8 through 11.

The Kunnemann Tract Excavations of Gerard Fowke

Until recently, it was believed that no excavations had been undertaken in the Kunnemann Tract Mounds 6, 7, 8 or 9 (Fowler 1989:68–70). However, John E. Kelly (pers. comm.) recently discovered documentation surrounding the excavation of two of these mounds by Gerard Fowke in 1905.

Between 1904 and 1921, there existed a group of St. Louis antiquarians called the Knockers[1] who, with the help of Bureau of American Ethnology archaeologists, conducted excavations at or sponsored the excavations of a number of sites on the Missouri and Illinois sides of the Mississippi River (Browman 1978; Pool 1989: 26–27).

> In 1905, the Knockers conducted several excavations on Illinois mounds—at Cahokia in Madison County, at the French Village site in St. Clair County, and at the Montezuma Mounds . . . in Pike County. [Browman 1978:4]

An article in the November 28, 1905, *Daily Advocate* (Belleville, Illinois) entitled "Looking for Relics" describes Fowke's work at Cahokia:

> In the interest of the Missouri historical society of St. Louis several mounds near Collinsville, Ill., are being opened, under the direction of Girard [*sic*] Fowke, formerly connected with the Smithsonian institute at Washington, D.C., and the author of several works on the mound builders, among them one treating [?] on their work in Ohio, of which state he is a native.
>
> The expense of this work is being borne by three St. Louisans, who are members of the Missouri historical society. They are Dr. W. F. Parks of 1022 [?] Goodfellow avenue[?], D. I. Bushnell of 1254 Olive street, and John M. Wulfing of 3448 Longfollow boulevard. The work has been in progress for over a week and is nearly completed. When finished a pamphlet will be issued giving the result.
>
> From an archaeological standpoint the investigation has not resulted as successfully as in other Illinois mounds, but of Indian skeletons, pottery, implements of warfare and shell ornaments enough have been found to reward the promoters of the research for their trouble and money. All artifacts found probably will be presented to the historical society.
>
> Dr. Parks visited the scene of the work Sunday and took back to St. Louis some of the pottery found. He was interested a short time since in prospecting in the mounds at Montezuma, Ill., and the result of that research was the finding of 1197 flint implements and fifty-two pearls. One of these pearls was of enormous size and would have been of great value had not its luster been dimmed by age.
>
> Dr. C. A. Peterson of 8 Shaw place, president of the Misouri [*sic*] historical society, and Judge Walter B. Douglas of 1205 Delmar boulevard, former president, are very much interested in the work which Mr. Fowke is doing for the members of the society. They regard Mr. Fowke as an authority on such matters.

Finally, we have the report of Fowke himself, published in *The Commerce Monthly* (a monthly magazine for the business community) in February, 1906. The portion of the article which pertains to the Kunnemann Tract excavations will be cited at length here.

> Half a mile north of Cahokia [Monks] mound, five mounds stand in a row along the north bank of the swamp bordering Cahokia creek. The largest was originally not less than fifty feet high; the others now have an elevation of four to eight feet above the base, but have been reduced by civilization. Two of these have been opened.
>
> The first one measures from 100 to 120 feet in diameter, and six feet high, from the level. Two trenches were carried in, one from the southeast and one from the southwest converging toward the center. In the first trench, ten feet from the center, was an extended skeleton with the head west; and in the second, thirty-five feet from the center, was another with head east. Both of these lay on the original surface, and no worked object of any sort was found with either. When the trenches met, an area at the center from ten to twelve feet across was thoroughly cleared out to undisturbed earth below the mound; but nothing whatever was found here, nor in any part of the mound examined, except such fragments of bones and pottery as would naturally be gathered up from the surface when building the mound. There were two parts to the structure: first, a cave of loose sand, which had been built up four feet; and above this a capping of "gumbo," very tenacious and heavy, with a present thickness of four feet. These figures show that the surrounding level has increased in height by about two feet since the construction of the mound was begun. The line of separation between the sand and the "gumbo" was practically horizontal, showing the sand cave had a level surface before the upper layer was placed on it.
>
> The second mound opened was six feet high; its outline was hard to trace but the original diameter was more than 100 feet. An area six by thirty feet was marked off on top, and all the earth within this removed. Next, a cross trench extended ten feet from each side of the first. Finally, the corners left at the intersection were cut off. In this way all the central portion of the mound was removed to the undisturbed earth beneath. Scattered at random in the structure were quantities of animal bones and pottery, all more or less broken; considerable ashes and charcoal; flint fragments; burned stone; mussel shells; and other debris and refuse such as will accumulate about an Indian wigwam. Among these were a few shell beads and bone perforators, evidently lost while the spot was occupied.
>
> The lower part of this mound was of clean sand which had a level surface as far as the digging extended. It had plainly been lived on for a number of years, at least, for the indicia of a campsite were abundant. This was about two feet high. The mound had then been additionally built up by sand around the margin and "gumbo" at the central portion, the two kinds of earth being carried in at the same time. There was finally a covering of sand.
>
> The conclusion is inevitable that both these mounds, and, inferentially, other low flat mounds in the vicinity, were intended as places of abode; perhaps permanently, perhaps only during high water or in rainy weather. A flat-topped mound would soon wear off, by erosion and particularly by cultivation and trampling of stock, into the flat dome shape which they now have. [Fowke 1906:26–27]

Fowke clearly states that he conducted excavations in two of five mounds on the Kunnemann Tract. He seems to have overlooked the sixth mound on the Tract, most likely one of the mounds at the extreme western or eastern end of the group, either Mound 6 or 12. It is not certain which of the low mounds—numbers 6, 7, 8, 9, or 12—he excavated, although it is likely for logistical reasons that he would have excavated two adjacent mounds, making the excavation of Mound 12 unlikely. Furthermore, the cache of celts which reportedly were found in Mound 12 around the turn of the century (some of which may have ended up at the Missouri Historical Society) were not associated in written accounts with Fowke, but could explain why Fowke, affiliated with the Missouri Historical Society, may have been lured into the excavation of two other Kunnemann Tract tumuli.

Evidently, these small mounds had already undergone substantial modification by the time of Fowke's exploration. Fowler (1989:68–70) observes that between the 1882 date of the McAdams map of Cahokia (or even the 1894 Cyrus Thomas map) and the 1906 Peterson-McAdams map, Mounds 6 through 9 were all reduced in height no less than 1.5 meters. The Peterson-McAdams map of 1906 gives the height of Mounds 6 through 9 at five feet (Fowler 1989: fig. 3.5) and Fowke (1906) measured the heights of two of them at six feet. Today, only the easternmost two of the four mounds, numbers 6 and 7, retain a height of over five feet, while the westernmost pair, 8 and 9, have been substantially lowered to 1.6 and 2.3 feet (Fowler 1989:70). On balance, it seems reasonable that Mounds 8 and 9 were the pair investigated by Fowke in 1905, for two reasons. First, Mounds 8 and 9 probably would have been the most visible and accessible of the four (a field road ran past them; see Fig. 2.2). Second, Fowke describes "thoroughly" excavating "all the central portion" of the two mounds (presumably reducing substantially their former heights in the process).

The findings of Fowke (1906) may be summarized as follows. In the first mound (Mound 9?), he found two burials on (or in) the submound surface without artifact accoutrements. He recovered ceramic and lithic refuse but concluded that it was accidental mound-fill inclusions. He identified two primary strata, a lower flat-topped sandy mound and an upper capping of gumbo or backswamp mud. In the second mound (Mound 8?), Fowke found domestic refuse, shell beads, and possibly bone awls on top of a low flat-topped sandy mound. Stratigraphically above this, he found additional mound-fill layers of both gumbo and sand fills. These brief observations of Fowke, to which we will return in Chapter 10, provide valuable information with which to compare the 1955–1956 excavation of the Mound 10/11 tumulus.

The Mound 10/11 Tumulus in the Twentieth Century

Except for the excavations by Gerard Fowke in 1905, which were largely forgotten within the span of two decades and seem to be unknown to recent Cahokia scholars, the first systematic investigation of any mound at Cahokia was carried out by Warren King Moorehead. Moorehead directed the testing or full-scale excavations of numerous mounds in the American Bottom region (Moorehead 1922, 1923, 1929). These included Mounds 11, 19–21, 24, 25, 32, 33, 39, 52, 64–66, 77–79, 82, 83, and others at Cahokia (Fowler 1989). Few of these were excavated in a manner which permits reanalysis of the structural or material remains uncovered.

Given our present concern with the Kunnemann Mound 10/11, we perhaps are fortunate to have as much documentation from Moorehead as we do. Moorehead was quite interested in the excavation of this mound. It had been, he thought, one of the larger mounds at the Cahokia site. Moorehead (1929:34) believed that Mound 11 originally

> was about four hundred feet [in] diameter and conical—not a pyramid. . . . Witnesses present during the previous work [i.e., the borrowing of the mound for fill] were questioned and all agreed that the mound was conical, or "pointed" as Mr. Kunnemann expressed it. The present diameter of the top is seventy-five by fifty-six feet. The sides are about twenty-five degrees slope. Restoring this same ratio of slope to the top would give fifteen to sixteen feet more elevation, as stated.

Most early maps do indeed show that Mound 11 was a steep circular mound (Bushnell 1904:10; Fowler 1989: chap. 3) with a small flattened surface that would have approached a conical shape, albeit slightly truncated. Bushnell (1904:10) notes that the diameter of Mound 11 by itself measured 200 feet or about 61 meters, without any mention of modern disturbance.

The Mound 11 Excavations of Warren K. Moorehead

"We wished," wrote Warren K. Moorehead, "to test one of the larger structures [at Cahokia], and as this one offered unusual facilities, we began work September 16, 1921" (Moorehead 1929:34). Moorehead proceeded to excavate the northern face of the mound (Moorehead 1922, 1923, 1929; see also Fowler 1989:70–73).[2] Moorehead (1929: plate I) presents a sketch map of his profile wall, about 35 feet high (Fig. 2.3), and describes these excavations as follows:

> Some three weeks were spent upon Kunnemann Mound. When we stopped work we were near the center and had excavated some eighty feet beyond the point reached by the dike builders. No skeletons were discovered, but in the earth were great

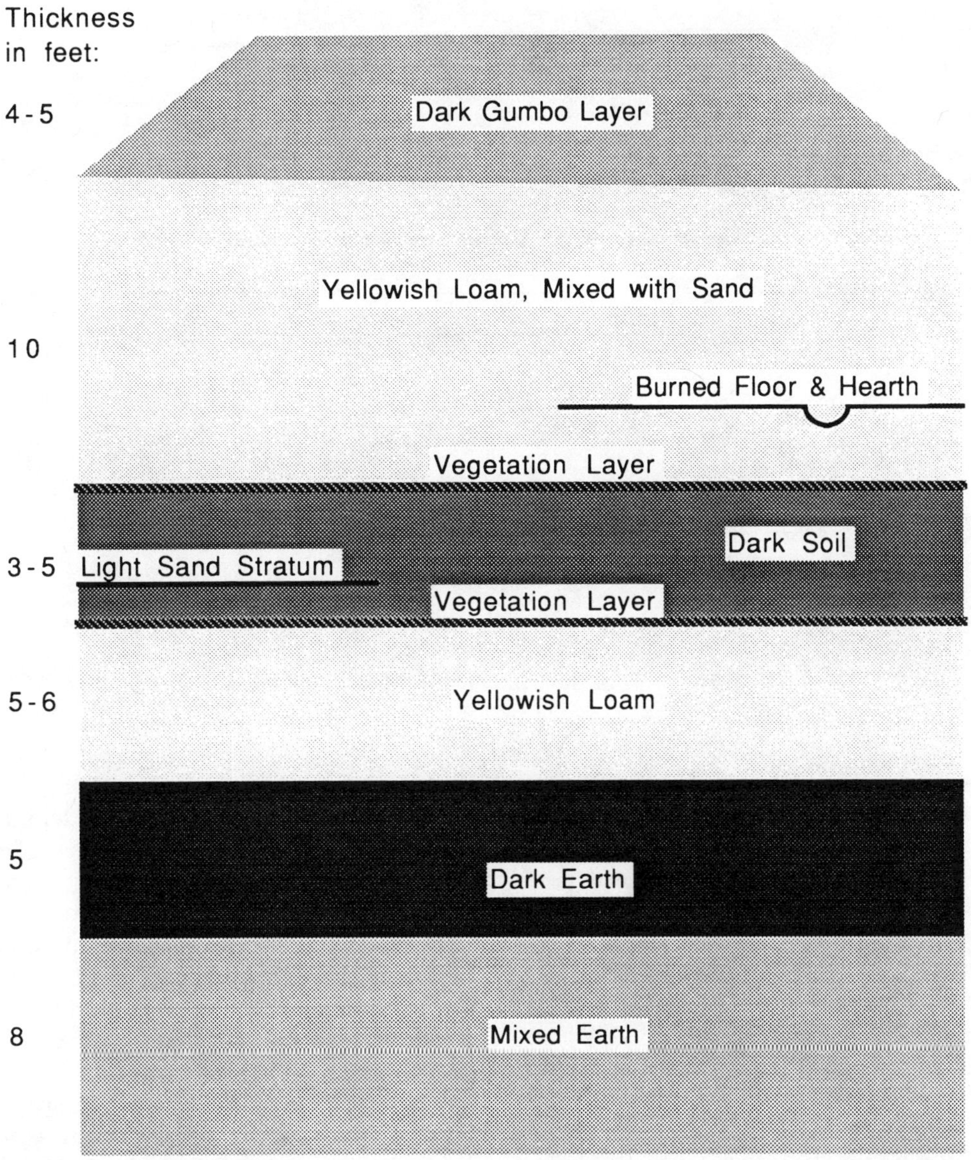

Figure 2.3. Moorehead's 1921 profile of the Kunnemann Mound (adapted from Mooreheard 1929).

quantities of flint chips, broken pottery, animal bones, and other refuse scooped up by the natives when they took the earth from about their cabins to build the mound.

It was found that the mound (that is, the portion we excavated) rested on a heavy layer of clear sand. Test pits sunk in this sand indicated that it was natural. . . . The lowest part of the mound is ordinary mixed earth and not stratified. About eight feet above the sand, or base, is dark earth in which are many broken artifacts; above this, some five or six feet of yellowish loam, then a rather distinct decayed vegetation layer running across the face of our fifty-foot trench. This is rather thin and even; then several feet of darker soil, but not gumbo, and above this the heaviest layer of decayed vegetation, in some spots about half an inch in thickness. Yellow loam containing some sand extends fully ten feet above. In this and the layer below the "dumps" or basketfuls of earth are noted. That is, natives carried the earth in loads varying from a trifle over a peck to a half bushel or more. Just below the summit is a four to five foot layer of heavy, compact gumbo.

After the work had progressed some days and when we were at a point north of the center, and where the mound was originally about forty-one feet high, we found a heavy layer of burned earth. This was almost floor-like in character. It was followed for a distance of thirty-five feet east and west, but was considerably narrower north and south. In the northern edge of this floor, eighteen feet above the base and eight feet below the present summit, we uncovered a circular, alter-like burned basin. . . . It was empty, but consisted of ordinary clay, hard burned. It was about a yard in diameter, ten or twelve inches deep and surrounded by a well

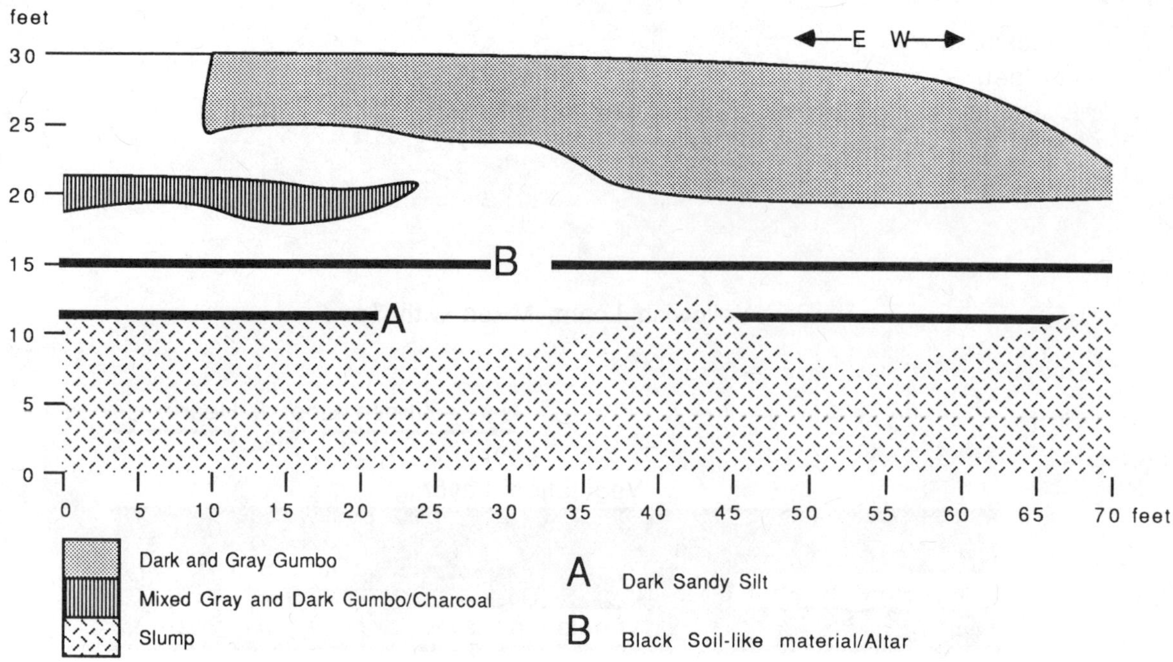

Figure 2.4. Leighton's 1921 profile of the Kunnemann Mound (adapted from Leighton 1929).

> defined, broad rim somewhat elevated. Extending in all directions beyond (save north) was the level, burned floor referred to.
>
> Near the center and twenty-seven feet from the base, Mr. Eldridge found the head of a frog effigy pipe and numerous fragments of fine pottery. Various large flat, shell beads were also discovered from time to time. [Moorehead 1929:35–36]

A description of the same trench was made by Morris M. Leighton, State Geologist with the Illinois Geological Survey, at some point during Moorehead's trenching of the Kunnemann Mound. His independent observations (Leighton 1923:86–87, 1929:133–34) vary somewhat from Moorehead's description and are probably the most accurate (Fig. 2.4). Leighton illustrates a cross-section with both vertical and horizontal scales; he shows the mound at about 30 feet (9.1 m) high. Unfortunately, when Leighton observed the trench, the "lower ten to fifteen feet" was covered with slump from the excavation.

Above the slump, Leighton observed a thin layer of "a dark sandy silt" above which was "a sand [fill] containing broken shells . . . [and] lumps of incoherent sandy silt." This was capped by a thin

> black soil-like material. . . . [This] was clearly not a soil in place, however, for the contact with the underlying materials is sharp. At this horizon a large bowl and a burned "altar" were found by Mr. Moorehead in the course of the excavations (Leighton 1929:133).

Above this was "a spotted sand [fill] with scattered charcoal, small shells, pottery, bones, and chips of flint." Within this matrix was a lens "of mixed gray and dark gumbo with charcoal. Its exposed length was twenty-four feet, and thickness two to three feet." The highest stratum observed was "a mixed dark and gray gumbo-like material showing no stratification" (Leighton 1929:134).

While the details do vary, the important conclusions to be drawn from Moorehead's and Leighton's description of the Kunnemann Mound include the identification of the underlying sterile soil, the assemblage of artifactual inclusions in the mound strata, the stratigraphic structure of the mound itself, and the features within these strata. Moorehead mentioned the basal natural sand underneath the mound. Both he and Leighton recognized the series of thick mound fills which contained refuse–including shell beads–redeposited from elsewhere. These fills were separated by thin layers of "dark earth," "black soil-like material," or "decayed vegetation" with "many broken artifacts." In one of these, Moorehead and Leighton noted the presence of a burned "floor-like" layer which featured a formal puddled hearth with a raised lip around its perimeter. Above this, Moorehead makes mention of another level in which elaborate artifacts–a fragmentary pipe and "fine" pottery were found. Lastly, both observers mention a thick gumbo fill as the uppermost mound stratum.

Two Episodes of Mound Borrowing

The 1882 McAdams, 1894 Thomas, and 1906 Peterson-McAdams maps list the height of Mound 11 between 30

Plate 2.2. Mound 11 in 1955 showing possible prehistoric dimensions (view to east).

and 35 feet, or about 9.1–10.6 m (Fowler 1989:47–51). Fowler (1989:70) records:

> Using 127 meters above sea level (416.7 feet) as the base, the Mound 10 portion extends from coordinates N1198 to N1244 and from E40 to E75 [using the Cahokia metric grid]. The E40 line, where Mound 11 begins, is taken as the division between the two areas. The Mound 10 section measures 46 meters (150.9 feet) north-south and 35 meters (114.8 feet) east-west. . . .
>
> The Mound 11 portion of this structure . . ., from a base elevation of 127 meters, is 7.5 meters (24.6 feet) high. That figure corresponds with the McAdams Map of 1882 and the Thomas Map of 1894, both of which give a height of approximately 30 feet (9.1 meters).

Fowke wrote of Mound 11 in 1906 that it "was originally not less than fifty feet high" (Fowke 1906:26). Writing in the early 1920s, Moorehead also records that "the tumulus was originally not below fifty . . . feet in altitude" (Moorehead 1929:34).

> Twenty years ago fifteen to sixteen feet of the summit was removed, and a trench run in from the north side some ninety feet, in order that earth to build a dike along Cahokia Creek might be obtained. Thus the mound had been seriously damaged. [Moorehead 1929:34]

Presumably, an agraded road or trail, visible in 1955, which led irregularly down the south face—debouching near the south end of the west face—was the path down which the wagons came carrying the borrowed fill around the turn of the century. However, if the Kunnemann Mound at one time was 50 feet in height, then it seems that the initial alteration of the mound must have taken place before the production of the 1882 McAdams map, which gives a height of 30 feet for the mound. Twenty years before Moorehead's 1921 excavation would place the initial removal of the conical summit before Fowke's excavations of the adjacent mounds but not as early as 1882. It is possible that neither Fowke's nor Moorehead's estimates of the original height are accurate. There is no hard evidence that Mound 11 was ever 50 feet high. It also is possible that both the McAdams 1882 and the Thomas 1894 maps are in error. The 1906 Peterson-McAdams map gives a height of 35 feet, or 10.64 meters, for Mound 11 (Fowler 1989:51).

Some years after Moorehead's 1921 excavations, around 1940, additional mound fill reportedly was removed by private landfill contractors. In 1955, the tenant farmer of the Kunnemann Tract told Preston Holder that 15 or more years prior to that time (around 1940) about 6 feet (1.8 m) of fill had been removed from the top of the mound, which fits the 1921 height as documented by Leighton. The mound also extended about 100 feet (30.5 m) west of its present western face prior to this fill removal. Between 1940 and 1955, the tenant had been removing sand in a desultory fashion from the dump heaps along the foot of the west face until he had made a considerable borrow pit of his own. By 1955, Holder estimated that only about one-half of Mound 11 remained. The heavily altered mound remnant (including both nos. 10 and 11) measured approximately 125 meters east–west by 75 meters north–south. It measured almost 7 meters in height.

If we accept as accurate the height of about 10.6 meters given on the 1882 McAdams map, then the 3.4-meter difference between the 1882 mound and the 1955 mound is less than the sum of what Moorehead (1929) and Holder's tenant informant (in 1955) estimated to have been removed from the mound top (Plate 2.2). Moorehead's estimate of the amount by which the mound was lowered may be inflated (see Fowler 1989:73) but it is intriguing that Fowke's information concerning the original height of the mound, from sources unknown, is consistent with Moorehead's projections (see Moorehead 1929:34).

It seems likely that the mound did witness two primary episodes of modification, one around the turn of the century and the other around 1940. However, it is possible that rather than the 4.5–4.8 meters of fill thought by Moorehead to have been removed around the turn of the century, the highest part of the mound might have been lowered a total of 2.0 meters or less at that time;[3] this does not negate the lowering of other portions to a greater extent, particularly to the north or west. Thus, subsequent to the fill borrowing which took place around 1940, the mound would have been lowered a maximum of roughly four meters.

The 1955–1956 Excavations

As if to add the final insult to twentieth-century injury, it was learned early in 1955 that Mound 10/11 on the Kunnemann Tract was scheduled to be destroyed in order that its fill could be used in elevating the berm under Sand Prairie Lane, the north–south county road which passes through the tract, in relation to upgrading the road and bridge over the Cahokia Canal. In a letter dated March 10, 1955, to Thorne Deuel, the Illinois state archaeologist at the Illinois State Museum, Holder wrote:

> Your information was correct. The county is planning on putting a bridge across Cahokia Canal and the bed of the old Cahokia Creek along Sand Prairie lane this spring and summer. There is a rumor that they may use part of one of the mounds as fill for their bridge approaches. I will know more after I talk to their engineers and see their plans on Friday. . . . I think I may try to get a modest foundation grant for this summer and try to do some "preventive" archaeology, and maybe we can salvage something when the machinery starts through.

Preston Holder obtained permission sometime between March and May of 1955 to conduct a salvage investigation of the mound before its planned destruction. In a letter to James B. Griffin dated June 3, 1955, Holder confides:

> I honestly had no hopes of getting such a break when I first broached this [with the Illinois State Highway Department]. Despite all the mess, maybe this will turn out to be a nice field session.

Two field excavation seasons were conducted at the Kunnemann Mound as the Illinois State Highway Department delayed the still-planned mound destruction. The work was supported by a grant from the American Philosophical Society (Holder 1957), with additional assistance from Washington University. The possibility that the mounds would be destroyed existed into the 1956 season, thereby setting the tone for the entire project. The first season's field work was done with a sense of urgency. The immediate and most important problem was to make a rapid analysis of the basic structure of the mound and, on that basis, identify priorities for later data retrieval.

During the opening week in 1955, a contour map was produced. An arbitrary datum was assigned an elevation of 100 meters,[4] and all elevations in the present volume are given in meters above arbitrary datum (a.d.). Holder established a metric grid system with alphanumeric coordinates and an arbitrary grid-zero point to the northwest of the mound. A points increase to the east; B points increase to the south; C points are opposite A points, and increase to the west. For instance, a coordinate position of A8, B37 thus translates into 8 meters east, 37 meters south, relative to the grid-zero point. The coordinate A10, B39 then is two meters further east and south of A8, B37.

A small crew of two to four laborers, two student archaeologists, and a number of volunteers was utilized in the field. The student archaeologists who assisted during the 1955 season included Marian E. White, a new Ph.D. from the University of Michigan, and Demaris Lou Nebgen, of Washington University (Plate 2.3). Regular laborers, who resided in East St. Louis, included Bell Cole, Sidney Sampson, and Claude Reed. Bell Cole, in particular, became a proficient archaeological technician. Holder and Cole were responsible for most of the field work in 1956 (Plates 2.4–2.5).

The archaeological excavation procedures involved exposing vertical profile walls and horizontal floors. Numerous section walls were profiled; those which best document the mound strata will be presented in this report. Mound surfaces and floors apparently were shovel-skimmed and troweled. The fills of these features and, it appears, all mound fill and floor zones excavated in 1955 and 1956 were dry-screened using quarter-inch mesh. Holder was responsible for the definition of most if not all mound zones and features in the western excavation areas; Marian White was responsible for some of the excavation and documentation of units in the eastern area. Features within the strata, like pits, hearths, and wall trenches, were profiled whenever possible and are presented in the following chapter.

Archaeology Since 1956 in the American Bottom

Fortunately, the Kunnemann Mound was not borrowed for fill by the Illinois State Highway Department in 1956. In fact, the mound was later purchased by the State of Illinois for inclusion within what is now the Cahokia Mounds State Historic Site. The State of Illinois ultimately purchased the entire Kunnemann Tract for incorporation into the park.

Because most of the remaining mounds of the Cahokia site are owned and administered by the State of Illinois (specifically, the Illinois Historic Preservation Agency) there has been little need to conduct excavations into them; those that have been excavated are reviewed in Chapter 10. However, large-scale archaeological surveys and excavations have taken place at Cahokia and in the surrounding floodplain since 1956. This work has included the large-scale salvage excavations of the Powell Tract and Tracts 15A and 15B at Cahokia in the early 1960s when interstate highways were planned to bisect the site (see Fowler and Hall 1975; O'Brien 1972; Vogel 1975). It has included excavations into Monks Mound (Bareis 1975; Benchly 1975; Reed Bennet and Porter 1968) and the Merrell Tract (Kelly 1980). Archaeological work since 1956 has included the University of Wisconsin–Milwaukee's mapping project and excavations of the palisade walls and Mound 72 mortuaries (Anderson 1977; Fowler 1977, 1989, 1991; Fowler and Anderson 1975; Pauketat 1987a, 1987b). Recent investigations include a series of small-scale surveys or excavations (see Gums et al. 1989; Holley 1990; Holley et al. 1990; Iseminger et al. 1990; Woods and Holley 1989) and a large-scale excavation of the Interpretive Center Tract II (Collins 1990; Holley 1989; Lopinot, Kelly, Milner and Paine 1991).

Outside the bounds of the Cahokia site, the 1970s and 1980s were dominated by the archaeological survey and excavations of the FAI-270 Project (Bareis and Porter 1984). The huge archaeological undertaking has been responsible for completely revising our perceptions of the late prehistory of the American Bottom, from artifact assemblages and chronology to subsistence and settlement patterns (see Johannessen 1984a; Kelly 1990a; Kelly et al. 1984; L. Kelly and Cross 1984; Milner et al. 1984; Pauketat 1989). Much of what we currently understand about Cahokia rests on these FAI-270 excavations outside of Cahokia (Milner 1990).

The archaeology of the American Bottom since 1956 bypassed Kunnemann Mound and now provides a baseline from which to analyze the Kunnemann Mound features and artifacts. It is now time for the Kunnemann Mound data to return the favor and contribute toward our future understanding of American Bottom archaeology. That it can is a clear indicator of the quality of the 1955–1956 excavations. A full description of these excavations is contained in Chapter 3.

CHAPTER 2 NOTES

1. "The core of the Knockers consisted of David Ives Bushnell, Sr., John Max Wulfing, and Mr. and Mrs. George S. Mepham. . . . Edgar L. Hewett, Earl H. Morris, Gerard Fowke, and of course, David I. Bushnell, Jr. all are found at some of their meetings" (Browman 1978:2).

2. Earning him, via the humor of Preston Holder's 1956 field assistant Bell Cole, the nickname "Professor Moorehog."

3. Calculation: *maximum documented height* (10.6 m) – *1955 height* (7.0 m) – *maximum thickness removed in 1940* (1.8 m) = *potential thickness removed ca. 1900* (1.6 m).

4. This corresponds to about 127 meters a.s.l. based on comparisons with the University of Wisconsin at Milwaukee map of the Kunnemann Tract and the USGS Monks Mound 7.5 minute quadrangle map.

Plate 2.3. Excavations in Exploration Area 1 in 1955: Preston Holder, sitting; Demaris Lou Nebgen, standing on the trench floor; Marian White, on the pedestal to the right.

Plate 2.4. Borrow pit area excavations in 1956: *top*, Bell Cole (foreground) and Preston Holder shovel-skimming Features 73 and 74 surfaces (view to south); *bottom*, Nebgen, Holder, and Cole (left to right) in the borrow pit area subsequent to the excavation of Feature 3–5 (view to southeast).

Plate 2.5. The 1956 excavations of Mound 11 (view to east).

Chapter 3

The Excavations

The 1955–56 Kunnemann Mound excavations focused on three primary excavation areas: the Moorehead profile, the exploration areas, and the borrow pit (Fig. 3.1). The Moorehead profile, as it was called in the field, was a stepped trench excavated into the side of the excavation scar created by Warren K. Moorehead in the autumn of 1921. The 1955 trench served as a stratigraphic guide for the rest of the excavations. As it turned out, it is particularly important since the more extensive excavation of the western portion of the mound provides little documentation of the mound's upper levels. A series of exploration areas, designated 1 through 3 in the field and consisting of several trenches, composed of squares, were dug in 1955 to resolve a number of specific problems surrounding mound construction. Finally, the borrow pit excavation was located in an area which, for several years prior to 1955, had been used as a source of fill by the tenant. The extensive excavation of this area in 1955 and 1956 provides the most insight into the structure and content of the mound.

Minor excavations took place in 1955 and 1956 in at least three other locations around the mound. One simply consisted of trimming the walls and inspecting the profiles of an old "pot hunter's" trench, located 3 m northeast of Exploration Area 3, trench 1, square B. The trench's dimensions were 4 m northeast–southwest by 2 m northwest–southeast by 1.5 m in depth. An inspection of the unit's walls and floor revealed basket-loaded sand fill. Another shallow trench, 7.2 m long and about 1.2 m wide, was excavated immediately northwest of Exploration Area 1 between grid coordinates A56–63, B5.5–8.4. Its exact depth is not known. It has been labeled "trench 5" since it is adjacent to Exploration Area 1 (Fig. 3.1) even though this was not the field designation. This unit revealed, in plan view, the junction of the upper "gumbo" fill zone of Mound 10, at an elevation of 100.88 m above the datum point (a.d.), and a lower sandy zone. This junction paralleled the long axis of the unit. The third excavation unit was referred to in the field as "Bell's Exploration" (BE) after its excavator, Bell Cole. This consisted of a test unit, dimensions unknown, south of the southern edge of the borrow pit area. No plan or profile maps exist and no locational information on this unit is available. A note, written by Holder, states that

> the work was unsupervised but Bell Cole was experienced and knew the site well. Since he was illiterate he could not maintain "sack data." Therefore, all . . . material is lumped together.

Features

Two major feature classes are recognized in the Kunnemann Mound excavations. The first consists of units of mound fill, slope wash, midden, and prepared surfaces, caps, or mantles. These features are substructural elements which need little explanation. The second class of features includes the remains of buildings, facilities, and burials which were found on or below mound surfaces.

Wall trenches, postmolds, floors, and basin fills are associated with structure remnants. At least 19 individual structures, as represented by wall trenches in profile or plan view, were encountered during the 1955–56 excavations (Table 3.1). Within these structures may be pits or hearths. Outside the structures are found pits, post pits, and postmolds. Sixteen formal puddled hearths, 10 formal pits, 3 large amorphous pits, and two (or perhaps three) post pits were recognized in the 1955–56 excavated sample from the Kunnemann Mound (Tables 3.2–3.3). Three submound pits contained human skeletal remains. Another hearth, it will be recalled, was excavated by Warren K. Moorehead in 1921.

The remains of structures, hearths, pits, post pits, and other cultural facilities are described in this chapter as they relate to various strata within the mound. Volume capacities of hearths and pits, all of which are basin-shaped in profile, have been estimated using the formula:

$$V = .16\pi d(3r_1r_2+d^2)$$

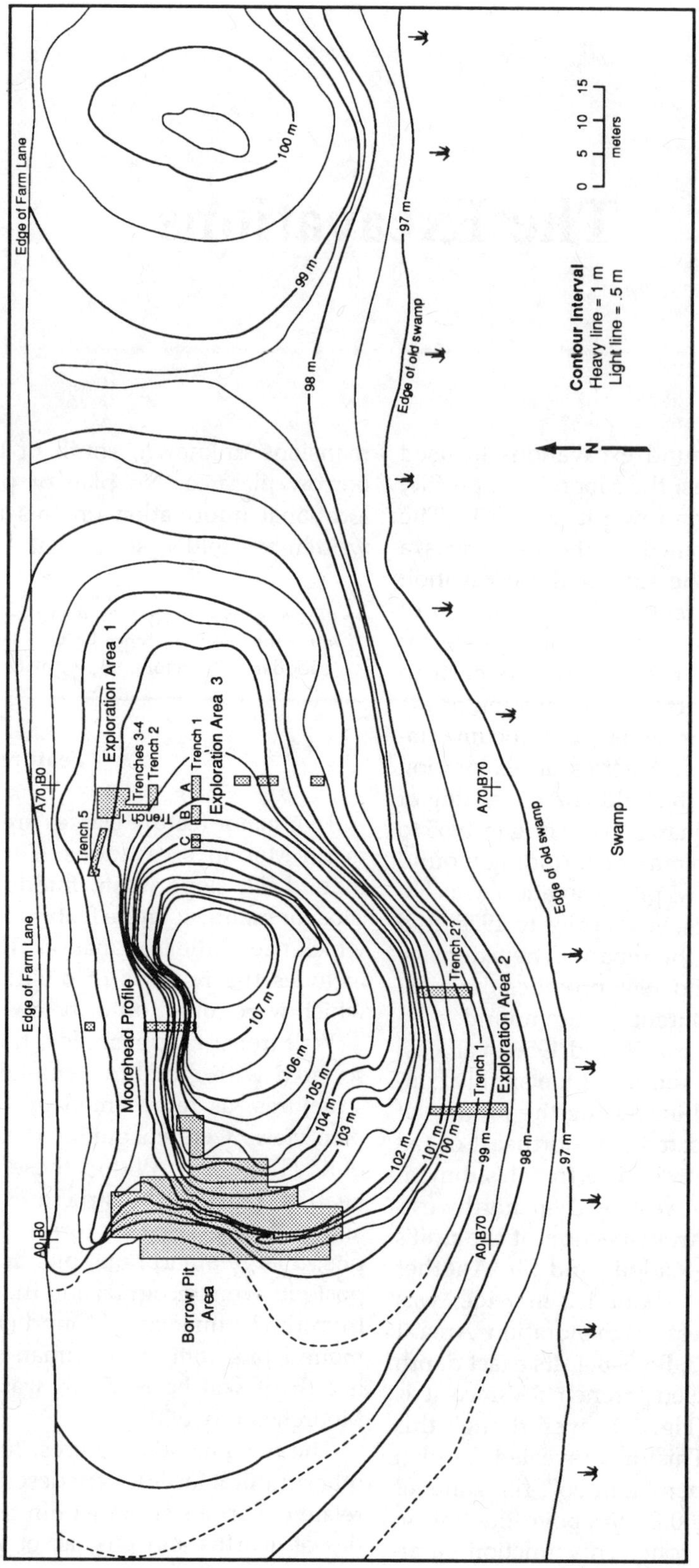

Figure 3.1. The 1955–1956 Kunnemann Mound excavation areas.

TABLE 3.1
Kunnemann Mound Structure Attributes

Feature	Stage	Shape	L(m)[a]	W(m)[a]	LxW(m^2)	W/L	Floor Notes	No. Hearths	Comments
BP AREA									
4 (3, 5, 11)	submound	L-shaped	6.1	3.6/4.6	25.7	0.59/0.75	sand layer	1	walls rebuilt; semi-subterranean; burned; basin 50cm deep
unnumbered	submound	rectangular?	?	?	-	-	-	?	partially defined wall trench adjacent to F83
72 (9, 70, 125)	south mound*	rectangular	9.1	6.9	62.8	.76	black clay	2	*north of south mound
106/107	south mound A	rectangular	?	2	-	-	-	?	partially exposed on early south mound (el.100.4 m)
105/134	south mound B	rectangular	≥8.4	>2.5	>21.0	-	-	?	partially exposed; associated with mound F133
95 (96, 138)	south mound C	rectangular	≥9.8	≥9.8	≥96.0	-	red film	1?	associated with mound F78
92	north mound (F75)	rectangular	≥5.2	≥4.0	≥20.8	-	plastered; clay	2	half of building destroyed by modern borrowing
119	F75/77/78	rectangular?	≥10.0	?	-	-	clay	(F97?)	only one wall exposed
121/122	F75/77/78	rectangular?	?	?	-	-	clay	(F97?)	two isolated and ill-defined wall trenches
74 rotunda	early F79 mound	circular	8.6	-	58.1	-	plastered; clay	4	mats
112/113	F79 mound	?	?	?	-	-	-	?	two ill-defined or short parallel wall trenches
84	later F79 mound	rectangular	≥4.7	4.7	≥22.1	-	-	1	-
94	later F79 mound	T-shaped	>2.4	8.1/4.6	>40.0	-	-	?	partially exposed and partially destroyed by borrowing
93	north F81/87 mound	?	?	?	-	-	-	?	defined only in profile
129	south sub-F81/87 md.	rectangular	?	2.2?	-	-	-	?	defined in profile only; above F114
36	F17 mound	?	?	?	-	-	-	?	wall trenches defined in profile in BP and MP areas
EXPLORATION AREA 1									
48	F41/md. 10 summit	rectangular?	?	?	-	-	-	?	unusually large wall trenches; a structure? partially exposed
54	later md. 10 summit	rectangular	>4.0	?	-	-	-	?	partially exposed
EXPLORATION AREA 3									
unnumbered	mound fill @101m	?	?	?	-	-	-	?	a single wall trench and prepared surface exposed in profile

[a]As measured from the midpoint of wall trench width.

TABLE 3.2
Kunnemann Mound Hearth Attributes

Feature	Diameter (cm)	Depth (cm)	Volume (m^3)
7	66	6	0.010
12a/b	45×22	?	?
13	50	5	0.005
14	84	9	0.024
15	60	14	0.020
71	70	0	0.000
85	64	20	0.016
97	56	10	0.012
103	50	?	?
110	60	11	0.016
116	60	11	0.016
117	60	12	0.017
118	47	9	0.017
123	55	13	0.016
123a	57	0	0.000
135	35	?	?

where V is volume, d is depth, r_1 is the radius of the feature length in plan view, and r_2 is the radius of the width in plan view (adapted from Fortier et al. 1983:112–13). Pits, post pits, hearths, and wall trenches—as well as the units of mound fill—were assigned individual feature numbers. Discussion of individual buildings will be facilitated by adopting one or a group of these numbers for each structure. A complete inventory of the Kunnemann Mound features, along with detailed information on those features for which it is available is summarized in Appendix I. The key used to interpret the symbols on the plans and profile maps which follow is presented in Figure 3.2.[1]

The Moorehead Profile

In September and October of 1921, Warren King Moorehead, with the assistance of a large crew of workers digging for some three weeks, cut away the northern face of the Kunnemann Mound. The scar from Moorehead's excavation is still clearly visible (Fig. 3.1). The profile trench that was excavated in 1955 into the northern face of the mound exposed a portion of the same surface examined 34 years earlier (Plate 3.1). In general terms, portions of the 1955 trench are comparable to that documented by Moorehead (1992, 1929:34–36) and Leighton (1929:133–134).

The 1955 excavation of the Moorehead profile found intact mound deposits a meter or less below mound fill slump. The 1955 trench ranged in width from a maximum of 130 cm at the top to 33 cm at its base. It exposed a cross-section of the Kunnemann Mound from its present-day surface to culturally sterile submound deposits (Figs. 3.3–3.4). Since the old face, as cut away by Moorehead (1929: pl. 7–8; Fowler 1989: fig. 4.9), was rather steep, the profile was excavated as a series of large steps (Plate 3.1).

The Moorehead profile reveals the primary strata of the mound. Beginning at the base and progressing up through the mound, these include a possible premound occupation zone designated F26 (as the features are numerous and mentioned often throughout this monograph, they will frequently be abbreviated thus), 10 cm thick (elevation 100.5 m a.d.), and a 30 cm-thick clay base mound fill, F25, surmounted by an occupation zone consisting of 3 distinct "floors" or living surfaces. These prepared surfaces, F22–24, reach a maximum thickness of 40 cm (elevation 101 m a.d.). Above this is a 165 cm-thick, sandy, mound fill deposit, Features 19–21, 27–30, and 37, which appears to contain a number of living surfaces not clearly defined here (Fig. 3.3). Feature 27, zones A-E, located stratigraphically above the putative living surfaces, may be additional living-surface strata or fill zones, with F21 perhaps representing a pit, 100 cm in depth, which superimposes these strata (Fig. 3.5).

Above this is found F18, a gumbo-clay (i.e., backswamp, silty, montmorillinitic clay) cap about 8 cm thick, labeled "Cap 1" by Holder. This particular feature is not found to the west in the BP area. On top of F18 is F17, 220 cm of sandy mound fill which is characterized by strata or laminations which dip to the east. The dip may be an indication of the marginal position of this area relative to the main body of Mound 11 at this point in time. An occupation zone is located at the top of F17 at an elevation of approximately 104.9 m a.d. A possible wall trench, F36, extends downward through F17 from this living surface at an unusual angle (Fig. 3.3).

This occupation zone and F17 are subsequently capped by a 6–12 cm thick clayey fill zone known as F35, called Cap 2 by Holder. More sandy mound fill, F34, was heaped above the former mound surface. As a single unit, F34 is approximately 110 cm thick, and is capped by another series of prepared surfaces, Features 32–33, having a maximum thickness of 13 cm (and called Cap 3 by Holder). However, it appears, based on the profile map, that F34 is actually two separate mound fill episodes, Features 34A-B making up an earlier platform stage and occupation surface at an elevation of 105.65 m a.d., and F34C, the later mound fill component.

The final stratum identified in the Moorehead Profile is a 110 cm-thick gumbo zone called F31. The original thickness of this cap zone or the presence of other strata above F31 is unknown since the top of the mound had been removed years earlier. It is possible that this gumbo fill was the last stage of the Kunnemann Mound, comprising the lower portion of the "conical" mound noted by various informants to have existed prior to twentieth-century borrowing activities. The present surface of F31 is located at an elevation of 107.3 m a.d. However, the tenant farmer of the Kunnemann Tract told Holder in 1955 that the gumbo clay layer, F31, had been about a foot higher and that a sand layer, 5–6 feet in

TABLE 3.3
Pit and Post Pit Attributes

Feature	Type	Plan Shape	Profile Shape	Length (cm)	Width (cm)	Depth (cm)	Volume (m^3)	Notes
8	pit	irregular oval	basin?	53	40	50	0.10	on floor of F3–5 structure
21	pit	?	basin?	?	?	≥100	–	exposed in profile, perhaps an unusual mound fill zone
46	post pit	elongate oval?	irregular	124	?	120	–	exposed in profile, not plan
58	pit	oval	basin	130	?	50	–	exposed in north profile of EA1, T2
60	post pit	elongate oval	irregular	240	75	137	–	exposed in plan and profile, two ramps?
83	amorphous pit	irregular	irregular	260	180	?	–	contains fetal skeleton and partial bundle
86	amorphous pit	irregular	basin	520	300	42	2.5	volume is rough estimate
89	amorphous pit	irregular	basin	≥420	≥200	15	0.5	volume is rough estimate of excavated portion
99	pit*	flat bottomed	?	140	?	70	–	*modern disturbance? exposed in profile only
100	?	irregular	irregular	230	100	80	–	historic-period disturbance?
101	?	irregular	irregular	208	110	64	–	historic-period disturbance?
104	post pit/w.t.	elongate	*	>600	100	≥50	–	*no longitudinal profile; plan not fully exposed
108	pit	oval	basin	126	92	30	0.14	superimposed by F95, so excavated volume less
127	pit?	oval	?	35	22	?	–	–
128	pit?	irregular oval	*	120	82	*	–	*only a few cm deep
unnumbered*	pit	?	basin	104	?	88	–	*exposed in profile of EA3, T2, Sq.B
unnumbered*	pit	oval	?	32	26	?	–	*in corner of F3–5; a postmold?
unnumbered*	pit	irregular oval	basin?	64	52	20	0.03	*in south-central portion of F3–5 floor

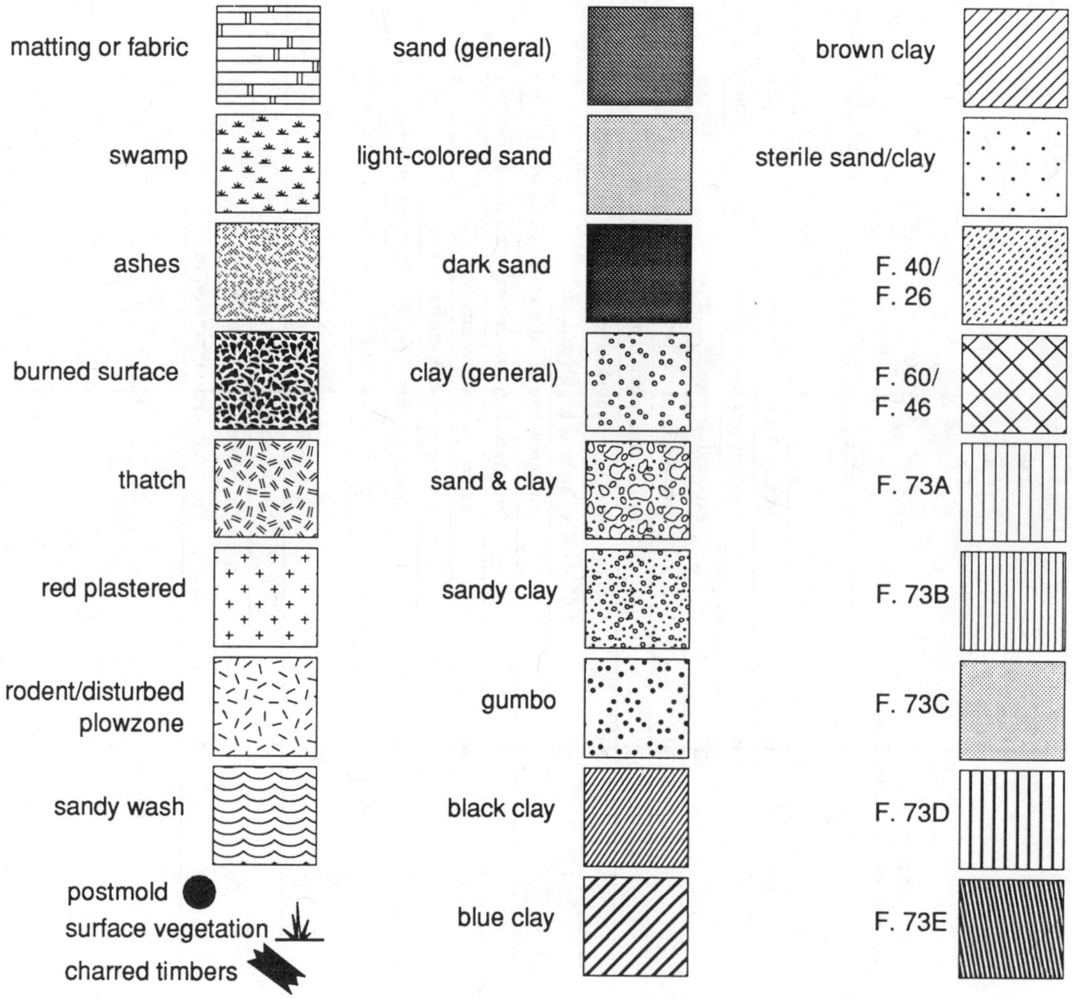

Figure 3.2. Map key.

thickness, was found on top of the F31 gumbo. This does not seem to correspond with the account of Moorehead (1929) and Leighton (1929) who observed a thick layer of gumbo on the mound surface in 1921.

Exploration Areas 1, 2, and 3

The exploration area (EA) excavations were intended to address specific problems related to the construction of the Mound 10/11 tumulus and historic-period modifications and disturbances. EA 1 was placed on the lowest tier of the mound, otherwise called Mound 10, where it abuts the mound's second tier, Mound 11. This exploration area was intended to resolve the problematic relationship between the two, establishing whether Mound 10 predated Mound 11 or whether it all was a single unit (Holder 1966). The purpose of EA2, trenches 1–2, and EA3, trench 2, involved evaluating the submound/mound interface. This was deemed important because, as of 1955, the entire mound was slated to be leveled for borrow in 1956 and knowledge of the depth of the submound surface could be used to prevent the contractor from proceeding down through these intact deposits as well (Holder 1955). EA 3, trench 1, was—like EA1—intended to clarify the relationship of Mound 10 to Mound 11. Furthermore, it was hoped that evidence of steps used to ascend the monument would be found in trench 1, EA3 (Holder 1966).

Of the three designated exploration areas, the first was most extensively investigated (Fig. 3.1). The complex layering of mound strata and cultural features in EA1 required extensive excavations (Holder 1966). EA 2 consisted of two

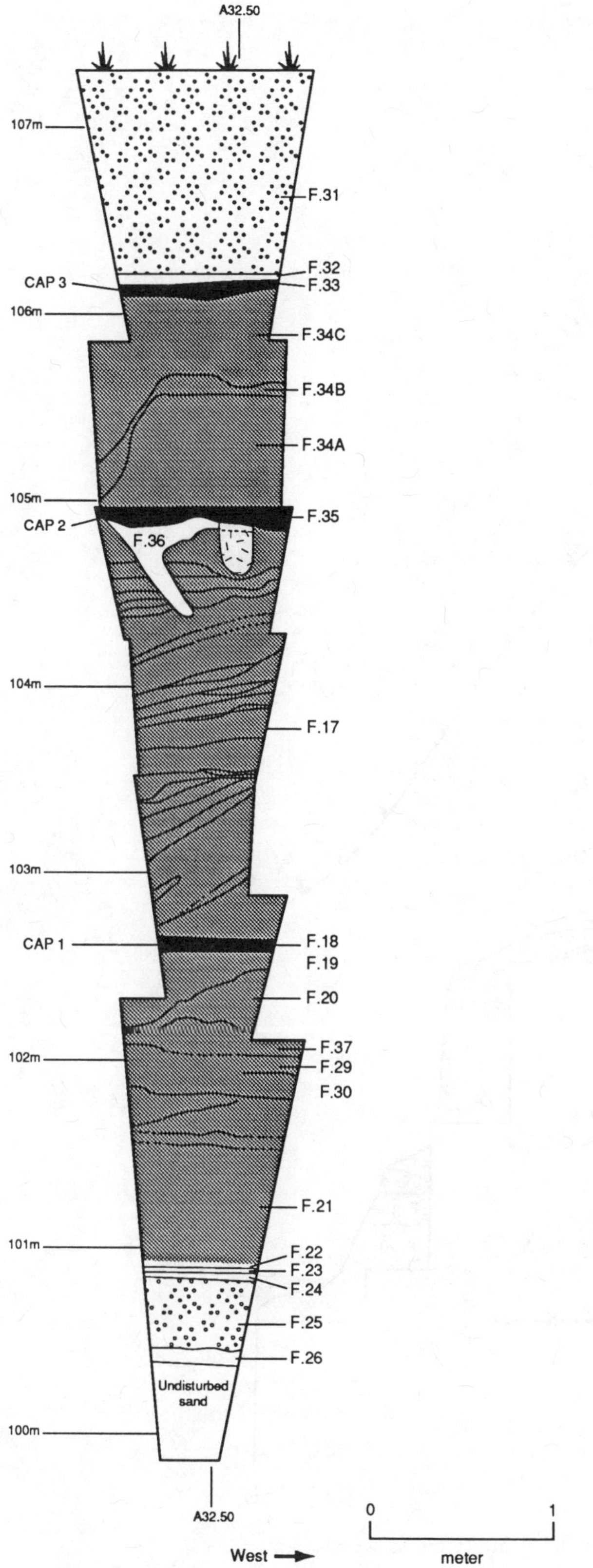

Figure 3.3. The 1955 Moorehead profile strata (view to south).

separate trenches. EA 3 consisted of two trenches of three units or squares each.

Exploration Area 1

During the early part of the 1955 season, two long narrow trenches were emplaced in the northwest corner of Mound 10. One of these, trench 1, was oriented north-south with a shallow enlarged square at the northern end. The other, trench 2, was oriented east-west (Plate 3.2). These trenches, along with trench 5 mentioned earlier, showed that Mound 10's

> gumbo capping was brought down the flanks [of the mound] in a fashion to seal off the underlying structures. . . . [U]nder this seal the layers and laminations ran horizontally. [Holder 1966]

In order to fully expose a series of features which appeared in these trenches, two other trenches, 3–4, were opened adjacent to the eastern side of trench 1. These four trenches are treated as a single unit (Fig. 3.6). As the profiles of EA1 illustrate, the northeastern portion of the unit was excavated through the mound and into sterile subsoils (Figs. 3.7–3.10). The lower portions of the unit exhibit alternating thick layers of sand and thin layers of clay, naturally deposited, all below an elevation of approximately 100.2 m a.d. The earliest cultural zone, as in the Moorehead profile and EA 3, consists of a pre-mound "midden." This zone, labeled F40, is approximately 13–30 cm in thickness with an undulating (and occasionally ill-defined) bottom. Features 52, 53, and 55 may be components of this same submound zone or may be mound fill components (Figs. 3.7–3.8).

The surface of F40 in EA1 is located at an elevation of 100.45 m a.d. A post pit, F46, superimposes F40 and marks the location where a large post was erected (Fig. 3.8). Subsequent to this, mound construction begins, here represented by a sandy fill, about 47 cm thick, called F41. The upper portion of F41 exhibited a darker appearance and an irregular stain line. This is interpreted to represent a stable surface upon which a soil was developing. Above this were two prepared surfaces, consisting of zones totaling 16 cm in thickness, the top of which reached an elevation of around 101 m a.d. These sandy floors are known as Features 42–43 on one profile (Fig. 3.8) and Features 61A-B on others (Figs. 3.9–3.10). They also seem to correspond to F56–57 in trench 2, the southern part of the unit.

Associated with this surface at an elevation of approximately 101 m a.d. are a number of different features. At the southern end of the unit (trench 2), a pit, F58, extends down 50 cm below the base of this prepared occupation surface (Fig. 3.6). In the northern area of the unit, an extremely wide and deep trench, F48, appears to indicate the corner of a possible wall-trench structure. Superimposed

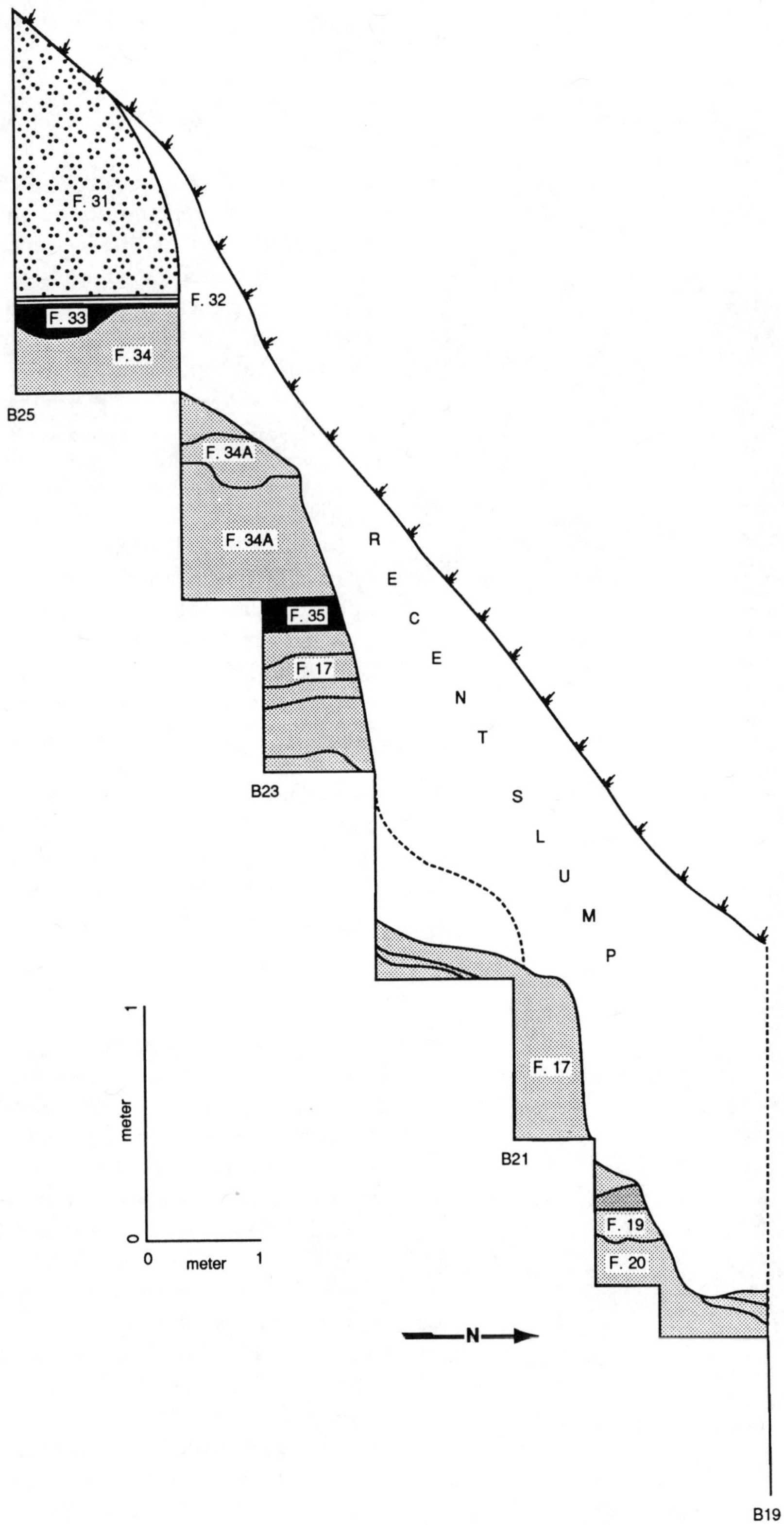

Figure 3.4. The 1955 Moorehead profile strata (view to west).

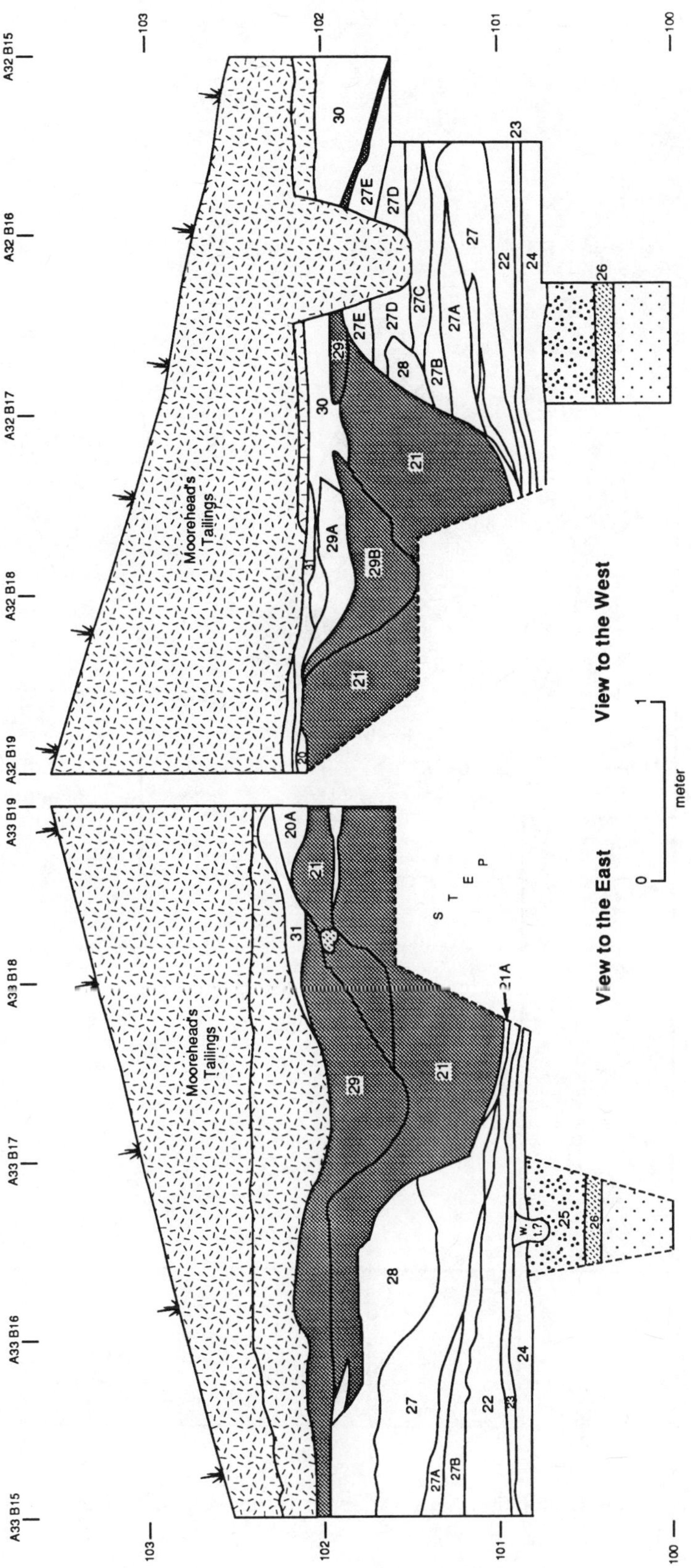

Figure 3.5. The lower section of the 1955 Moorehead profile.

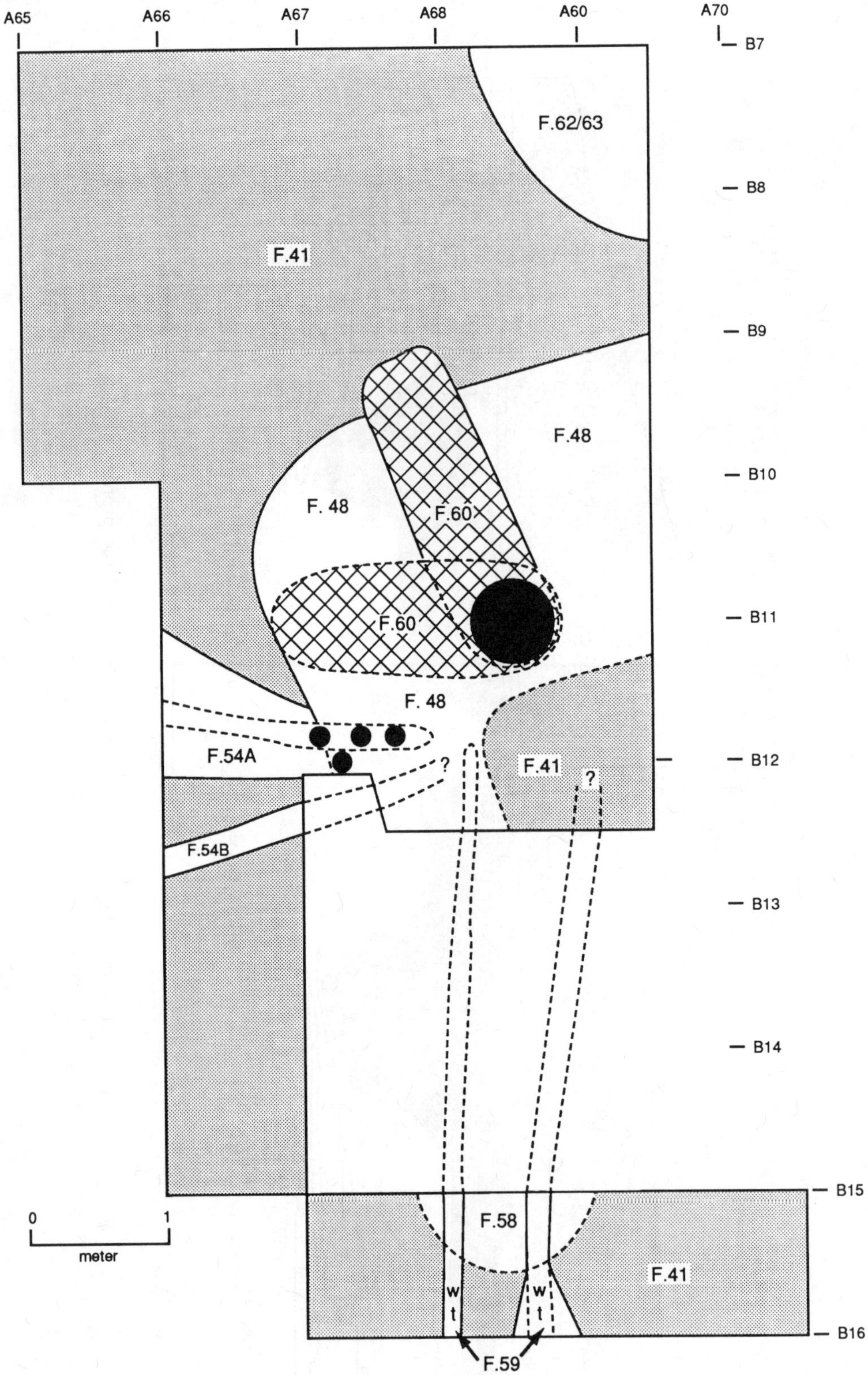

Figure 3.6. Exploration Area 1 at about 101 m, composite plan.

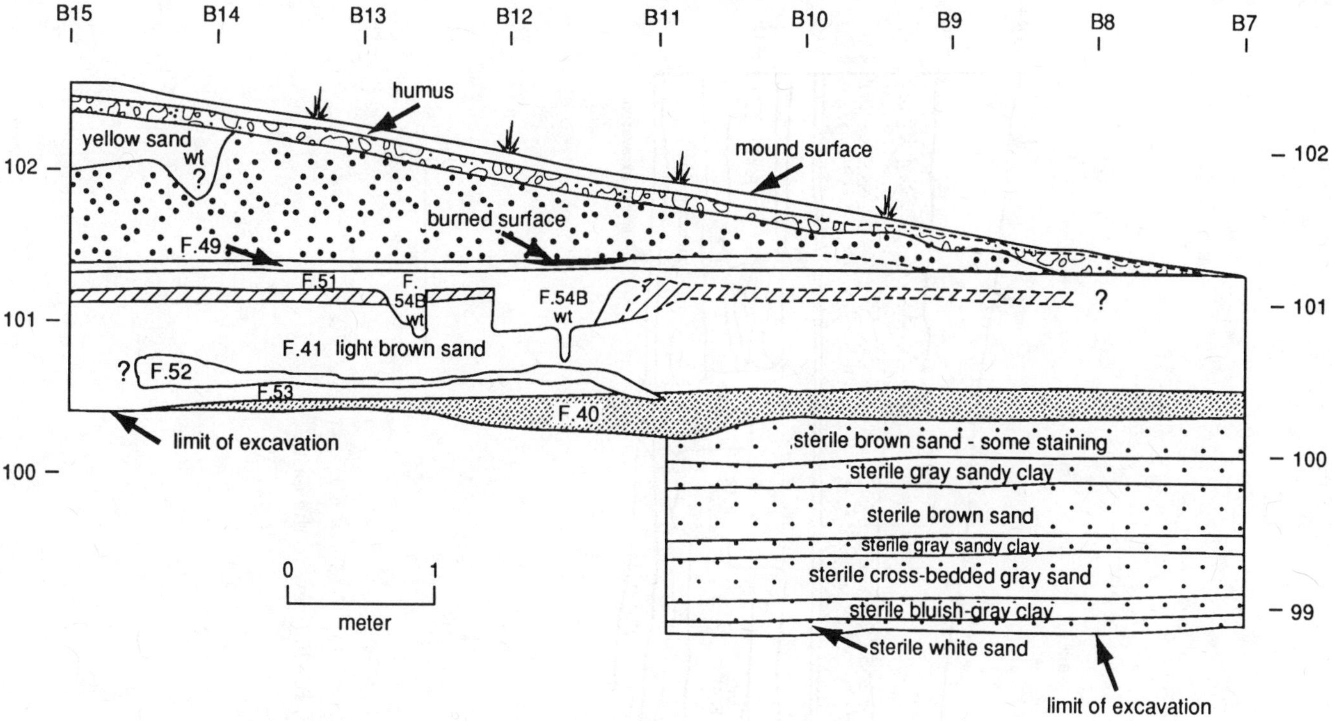

Figure 3.7. Exploration Area 1 profile at A66, B7–15 (view to the west).

upon both the pit and the possible structure F48 are other wall trenches. Two unnumbered wall trenches parallel each other in the southern portion of EA1 and extend northward, where they appear to meet an east–west wall trench, F54A. Another southwest-northeast trending wall trench, F54D, may be related to a rebuilding of this same structure (Figs. 3.6–3.8).

Also superimposed upon F48 is a large post pit, F60 (the postmold itself, about 60 cm in diameter, is called F65). As identified in plan view at an elevation of 101 m a.d., F60 is an elongate oval trending northwest-southeast (Fig. 3.6, see Plate 3.3). A ramp that meets the surface at the feature's northern end was probably used to remove the post set in the deep southern end. Another ramp found to the west of the post, but not defined in plan view in the field, had probably been dug to insert the post. Fill zones 60D-G represent fill episodes that occurred while the post was in place (Fig 3.9) This proposed insertion ramp has been noted on the composite plan as a dashed outline (Fig. 3.6).

The next phase of mound construction in EA1 consists of additional mound fill, F51. This zone averages approximately 20 cm in thickness in the northern end of EA1. A thin occupation surface, F49, is located on top of F51. Its upper surface has an elevation of about 101.3 m a.d. In trench 2 of EA1, slightly upslope from the other trenches, both F51 and F49 appear as thin occupation surfaces stratigraphically above F56–57. Thus, F51 may be a prepared floor, comparable to Features 42–43, 56–57, or 61A-B, simply becoming thicker around the lower margins of the mound (Figs. 3.7–3.10). Additionally, it appears, on one profile, that a portion of F51 was scooped out or eroded, weathered, and then filled prior to the deposition of F49 (Fig. 3.9). It is unclear what this feature, designated 50 and 51A, represents.

A final mound construction stage of the Kunnemann Mound 10 terrace appears to be gumbo (Figs. 3.8–3.10). The western profile wall of EA1 exposed a fill zone up to 90 cm thick. A plow zone has disturbed the upper levels of EA1 to the east (Fig. 3.9), but along the west an undisturbed surface, consisting of a weathered sandy upper zone and humus is evident. A possible structure basin and wall trench are located at an elevation of approximately 102 m a.d. in the southwest corner of the exploration area, trench 1 (Fig. 3.7).

Exploration Area 2

Trench 1 of EA2 was excavated along grid coordinates A20–21, from B61–74. The northern half of this trench was one meter wide, while the southern half was 1.5 m wide; the depth of the trench is unknown. Trench 2, EA2, was poorly documented and no profiles are available. Its di-

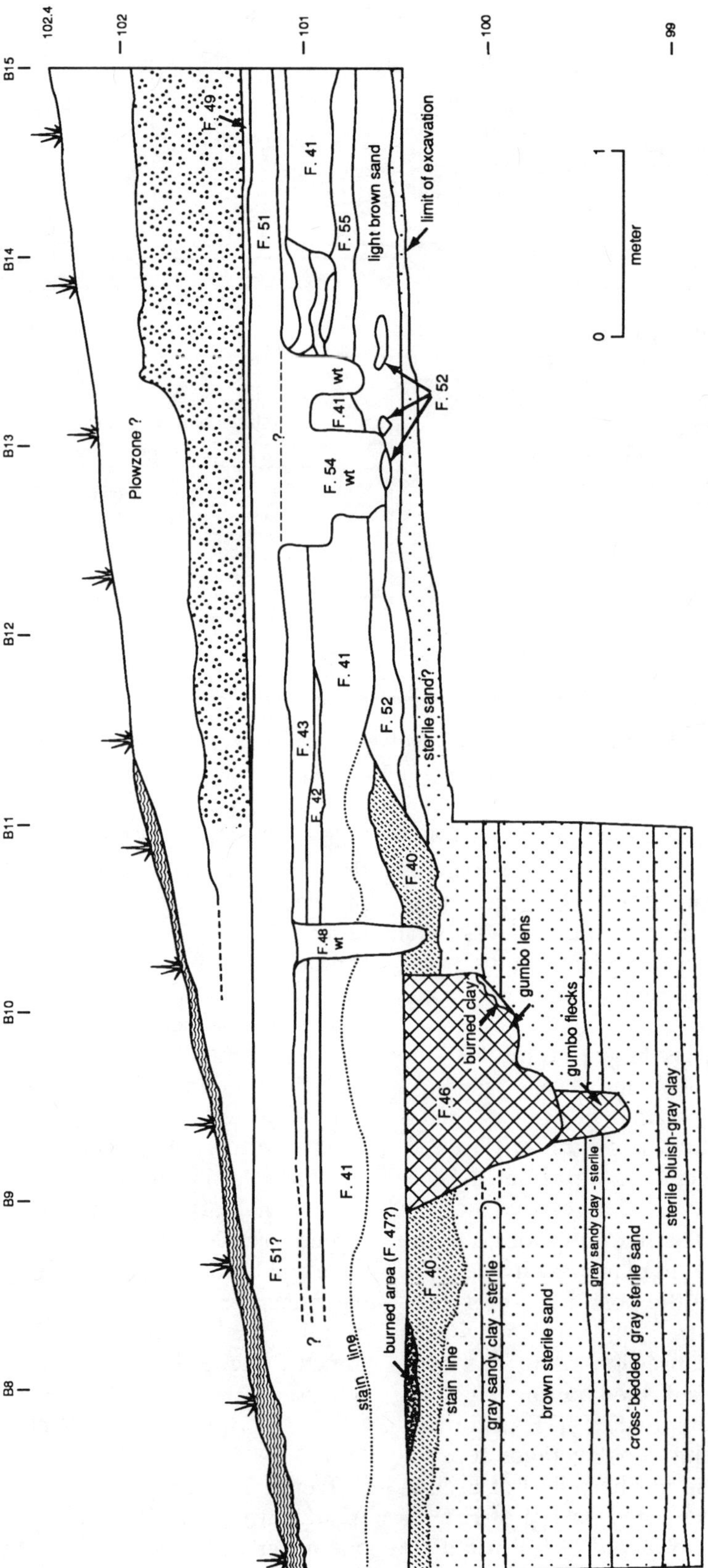

Figure 3.8. Exploration Area 1 profile at A67, B7–15 (view to the east).

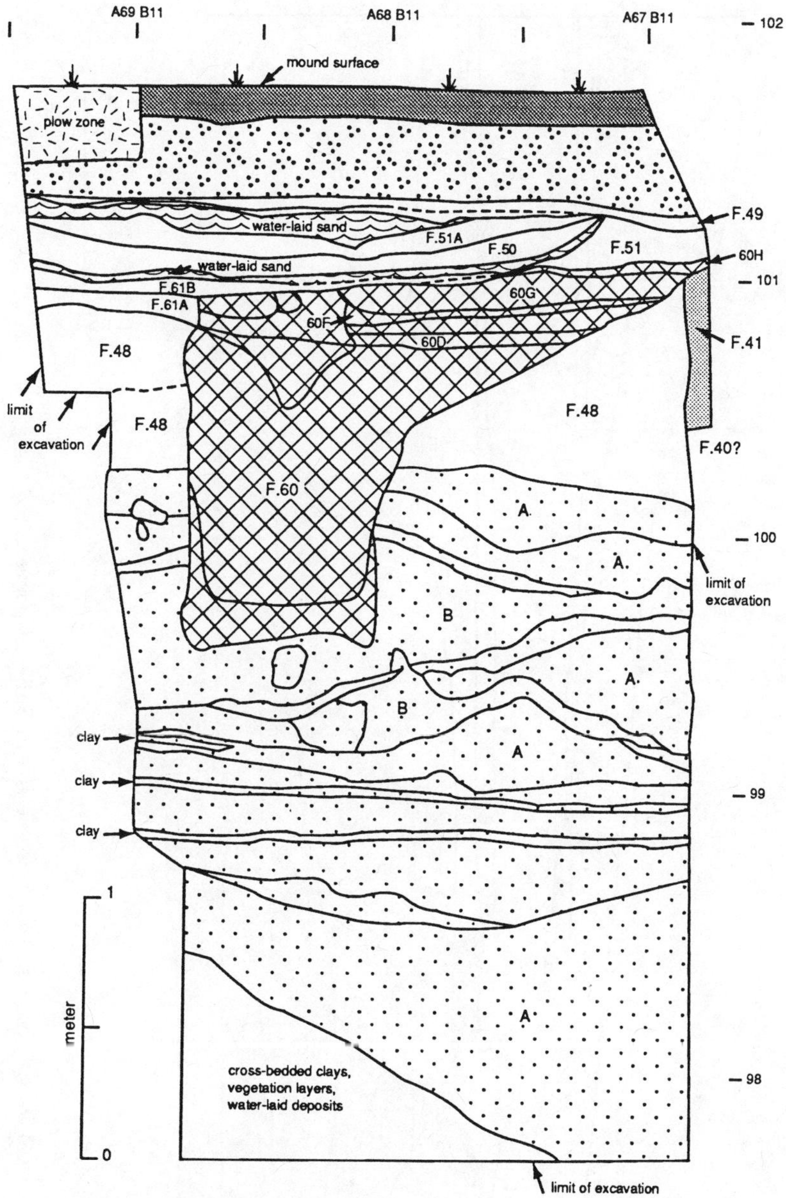

Figure 3.9. Exploration Area 1 profile at B11, A67–69.5 (view to the south).

mensions and precise location are uncertain (see Fig. 3.1). The profile walls of both trenches showed signs of historic-period disturbance.

Exploration Area 3

The two EA3 trenches each consist of three excavation units (Fig. 3.1). The strata of trench 1 (EA3) vary between these squares. The profile of the easternmost square A, located on Mound 10, shows sandy mound fill below a sandy clay prepared surface at an elevation of about 101 m a.d. This is surmounted by a 70 cm-thick gumbo component, a 60 to 70 cm-thick "mixed sand" zone, and 30 to 40 cm of plow zone (Fig. 3.11).

The excavation of the square B upslope revealed only one basket-loaded sandy mound stratum evident to a depth of approximately 1.4 m below surface (Fig. 3.11). Further upslope and now on Mound 11, square C exposed gumbo at an elevation of 101.4 m. Above this was a 40 cm-thick "mixed sand" zone, a sandy clay floor (plastered red?) at an elevation of about 101.8 m a.d.; a "mixed sand" fill zone, 32–34 cm thick; a humus-stained sand layer, 5–10

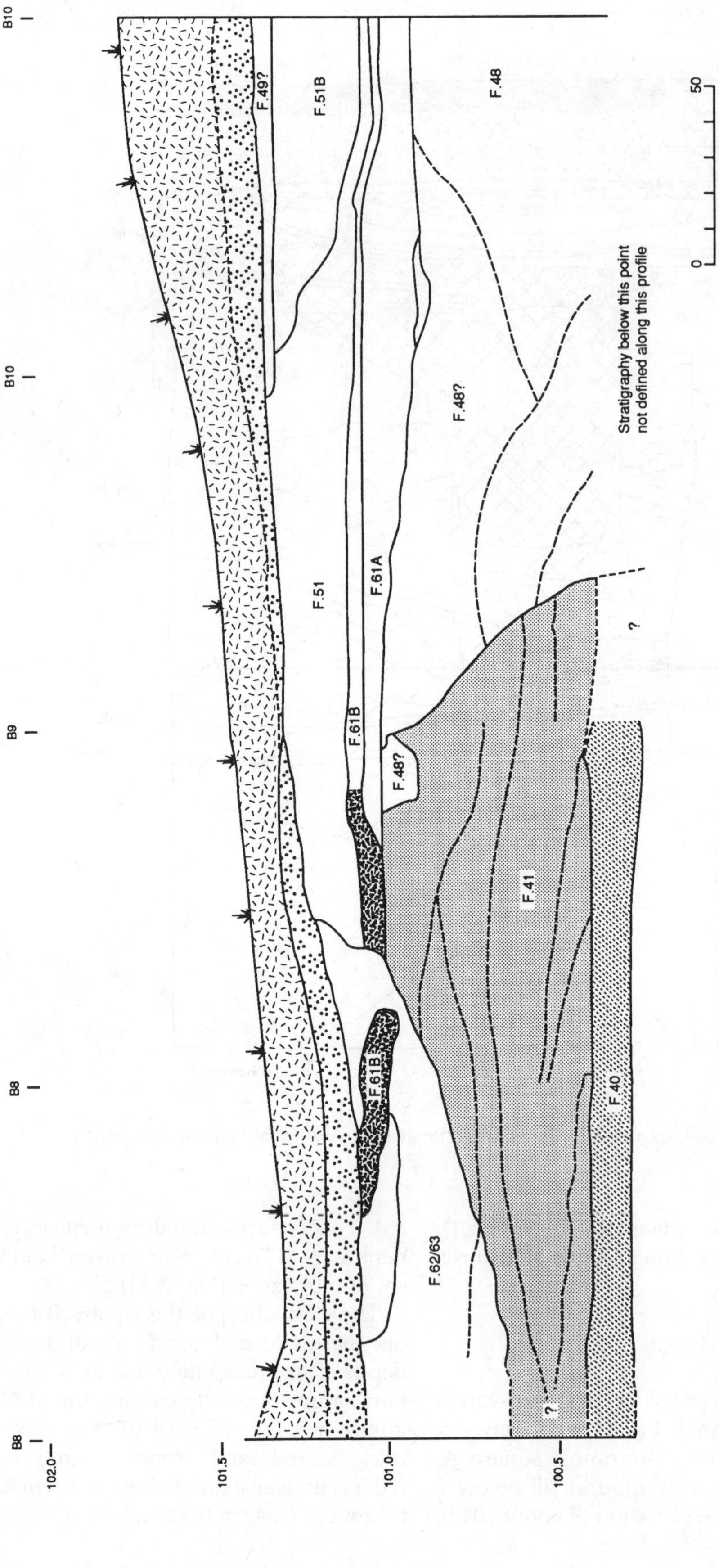

Figure 3.10. Exploration Area 1 profile at A69.5, B7–11 (view to the east).

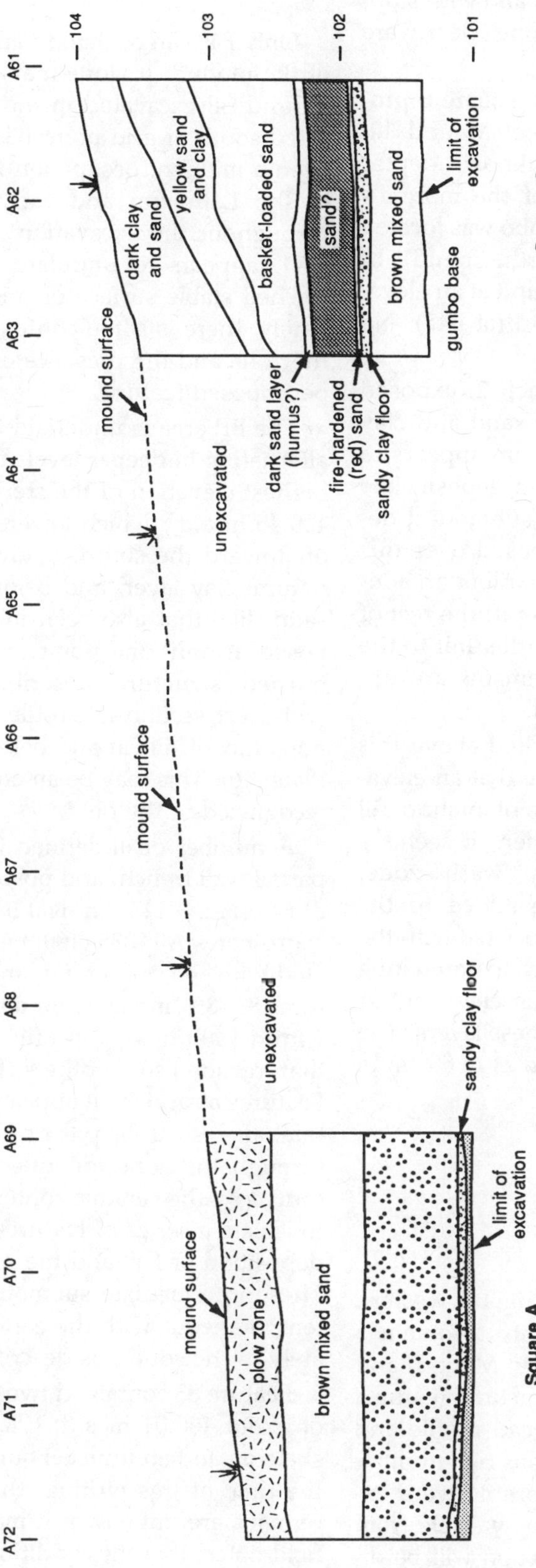

Figure 3.11. Exploration Area 3 profile: trench 1, south wall.

cm thick (102.3 m a.d.); and sand, yellow sand and clay, and gumbo fill zones of varying thicknesses and with sloping surfaces (Fig. 3.11). These latter three zones clearly are fill on the eastern slope of Mound 11.

Of the three units within trench 2 (EA3), square B provided the most insight into the structure of Mound 10. Squares A and C were excavated to an unknown depth, providing information on the elevation of the mound's gumbo cap. In square A, the top of the gumbo was located at an elevation of 101.8 m a.d. (at the northern end). In square C, the edge of the gumbo fill was found at an elevation of 101.2 m a.d., on top of sterile sand (at B42). No profiles are available for inclusion here.

Square B excavations within EA3, trench 2, exposed seven cultural strata, underlaid by sterile sand and clay strata (Fig. 3.12). The lowest cultural stratum appears to be a submound occupation surface/midden deposit, like F26 or F40. The EA3, trench 2, square B submound deposit is 48 cm thick. Within or superimposed over this deposit was a burial pit. Apparently, the skull of an adolescent individual was recovered from this pit; the rest of the burial extended outside the bounds of the unit to the west. The whereabouts of the skeletal remains are unknown.

A clay floor, 10 cm in thickness, is located above this submound surface in EA3, trench 2, square B at an elevation of 100.5–100.6 m a.d. Another layer of mound fill (sand?), 40 cm thick, covers this floor. Then, it seems a second prepared clay surface and a sandy "wash" zone, totaling about 16 cm in thickness, were added to the mound fill. A wall trench appears to be associated with the clay floor (101 m a.d.). A pit, although perhaps predating the clay layer, also is associated with this elevation. A gumbo layer, 70 cm thick, rests atop all of these layers. The uppermost zone is plow zone ranging from 24 to 58 cm in thickness (Fig. 3.12).

The Borrow Pit Area

The existence of a modern borrow pit along the western side of the mound afforded an opportunity to obtain a north-south profile through the Kunnemann Mound, and to examine in more detail some of the structural features which had been identified in the Moorehead profile and exploration areas. The horizontal dimensions of a number of the occupation surfaces identified in profile were exposed. Consequently, a series of plans are available from the various stages of the mound. This section will be divided according to these feature groups and stratigraphic stages.

Feature 40 and the Amorphous Pits

Only F40 can be dated to the period prior to the erection of the mound. It alone may be isolated under the earliest mound fill excavated in the BP Area, F109 and F133, located south of grid point B36. Feature 40 appears to have been a midden, occupation zone, or stable surface dating to the Lohmann and early Stirling phases and found throughout the excavation. The base of the zone, as in EA1, appears to undulate, which is characteristic of a leached stable surface or midden accumulation. Unfortunately, there is some confusion concerning the bottom of the zone and the presence of other fill components or superimposed features.

The BP area is underlaid by a light-colored sterile sand alternating in deeper levels with bands of sterile clay. The highest elevation of the sterile sand within the BP area is 100.45 m a.d., which lowers as the ridge naturally drops off toward the south. Below this (99.7 m a.d.) is a thin natural clay layer, and below this, a naturally deposited sand, like that also seen in EA1. The clay layer was exposed at only one point in the BP excavations, below a burned structure described below (Fig. 3.13). The east–west section in profile appears to show a heterogenous mix of fills at and below F40 (the shaded portion of Plate 3.6). This may be an amorphous pit or a fill zone not recognized in the field.

A number of ill-defined features, a small pit (F127), a partial wall trench, and postmolds were defined at the top of F40 (Fig. 3.14). An oval basin pit (F108) exposed at grid coordinates A0, B35 (100.3 m a.d.) probably also is associated with the premound surface (also F128 nearby?). Features 83, 86, and 89 were defined as amorphous fill zones within F40 on some profile maps and as irregular basins that intrude F40 on others (Figs. 3.15–3.18). In the case of Features 83 and 89, it appears that they were judged in the final analysis to be pits or fill zones which did indeed cut through the zone identified as F40. This is clearly supported by the ceramic contents of F89. Thus, it is possible to isolate a series of features as intermediate between the deposition of F40 and the mound fill immediately above. These intermediate submound features still may be contemporaneous with the earliest Mound 11 stages immediately to the south, as described below.

Feature 83 contained two human burials at an elevation of about 100.01 m a.d. (Plate 3.4). These include a fetal skeleton and an unusual bundled burial. Unfortunately, at the time of this writing, the whereabouts of the human remains are unknown. It may be supposed, based on the field notes, that the condition of the fetal skeleton was too poor to permit retrieval. Holder's (March 1956) field notes about the fetal remains read as follows:

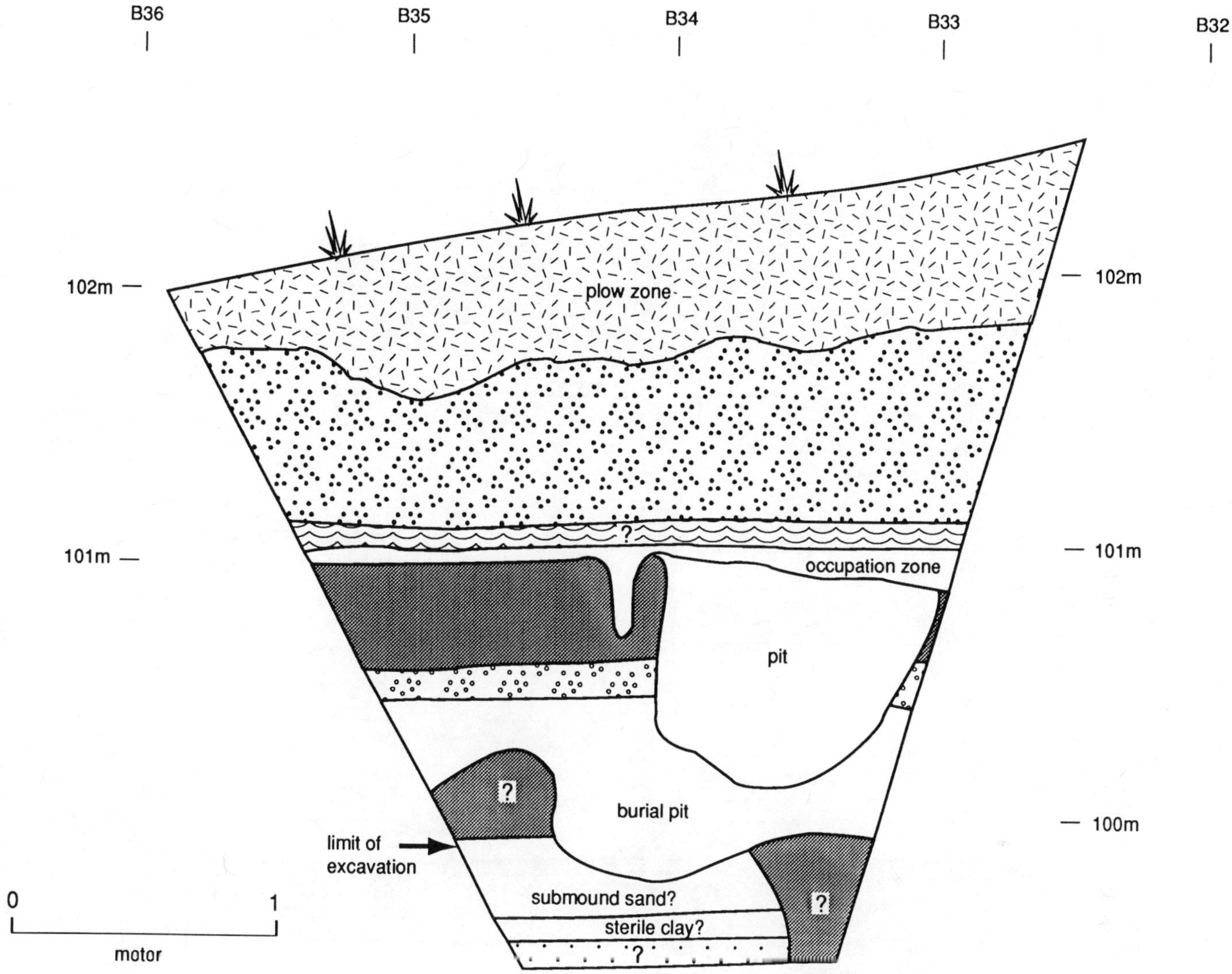

Figure 3.12. Exploration Area 3 profile: trench 2, square B, west wall.

> Small parietal plates with frilled edges no face found, extremely small long bones and pelvic plates. Tried to save some of these bones but doubt that they will survive to lab. Arrangement of bones made it clear that skeleton was in complete articulation at time of burial.

Of the other burial, Holder's field notes read as follows:

> A most peculiar "burial" the skull & jaw—note that the mandible was broken before burial & the 2 parts thrown in—are clearly those of an adult male, heavy supraorbitals, "wings" on gonial angle, large caries in r. lower 3rd molar—skull may have pre-burial fractures. But the left leg and r. tibia look like adolescent or at best female also thoracic vertebrae look "young." This can hardly be called a "bundle" burial. Looks more like a skull burial with associated non-related long bones and ribs, looks like some sort of cannibalism or "trophy" deal.
>
> Note: the bones are covered at surface with reddish greasy clay-like layer gives field impression was fabric but no weave visible, or maybe meat?

Likewise, a human skull fragment, possibly a parietal fragment, weighing 3.9 grams (measuring 33.2 mm by 29.2 mm by 5.6 mm), was recovered from F89 (John R. Bozell, pers. comm.). This was the only such fragment found in this amorphous feature.

The Burned Structure (Feature 3-5)

The remains of a rectangular structure with an *L*-shaped room extension was found to have superimposed F40—like Features 83, 89, and 127—and to have been burned down. This Mississippian structure had been erected in a 50 cm-

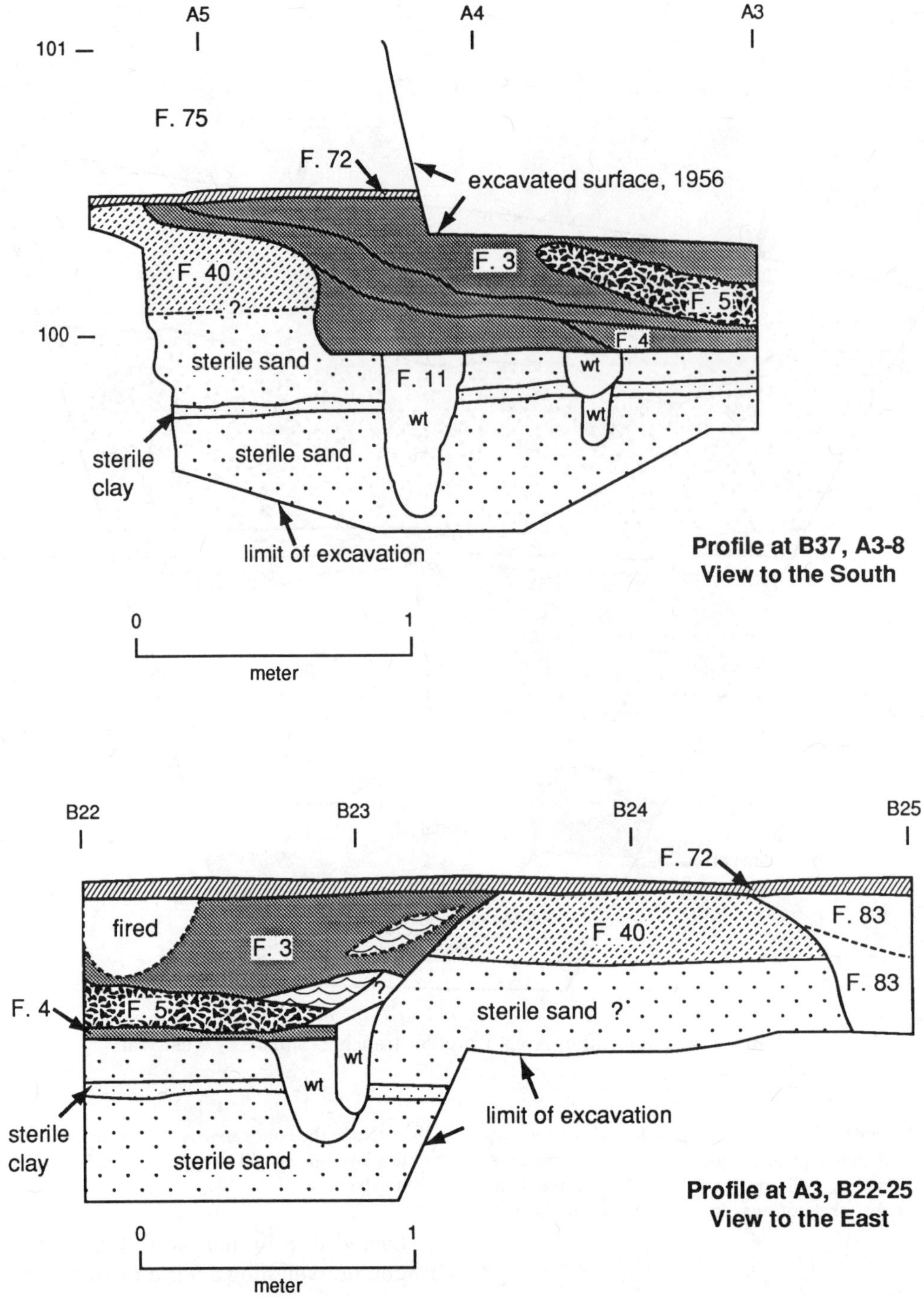

Figure 3.13. Borrow pit area profile of Feature 3–5.

deep basin. The cross-section of the feature reveals that the wall-trench building had a recognizable (prepared?) sand floor, labeled F4 (Fig. 3.13; Plate 3.4). Actually, F4 may be an earlier floor of another structure not delineated by Holder; the F4 ceramics (see Chapter 4) seem to date earlier than F3 and F5 pottery from the floor of the structure at the time it burned down and from the basin fill above this burned floor. It also is possible that F4 is a sandy wash or intentional floor fill zone derived from the F40 midden thus accounting for the earlier artifacts recovered from F4. Consequently, it was sorted separately from F3 and F5, but the present discussion will retain the F3–5 designation.

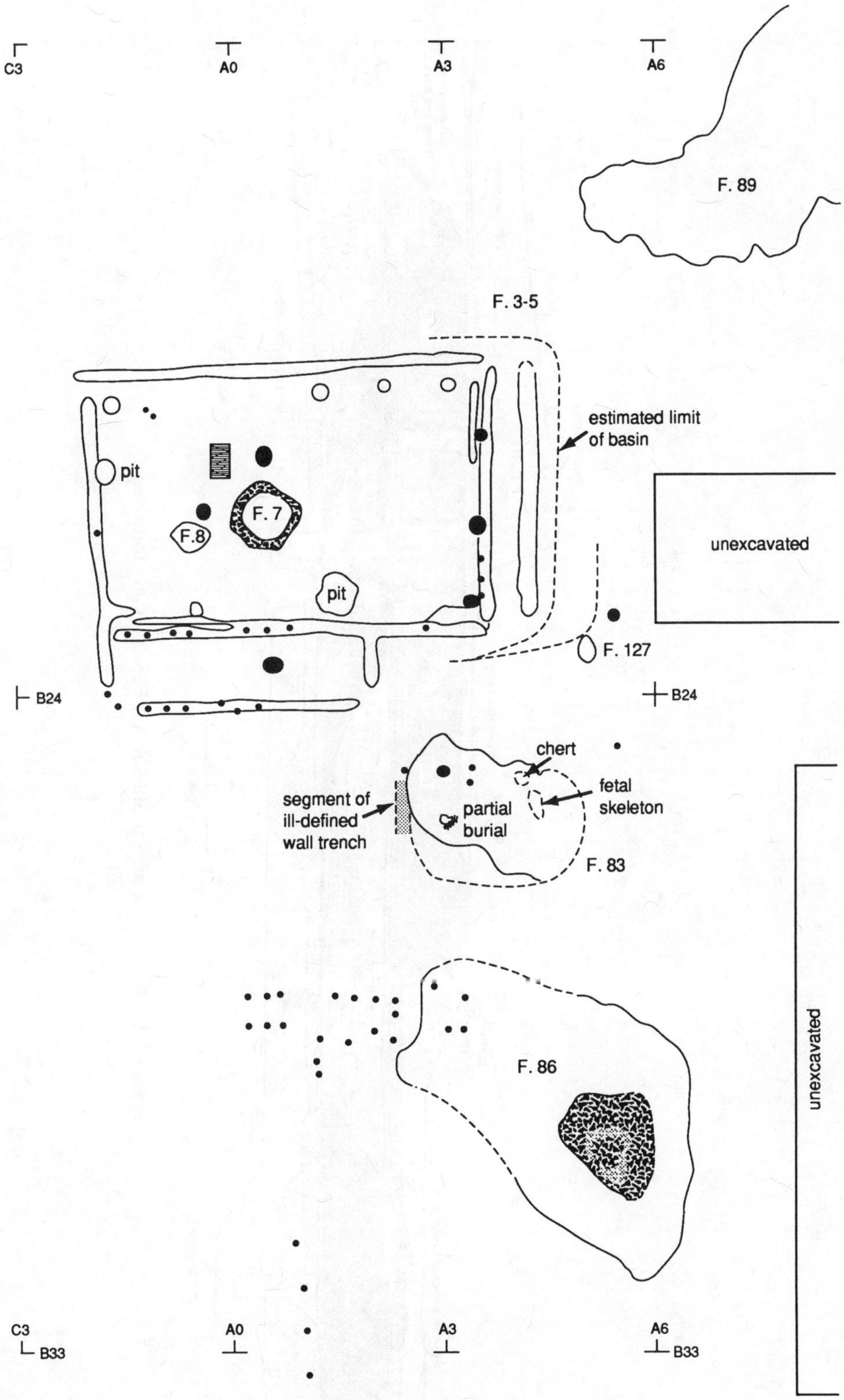

Figure 3.14. Borrow pit area submound features.

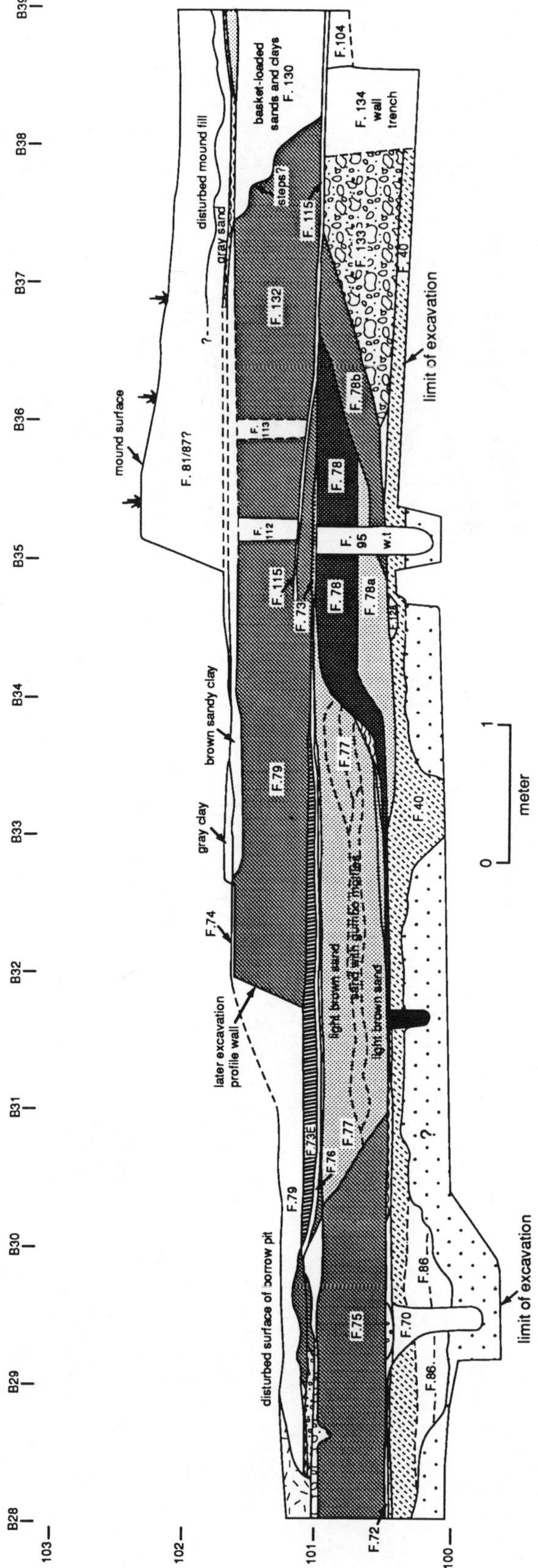

Figure 3.15. Borrow pit area profile at A3, B28–39 (view to the east).

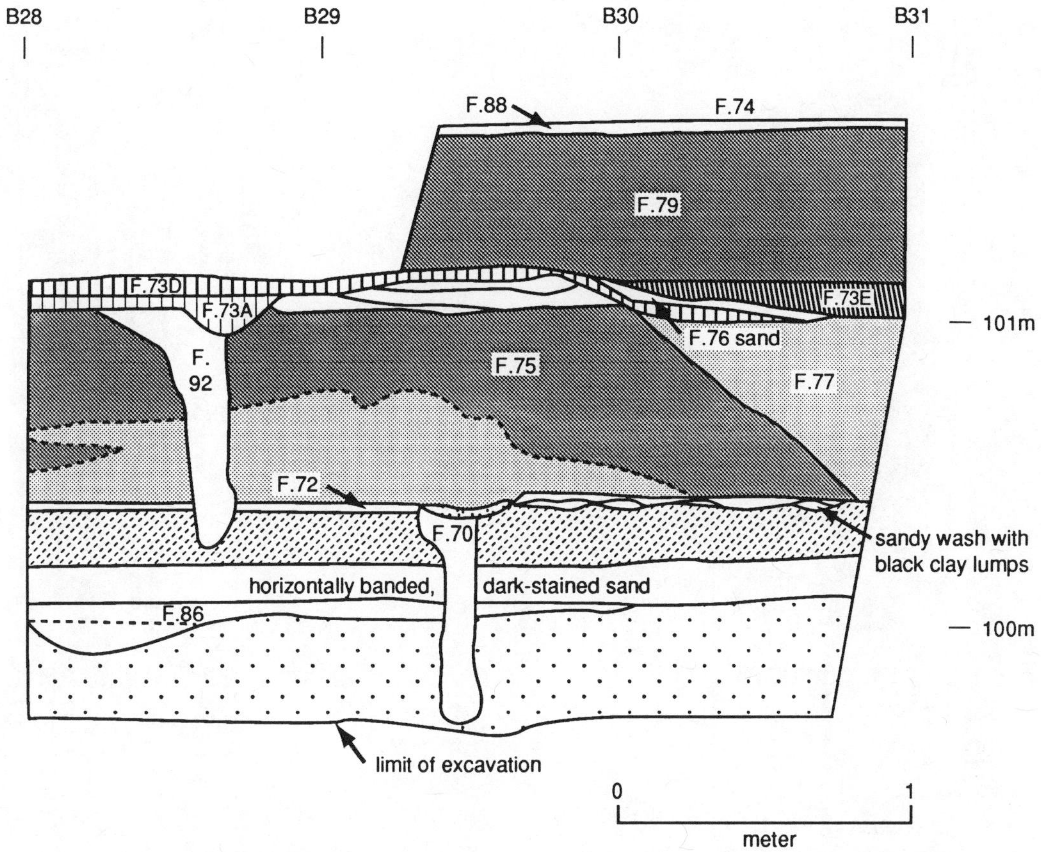

Figure 3.16. Borrow pit area profile at A4, B28–31 (view to the east).

The burned debris layer above the floor has been labeled F5, and the upper postabandonment basin fill has been called F3. The top of the basin, and that of F40, is at an elevation of about 100.4 m a.d. (Fig. 3.13; Plate 3.4). Marian White's field notes state that in "the north part of the area uncovered, there was no grass or roof-fall so some of the artifacts from there designated Feature 3 in Feature 5 may have been within the house." Another note states that F3 was everything down to the house floor (F4). Feature 5 was then a general designation for the structure as a whole. It is probably best to lump F3 and F5 together (Plate 3.5).

The building itself is a somewhat atypical wall-trench structure with a narrow rectangular room wing or an expanded rebuilt wall on its south side (Fig. 3.14; Table 3.1). The south and east structure walls had been rebuilt at least one time, visible in both plan and profile (Figs. 3.13–3.14). A single wall trench of this structure was labeled F11.

A large circular hearth, F7, located in the center of the floor space, appears to have been cleaned out or re-established about three times. In the 1955 field notes, this hearth was described as a

> puddled clay fire basin, heavily burned. Saucer shaped, about 10 cm deep, 1 meter in diameter. No raised lip merely round up to floor surface[.] Fire place was disturbed by wall trench of later house [F72] and showed considerably early disturbance along the northern edge. Central portion contained some ashes at time of discovery. This is apparently the last of 3 sequential, each of which had been located roughly on the same place as the one prior.

The earliest zone of the hearth apparently involved "7 cm of red burned sand." This was superimposed by the next hearth, measuring about 80 cm in diameter and 8 cm in depth, "roughly 10 cm below [the] lip of [feature] #7 and separated [from F7] by fine gray ash fill." Adjacent to these hearths, though unclear whether level with the first or second hearth, a "level fired floor" was found, which exhibited what may have been "patches of salmon colored pink plaster," in turn covered by a very thin and black sooty layer (1955 field notes).

A number of postmolds on the F3–5 floor may have contained roof support posts. These include two postmolds in the central area (25 and 28 cm deep), one along the east wall, and one in the southern room wing (both 30 cm deep). Other postmolds within the structure have

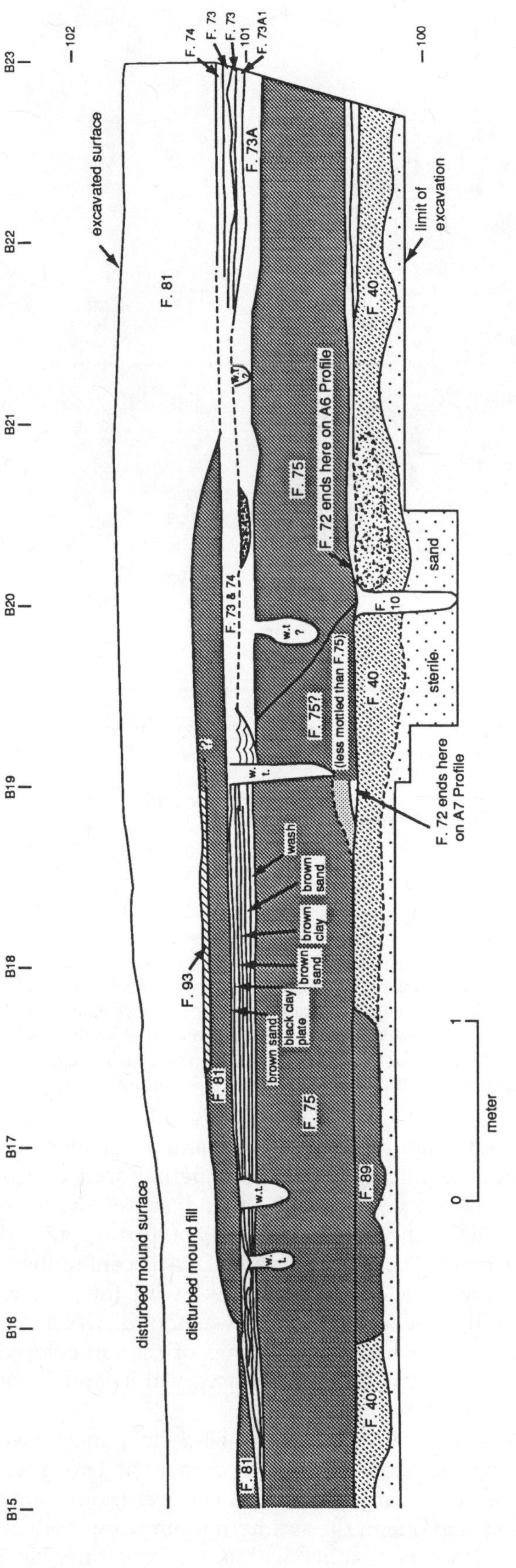

Figure 3.17. Borrow pit area profile at A7, B15–19 and A6, B19–23 (view to the east).

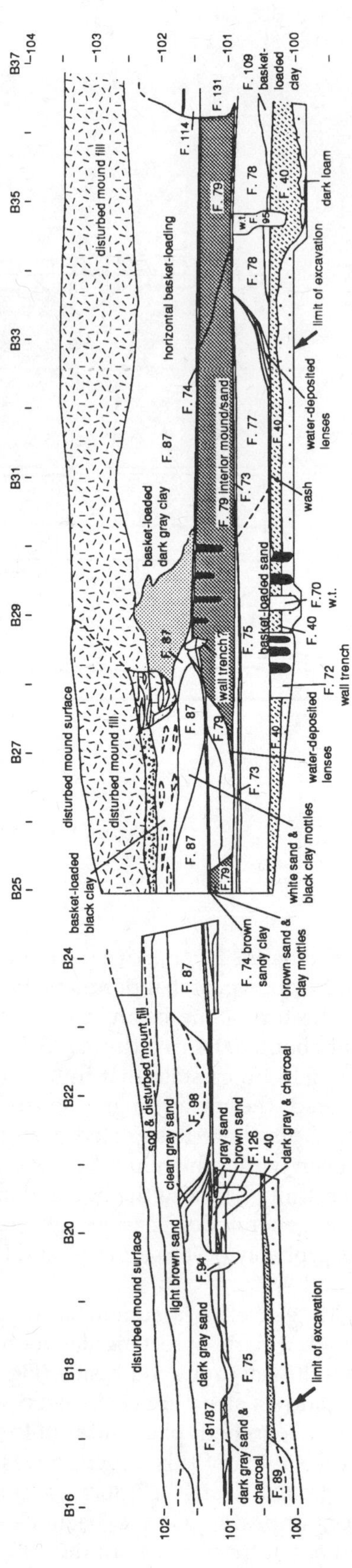

Figure 3.18. Borrow pit area profile at A9, B16–24.5 and A8, B25–37 (view to the east).

depths of 6, 8, and 15 cm. Four small postmoldlike pits lined the structure's northern wall. These were found to contain charred maize cobs. The depths of the easternmost three features measured 25 cm. Along the southern wall of the main room, a similar postmold or pit (25 cm deep) contained a bone awl.

Three other pits were defined on the F3–5 floor. One such pit was located along the west wall of F3–5 and is of unknown depth. Two other pits, F8 and an unnumbered feature, are amorphous oval basins. Feature 8 contained burned wood and twigs indicating that it was open at the time of structure incineration (see Chapter 8). The unnumbered feature contained no artifacts.

The burning of the F3–5 structure sealed the floor, preserving the living surface and, presumably, the material distribution reflects the use of space prior to incineration. In the upper levels of the basin were scattered small pieces of charred wood debris, burned clay, and—as identified in the field (but apparently not saved)—small "pebbles" of limestone (Fig. 3.19). Below this were patches of burned thatch, up to 3 cm thick in places. In one patch, Nebgen noted that some

> evidence of weaving of grass fibers was found. Although only a few cross members still remained, there were impressions or crinkles in the grass which might suggest weaving.

Nebgen continued:

> All through the thatch were braided cords, which we interpreted as being used to secure thatch to poles. They were usually 5 to 8 cm. long, made of a simple 3 strand braid. These were of a much different quality than that of the fabric.

The fabric referred to by Nebgen was uncovered directly below the thatch and charred wood in one portion of the floor (see Chapter 9). It appears to have either covered the floor or the wall interior when the building burned down.

> Probably this structure burned on a south wind and complete or nearly complete combustion took place on that side. Also in areas of considerable thicknesses of thatch and wood charcoal, there seemed to be a layer of sand that might have been used to extinguish the fire. [D.L. Nebgen, field notes, 1955]

In one portion of the structure, Nebgen noted that two thatch layers seemed to be separated by a thin layer of sand.

A number of complete, or nearly complete, remains can be associated with the burned structure floor (Fig. 3.19). These include at least one ceramic vessel and perhaps another—a bowl—in the northwest corner of the floor space. Mussel-shell hoe blades were recovered from the northwest corner. Cut and smoothed antler, bone, and, possibly, wood were among a cluster of items recovered from the southeastern corner of the main room floor. A cluster of items—a chert hoe blade, hammerstone, bone, shell, chert, and charred botanical remains—was located south of the hearth (F7). An unfinished shell pendant or gorget and charred cordage were found in the northeast quadrant of the floor. A lump of clay, a sandstone saw fragment, a mussel-shell valve, and other shell artifacts were found in the extreme southeast corner. A deer scapula hoe blade, a pair of "grinding stones," unfinished marine shell beads, mussel shells, chert, and sherds were among the items recovered from the southern room wing. Maize kernels were found in places within the structure (Finds 13, 21). One instance consisted of 50 or 60 kernels on the floor.

The distribution of materials on the F3–5 floor seems consistent with the structured use of "dead space" (Hayden and Cannon 1983) observed in other Mississippian domiciles (Pauketat 1987a:226). Burned structures are known throughout the midcontinent. Most of them—by virtue of their cleaned-out look—seem to have been intentionally burned to rid the area of the building (Pauketat 1987a:228–33). At Cahokia, two other burned structures are, like F3–5, full of often-unbroken material objects (Collins 1990:150–53; Pauketat 1987a, 1987b): House 4 and Feature 178. These two late Stirling phase features contained numerous ceramic vessels and an array of other complete or fire-damaged items. The significance of this will be explored in Chapter 10.

The South Mound and Prepared Surface Feature 72

Two deposits represent the beginning of mound construction as visible in the BP excavations. The first of these is a low flat-topped mound exposed in the southern portion of the BP area (Figs. 3.18, 3.20). This is the earliest uncovered culturally prepared mound surface in the BP area. It was exposed in the southernmost end of the BP area excavations; the areal extent of this earliest of mound stages is unknown. In the exposed profile, the early mound consists of three unlabeled grey and black clay or sandy-clay mantles, about 25 cm thick, resting on top of "brown sand wash," south of grid point B40 at an elevation of 100.38 m a.d. (Fig. 3.20). No feature number was assigned to these three mound fill zones, the largest of which is a 16 cm-thick mound fill deposit. These earliest zones of a south mound reach a height of about 100.54 m a.d.

Sandy wash redeposited from a higher elevation is visible along the northern face of this earliest unnumbered mound, a characteristic seen in later mound stages exposed in the BP area as well. A narrow wall-trench structure was partially exposed in this area. Its east–west wall trenches, Features 106 and 107, were defined at an elevation of 100.4 m a.d. (Fig. 3.20; Table 3.1). The top of F40 in this area dips to an elevation of about 100.2 m a.d. Thus, it is possible that the F106/107 structure surmounted an early

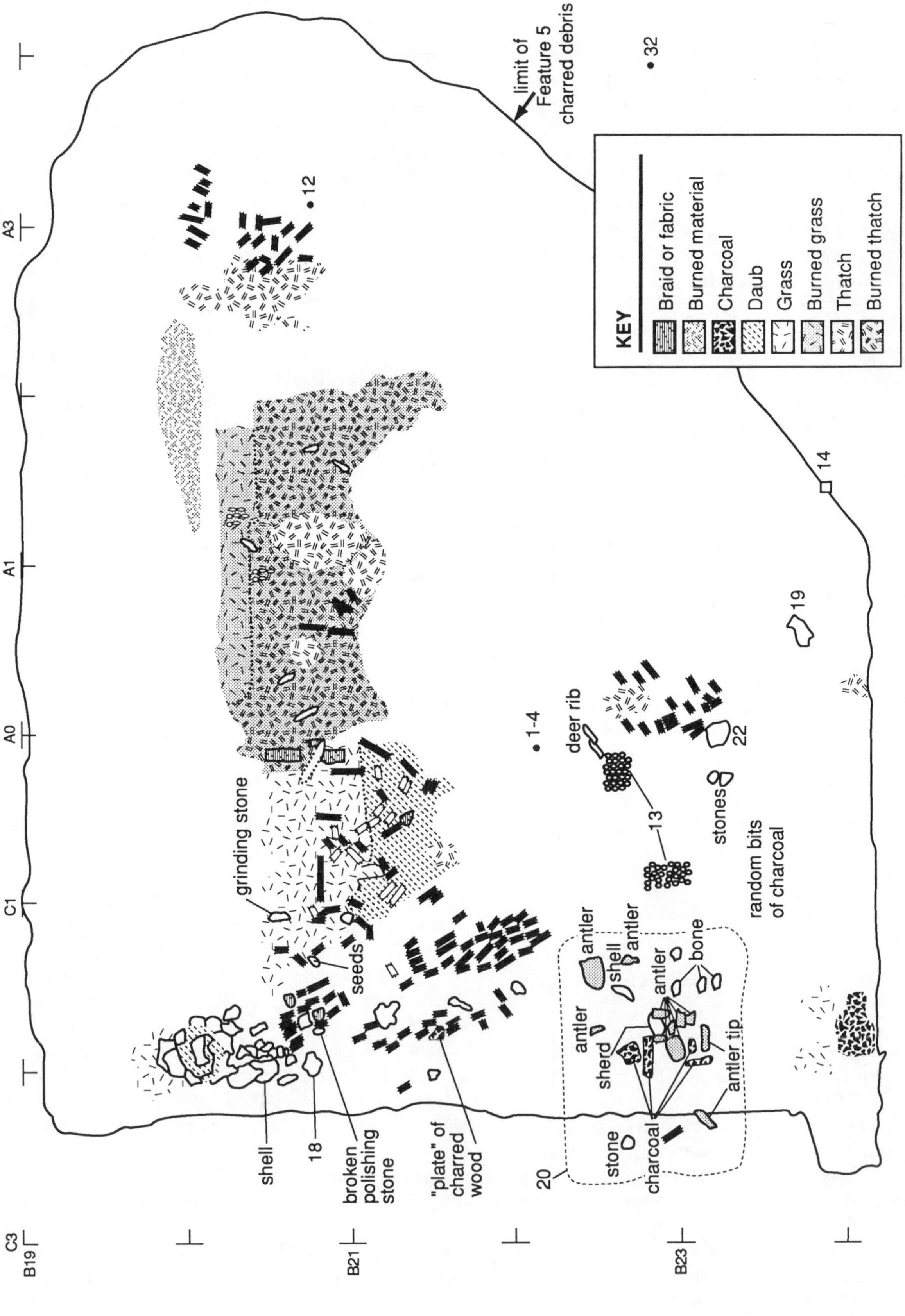

Figure 3.19. Plan of Feature 3-5 with *in situ* artifacts and debris.

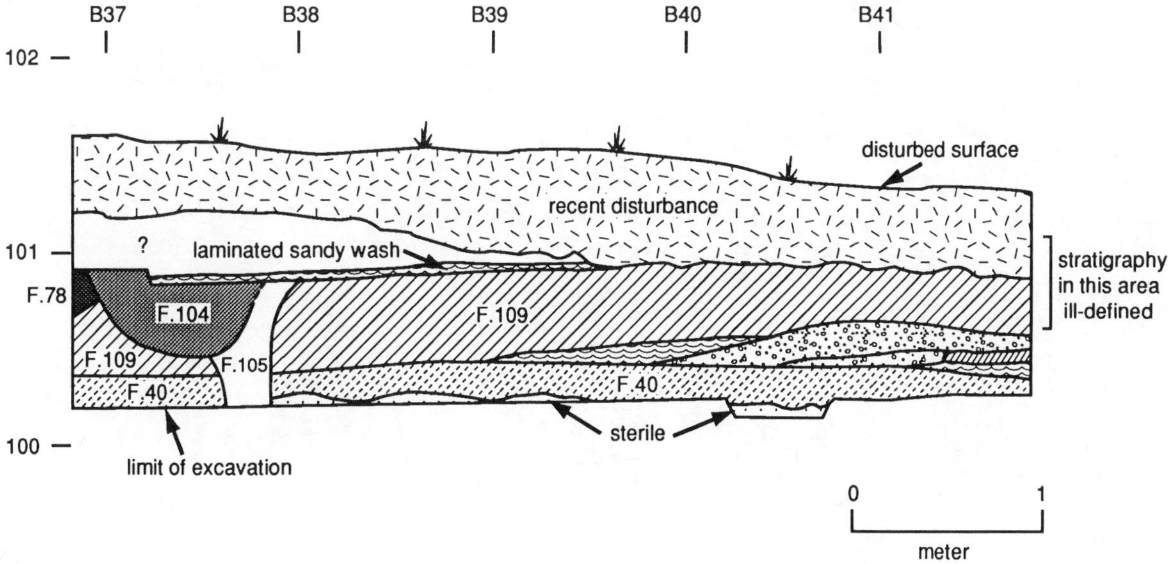

Figure 3.20. Borrow pit area profile at A0, B37–42 (view to the east).

stage of this south mound. It may be of importance that F106/107 is oriented with the cardinal directions comparable to structure F3–5, while later structures in the BP area are fairly consistently oriented 5 to 8 degrees west of north.

Features 109 and 133 are fill elements representing enlargements of the south mound to a height of 100.88 m a.d., clearly a flat-topped platform (Figs. 3.15, 3.18, 3.20). The northernmost edge of the south mound base at this point is found at grid point B36. A large structure, represented by wall-trench Features 105 and 134, is fairly securely associated with the F133 mound surface (Fig. 3.21). The building's wall trenches parallel the mound's northern edge; thus, the south mound probably was a rectangular truncated pyramid (Figs. 3.18–3.20). A later structure (F95/96) associated with mound F78 superimposes this F105/134 building.

At this point in the sequence, it is not certain whether some of the features to the north—the burned structure F3–5 and fill zone Features 83, 86, and 89—predate or are contemporaneous with the early south mound. It is certain that at some point after the incineration of the F3–5 structure, the northern features were capped by a 5 cm-thick black clay floor—F72—associated with a rectangular wall-trench structure erected in this area (Fig. 3.22; Table 3.1; see also Figs. 3.13, 3.15–3.18). One small area on the floor appeared to reveal the manner in which the black clay had been applied. The floor in this spot had a brushed, or splashed, appearance (see Fig. 3.22).[2] The F72 building is quite large (62.8 m^2) and contains two circular hearths (F13 and F85), one in the north-central portion of the floor and the other in the south-central floor area (Figs. 3.22–3.23; Tables 3.1–3.2). Another circular burned surface (F71) and two central postmolds (F90) also are located on the F72 floor. The depth of one of the F90 postmolds was recorded to be 70 cm, a substantial depth. The F72 wall trenches, labeled Features 9, 10, 70, and 125, contained slender postmolds, some about 6 cm in diameter and spaced about 30 cm apart.

The F72 structure was probably contemporaneous with some stage of the south mound, and it is worthy of note that this elaborate building itself was not on a "mound" per se. A wash zone derived from the latest stage of the south mound, a horizontal enlargement (perhaps itself constructed in two stages) called F78, appears to postdate the construction of F72. As Holder noted in the field, this single F78 wash zone seems to superimpose the edge of F72 (Fig. 3.18). This does not necessarily mean, however, that the two were not contemporaneous, but may only suggest that a particular erosion event associated with an extant mound postdated the initial construction of the northern building (F72).

A new building was constructed on the south mound subsequent to its F78 enlargement (northern surface, 100.9 m a.d.). This structure, outlined by wall-trench Features 95/138 and 96, appears larger than its F72 counterpart to the north (Fig. 3.21; Table 3.1). In profile, it may be observed that this F95/96 building skirted the edge of the flattened top of the F78 mound (Figs. 3.15, 3.18), like the preceding building (F105/134) atop the earlier F133 south mound. Consequently, it is reasonable to surmise that the

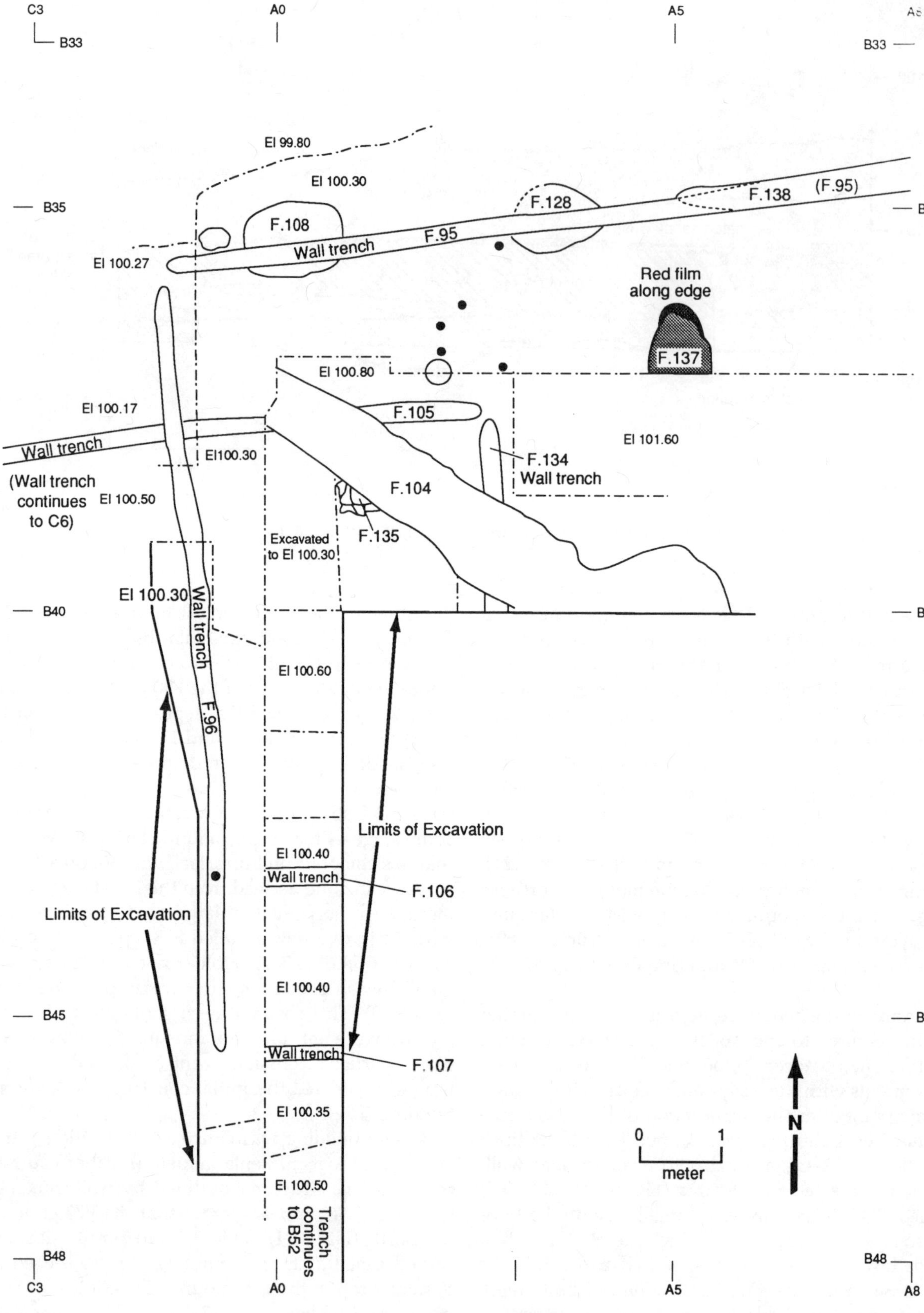

Figure 3.21. Plan of structures associated with the south mound (Features 95, 96, 106, 107, 134).

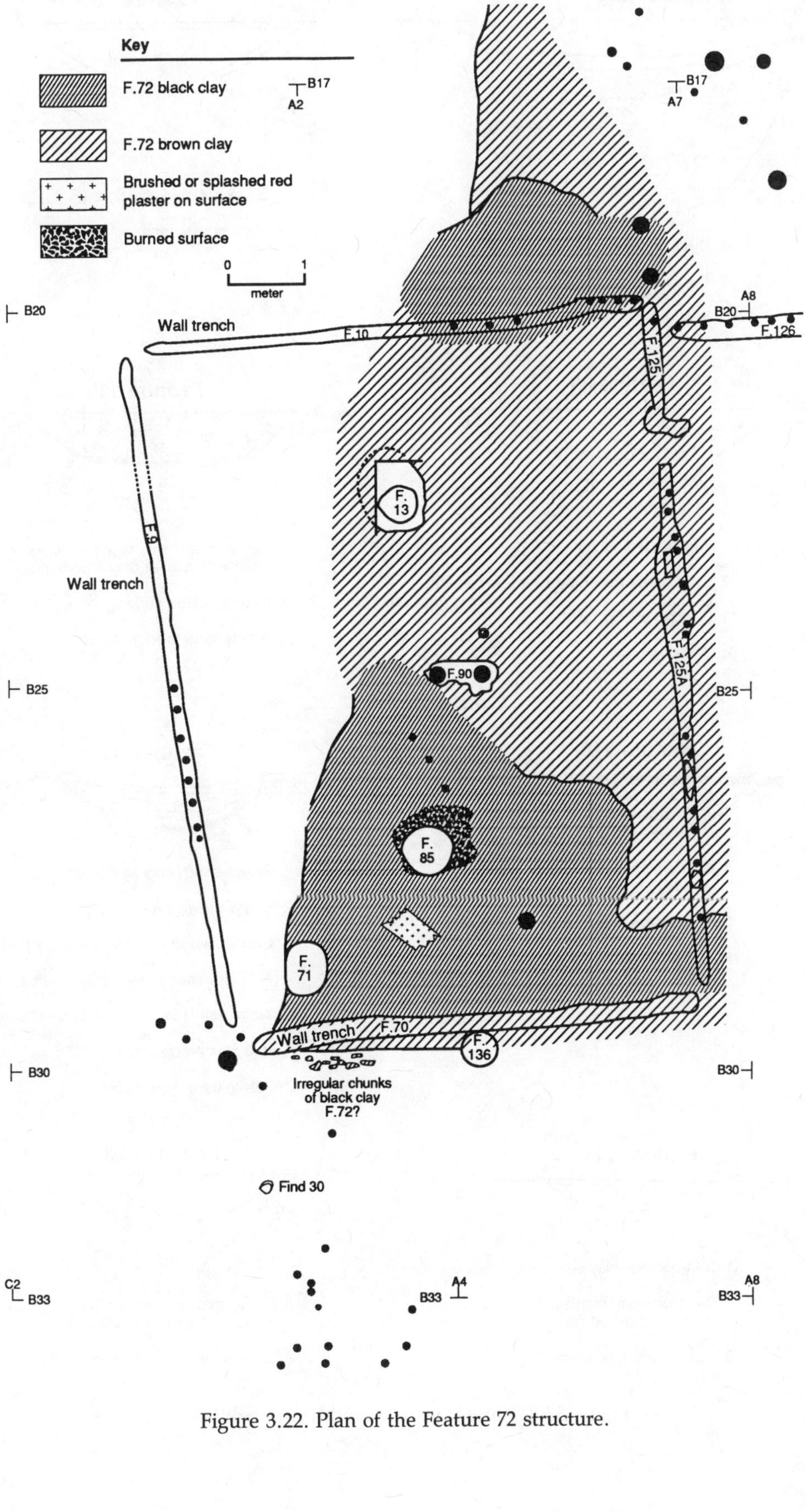

Figure 3.22. Plan of the Feature 72 structure.

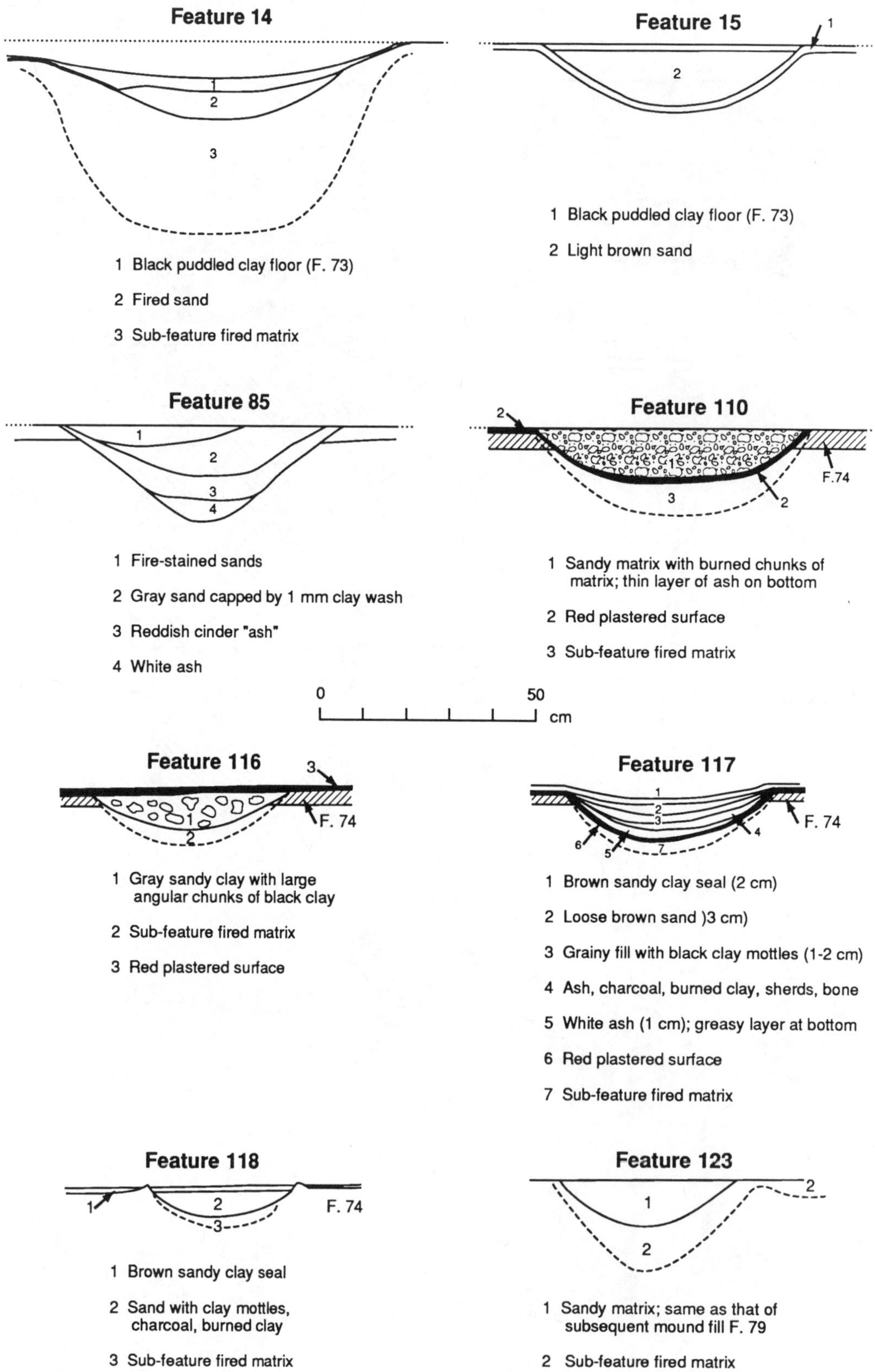

Figure 3.23. Kunnemann Mound hearth profiles.

late-stage south mound also was a rectangular platform, like the earlier south mound. A hearth, F135, may be associated with the F95/96 structure floor. What appears to be a small partially defined pit (F137) may be associated with this mound stage; a "red film" (plaster on the floor?) was observed around the perimeter of F137. The ramp to a post pit, F104, may be associated with the insertion or extraction of a roof support post for the F95/96 structure (Fig. 3.21).

Mound Fill Features 75 and 77, Prepared Surface(s) Feature 73

At some point, perhaps while the south mound was still in use, the structure associated with F72 was dismantled and covered with another flat-topped mound (Plate 3.6). The southern face of this mound, F75, was less than 2 meters north of the south mound, and was raised to the same elevation as that of F78 to the south (Figs. 3.15, 3.17, 3.18; Plate 3.6). This "north mound" (F75) existed as an entity separate from the south mound; this is suggested by the existence of a southern face, and by prepared floor zones that cover only the F75 surface (Fig. 3.15).

Based on its stratigraphic position below the prepared floors (F73) on the F75 mound surface, wall trench F92 would appear to be the primary candidate for the earliest structure surmounting the F75 mound (Fig. 3.16). Unfortunately, only the southeast portion of the F92 structure remained intact (Fig. 3.24) and, assuming that the associated hearth F123 was located near its center, it appears that this building was not as large as other previous examples on mound surfaces (Table 3.1). However, the portion that does remain tells of a unique building with a wide wall trench (which probably amounted to an interior lip which gradually dropped off into the main trench, Fig. 3.16). Wall posts about 5 to 8 cm in diameter were set at regular 20 cm intervals. In addition, two other features distinguish this building from previous examples. The first of these is the hearth and the second is an apparent red-plastered floor. The F92 red-plastered floor was not well preserved within the structure. Only an isolated portion of it—called F91—remained adjacent to the south wall of the structure (not illustrated).

The F123 hearth on the floor of F92 is the most elaborate example excavated at the Kunnemann Mound. It superimposes an earlier hearth, F123A, a shallow, well-defined circular basin (Figs. 3.23–3.24; Table 3.2). Feature 123, on the other hand, is a circular basin with an extraordinary groove surrounding it (Plate 3.7). This groove, 10 mm wide and 3 mm deep, is *v*-shaped in cross-section. In plan, it outlines a perfect square enclosing the circular hearth. Nothing similar to this square v-shaped groove has been reported from Cahokia in the past. It is not clear what left the groove. It may have been the result of some kind of box containing the fire inside; the burned area surrounding the circular hearth appears largely contained within this square (Plate 3.7). The burned area within the bounds of the square groove has a dark-brown to black color, apparently a consequence of a reducing atmosphere contained inside the square. If this was a fire box, then the groove would have been left behind by some nonflammable yet straight or flat object (perhaps like a laminated sandstone, although it is difficult to envision such large and thin sandstone slabs). For the time being, this F123 groove will remain a mystery (compare the hearths illustrated by Lewis and Kneberg 1946:55). Two other hearths, F14 and F15, were probably associated with the F92 structure or a subsequent F73 building (Fig. 3.23). Both hearths, their centers located at grid coordinates A3.1, B24.7 (F14) and A3.45, B26.45 (F15), were excavated early in 1955 prior to the recognition of an associated F73-level structure.

A series of other partially exposed structures are associated with floor zones of F73 (atop the north mound F75). A wall trench of considerable length, F119, may be the second in the sequence of F73 structures. It apparently was defined in zone A of F73. A hearth (F97), postmolds, and segments of ill-defined wall trenches (F121–122 and unnumbered trenches) probably are associated with later F73 surfaces. A poorly preserved red-plastered floor was found associated with the F73E surface (Figs. 3.15–3.18 and 3.24).

Given the apparent lack of mound wash on the southern face of the F75 mound, it is possible that it was not long in place before another modification occurred. This modification appears as an horizontal enlargement, F77, linking the south mound F78 (etc.) with the north mound F75 (Figs. 3.15, 3.16, 3.18); on certain profile maps (e.g., Fig. 3.17), Holder retained the F75 designation for this intermediate fill zone. A number of structures and corresponding floors (zones of F73) and one hearth (F97) are located on the summit of the northern portion of the newly expanded mound (Figs. 3.15–3.17, 3.24; Table 3.1). The final elevation of this mound stage is around 101 m a.d.

The southern end, old mound fill Feature 78, appears to have witnessed little in the way of layers of (F73) prepared floors. It is possible that the large trench F104, located on the surface of the southern mound, dates to the later period of this mound stage (Figs. 3.20–3.21). It superimposes other features in the area supposedly associated with the earlier structures. Given the proportions of this feature, F104 is probably the ramp portion of a large post pit, the postmold itself falling outside the limits of excavation.

Mound Fill Features 79, 130, 131, 132 and Prepared Surface Feature 74

The next major construction event represented in the BP area was the vertical and horizontal enlargement of the now-combined (north and south) Kunnemann Mound.

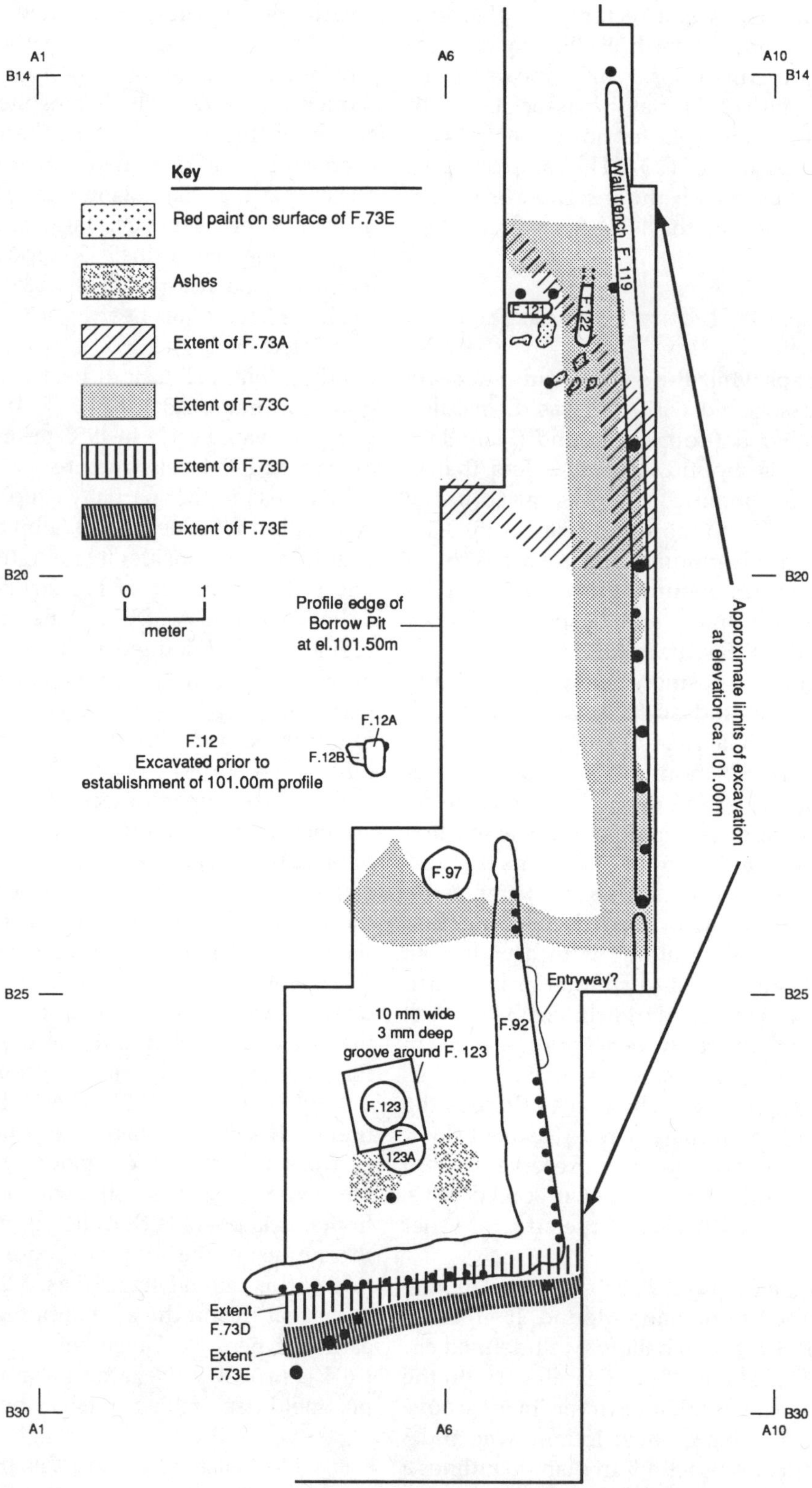

Figure 3.24. Plan of Feature 73 structures.

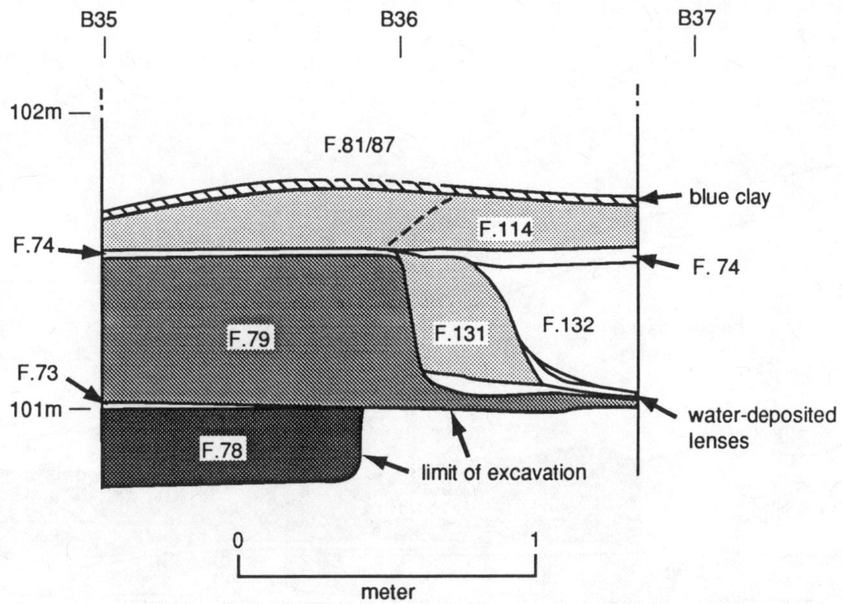

Figure 3.25. Borrow pit area profile at A4.5, B35–37 (view to the east).

Again, however, this enlargement actually was two distinct enlargements. Two new upper platforms, perhaps sequential constructions, were added. Only later were these combined into one.

To the south was an earthen platform (F79) covering only part of the larger (and earlier) first terrace (i.e., the combined F75/77 mound capped by F73 layers). In the BP profile, this upper and southern mound terrace F79 was at least 8 m in length (between grid points B28 and B36), with some evidence that it had been narrower prior to a horizontal enlargement episode (Fig. 3.18). This portion of F79 was approximately 55 cm thick and was capped by a prepared surface (F74). Both the northern and the southern faces of this particular southern F79 terrace exhibit water-deposited sand lenses (Figs. 3.18, 3.25).

Evidence suggests that the southern face of this mound at least twice was enlarged horizontally (Figs. 3.15, 3.18, 3.25). Feature 131 comprises a seemingly small addition which at one point during the excavation was thought to be a trench due to its regularity. In one profile, however, Holder depicts it as a small horizontal mound addition with wash laminations (Fig. 3.26). As it turns out, this particular occurrence of F131 in profile is in the exact position where a wall trench would be expected (see below). On the other hand, an east–west profile clearly shows F131 as mound fill stratigraphically above F79 (Fig. 3.26). The mound wash presumably eroding off of the F131 mound has been labeled F115 (Fig. 3.26). Feature 115 appears in other profiles as something of a mysterious poorly defined zone (Fig. 3.15). In another east–west profile, F115 exhibited a small slip fault (Fig. 3.27).

A single building, whose size closely matches the horizontal dimensions of the southern mound F79/131, appears to have occupied the surface of this stage. This unique structure, situated atop the prepared surface F74, has a circular shape in plan view. No wall trenches were discerned in profile (except perhaps for F131), but the plan map and photographs betray a sandy circumferential band that in fact appears to be a wall trench (Fig. 3.28; Plate 3.18). Additionally, a field note states that the circular structure had a "ring of mottled fill around it." Perhaps the curvilinear nature of this trench made it difficult to identify in profile, especially since the underlying mound was also comprised of sandy fill and perhaps because it was confused with a horizontal mound enlargement.

The unique qualities of this circular structure go beyond its shape. This circular building or "rotunda" (see DePratter 1983; Mehrer 1988: Table 26) had a plastered, dark-colored clay floor (part of F74). Red plaster showed up across much of the building floor. Holder more than once uses the term "splattered" to describe its appearance within the circular F74 building. Black plaster also was noted in the field, but this simply may be reduced red plaster, a consequence perhaps of close proximity to some hearth area within the rotunda and the sooting of the red plaster. One small cross-section of the floor exposed a sequence including, from top to bottom, a thin film of "greasy" red plaster (0.5 mm thick), a thin film of "flakey" white plaster (0.5 mm thick), and finally a layer of buff-

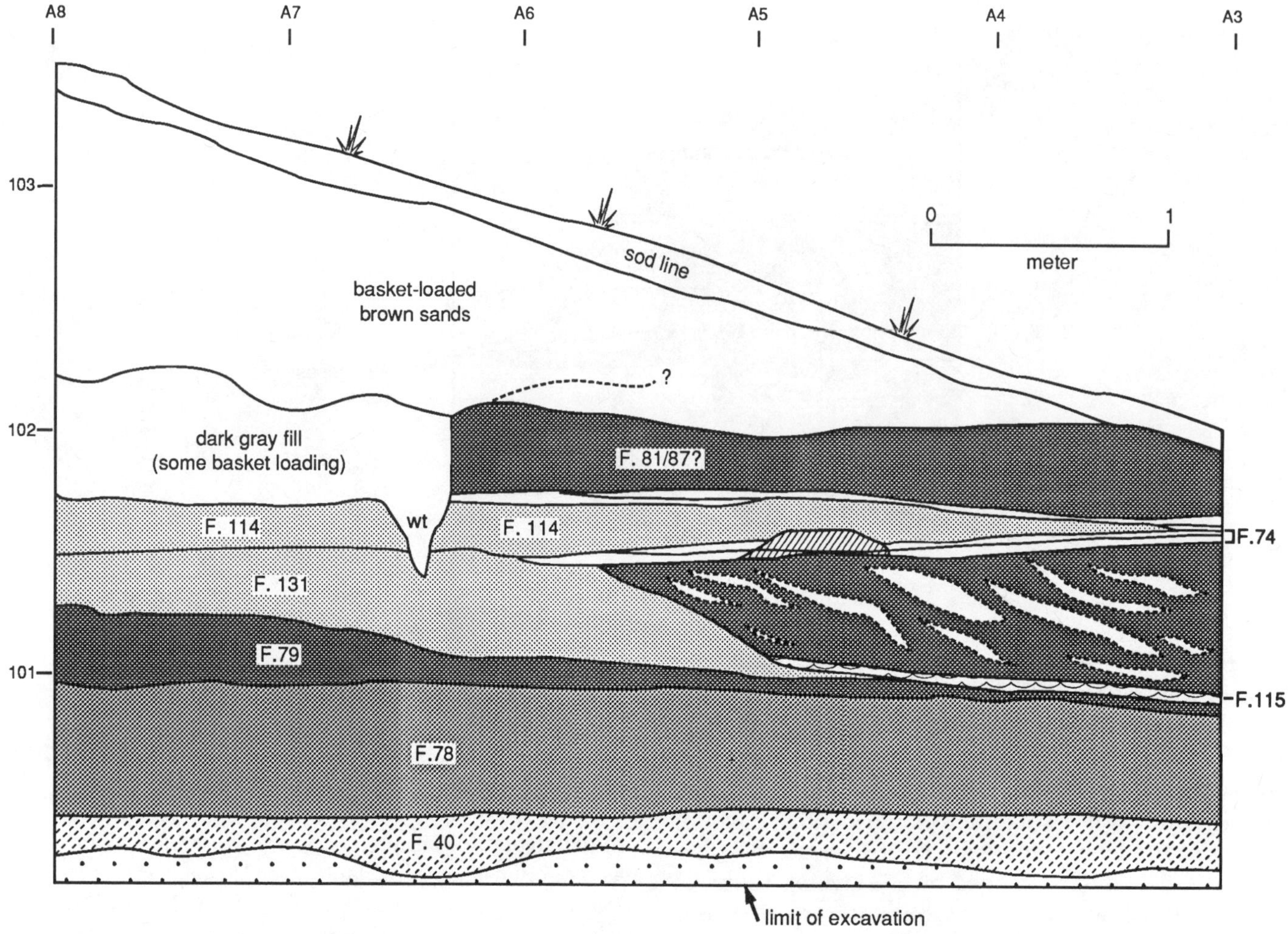

Figure 3.26. Borrow pit area profile at B37, A3–8 (view to the south).

colored sandy clay (1.5–2.0 mm thick). Another field note makes reference to "yellow plaster" on the F74 surface in association with a burned area (F88). Just outside the structure, a "blue-grey clay" version of the F74 black clay surface (also called "plate") extended to the south. Holder suspected that this might be a "paving"—the specially prepared and compacted entrance to the rotunda.

Clearly evident on portions of the rotunda floor were impressions of mats (Fig. 3.28; Plate 3.8). These impressions were sunk into the surface of the F74 black clay floor to a depth of a millimeter or so. The warp elements of these mats in the two documented areas on the floor appear to have been oriented parallel to the tangent of the perimeter of the rotunda. If these were wall hanging imprints, then the walls had to have collapsed and been left in place for a period of time or immediately buried by additional mound fill. (A modern analog for the appearance of these imprints might be straw-bamboo blinds.) For this reason, floor mats might be the most reasonable inference to be drawn. Holder noted that some clay, 5 to 8 cm thick, covered a portion of the floor in northern and western areas of the building. This clay Holder thought to be remnant wall/roof earthen cover or daub which fell onto the floor (perhaps resulting in the wall hanging impressions being made on the floor).

The floor of the circular structure witnessed a sequence of four formal hearths (Table 3.2). Of these four, Features 116 and 118 appear to have been the earliest (Fig. 3.28; Plate 3.9). Both were filled prior to the time when the entire circular floor was plastered red (Fig. 3.23). Interestingly, these were located in the north-central and south-central portions of the building and may have been in use at the same time. Feature 117 appears to have been used next. It had a red-plastered floor, but also seems to have

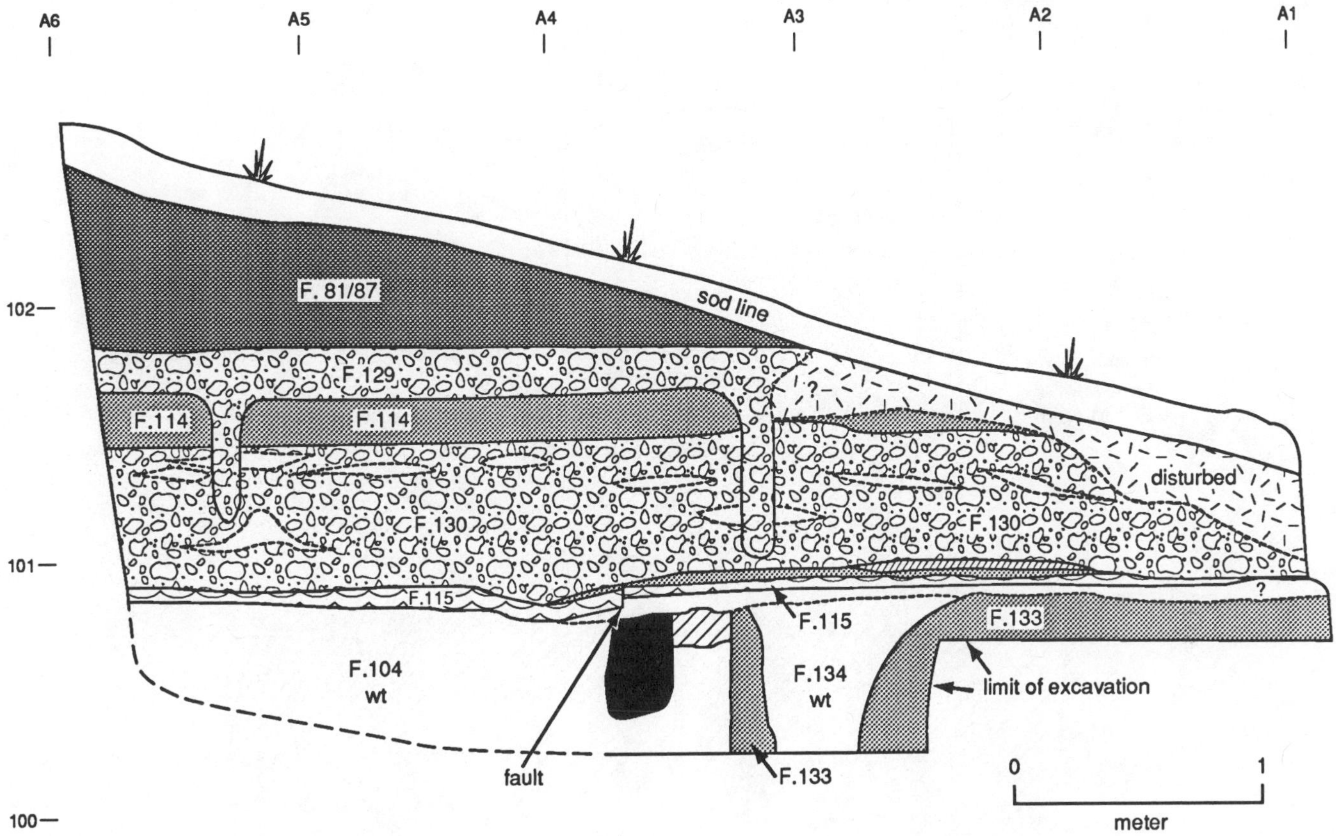

Figure 3.27. Borrow pit area profile at B40, A1-6 (view to the south).

been backfilled and partially covered over with a floor zone and red plaster (according to a field note). Feature 110 has a red-plastered base, a single fill zone, and no prepared floor covering it. Therefore, it is believed to be the most recent of the series. It should be noted also that other burned or fired surfaces, perhaps informal hearths, are located on the floor as well (Fig. 3.28).

A final unique feature of the circular structure is the presence of interior structural features. Most notably these include lines of postmolds traversing the northern and southwestern portions of the floor, and narrow linear grooves, 1 cm wide (such as those seen around F123). These grooves run approximately north–south across the western side of the circular floor and east–west across the south-central structure floor. Another small segment was oriented approximately north–south in the east-central floor area; this particular groove also featured a postmold within its bounds (Fig. 3.28). The function of the grooves on the floor of the F74 circular building in part may have been related to the hearth features on the floor (as is suspected of the F123 hearth grooves mentioned previously). They also may have served to somehow partition interior space. We might be wise to examine the east–west groove on the F74 surface (and some short nearby grooves) in relation to F110 and the "fired area" along the eastern side of the floor space.

Certainly the postmolds, with the possible exception of the row oriented northwest–southeast across the southwestern floor area, may have partitioned the interior space of the circular structure. The southwestern postmold row appears to cut through and hence probably postdates the prepared F74 structure floors associated with the rotunda. The two stray wall trenches, F112 and F113, also may postdate the rotunda, although Holder felt otherwise (Fig. 3.28; Plate 3.9).

At some point, perhaps while the circular structure was in use, the F79/131 mound upon which it sat was enlarged, again in a horizontal direction. This southern expansion, recognized as F132, extended the surface of the mound three or four meters. Undulations in the south face of this mound extension are possible steps (Fig. 3.15). A second horizontal expansion to the south is labeled F130.

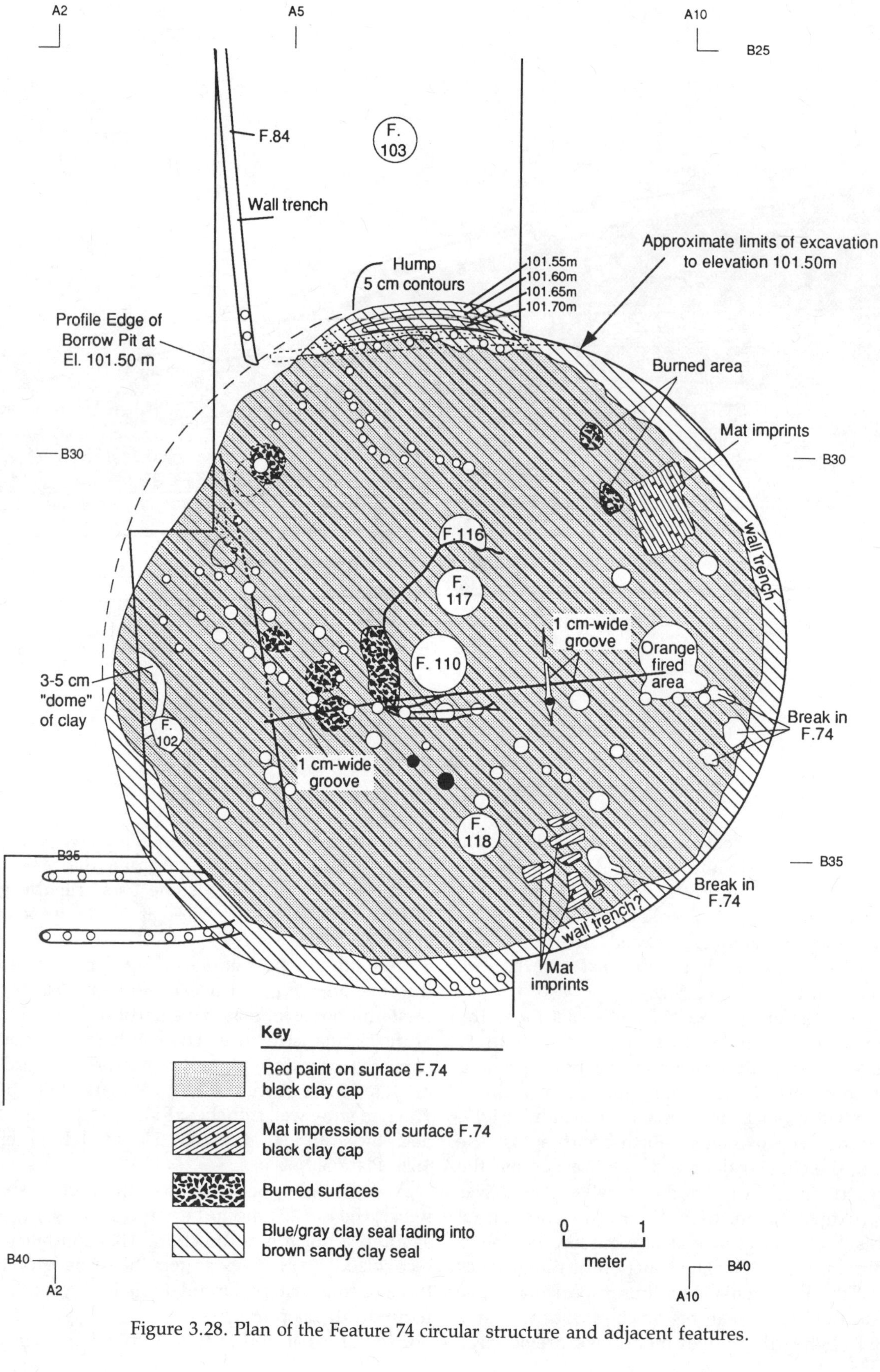

Figure 3.28. Plan of the Feature 74 circular structure and adjacent features.

A small northern F79 platform terrace was constructed at some point after the construction of the southern F79 terrace, the south face of which, in one profile, is located around grid point A8, B25.5 (Fig. 3.18). Shortly thereafter, the two-meter gap between this terrace and the initial (southern) F79 terrace was bridged making a single mound surface along the entire course of the BP area (Fig. 3.18). This platform (made up of mound fill F79 and F130–132), however, dips noticably toward the north. In fact, while the southern portion (F130) is elevated at 101.5 m, the northern portion slopes down to meet the earlier stage. North of grid point B23.5, the F79 mound fill disappears (Figs. 3.17–3.18). The F74 prepared surface continues to the north located directly on top of the older stage F73 prepared surface. The northern limit to F73/74 (along the A9 profile) is located between grid points B15.5 and B16 (Fig. 3.17). The elevation of this mound, the top of F74, is 101.16 m a.d. at the northern end. Consequently, the F79/130–132 mound, easily identified by following the course of the prepared surface F74, dips to the north at about a four-degree angle, losing 34 cm in height from the south to the north.

A rectangular wall-trench structure, F84, and its internal hearth (F103) are associated with the F74 surface which spans the distance between the initial F79 mound and the low northern mound (which merges with F73). This structure also superimposes the floor and wall trench of the former circular structure to the south (Figs. 3.28–3.29; Table 3.1). A possible *T*-shaped structure, F94, is located to the north of F84 (Fig. 3.30). It superimposes an earlier F73 structure wall and also cuts through the prepared F74 floor. Its wall trenches are filled with the same matrix as the F81 mound fill subsequently placed over it (Figs. 3.17–3.18). It probably represents the last in the series of F73/74 buildings at this location.

Mound Fill Features 81, 87, 114, and 129

The subsequent phase of mound construction is poorly understood because of modern-disturbed upper zones in this area (Plate 3.10). No structure plans were exposed in plan view at or above this level. An additional east–west trench, however, was excavated between grid points A5 to A19 to provide clarity into the upper zones of the BP area of the Kunnemann Mound (Plate 3.11; Fig. 3.31). In notes and records this is called the Moorehead profile cut 2 (MP2) and appears as the easternmost extension of the excavated BP Area in Fig. 3.1.

Isolated mantles of earth were added to the top of the northern, central, and southern portions of the F74 surface as exposed in the BP profile on top of the F74 surface. In the northern area, this addition appears to take the form of a terrace raised 50 cm above the old F74 surface, approximately between grid points B16–21 along the A9 profile. The highest elevation of this terrace is 101.74 m (Fig. 3.18). The mantle is variously refered to as F81, 87, or 81/87 on field maps. There is some indication of a prepared surface F93 on top of this platform (Fig. 3.17) and redeposited wash lenses on the south face of this terrace (Fig. 3.18).

In the central portion of the BP area, a second fill mantle was laid down between grid points B22.5–29.0 along the A8 profile (Fig. 3.18). This fill, called F87 (and F81), apparently was a mound terrace (101.9 m a.d.) isolated for a time from the northern F81/87 terrace. Only about two meters separate the central F81/87 terrace from its northern counterpart (Fig. 3.18). A number of slightly different fill zones comprise this central terrace, but these may represent fills laid down during a single construction event. The west face of this mound tier exhibits lenses of water-redeposited fill (Fig. 3.31). The north face does not exhibit such clearly defined wash zones. Perhaps the northern and central mound terraces were not separate for a significant length of time. The fill zone between and joining the two is known as F98 (Fig. 3.18).

In the southern BP area, a mantle of earth called F114 appears almost as an initial counterpart to the northern and central Features 81 and 87 (Figs. 3.18, 3.25–27). This southern fill is only about 20 cm in thickness, reaching an elevation of about 101.7 m, and is capped by thin "blue" and black clay prepared surfaces. Another 15 cm of possible mound fill, F129, was heaped above F114. The upper surface of F129 is found at 101.83 m a.d. In one profile, F129 appears almost as basin fill to a wall trench structure (Fig. 3.27). The same structure is probably represented in Figure 3.26 (unlabeled). A third mound fill zone, identified as F81/87, also is found in this area above (and possibly beside) F129. The poorly defined upper surface of this substage seems to be elevated to a height of 102.2 m a.d. (Figs. 3.26–3.27).

Upper Mound Strata

At some point after the two or three lower F81/87/98 and F114/129 terraces had been constructed, the entire area was covered with additional mound fill. Unfortunately, soil disturbances created by modern modification to the mound engendered confusion in the field, evident in the north–south profiles of the BP area (Figs. 3.15, 3.17, 3.18). For instance, three possible features (F99–101) were defined at the base of the disturbed zone between elevations 102.00–102.35 m a.d. These features may be modern disturbances, perhaps even the potholes of unscrupulous artifact collectors (Fig. 3.32, compare with Fig. 3.18).

Upon hindsight, it seems that the mound fill above 101.5 m between grid points B29–36.5, and above 102 m elsewhere, was deposited during one construction event or a series of related construction episodes. This is clarified

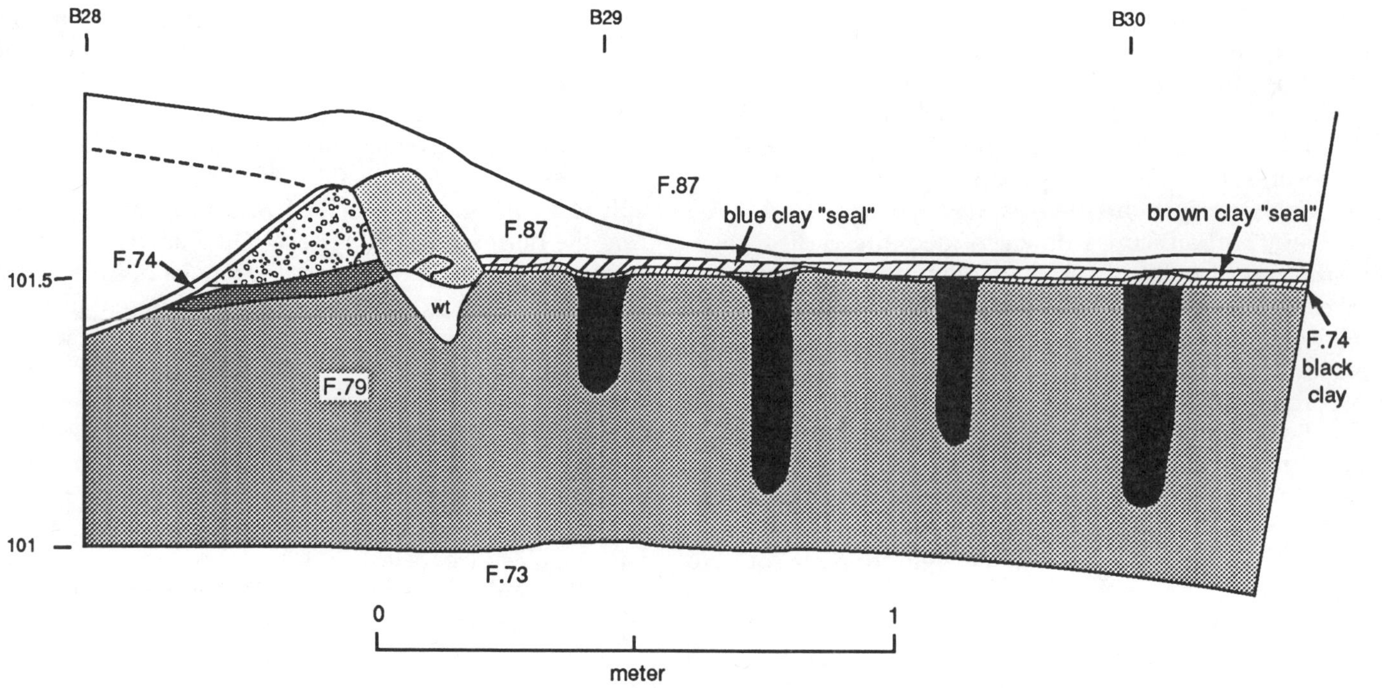

Figure 3.29. Borrow pit area profile at A8, B28–31 (view to the south).

by the east–west trench extension of the BP excavations (MP2), the stratigraphic sequence of which is comparable to that documented in the Moorehead profile (Figs. 3.3, 3.4, 3.31).

A thick deposit of mound fill is found above an elevation of 102 m a.d. This deposit of sandy fill is called F17. It is fully three meters thick and is capped at an elevation of 104.8–105.0 m a.d. by four prepared surface and sandy "wash" layers. Three wall trenches were cross-sectioned on the flat surface of F17.

No F18 "cap" or prepared surface features were observed at an elevation of 102.6 m a.d. as was recorded in the Moorehead profile (Figs. 3.3–3.4). However, if the prepared surface visible in the Moorehead profile did not extend to the BP area, it is conceivable that the small vertical MP2 exposure in the BP area would fail to identify its presence. It should be noted that "sandy wash" laminations were found at an elevation of 103.7–103.9 m a.d. and may hint at a different stable surface within F17.

Above the four sequential prepared surfaces covering F17 was a clayey cap F35, the same as appeared in the Moorehead profile. This cap measured 14 cm in thickness. Above this prepared surface was another sandy mound fill component, F34 (Fig. 3.31). Feature 34 was the uppermost mound element exposed in the BP area.

Summary and Discussion

A submound occupation zone or midden is evident everywhere under the Kunnemann Mound. The surface of this occupation zone typically is found between 100.4 and 100.5 m a.d. Based on ceramic refuse (see Chapter 4), this zone has been dated to the Lohmann phase. A number of Lohmann or early Stirling phase features are found in or on this occupation zone including pits, postmolds, amorphous pits, structures, a post pit, and human burials (in amorphous fill zones).

An early platform mound was situated on the crest of a natural point bar ridge as identified in the BP area profile. A structure (F106/107), of a size typical of domestic dwellings at Cahokia, may have occupied its raised surface (Fig. 3.33a). Feature 3–5, an *L*-shaped domicile containing a series of puddled central hearths, may have been occupied at the same time on the pre-mound surface immediately to the north. This structure was destroyed by fire.

Subsequent to the incineration of this dwelling, a large rectangular structure with a prepared clay floor (F72), deep central posts and opposing hearths was constructed in the BP area. By this time, the small platform mound to the south had been enlarged (F109/133) and a large rectangular building (F105/134) had been erected on its flat top (Fig.

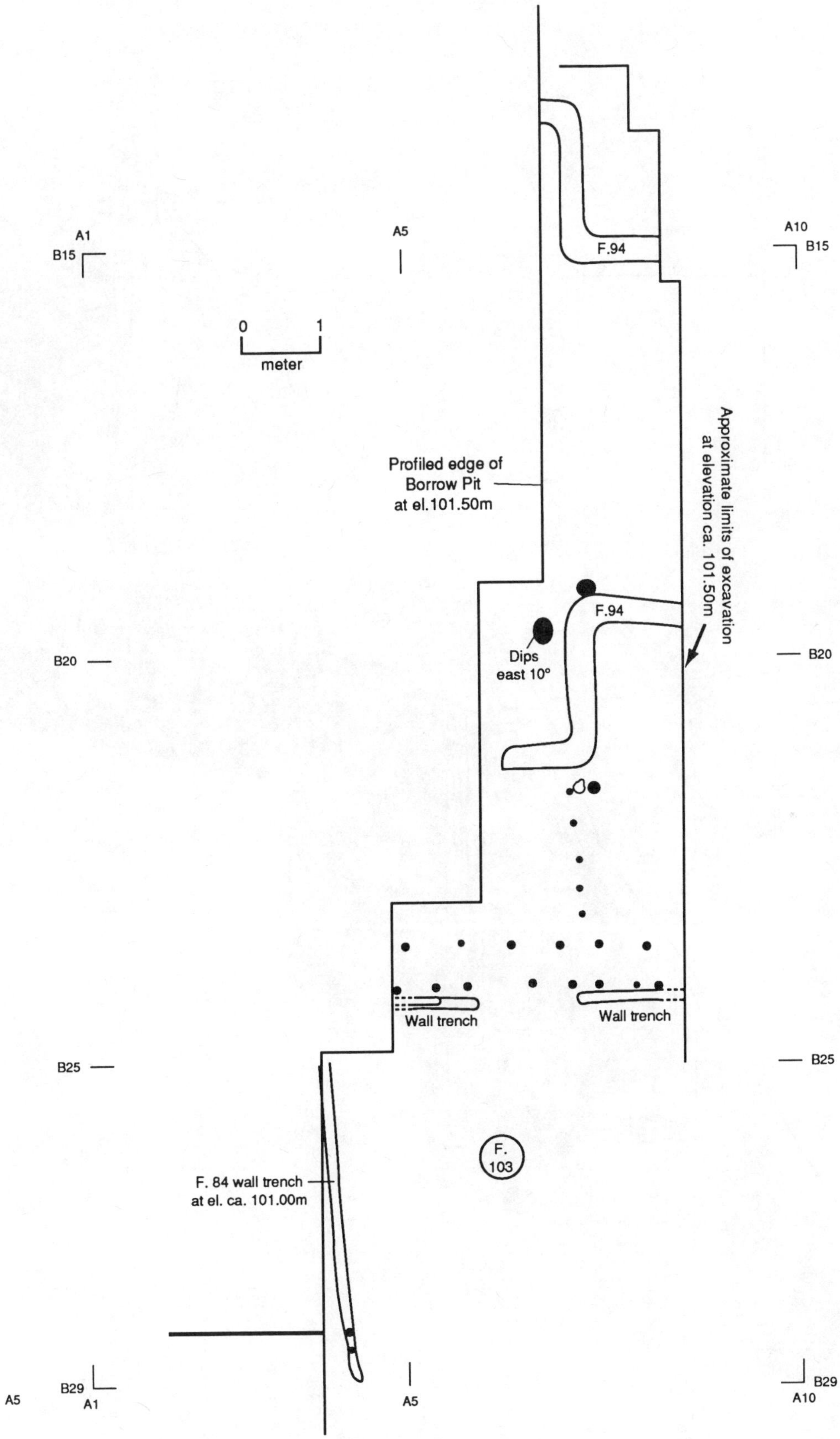

Figure 3.30. Plan of Feature 74 structures north of the rotunda.

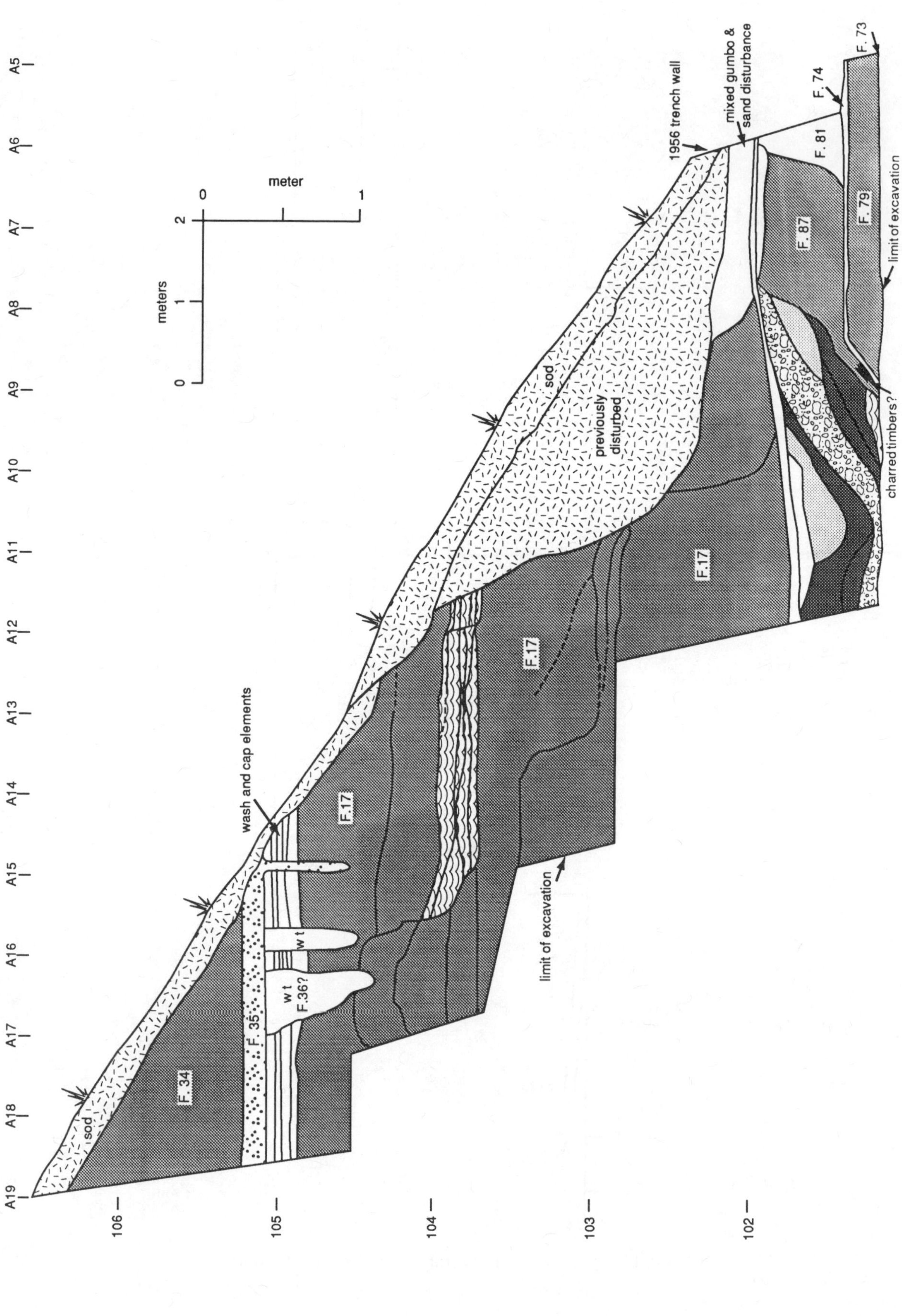

Figure 3.31. Borrow pit area profile (MP2) at B25, A5–19 (view to the south).

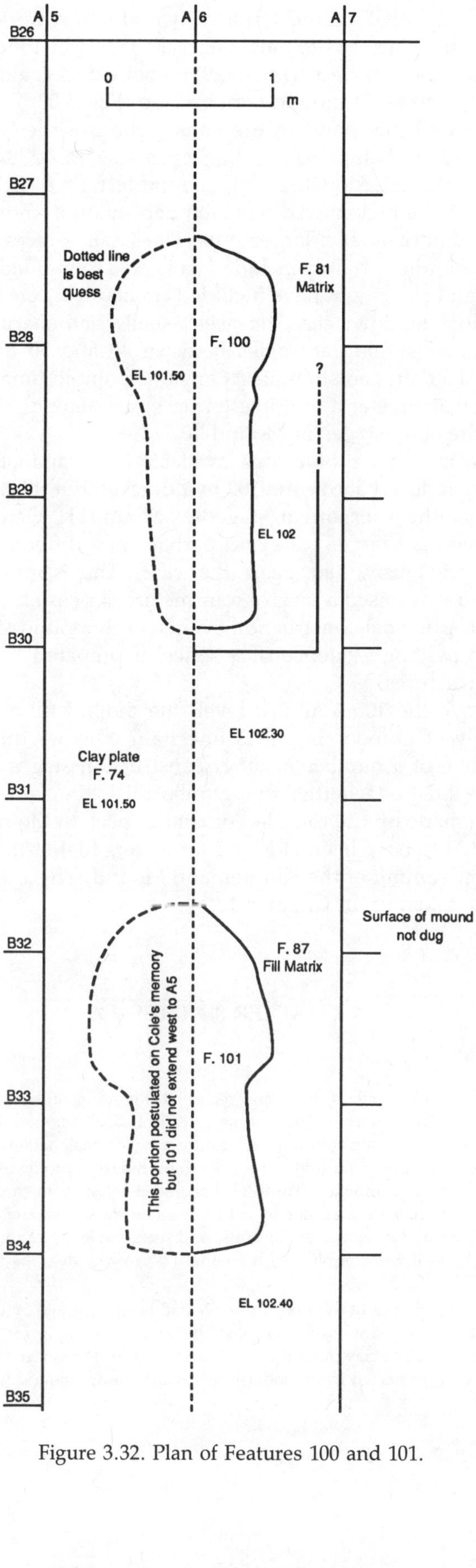

Figure 3.32. Plan of Features 100 and 101.

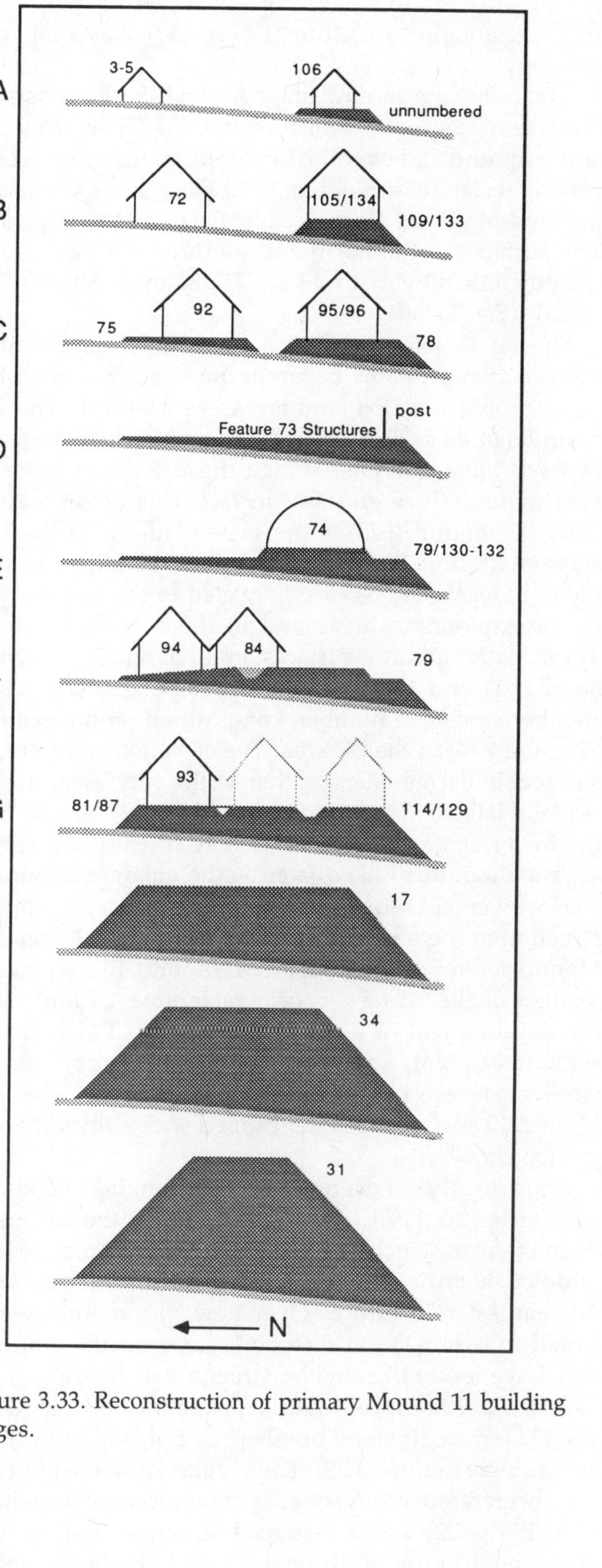

Figure 3.33. Reconstruction of primary Mound 11 building stages.

3.33b). This "south mound" was enlarged again (F78) and a new rectangular structure (F95/96/138) was built on its summit.

The following mound stage in the BP area consisted of the construction of a "north mound" (F75) adjacent to the south mound and over the former location of the F72 structure. A rectangular building (F92) with an elaborate hearth and red-plastered floor occupied its surface (Fig. 3.33c). The surfaces of the north and south mounds were subsequently linked by mound fill (F77), at an elevation of 100.9 m a.d. (Fig. 3.33d).

During this time, or perhaps slightly earlier, mound construction probably began in the vicinity of the Moorehead profile and Exploration Areas 1 and 3. The initial mounds in these areas (F25/41) were raised to an elevation of about 100.7–101.1 m a.d., like those of the early-stage BP area mounds (F75 and 78). In fact, it is possible that an early BP mound (F75) is the same platform as the F25/41 stage of Mound 10 in EA1, EA3, and the Moorehead profile or at least may be closely related to the strata exposed in the exploration areas and in the Moorehead profile. These early mound surfaces in EA1 and EA3 (F49–51, 56–57, 61) and the Moorehead profile (F22–24) also are roughly similar in number, composition, and elevation to F73 (and F74) in the BP area. The elevations and prepared surface similarities suggest that, at the very least, they represent related construction events. At most, Mound 10 and the lower stages of Mound 11 may constitute a series of separate mounds linked later by the enlarged Mound 11.

However, subsequent to this point in time, mound construction in the east and west portions of the Kunnemann Mound follow different courses. Mound 10 may have remained unaltered for a considerable time, as hinted at by the development of a soil horizon on the F41 surface. At some later point, structures were built, and one or more large posts erected in the vicinity of EA1. The entire Mound 10 surface was later capped with a thick mantle of gumbo clay.

Prior to these events in EA1, another sand-based mound terrace, F79, was constructed in the BP area. A large circular structure, possessing a plastered floor and puddled hearths, was constructed on the flat surface of this earliest F79 terrace. Over time, the mound was enlarged in a horizontal direction; steps on the south face may have led to the circular structure at the top.

A small F79 terrace was built just to the north of the F79/131/132 terrace. It stood briefly prior to being incorporated into a single mound (F79). The circular structure appears to have been removed. A series of other rectangular buildings (F84, F119–122) and a *T*-shaped structure (F94) occupied the summit to the north (Fig. 3.33f). Subsequent enlargement of the mound seems to have included the building of three individual mound terraces, two of which were combined into one (F81/87) after a brief period of time. The southernmost terrace (F114/129) remained isolated until the next phase of mound construction (Fig. 3.33g).

Up until this point in the construction of the Kunnemann Mound, mound-building events seem to have included the occasional, small, mound-terrace addition in between the regular and repeated deposition of thin mantles and horizontal enlargements. The small terraces of the lower mound certainly included truncated four-sided pyramids and also might have included circular truncated-cone mounds. In either case, terraces usually had sharply angled sides sloping at angles between 40 and 50 degrees toward a flattened summit. At any one point in time, multiple structures and multiple terraces may have characterized the early stages of Mound 10/11.

The exposed profile area available for examination is greatly reduced above the 102 m a.d. level, but it is arguable that the subsequent stages of Mound 11 were constructed on a larger scale and perhaps at a different pace than previously had been the case. The Kunnemann Mound was raised a total of four meters in possibly as few as four principal construction events, each mound surface also providing evidence of a series of prepared surfaces and structures.

Above the 106.2 m a.d. level, the mound fill consists entirely of gumbo clay. It is uncertain whether this was only one of a number of other construction stages above 107 m a.d., or whether this gumbo fill is the same zone which made up the rounded or conical peak to Mound 11, reported to have been at least four meters higher than the present summit of the Kunnemann Mound. This question will be taken up in Chapter 10.

CHAPTER 3 NOTES

1. Holder took excellent notes and recorded the mound fills in minute detail. His notes from time to time contain a small number of minor inconsistencies surrounding the feature-number designations or the texture of a particular unit of mound fill on different profile maps, or stratigraphic anomalies. These all have been retained in the profile maps to enable the reader to better evaluate the fill variability, the integrity of the feature or fill units, and the complexity of the stratigraphy as it was complicated by modern borrowing disturbances.

2. The western half of the floor probably had been damaged by the tenant farmer's borrowing activities in this area (accounting for the absence of a black clay floor along the eastern side). The eastern portion had been protected from modern disturbance under mound fill.

Plate 3.1. The 1955 Moorehead profile and Preston Holder (view to south).

Plate 3.2. Exploration Area 1 in its early stages: *left*, trench 1 (A66–67, B7–15) view to north; *right*, trench 2 (A67–70.5, B15–16) view to northwest.

Plate 3.3. Features 48 and 60 in Exploration Area 1: *top,* Marian White and Finds 45 and 46; *bottom,* a Feature 60 ramp superimposing Features 40 and 48.

Plate 3.4. Borrow pit area submound features: *top*, bundle burial in Feature 83; *bottom*, profile of Feature 3-5 in relation to submound and mound features.

Plate 3.5. Submound structure Feature 3–5 during excavation (view to northwest, from left to right: Holder, Nebgen, and White).

Plate 3.6. Lower mound fill elements in the borrow pit area profile (at about A6, B19–23).

Plate 3.7. Feature 123 hearth and square groove.

Plate 3.8. Feature 74 circular structure: *top*, eastern half of the floor; *bottom*, mat impressions on the floor (black plate).

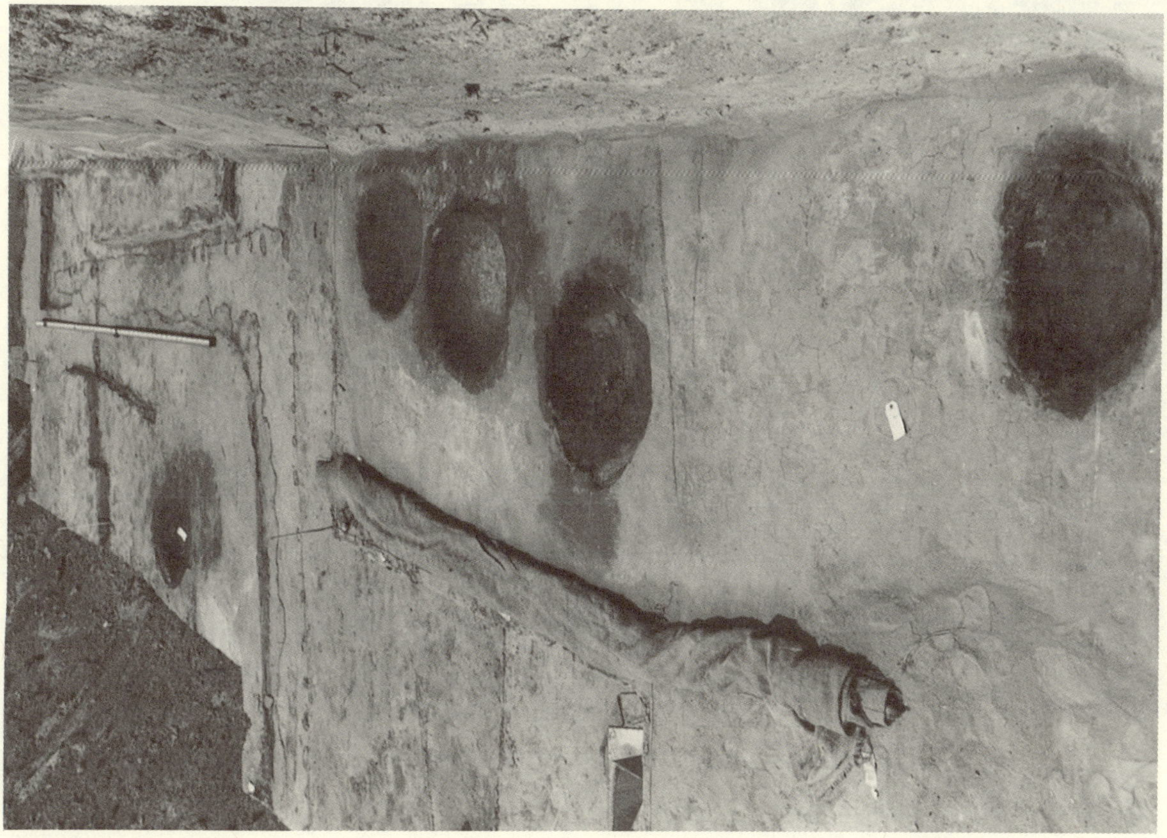

Plate 3.9. Feature 74 hearths and wall trenches: *left*, hearths (Features 110, 116, 117, 118) on the rotunda floor; *right*, Features 112 and 113 wall trenches.

Plate 3.10. The borrow pit area profile, view to northeast.

Plate 3.11. The eastern extension of the borrow pit area excavations (Moorehead profile, cut 2).

Chapter 4

Ceramics

Pottery remains can give us information on both the temporal and social dimensions of the Kunnemann Mound. The ceramics were embedded in discrete strata and, thus, temporal change in ceramic attributes may be measured and compared to the established Cahokia ceramic chronology. However, the construction and maintenance of the earthen pyramid and its buildings were probably responsibilities of an elite subgroup of the population and–assuming that the style, use, and breakage of pots were in part related to social status and sacred/secular distinctions–it is reasonable to suspect that the ceramic assemblage associated with monument-related activities differs from contemporaneous assemblages elsewhere in the American Bottom, even elsewhere at Cahokia (Holder 1966).

Unfortunately, many of the ceramic sherds recovered probably were unintentional inclusions in mound fill obtained from former living areas. These are of limited value in identifying social and temporal variability. On the other hand, a subset of the ceramic assemblage is associated either with refuse accumulations on living surfaces or discrete episodes of refuse disposal in pits or in basins associated with abandoned buildings. Most of the latter are from submound deposits, a number of which probably came from a residential occupation adjacent to the earliest stages of the Kunnemann Mound.

Method of Analysis

All sherds from the 1955–56 excavations were included in this analysis, but sherds from Preston Holder's general collection of the Kunnemann Mound surface or the surrounding Kunnemann Tract were excluded. A minimum number of vessels (MNV) was reconstructed based on container rim sherds. A vessel number was assigned to one or more rim sherds representing a single container. This vessel number consists of a feature or excavation area designation and a consecutive number. For example, the third container recognized in F78 would be referred to as 78–3. The nineteenth vessel from general borrow pit contexts would be BP-19.

A number of discrete and continuous variables were recognized as part of the analysis. Discrete variables include vessel form, temper, and surface treatment. Orifice diameter, the percent of orifice represented by the rim segment, and sherd weight are continuous variables. Orifice diameter was measured by aligning rim segments with concentric arcs drawn on a chart at 1 cm intervals. Rim profiles were oriented relative to the plane of the orifice. Those vessels represented by rim segments too small to measure accurately orifice diameter or wall orientation are illustrated with a dashed orientation line.

Additionally, a series of indices and an angle measurement are used to quantify the continuous variation represented in jar morphology. A lip protrusion (LP) index was used to standardize observations of lip length, to account for jar size variability (see Pauketat 1991). Lip length was divided by wall thickness at the point where the lip meets the vessel wall, and is essentially the same measurement as Holley's (1989) "rim protrusion ratio" (RPR). Another index used in this analysis is the lip thickness/lip length index (LTLL), another means of quantifying lip form. A final index measures rim curvature (RC), the straight-line distance (x) of the exterior rim wall (between where it joins the lip and where it joins the shoulder) divided by the distance (positive or negative y) between the midpoint of x and the rim wall. The last continuous variable measured is the rim angle (RA), measured only on jars with RC indices of 00.03 or less (see Pauketat n.d.).

Several morphological forms are recognized among the Kunnemann Mound vessels: jars, seed jars, bowls, beakers, jugs, funnels, and stumpware pots (see Esarey and Pauketat 1992; Kelly 1980, 1990a; Kelly et al. 1984; Holley 1989; Milner et al. 1984; Pauketat 1990, 1991; Vogel 1975). I have distinguished these forms in metric and morphological terms previously and will provide only a brief description here (see Esarey and Pauketat 1992; Pauketat

TABLE 4.1
Vessel Orifice Diameter Summary Data

Vessel Form	Mean Orifice Dia. (cm)	s.d.	Total n
Jar	24	10	109
Seed jar	18	12	9
Bowl/beaker/pan	18	12	45
Jug	12	4	17
Funnel/stump	14	5	7
TOTAL			187

1987b:4ff.). Following Shepard (1980:230), the Kunnemann Mound jars are "dependent restricted" forms with "composite" contours. They are semiglobular with pronounced angled shoulders and inward-leaning rims. Seed jars are "simple restricted" forms with "simple" contours, the Cahokia version of the tecomate.

Bowls are "unrestricted," or occasionally "restricted" forms with simple or composite contours and orifice diameter:depth ratios greater than or equal to one. One restricted form with simple contours elsewhere has been called a "constricted bowl" (c-bowl) and this designation has been retained here (see Esarey and Pauketat 1992). Another large, shallow bowl form with interior red slipping is commonly referred to as a "pan" or "basin" (Pauketat and Woods 1986; Holley 1989). Beaker morphology is similar to that of bowls but beakers usually have straight, vertical, or inward-leaning rims, composite contours, and orifice diameter:depth ratios of less than one. The two often are difficult to distinguish among the Kunnemann Mound sherds and indeed appear to represent a shape continuum. Consequently, I refer to some containers as "bowl-beakers."

Jugs (or bottles) in the Kunnemann Mound pottery assemblage are "independent restricted" containers with composite contours. These vessels usually have globular bodies with vertical, extended necks and small orifices. Funnels and stumpware pots are conelike, ellipsoidal, or ovaloidal vessels with thick walls, wide mouths, and small lower orifices; stumpware features flat bases and footlike projections (Kelly et al. 1984). These vessels may have served in some cases as strainers and funnels or were used in an inverted position as supports for other vessels (Kelly 1990a:128; Wesler 1986).

Recognized vessel tempers include crushed mussel shell (SH), limestone (LS), grit (GT), and grog or crushed sherd (GG). The surfaces of vessels are smoothed, or plain (PL), slipped (S), or cordmarked (CM). These finishes may, in turn, be polished (P), trailed, incised, and excised. In most cases, surface color is brown or black, presumably reflecting the firing of vessels under a reducing atmosphere. Under oxidizing conditions, soot would not have become impregnated in vessel surfaces and these same pots ordinarily would have possessed a tan or buff color. Some vessel slips are red (here noted as RS). A series of bowls and beakers, usually compact-paste fine ware, typically exhibit a brownish-red burnished or slipped surface (BRS). Lastly, postmanufacturing use-related alteration of vessel surfaces is noted, particularly in the case of jars which often exhibit soot or heat spalls.

Kunnemann Mound Ceramics

Ceramic sherds weighing a total of 40.9 kg were recovered from excavated contexts at the Kunnemann Mound (Appendices II–VI). Ninety-nine percent of this total is shell tempered. Grog or grog-shell tempered fine ware, funnel and stumpware, and limestone-tempered sherds comprise the other one percent.

A minimum number of 272 vessels is recognized in the Kunnemann Mound ceramic assemblage (Appendices II-IV). This includes 162 jars (59.6%), 16 seed jars (5.9%), 65 bowls and beakers (23.9%), 19 jugs (7.0%), 8 funnels (2.9%), and 2 stumpware pots (0.7%). Vessel size in combination with form probably was related to container function and provides hints of subcategories within the morphological types. For present purposes, orifice diameter will be relied upon to provide an indirect (although not necessarily linear) measure of vessel size (Table 4.1).

As with other comparable vessel assemblages from the American Bottom (Pauketat 1989:299), the Kunnemann Mound jars hint of size modes. Likewise, the orifice diameters of jugs may be used to suggest that two principal modes might have existed (Fig. 4.1). The first of these, the small-mouthed mode, is what most researchers have called "bottles," while the larger-mouthed jugs have been called "straight rim jars" by Emerson and Jackson (1984:288). I have referred to both of these elsewhere simply as jugs (Pauketat 1987b).

The orifice diameters of bowls and beakers reveal a primary mode between about 6 to 28 cm, indicative of the beaker-bowl continuum earlier mentioned. The largest of bowls belong to the pan or basin subcategory (Fig. 4.1). Within the bowl and beaker grouping, there are 28 simple or composite bowls, 13 beakers, 12 bowl-beakers, 5 pans, 5 constricted bowls, and 2 mini-bowls (Figs. 4.4–4.7).

Other ceramic artifacts include fragments of a single pottery trowel and 10 recycled vessel fragments (Appendix VI). Three of the latter are disks, of which two are drilled. Seven other sherds have modified edges including six with ground edges and one which appears to have been sawed or filed and then snapped. With two exceptions, the sherds with ground edges were fragments of larger recycled vessel sections. One sherd might have been a scoop. It exhibits wear on opposing edges. Another small sherd from F89 had its edges ground smooth, probably modified

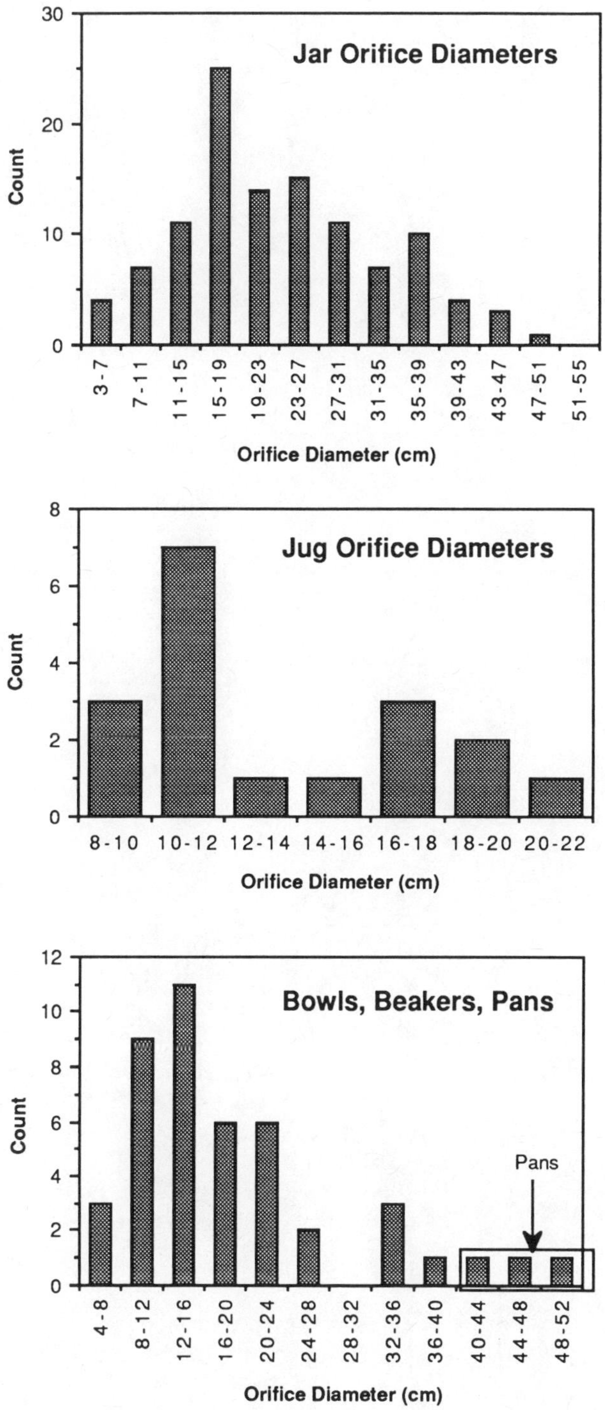

Figure 4.1. Vessel orifice diameters.

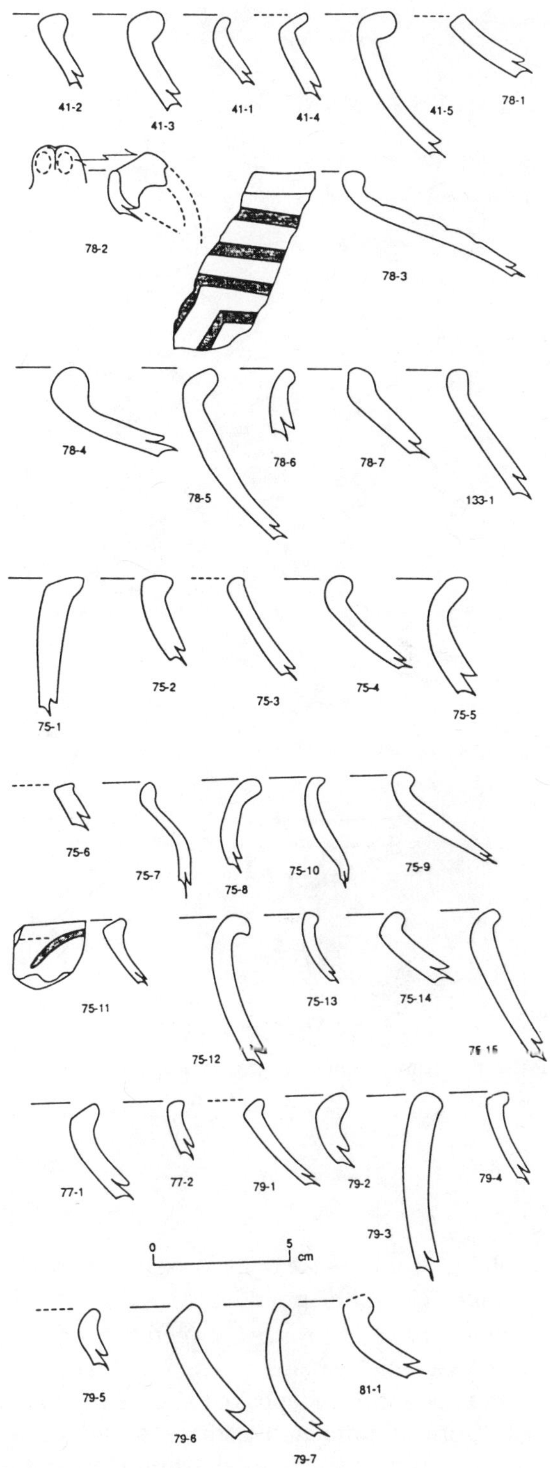

Figure 4.2. Rim profiles of jars from basal mound stages.

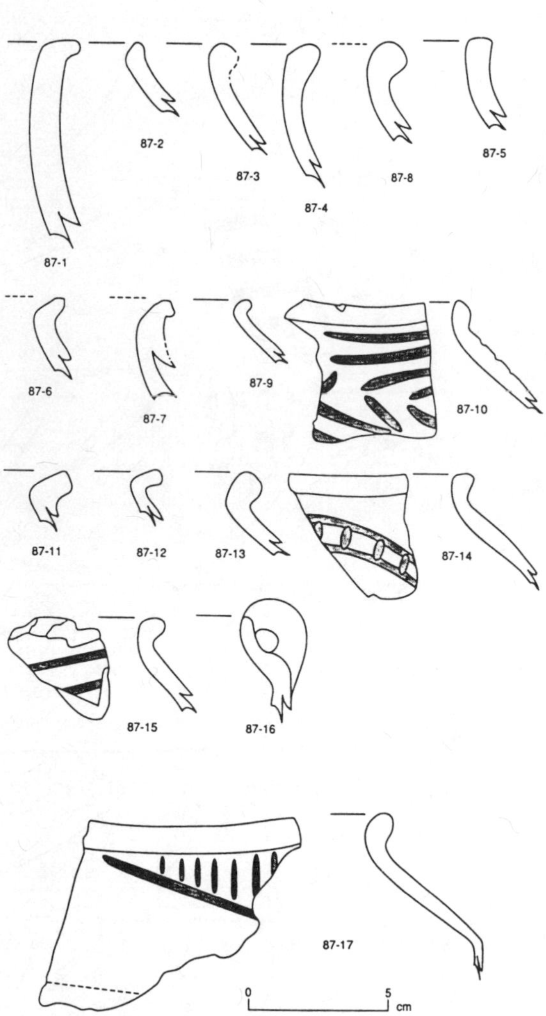

Figure 4.3. Rim profiles of jars from upper basal mound stage Feature 87.

and retained for the sake of its Ramey Incised weeping eye decoration (Fig. 4.8, Appendix VI).

Distinctions can be made between the types of deposits in which ceramic remains were found. The primary distinction is between redeposited sherds in mound fill and sherds from accumulated garbage or living surface deposits. The redeposited sherds—unintentional inclusions in the matrix of the mound—are of limited use in this analysis although they provide some help in determining the earliest possible phase in which a construction event occurred. The sherd accumulations in garbage deposits on living surfaces are of primary concern in this analysis and will be described in detail.

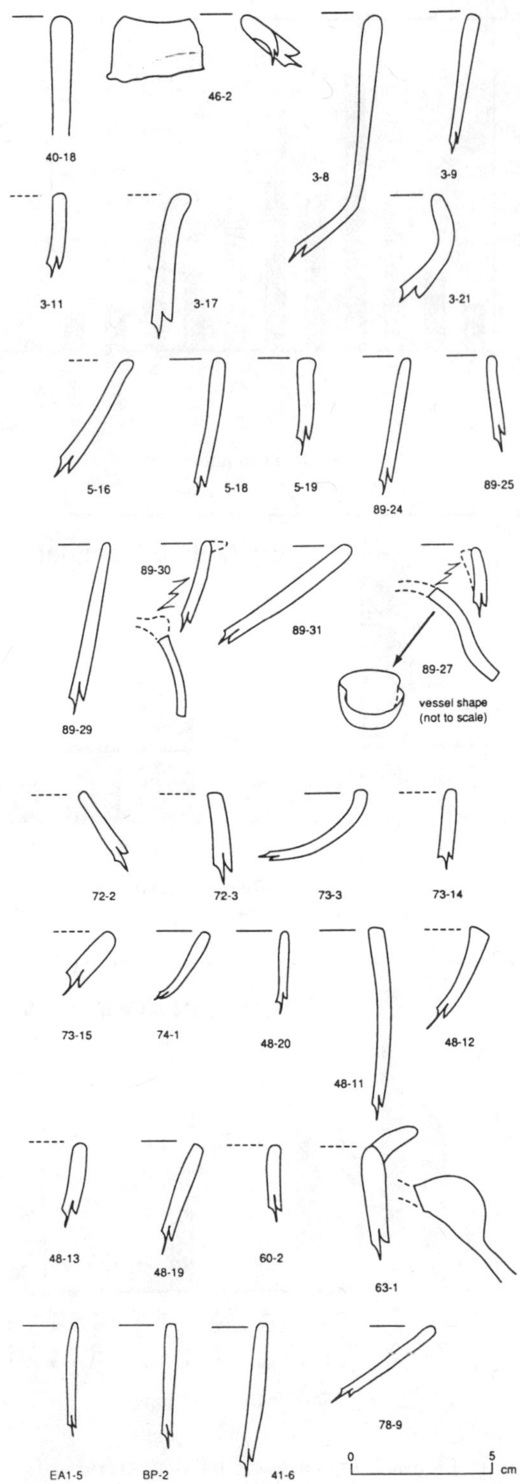

Figure 4.4. Rim profiles of bowls and beakers.

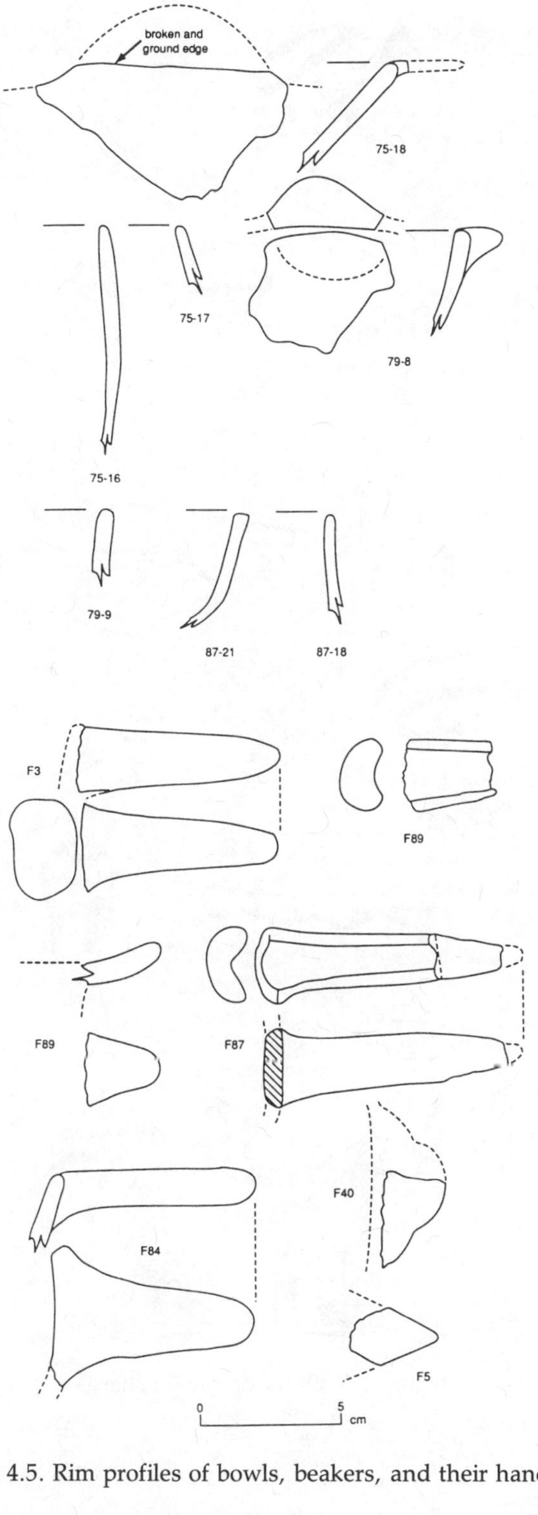

Figure 4.5. Rim profiles of bowls, beakers, and their handles.

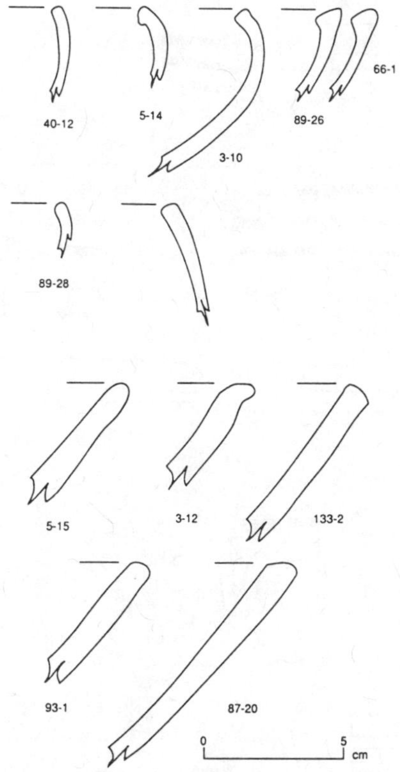

Figure 4.6. Rim profiles of constricted bowls (*top*) and pans (*bottom*).

Mound Fill Sherds

A minimum of 62 jars, 6 seed jars, 11 bowls and beakers, 2 pans, 4 jugs, 1 funnel, and 1 stumpware vessel are associated with mound fill Features 17, 41, 75, 77, 78, 79, 81, 87, 133, and other general proveniences within the exploration areas and the Moorehead profile (Table 4.2; Figs. 4.3–4.7). Among the body sherds are fragments of Ramey Incised jars, decorated fine ware, a ceramic disk, and a Middle Woodland jar rim sherd (Appendix VI).

It is noteworthy that all mound fill zones contain Lohmann phase sherds. Most also contain Stirling phase sherds. For instance, the earliest mound fill, BP area F109/133 and Exploration Area F41, contains Lohmann phase ceramics (Fig. 4.2). Both lie over features which date to the Lohmann phase or are ambiguous with regard to phase. Thus, these earliest mound stages, particularly in the BP area, may date either to the Lohmann or early Stirling phase. The subsequent F78 fill of the south mound contained early Stirling phase rim sherds (Fig. 4.2). Later mound fill, for example F87, contains jar sherds which probably date slightly later in the Stirling phase (Fig. 4.3). Three jars from F87 (vessels 1, 11, 12) have low LP indices (mean = 0.47) identifying them as relatively late vessels (see below).

Lohmann Phase Vessels

Ceramics from the submound Feature 40 (the submound midden) are representative of the Lohmann phase.

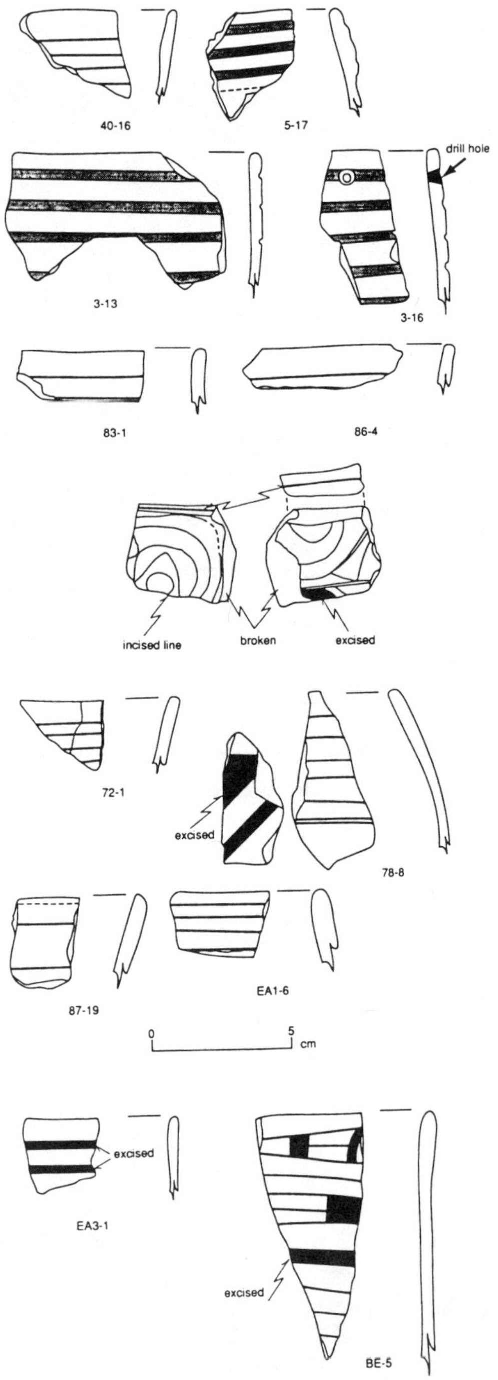

Figure 4.7. Rim profiles of decorated bowls and beakers.

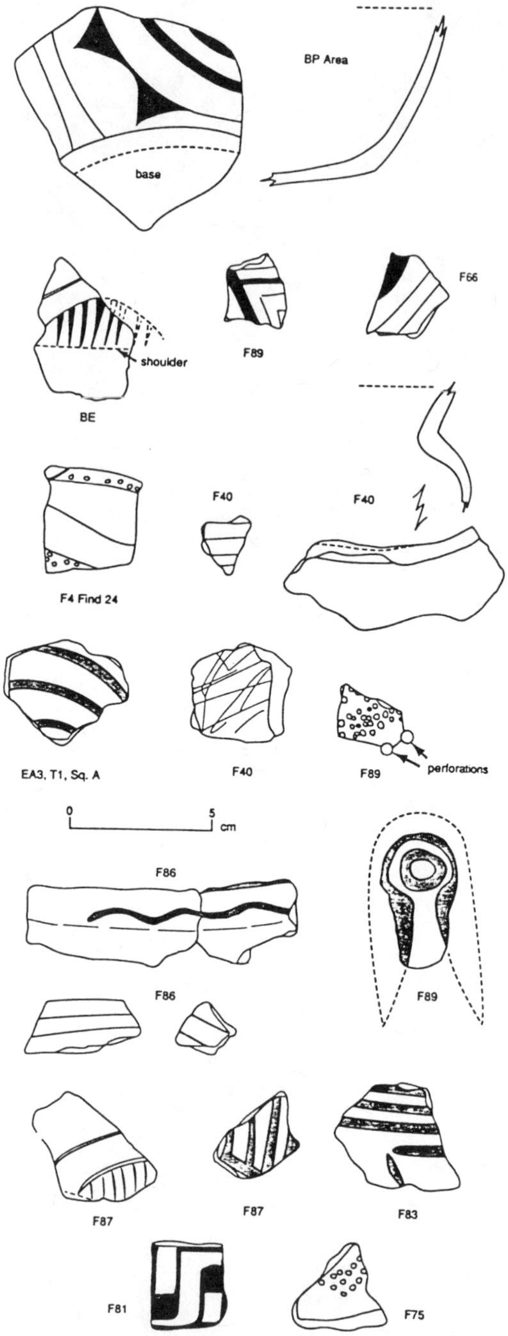

Figure 4.8. Other decorated sherds.

Other sherds from Features 4, 7 (components of F3–5), and 46 (a post pit superimposed on F40) may also date to the Lohmann phase (or the early Stirling phase), as may a possibly redeposited jar rim sherd from F58 (redeposited?). The latter vessel, 58–1, is associated with an early Mound 10 surface and was not tabulated with the Lohmann phase vessel assemblage.

Additionally, a vessel perhaps smashed in a corner of the burned structure F3–5 was given the number 5–25 (Fig. 4.12). It has a Lohmann phase shape and the unique feature of four broad lip tabs giving the lip (but not the orifice) a rectangular plan shape. This vessel was curated by the Illinois State Museum without any numbering information written on the sherds. Preston Holder's personal slide collection (now the possession of the University of Michigan Museum of Anthropology) shows a vessel similar to 5–25 from a submound structure beneath the Wilson ("Junkyard") Mound, excavated by Holder in 1954. Given the similarities in the excavated contexts, the questions surrounding this particular vessel's provenience—although tentatively listed here as F3–5—remain unresolved.

Sherds from a red-slipped bowl (Find 16) associated with the F4 floor had been sent to the Illinois State Museum in 1957 but these could not be relocated in 1990. The minimum number of pots from these four features, including the 5–25 jar, but not the missing red-slipped bowl, includes 18 jars (53%), 6 seed jars (18%), 3 bowls (9%), 1 beaker (3%), and 6 jugs (18%) (see Figs. 4.4–4.11; Table 4.2). All vessels are tempered with shell except for one limestone-tempered seed jar and the beaker tempered with finely crushed grog.

Nine of the Lohmann phase jars have red-slipped lips and upper interiors and plain or eroded exteriors. Seven of the remaining jars have plain interiors and slipped exteriors; two are slipped on interior and exterior surfaces. The mean LP, LTLL, and RC values distinguish them from later Stirling phase vessels (Table 4.3). One of the jars, vessel 4–5, has a distinctive modeled loop handle. Jar 4–5 in particular, associated with the burned building floor, probably dates to the early Stirling phase. The handle has an elbow joint at about its midsection and a gouged-out area where it meets the jar lip, creating a distinctive bifurcated or bi-knobbed appearance (Fig. 4.9, bottom). Similar handles are found in late Lohmann and early Stirling phase ceramic assemblages at Cahokia's ICT-II (Holley 1989) and Tract 15A (Pauketat n.d.) and at outlying sites (Hall 1980: figs. 11–20 and 11–21; Porter 1974:716). These may be reliable diagnostics of the period.

All of the remaining vessels are slipped except for one plain-surfaced jug. About 53 percent of these slipped containers are red in color. Two of the seed jars, vessels 40–4 and 40–24, have punctate decorations on their exterior surfaces (Fig. 4.10). The beaker, vessel 40–16, has a reddish-brown slip and finely incised/engraved circumferential lines on its exterior surface. One of the bowls (46–2) has a constricted mouth and an unusual complex shape (Fig. 4.4).

Other F40 sherds from vessels not counted in the MNV include a delicately engraved, fine-grog tempered sherd, a shell tempered bowl (tail effigy?) tab, a fine-grog tempered, constricted-mouth bowl with an everted lip, and a shell tempered sherd with a scratched/engraved surface. Another sherd from F4 (Find 24) is tempered with fine shell and has highly polished surfaces and exterior engraved lines and dots (Fig. 4.8).

Early Stirling Phase Vessels: Submound and Early Mound

A pit on the F41 mound surface in EA1 (Mound 10) contains a meager assemblage of pottery including a single insloped-rim jar (LP = 0.65), which probably indicates that it dates to the Lohmann or early Stirling phase. As earlier stated, it is possible that the F109/133 mound in the BP area also dates as early as the Lohmann phase, although a jar shoulder segment found beneath this mound fill, having a RA value of about 110 degrees, is typical of the Stirling phase.

The early Stirling phase features recognized here were situated adjacent to or below the mound surfaces themselves. The early Stirling phase ceramic assemblage is isolated in a series of submound fill zones or amorphous pits (F83, F86, F89) and a structure (F3–5). Early Stirling phase ceramics also are associated with mound fill F78, including a Ramey Incised jar and a jar with a bifurcated loop handle. However, this mound fill may contain mixed Lohmann phase pottery admixture.

Given that a floor (F4) of the burned submound structure (F3–5) and one or more of a series of hearths (F7) contained Lohmann (and possibly early Stirling) phase pottery, while the fill of this same structure's basin contained early Stirling phase ceramics, it is either the case that the F4 and F7 fills date to the early Stirling phase but contain redeposited Lohmann phase sherds, or that the actual temporal separation of the Lohmann phase (as represented by F4 and F7) and the early Stirling phase (as represented by F3 and F5) is not great. Elsewhere at Cahokia, Lohmann phase forms can be found alongside Stirling phase forms in the early Stirling phase feature fills (see Holley 1989; Pauketat 1991). The same may be true of F3–5 and all of its associated features. Only F3–5 and not F4 or F7 will be used in reconstructing an early Stirling phase vessel assemblage.

A minimum of 87 vessels make up the early Stirling phase ceramic assemblage from submound features: 50 jars (57.5%), 2 seed jars (2.3%), 12 bowls (13.8%), 7 beakers or bowl-beakers (8.0%), 3 constricted bowls (3.4%), 2 pans (2.3%), 8 jugs (9.2%), and 3 funnels (3.4%). About 93 percent of this MNV is made up of vessels tempered with shell (see Figs. 4.4–4.8, 4.10–4.14; Table 4.2). Grog or grog-shell tempered vessels include a jar, a seed jar, two fine-grog bowl-beakers, and two funnels. Fewer early Stirling phase vessels have red slipped finishes compared to the Lohmann phase materials. Only 14 percent of the early Stirling phase jars jars have red-slipped upper-interior surfaces or lips and plain-exterior surfaces. Another 14 percent of the jars are completely plain-surfaced. The remaining jars have brown or black slips on exterior surfaces only.

Besides changes in surface finish, early Stirling phase jars on average have straighter inslanted rims than their Lohmann phase counterparts, visible in the decreased

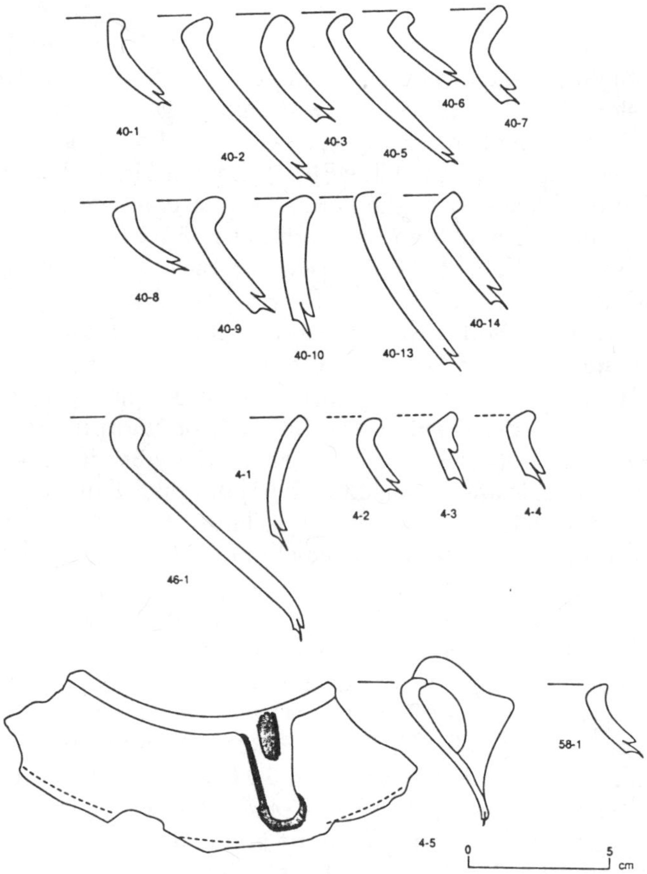

Figure 4.9. Rim profiles of Lohmann phase jars.

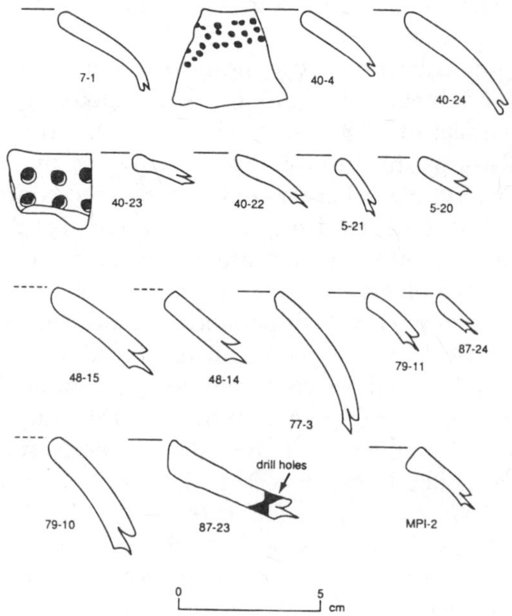

Figure 4.10. Rim profiles of seed jars.

mean RC value (Table 4.3). Additionally, the rim angles of the early Stirling phase jars are consistently lower than Lohmann phase jars (Table 4.3). The lips of early Stirling phase jars increase in length relative to wall thickness and vessel size (Table 4.3). Most visibly, a decorated jar style called Ramey Incised made its appearance during the early Stirling phase. Ramey Incised jars, like other early Stirling phase examples, consistently lack flared rims, instead possessing straight, inslanted walls (i.e., low RC indices), sharp shoulder angles, slipped and polished exteriors, and broad-trailed motifs on jar shoulders. Three motifs may be identified among the Kunnemann Mound early Stirling phase pottery: concentric arcs, a nested scroll-in-line, and a weeping eye. A fourth partially represented motif on a F86 sherd consists of an unusual wavy trailed line (Figs. 4.8, 4.12–4.13; Appendices II and VI).

A number of early Stirling phase seed jars, funnels, bowls, and beakers from the Kunnemann Mound stand out from the rest of the assemblage and from their Lohmann phase counterparts. The seed jars are small (orifice diameters less than 14 cm); one is slipped but the other has plain or polished surfaces. Three funnels have thickened lips and insloped rims reminiscent of the jar shape. The bowls and beakers include a number of decorated vessels.

Fine-incised beakers and bowls are prominent components of the early Stirling phase assemblage. Compared to the Lohmann phase, these appear to make up a larger proportion of the early Stirling phase ceramic assemblage. Two shell tempered and one grog-shell tempered beaker handles and a single shell tempered bowl tab were unassociated with rim sherds (Appendix VI). All had pointed or spurred ends, flattened superior surfaces, and trianguloidal shapes in plan view (Fig. 4.5). One bowl (86–5), tempered with finely crushed shell, appears to have had a rectangular orifice. It has fine-incised lines and an excised portion on its surfaces and on the superior surface of the lip. These incisions and excisions appear to have been made when the pre-fired paste had hardened.

The early Stirling phase ceramic assemblage also features the following shell tempered bowls and beakers: a bowl with opposing indented rim walls (89–27), a red-slipped constricted bowl (89–26) identical to a vessel found associated with the ill-defined F66 in EA1, and three bowl-beakers with broad-trailed lines around the circumference of their rims (3–13, 3–15, 5–17). These latter containers have been called "Mound Place Incised" in the American Bottom region (Milner et al. 1984:170). The trailed lines on one of the vessels (5–17) are located on a thickened rim (Fig. 4.7).

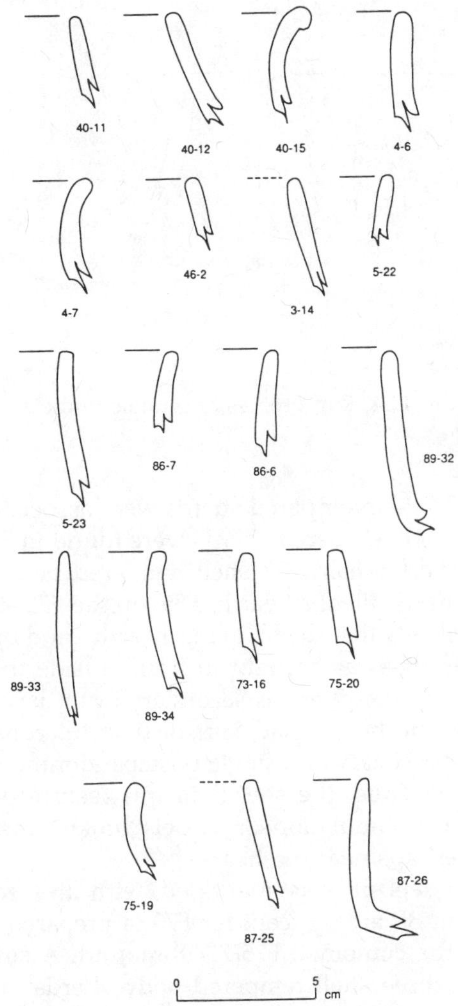

Figure 4.11. Rim profiles of jugs.

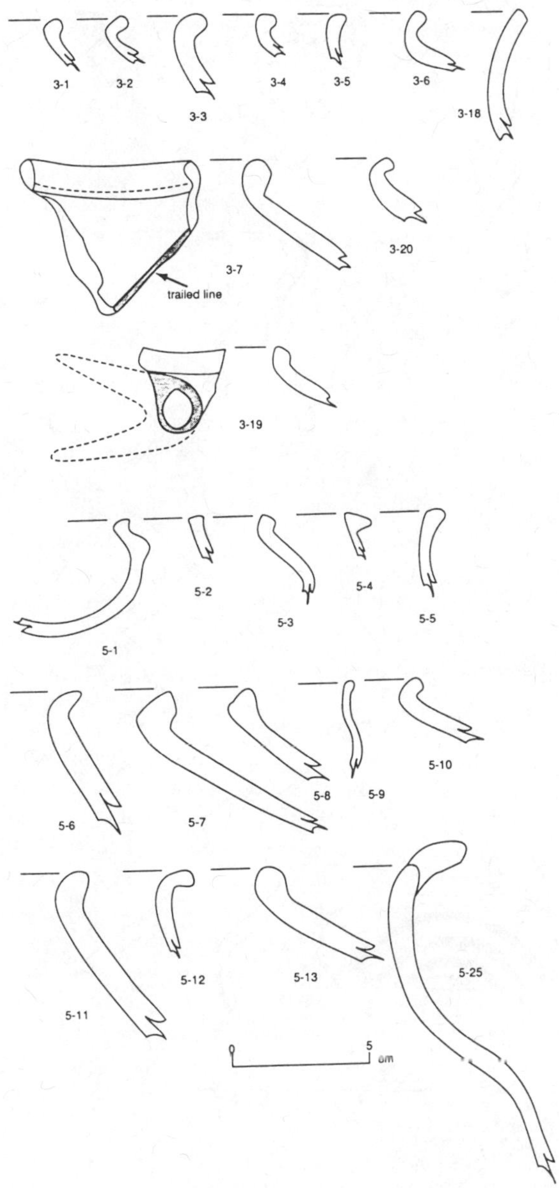

Figure 4.12. Rim profiles of early Stirling phase jars from Feature 3–5.

Other ceramic artifacts from early Stirling phase deposits include two pottery disks, six sherds with ground edges, a sherd with a straight, broken edge (evidently produced by sawing or filing a line and then snapping the sherd along this filed line), and a body sherd from a F89 vessel which had a series of dots drilled through the post-fired black-slipped surface (Fig. 4.8, upper right). Only one of the disks had a central drill hole. Another sherd had opposing ground (or worn) edges, perhaps indicating that it had been used as a scoop. A final sherd was the central portion of a Ramey Incised weeping eye motif from F89, smoothed along its perimeter (Fig. 4.8).

Stirling Phase Prepared Surface Feature 72 Ceramics

The prepared surface of a large rectangular structure, F72, which superimposed the early Stirling phase Features 3–5, 83, and 86, contained a number of small sherds which appear to have been primary refuse (Schiffer 1976:30; DeBoer 1983) left on the floor of the F72 structure. In more than one case, the field description of the sherds in question mentions their being embedded in the F72 surface. The ceramic assemblage from F72 and its wall trenches, F9 and F70, consists of a single jar (LP=0.62), a shell tempered, red-slipped bowl, and two beakers (Table 4.2). The beakers include a specimen (72–2) tempered with fine shell and having slipped and polished surfaces, and a fine-grog tempered, slipped and polished container (72–1) with fine-incised lines around the circumference of its exterior (Ap-

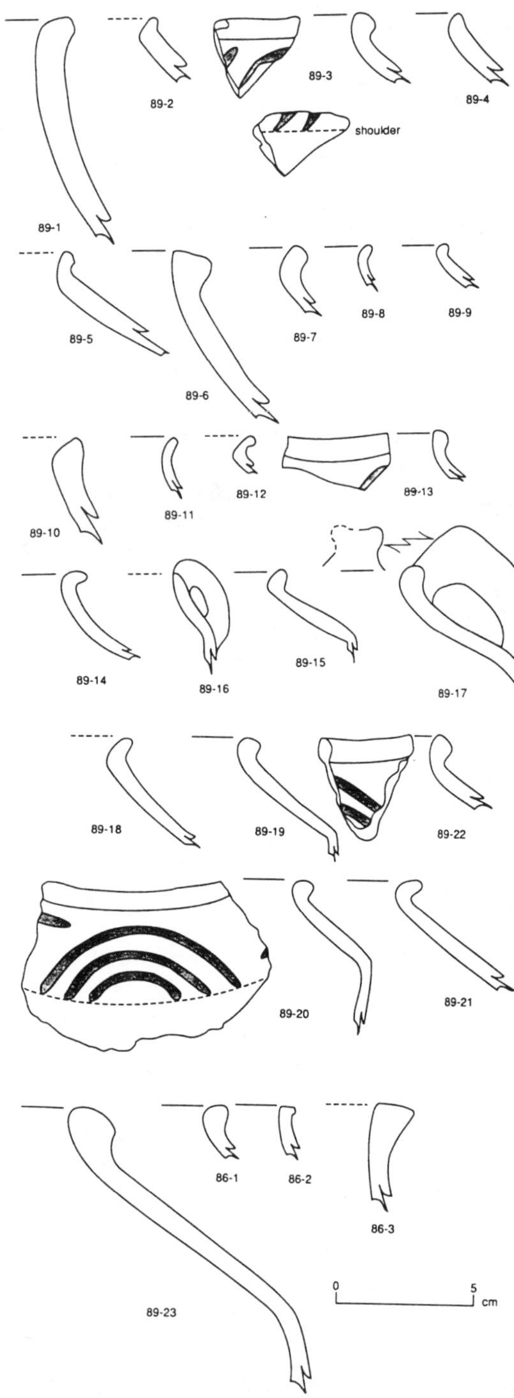

Figure 4.13. Rim profiles of early Stirling phase jars from Features 86 and 89.

pendix III; Fig. 4.7). Fourteen body sherds from this latter beaker were recovered from the structure floor. Another sherd from this finely made pot was found on the F72 floor at its interface with the F9 wall trench, again representing primary or abandonment refuse (see Deal 1985).

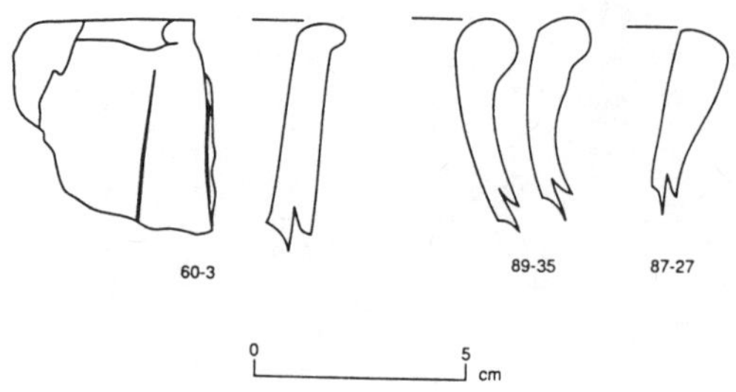

Figure 4.14. Rim profiles of ceramic funnels.

Another 27 shell tempered sherds were associated with F72, and 14 shell tempered sherds were found in F70 (Appendix V). Additionally, 47 shell tempered body sherds were found in the fill of a hearth, F85, on the F72 structure floor. It is unlikely that the fill in this hearth—and by extension, the sherds—was brought in from outside the structure and redeposited here as secondary or tertiary refuse. Besides this, the hearth had four distinct fill zones, precluding the possibility of a single postabandonment depositional event. Thus, the sherds in this feature probably represent an accumulation of vessels broken inside the structure, perhaps near the hearth.

No floor deposit was identified with the southern mound in the BP area, except for F73, a prepared surface which caps the combined F75/77/78 mound. A single jar, vessel 95-1, three shell tempered body sherds, and one fine-grog tempered body sherd are represented in the wall trench of the F95/96 structure on top of the F78 mound, which is interpreted to be contemporaneous with or to slightly postdate F72. The jar sherd in the F95 wall trench may derive from the activities on the surface of this mound, but wall trench fill is inherently unreliable.

Stirling Phase Prepared Surface Feature 73 Ceramics

The next series of structures and prepared surfaces are found on top of mound Features 75 and 77 (and 78 when subsumed within the F75/77/78 mound with its F73 occupation surfaces). This series of at least five distinct F73 prepared surfaces contained a minimum number of 16 vessels. The F73 rim sherds represent a minimum of 12 jars (75%), 2 bowls and a possible beaker (19%), and a jug (6%) (Figs. 4.4, 4.11, 4.15; Table 4.2; Appendices II-IV). About 120 shell tempered body sherds were recovered from these prepared surfaces (includes F73 and F73/74 sherds; Appendices V-VI). Additionally, a sherd was recovered from F91, a remnant red-plastered floor at the base of F73, probably the floor of a structure whose wall trenches are labeled

TABLE 4.2
Reconstructed Ceramic Vessel Assemblages

Assemblage	Jars		Seed Jars		Bowl		Beaker/Bowl		Pan		Jug		Funnel/Stump		Total n
	n	%	n	%	n	%	n	%	n	%	n	%	n	%	
Lohmann	18	53	6	18	3	9	1	3	0	0	6	18	0	0	34
Early Stirling	50	58	2	2	15	17	7	8	2	2	8	9	3	3	87
F72 Stirling	1	25	0	0	1	25	2	50	0	0	0	0	0	0	4
F73 Stirling	12	75	0	0	2	13	1	6	0	0	1	6	0	0	16
F93 Stirling	0	0	0	0	0	0	0	0	1	100	0	0	0	0	1
Late Stirling[a]	11	49	2	9	6	26	0	0	0	0	0	0	4	17	23
EA1 T2 General	5	71	0	0	0	0	2	29	0	0	0	0	0	0	7
Mound fill	62	71	6	7	5	6	6	7	2	2	4	5	2	2	87
Miscellaneous	3	23	0	0	3	23	6	46	0	0	0	0	1	8	13
Total n	162	60	16	6	35	13	25	9	5	2	19	7	10	4	272

[a]Probably a late Stirling phase assemblage mixed with earlier vessels.

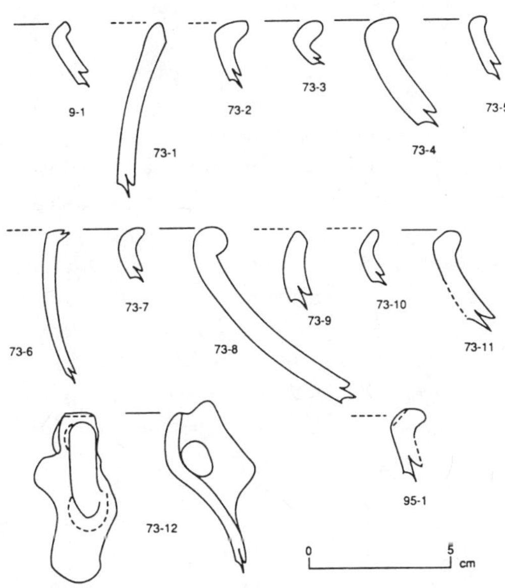

Figure 4.15. Rim profiles of jars from Features 9, 73, and 95.

F92. Two other sherds were found within the wall trench fill of F92.

While some of the F73 jars exhibit characteristics of Lohmann and early Stirling phase jars, a subset exists which displays the longer rolled and everted lips characteristic of later Stirling phase containers (Table 4.3; Fig. 4.15; Appendix II). Interestingly, although there are three trailed body sherds, none of the jars in the MNV are decorated. Three exhibit exterior blackening or soot from use over a fire. It is not clear whether all vessels from F73 were associated with activities that took place there, but it is possible they were. It seems unlikely, given the debris-free fills usually associated with prepared surfaces, that the F73 surface mantles when initially deposited were laden with garbage. Certainly the primary or abandonment (sherd) refuse on other floors (F72, F74) supports the contention that ceramic containers were used and broken within structures atop the Kunnemann Mound. Unfortunately, the origin of the F73 vessels will remain unresolved.

Stirling Phase Prepared Surface Feature 74 Ceramics

Concerning the prepared floor of the F74 circular structure which lies on top of a F79 mound, a field note states that 22 shell tempered, slipped and polished sherds were found "tramped into [the] black clay surface which show[s] red painting of some sort." This concentration of 22 body sherds was found embedded in the floor around grid coordinates A4, B31.5. Twenty-one of these are from a moderate-sized, thin-walled (2.0–2.5 mm) container which had a polished, black-colored slip on its exterior surface and a polished and lightly slipped interior finish. The last sherd was from a second vessel (Appendix V). Two additional shell tempered body sherds were found in a hearth (F118) inside the F74 rotunda. Another 17 shell tempered body sherds were found elsewhere in the F74 matrix, including a rim sherd from a plain-surfaced mini-bowl (Appendix V).

A rectangular structure, F84, on the F74 surface postdates the circular building and contains an uncertain number of ceramic sherds, including a shell tempered, slipped and polished beaker handle in its wall trenches (Fig. 4.7; Appendices V–VI). Two shell tempered sherds were contained in the fill of the building's interior hearth, F103.

Stirling Phase Prepared Surface Feature 93 Ceramics

The final prepared surface in the BP area found to be associated with ceramic refuse is F93, an ill-defined floor atop F81 mound fill. The sole sherd recovered was a rim segment of a shell tempered pan, vessel 93-1 (Fig. 4.6; Appendix II).

A pit, thought to be modern, F100, which superimposes the F87 mound fill, contained a couple of sherds. One was a rim sherd from a jar (100–1). Based on a low LP index of 0.45, it is likely that this jar was manufactured during the late Stirling (or even Moorehead) phase (Fig. 4.16). The pit itself, however, may be a fairly modern feature containing redeposited sherds from upper mound fill levels. The jar LP index is comparable to some from F87 (Table 4.3).

Late Stirling Phase Vessels in EA1

The fills of F48, an unusually large wall trench or post pit in EA1, and F60, a large post pit that superimposed F48, contain ceramics which may be used to place them later in the Kunnemann Mound sequence than most of the Stirling phase components of the lower BP area mound. Most of the F48 and F60 ceramics from the features appear to date to the late Stirling phase. A concentration of artifacts in F48 (Finds 45 and 46) are clearly dumping/fill episodes which date to the late Stirling phase. Large sections of two Ramey Incised jars; a funnel; and a thick grog-shell tempered plug with a circular appendagelike scar were found in this concentration (Appendices II, IV, VI).

The fill of F48 and F60 contains sherds from late Stirling phase containers mixed with Lohmann and early Stirling phase vessels. A minimum of 23 ceramic containers comprise the ceramic assemblage from F48 and F60. There are 11 jars (49%), 2 seed jars (9%), 6 bowls (26%), 3 funnels (13%), and 1 stumpware vessel (4%) (Figs. 4.4–4.6, 4.10, 4.14, 4.16–4.17; Table 4.2). Four of the 11 jars have trailed Ramey Incised motifs (Figs. 4.16 and 4.17; Plate 4.1). Identifiable late Stirling phase Ramey motifs include three scrolls and a ladder arc. Two of these Ramey Incised containers have trailed lines embellishing the superior surface of their lips (Fig. 4.17).

A few vessels may derive from the floor(s) above F48 and F60. For instance, although the depositional context remains unclear, five jars (50–1; EA1–1 through 4) and two fine-ware beakers (EA1–5, EA1–6) may have been deposited in these upper prepared surface zones just below the Mound 10 gumbo cap in EA1, trench 2. A single Ramey Incised body sherd may originate from this same subgumbo context (Appendices II, III, VI).

One of these jars, vessel EA1–2, has attributes that may be used to date it to the period after the Stirling phase, probably either to the late Moorehead or Sand Prairie phase. A similar jar, vessel EA2–2, was found along the south side of Mound 11, though it was possibly redeposited. These two vessels have LP indices of 0.30 and 0.31, respectively, and are the only post-Stirling phase vessels in the Kunnemann Mound ceramic assemblage outside of F100 (Table 4.3; Fig. 4.16).

Discussion

The ceramics from the Kunnemann Mound may be used to establish three primary Mississippian components: the Lohmann phase, the early Stirling phase, and the late Stirling phase. Ceramics from the F72–74 surfaces represent Stirling phase assemblages which are intermediate between the early and late aspects of the Stirling phase as defined in the Kunnemann Mound excavations.

Temporal Trends

The jar-rim shape indices provide a means of evaluating temporal trends in vessel morphology (Table 4.3). The mean RC values decrease through time as well, excluding the three F72–74 intermediate ceramic assemblages. Rim angle (RA) shows a sharpening of the inward-leaning jar shape from the Lohmann to early Stirling phase, but a lessening of this by the late Stirling phase (Fig. 4.18). The mean LP index decreases through time, while the related LTLL index increases through time (Fig. 4.18). The jar lips, in other words, become longer and thicker through time. The standard deviations for these same indices both increase through time (Fig. 4.18), an interesting phenomenon in the case of the LP index, which decreases. The decreasing LP index concomitant with increasing LP index variability (reflected in the standard devations) may be a function of the admixture of earlier high LP rims with late Stirling phase low LP jars. Conversely, the low LTLL standard deviation for the F73 jar assemblage may indicate an unmixed assemblage.

The mean jar LP indices from mound fill contexts replicate the general trend of the ceramic data from features and occupation zones, although the values themselves are greater, probably due to the incidence of Lohmann phase admixture in their fills (Fig. 4.18). The south mound (F75/77) reversal of the decreasing-LP trend may be due to the fact that a number of rims in the south mound may be primary refuse (derived from early Stirling phase mound-related activities) rather than Lohmann phase admixture (as in F75/77).

The Lohmann phase vessel assemblage is similar, in gross terms, to other contemporaneous assemblages from American Bottom sites (see Milner et al. 1984). It is comparable to the extensive Lohmann phase ceramic assemblages documented from the communities at the ICT-II Tract (Holley 1989) and at Tract 15A at Cahokia (Pauketat 1991; n.d.). However, in proportional terms, the Kunnemann Mound collection has more seed jars and jugs and fewer bowls and beakers (Table 4.2; Fig. 4.19). This is perhaps a chance consequence of the rather small Kunnemann Mound Lohmann phase sample size (MNV = 34).

Two of the features included in the Lohmann phase totals, a structure floor (F4) and a possible associated

TABLE 4.3
Ceramic Jar Rim and Lip Shape Indices

Vessel #		LP	LTLL	RC	RA
LOHMANN PHASE JARS					
4	2	0.46	0.56		
4	3	0.64	0.53		
4	4	0.65	0.65		
4	5	0.50	0.50	0.00	52
5	25			0.1	
40	1	0.92			
40	2	0.61	0.51		50
40	3	0.57	0.60		
40	5	0.54	0.40	0.02	
40	6	0.53	0.43		
40	8	0.61			
40	9	0.52	0.71		
40	10	0.74			
40	13	0.78	0.36	0.04	
40	14	0.58	0.51	0.00	56
46	1	0.46	0.58	0.00	43
Mean		0.61	0.53	0.03	50
s.d.		0.13	0.10	0.04	5
EARLY STIRLING PHASE JARS					
3	1	0.58	0.92		
3	2	0.42	0.42		
3	3	0.48	0.56		
3	4	0.59	0.72		
3	5	0.68			
3	6	0.39	0.29		33
3	7	0.38	0.72	0.0	34
3	19	0.61	0.73	0.0	33
3	20	0.68	0.47		
5	5	0.71			
5	6	0.66	0.46		
5	7	0.44	0.65	0.03	31
5	8	0.59	0.92		
5	10	0.56	0.42	0.01	31
5	11	0.69	0.78	0.04	
5	12	0.42	0.42		
5	13	0.70	1.11	0.00	31
86	1	0.48	1.30		
86	3	0.44			
89	1	0.87		0.08	
89	2	0.76	0.54		
89	3	0.59	1.13		
89	5	0.64	0.41		
89	6	0.66			
89	7	0.37	0.55		
89	9	0.73	0.77		
89	10	0.69			
89	13	0.74	1.23		
89	14	0.49	0.51	0.10	
89	15	0.49	0.79	0.00	29
89	17			0.05	
89	18	0.53	0.50	0.05	
89	19	0.70	0.92	0.03	39
89	20	0.56	0.88	0.00	41
89	21	0.45	0.45	0.00	37
89	22	0.54		0.00	36
89	23	0.50	1.14	0.00	38
Mean		0.58	0.71	0.02	34
s.d.		0.13	0.28	0.03	4
FEATURE 72 STRUCTURE					
9	1	0.62	0.51		58
EARLY MOUND 10					
58	1	0.65			
EARLY STIRLING PHASE SOUTH MOUND					
78	3	0.68	0.80	-0.02	24
78	4	0.49	0.87		
78	5	0.55	0.62	0.05	
78	7	0.78			
95	1	0.58			
133	1	0.87	1.34	0.00	53
Mean		0.66	0.91	0.01	39
s.d.		0.15	0.31	0.04	21

Vessel #		LP	LTLL	RC	RA
STIRLING PHASE MOUND FILL (F75/77)					
75	1	0.74			
75	2	0.71	0.70		
75	4	0.52	0.80	0.03	40
75	7	0.62		0.00	49
75	9	0.80	0.54	0.01	39
75	10	0.91	0.90	0.08	
75	11	0.51			
75	12	0.69	0.58	0.05	
75	13	0.76		0.07	
75	14	0.69	0.56		
75	15	0.72	0.45		
77	1	0.60	0.63		
77	2	0.78			
Mean		0.70	0.65	0.04	43
s.d.		0.11	0.15	0.03	6
STIRLING PHASE PREPARED SURFACE F73					
73	2	0.38	0.78		
73	3	0.34	0.69		
73	4	0.73	0.63		
73	5	0.73	0.78		
73	7	0.55			
73	8	0.68	0.86	0.08	
73	10	0.46	0.38		
73	11	0.59	0.71		
Mean		0.56	0.69	0.08	
s.d.		0.15	0.16	0.00	
STIRLING PHASE MOUND FILL F79					
79	1	0.58	0.43	0.07	
79	2	0.61	0.76		
79	4	0.64	0.64		64
79	5	0.66			
79	6	0.63	0.63		
Mean		0.62	0.62	0.07	64
s.d.		0.03	0.14	0.00	0
STIRLING PHASE MOUND FILL F87					
87	1	0.75	0.46	0.08	
87	2	0.78			
87	4	0.60			
87	5	0.92			
87	6	0.56	0.64		
87	8	0.65			
87	9	0.57	0.67		46
87	10	0.88		0.00	45
87	11	0.42	0.47		
87	12	0.48	0.48		60
87	13	0.50	0.73		47
87	14	0.60	1.25	-0.03	41
87	15	0.46	0.65	0.00	
87	17	0.46	0.87	0.01	41
100	1	0.45	0.64		
Mean		0.61	0.69	0.01	47
s.d.		0.16	0.24	0.04	7
LATE STIRLING PHASE JARS					
48	1	0.46	0.46		
48	2	0.29	0.51		51
48	6	0.33	0.94		44
48	7	0.55	0.99		49
48	8	0.97	1.32	0.00	32
48	9	0.20	0.36	0.00	41
48	10	0.29	0.70	-0.02	31
50	1	0.50	0.92		
60	1	0.41	0.78		
Mean		0.44	0.78	-0.01	41
s.d.		0.23	0.30	0.01	8
MOOREHEAD-SAND PRAIRIE PHASE JARS?					
EA1	2	0.30	0.25	-0.05	
EA2	2	0.31	0.31	-0.07	
Mean		0.31	0.28	-0.06	
s.d.		0.01	0.04	0.01	

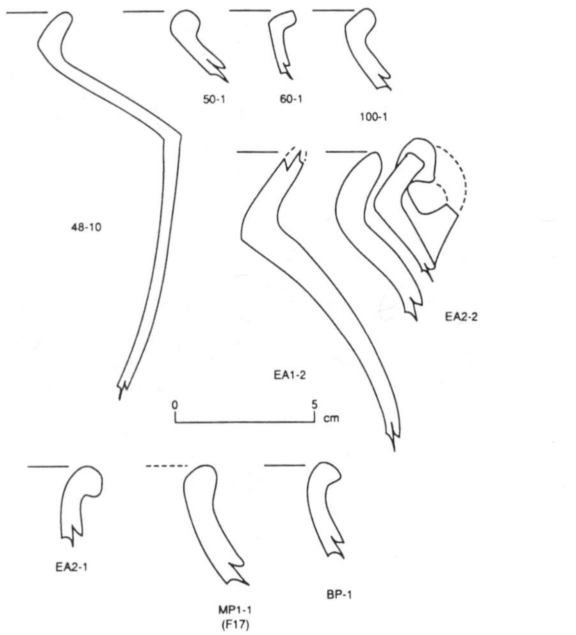

Figure 4.16. Rim profiles of late Stirling phase and miscellaneous jars.

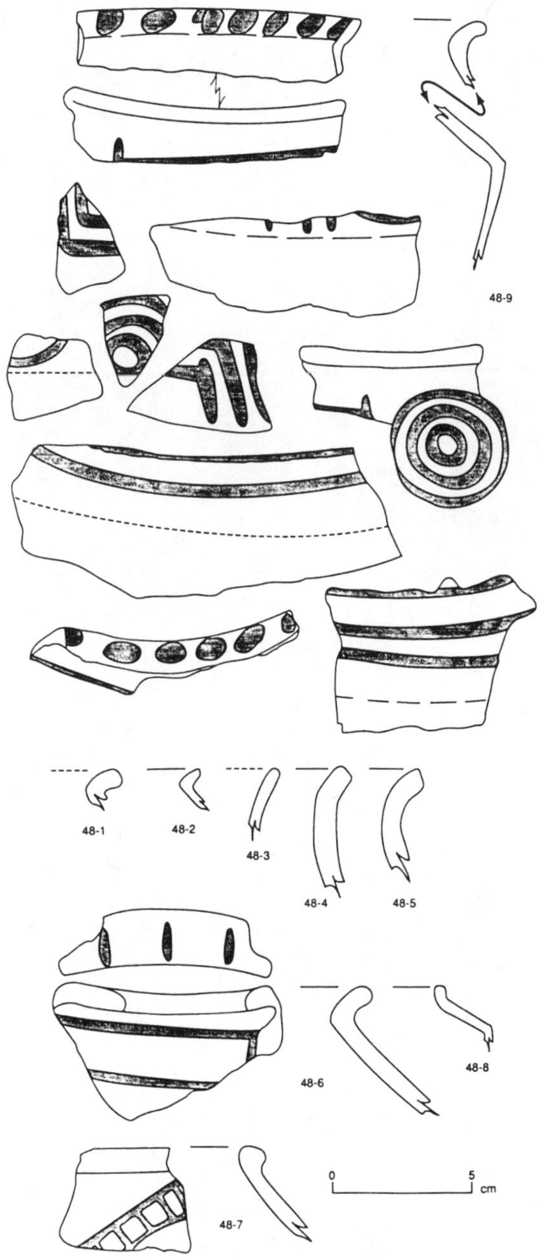

Figure 4.17. Rim profiles of jars in late Stirling phase Feature 48.

hearth (F7), actually may date to the early Stirling phase. It is not known what the F4 and F7 deposits represent (whether primary, secondary, or tertiary remains, or an earlier superimposed structure not defined in plan view). The basin fill above the burned structural elements clearly contained early Stirling phase ceramics. Perhaps the structure itself was occupied for the period of years that spanned the terminal Lohmann-early Stirling divide. The fact that the building walls were rebuilt at least once, along with the cleaning-out and relining of the central hearth, may mean that the building was standing for more than a decade (Pauketat 1989:304). The higher elevation of the second and later wall trench may provide confirmation that F4 was associated with the earliest usage of the structure (F3–5).

The early Stirling phase in the BP area is well represented by ceramic refuse. Several large amorphous basins were filled during this subphase. A total of 87 vessels have been identified in the submound features. Among this number are fewer seed jars but more bowls and beakers relative to the Lohmann phase ceramic assemblage (Table 4.2; Fig. 4.19). A decorated jar form (Ramey Incised), representing 10 percent of the total number of jars, and a decorated bowl-beaker form (Mound Place Incised) making up 14 percent of the 22 bowls and beakers, are new additions to the ceramic assemblage. The Mound Place Incised bowls in early Stirling phase contexts are the earliest known at Cahokia. Few early Stirling phase vessel surfaces are red slipped, in contrast to the Lohmann phase containers (see Holley 1989; Pauketat 1991: chap. 4). Stirling phase jar lips, as visible in the LP and LTLL indices, become more pronounced than their Lohmann phase counterparts.

Late Stirling phase ceramics were associated with the summit of Mound 10 (in EA1). These vessels include decorated and undecorated jars and a funnel. The array of vessel forms in this small refuse assemblage, ignoring extrane-

Plate 4.1. Late Stirling phase Ramey Incised jar (48–10).

ous sherds derived from earlier components, is reminiscent of the submound deposits and is comparable to the late Stirling phase ceramic assemblage from the ICT-II. The LP and RC indices are low and Ramey Incised jars make up a large portion of the late Stirling phase ceramic assemblage, like other roughly contemporaneous pottery collections (Holley 1989; Pauketat 1991).

Possible Sacred-Elite Wares

The material remains from the Stirling phase mantles or prepared surfaces and associated structures excavated in the BP area presumably were deposited under circumstances different from those which resulted in the submound and perhaps the late Stirling phase refuse. Generally speaking, the prepared mound surfaces and structure floors were quite clean. Nonetheless, nearly all of the floors and/or mound caps whose surfaces were horizontally examined produced some sign of vessel usage and breakage.

Within Features 72 and 74 were embedded fragmented portions of finely made shell or grog tempered pots. Feature 73 contained an array of fragments from apparent utilitarian containers. Sherds were found within hearths associated with the structures associated with F72, F84, and F74. Fine-ware sherds from the south mound (F78) and from Mound 10 (EA1) might be related to mound-top activities, as may the pan sherd from F93. It will be recalled that Moorehead (1929:36) mentioned finding "fine" pottery associated with a floor higher up in the mound.

Based on this meager ceramic assemblage, it seems likely that ordinary domestic activities involving the use of utilitarian pots were seldom conducted on the mound summit(s), although decorated or finely crafted vessels—Ramey Incised jars and fine-ware beakers and bowls—were regularly used there. Further, while the Lohmann and early Stirling phase submound ceramics appear to be domestic refuse, the composition of the assemblages in both cases differs in some manner from other documented refuse both at Cahokia and elsewhere in the American Bottom (see Holley 1989; Milner et al. 1984; Pauketat 1991: chap. 4).

There exists no definitive study of sacred and secular Mississippian wares from the American Bottom, in part because of unsuitable samples and in part because there does not seem to have been an absolute segregation of wares according to the context of use or social status. However, there are indications of the restricted manufacture and use of decorated fine-ware bowls and beakers and Ramey Incised jars.

Holley (1989:61) thinks that this might be true of Lohmann phase garbage beneath Mound 72. I have argued

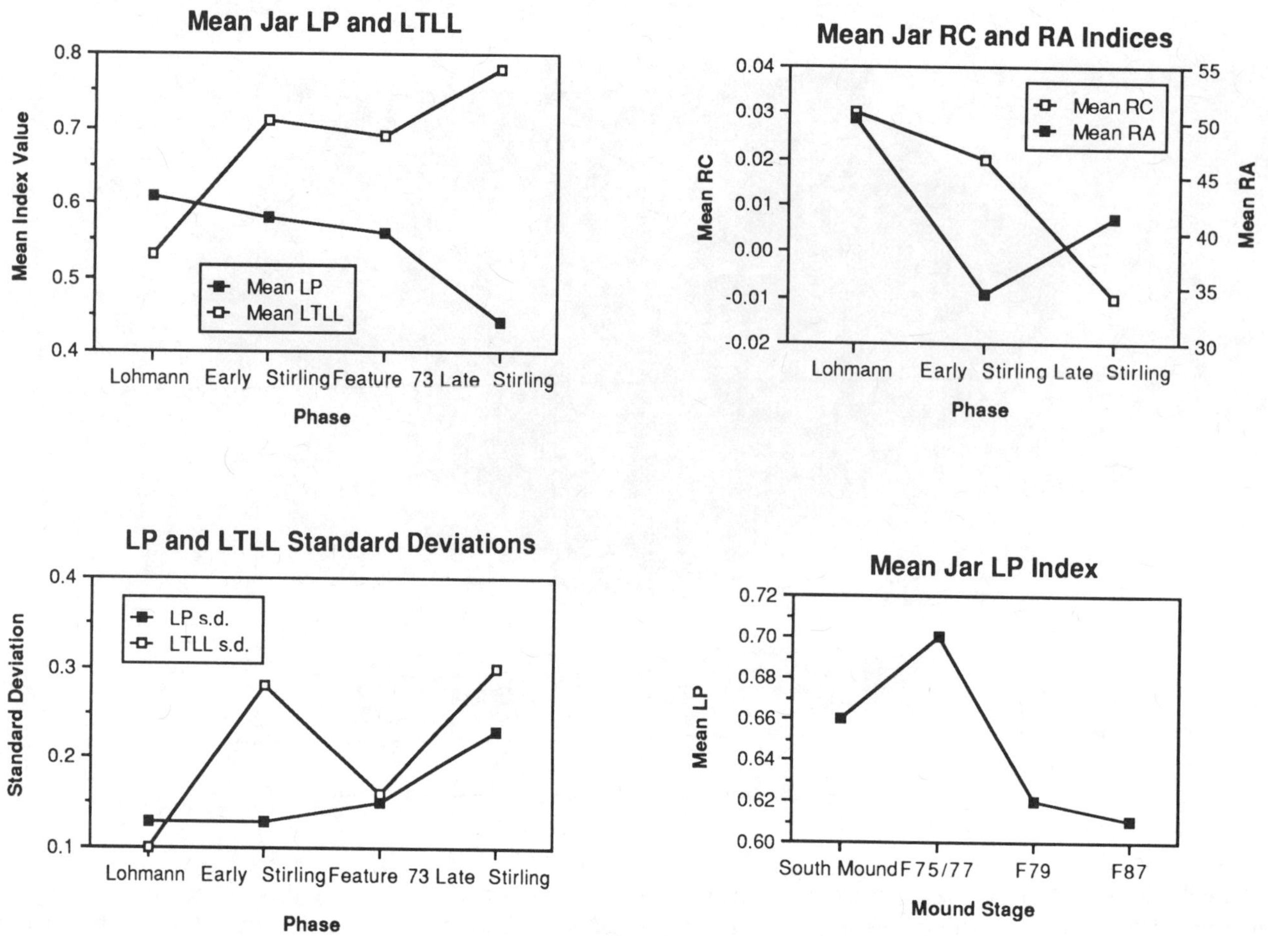

Figure 4.18. Temporal trends in jar rim and lip shape.

that the same may be true of Tract 15A (Pauketat 1991:195). In the past, the grog tempered fine-ware, found mostly in Lohmann and Stirling phase features at Cahokia and surrounding sites, has been assumed to consist of Caddoan and Coles Creek "trade" vessels made in the mid-South (e.g., Fowler and Hall 1975; O'Brien 1977; Pauketat 1984). Undoubtedly, some of the fine-ware vessels are from these distant regions (Kelly 1991b). However, it is likely that many Lohmann and Stirling phase fine-ware beakers and bowls featuring fine-grog temper, brown paste, and reddish-brown slips are a product of Cahokia and other Mississippian centers in the American Bottom (Holley 1989:107). Elsewhere, I have argued that there is a marked increase in the density of these fine-ware sherds at the beginning of the Mississippi Period (Pauketat 1991:288). Fine-ware sherd densities at Tract 15A and the Dunham Tract are greatest during the Stirling phase, when this area of Cahokia hosted the elite "post-circle monument" and presumed elite domiciles (Pauketat 1991:231–36).

There is at present inconclusive evidence directly addressing where or when these fine-ware containers were manufactured. In contrast, there is evidence to argue that the well-made and decorated Ramey Incised jars were manufactured under restricted and centralized conditions for use in the distribution of comestibles (Emerson 1989; Pauketat and Emerson 1991). Ramey Incised jars are represented in most Stirling phase refuse in the American Bottom, particularly in and around Cahokia. While clearly not restricted to elite or sacred contexts, these shell tempered jars are associated with the activities and facilities surmounting earthen platforms like the Kunnemann Mound, Murdock Mound (H. Smith 1977), and Mound 34 (UMMA collections).

Conclusions

The Lohmann and early Stirling phase occupations below or adjacent to the early Kunnemann Mound stages appear to have produced the usual array of Cahokia do-

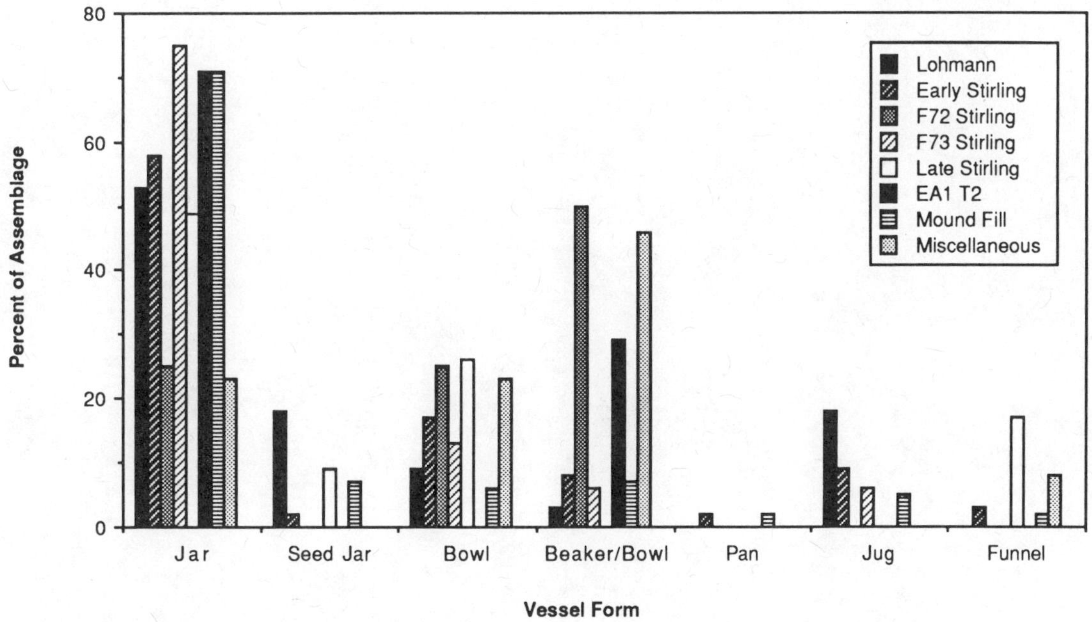

Figure 4.19. Vessel assemblages.

mestic vessel forms in the usual proportions with the possible exception of jugs and, in the early Stirling phase features, Mound Place Incised bowls. Early Stirling phase jar lips were relatively small. Jar rims sloped inward. Bifurcated loop handles were common. Trailed Mound Place Incised bowls make their appearance along with trailed Ramey Incised jars.

Stirling phase mound activities included the use and breakage of finely made shell and grog tempered bowls, beakers, and Ramey Incised jars. Late Stirling phase jars had larger lips, straight inward-slanting rims, and trailed decorations on rim exteriors and lip-superior surfaces. Two probable post-Stirling phase containers were found from disturbed contexts.

While small, the excavated Kunnemann Mound ceramic assemblage provides further support for previously observed temporal trends and social-contextual distinctions among ceramic wares at Cahokia. The ceramics also are the basis of the definitions of phase units (i.e., feature groups) whereby the remaining artifact classes (lithics, faunal remains, and plant remains) are ordered and interpreted. These analyses follow in Chapters 5 through 9.

CHAPTER 5

Lithics

Approximately ten kilograms of lithic artifacts were recovered from excavated contexts during the 1955–1956 excavations at the Kunnemann Mound. These artifacts may be sorted into four primary lithic classes: chert tools and debitage, sandstone sawing and smoothing equipment, miscellaneous sedimentary and igneous rock tools, and copper.

Chert artifacts make up 6.5 kg or 65 percent of the total recovered lithic artifact weight. Only three chert types (or geological formations) are represented in the chert artifact assemblage from the Kunnemann Mound excavations: Burlington, Kaolin, and Mill Creek. The first probably was derived from the Crescent Hills area of St. Louis and Jefferson counties, Missouri, while the last two came from Union County, Illinois (see Kelly 1984; Koldehoff 1990b:78ff.).

The 540 individual Burlington chert artifacts represent 84 percent of the chert artifact assemblage by weight (Table 5.1). Most of this total is debitage from chert-working activities. The chert-working activities have been discussed in the past in terms of distinct industries (Esarey and Pauketat 1992; Kelly 1984; Koldehoff 1987, 1990a; Morse 1974; Pauketat and Woods 1986; Perino 1960). Two of these industries are evident in the chert artifacts from the Kunnemann Mound excavations.

Expedient Tool Industry

A late prehistoric expedient tool or flake tool industry has been recognized in the American Bottom (see Esarey and Pauketat 1992; Koldehoff 1990a:63ff., 1990b:77). Informal chert flake tools were produced by striking flakes from cores in a rather haphazard and free-hand manner. The amorphous shapes of debitage and flake tools, cores struck from multiple directions, and large quantities of debitage, attest to the existence of this common household industry (see Kelly 1980, 1984; Koldehoff 1990a, 1990b).

Eight multidirectional cores and 326 flakes are by-products of expedient-tool manufacture at or around the Kunnemann Mound. About 1.6 kg or 68 percent of these Burlington and Kaolin chert flakes and cores were associated with F89. Surprisingly few flakes or cores were found in the F3–5 fills associated with the submound burned structure. Twenty-seven flakes were found on the F73 surfaces, and the remainder were found in mound fill (Tables 5.1–5.2). A macroscopic examination revealed 13 flakes with utilized edges (UE) or retouched edges (RT). One of these had a steeply retouched, convex edge, suitable for scraping soft hides, among other things. A single flake was retouched into a graver having a single spur showing macroscopic traces of use-wear. Other utilized or retouched flakes probably were used as cutting or sawing tools.

Microlithic Industry

The second industry identified in the Kunnemann Mound chert assemblage involved the production of microliths. The Kunnemann Tract is well known for the high density of microlithic tools and debitage (Holley 1990; Mason and Perino 1961; Morse 1974; Perino 1960). The large quantities of these lithic artifacts recovered from the plow zone of the Kunnemann Tract have been thought to indicate craft specialization at Cahokia (Prentice 1985:95; Yerkes 1983, 1989, 1991). The following represents the only excavated sample of microliths from this tract.

Sixty-eight unmodified bladelets, or microblades, were found during the 1955 and 1956 excavations (Plate 5.1). These are small, thick, elongate spalls detached from small microblade cores (Koldehoff 1990a:74). Microblades probably were manufactured to be used as microdrills, used to drill mollusc shell (Mason and Perino 1961; Yerkes 1983, 1989, 1991), although the large numbers in the Kunnemann Mound sample may indicate either the large number of microblade by-products per usable microdrill blank or the production of microblades for some other purpose. Approximately 84 percent of the Kunnemann Mound microblades were recovered from three early Stirling phase

TABLE 5.1
Burlington Chert Artifacts

Feature	Cores	Wt.(g)	mbCores	Wt.(g)	Flakes	Wt.(g)	Microblades	Wt.(g)	Informal Tools
3					2	4.8			
5					2	17.6	5	10.6	
3+5					1	2.0			flake is M.Woodland blade?
40			4	84.1	27	94.5	1	2.6	
41					1	3.3			
46					16	16.4			
70					2	5.0			
72							9	4.6	
73			1	1.9	2	5.0	1	0.9	
73A			1	12.6	7	43.5			
75			1	8.9	20	116.9			
77					3	26.1			1 heavily UE flake
78			2	18.7	3	28.8			2 heavily UE flakes
79			1	18.1	5	18.3			
80					2	10.5			
83			1	9.6					
86					24	88.8	47	83.1	1 UE flake; 1 UE microblade
87	2	64.2	4	95.1	12	130.7			1 convex-RT flake (scraper); 1 UE flake
89	6	347.5	120	3092.3	187	1224.1	5	7.8	3 gravers on microblades; 2 RT flakes; 3 UE flakes;
89 (cont'd)									6 perforators on flakes; 1 core-biface with UE
108					1	4.6			
109					1	1.5			
BP			2	82.8	6	35.4			1 steep-RT mbcore; 1 graver on flake
EA (?)			1	33.4	2	20.3			1 UE flake
Total:	8	411.7	138	3457.5	326	1898.1	68	109.6	24 informal tools

TABLE 5.2
Other Chert Artifacts

Feature	Kaolin Flakes	Wt.(g)	MC Flakes/Shatter	Wt.(g)	Informal Tools
5			23	132	
40	1	2			
41			28	91	
74	1	6			1 graver
87	1	12			
89	1	3			
TOTAL	4	23	51	223	1 informal tool

features. One microblade was found in the Lohmann phase Feature 40. Nine others (13%) were found on the F72 surface, and one was associated with F73 on the mound top. One unmodified bladelet from F86 exhibits a utilized edge; three from F89 have delicately retouched graver spurs at one end (Table 5.1). The others show no macroscopic signs of utilization.

The microblade cores (mbCores) include a subset longitudinally faceted and roughly columnar in shape (Mason and Perino 1961:556).

> Some researchers have described these cores as bipolar; this term is a misnomer. . . . [T]he . . . microblades were not produced with the bipolar flaking techniques but were detached from opposite ends (or poles) of cores. [Koldehoff 1990a:76]

Microblade cores sometimes resemble the prismatic or polyhedral cores of other formal core-and-blade technologies (Plate 5.1; see Mason and Perino 1961:556; see also Koldehoff 1987). Another subset includes microblade cores with amorphous shapes. These are simply flakes or fragments of block shatter from which one or more bladelets have been removed, sometimes giving the core a burinlike appearance (Mason and Perino 1961; Yerkes 1983:500). In fact, even the columnar cores may have started out as large

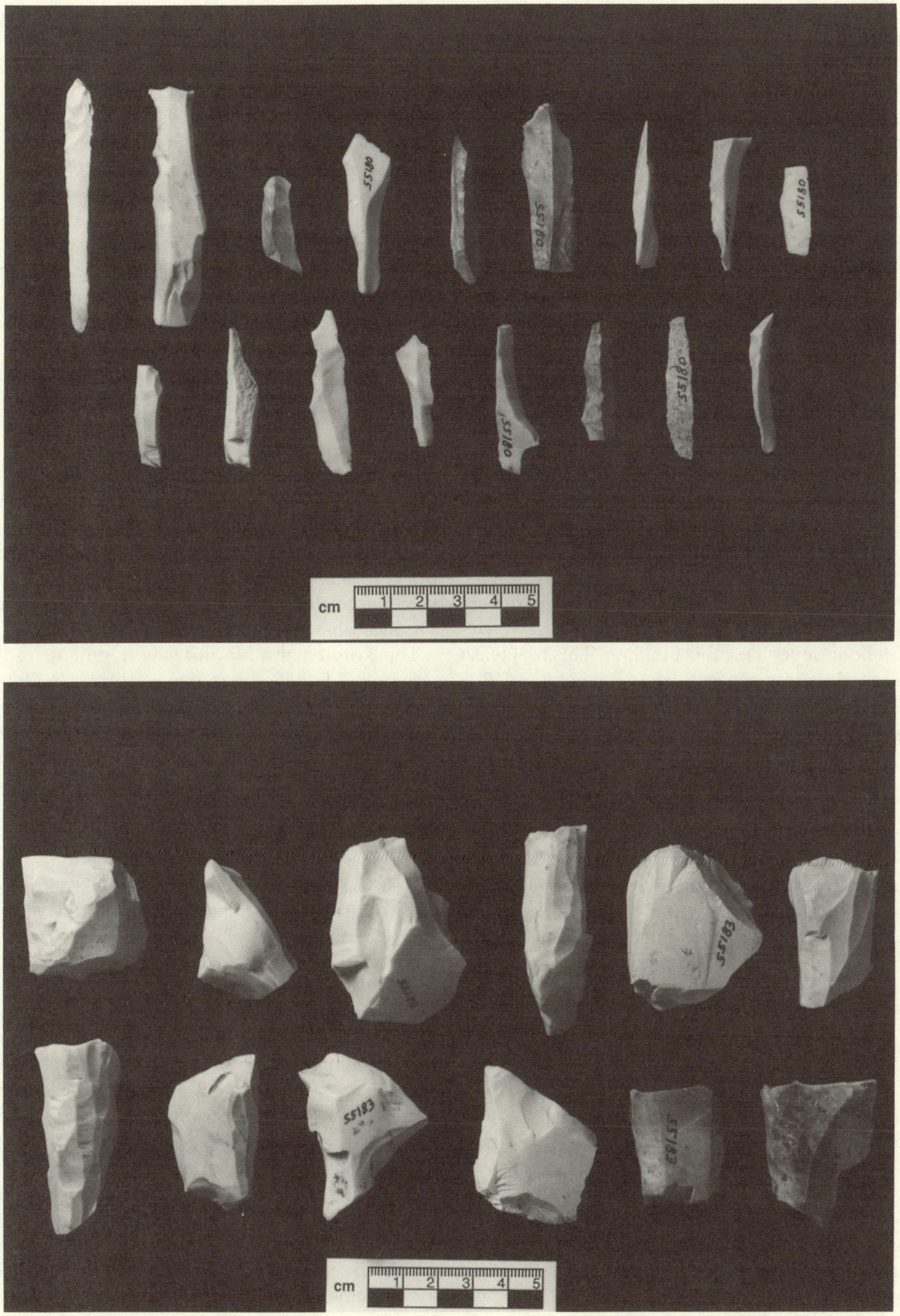

Plate 5.1. Microlithic artifacts: *top*, microblades and drill; *bottom*, microblade cores.

flakes or block shatter. The chance fracture pattern of a particular core may have determined its continued use as a core, and ultimately its final shape. A single microblade core had a steep, retouched edge, suggesting it was used as a scraping tool after its use as a core.

The assemblage of chert artifacts included six perforators (mean length = 54 mm, s.d. = 11.3; Table 5.1; Plate 5.1), all are from F89. One could be called a microdrill (length, 39 mm), but two of the perforators were manufactured from larger bladelets (length = 55 mm and 69 mm). The other three perforators are thick retouched flakes. All show macroscopic traces of use-wear from simple perforation or drilling tasks.

Formal Chert Tools

Four formal chert tools are represented in the lithic artifact assemblage. A small projectile point of undetermined chert type was found in F5 (Table 5.3). This might have been associated with the *in situ* deposits on the burned building floor. A hoe blade, manufactured from Mill Creek chert, was found on the floor of this same structure (Table 5.3; Plate 5.2). The burned and heat-shattered fragments of another Mill Creek-chert hoe blade also were associated with the *in situ* floor deposits of this building. This tool was probably damaged during the building's incineration. Finally, 28 Mill Creek hoe-blade resharpening flakes were recovered from the F41 mound fill (EA1).

Sandstone Artifacts

By weight, sandstone artifacts (500.6 g) constitute 15 percent of the lithic artifacts found during the excavations at Kunnemann Mound. Among their numbers are four types of tools—saws, chisels, abraders, and palettes (Table 5.4). Additionally, a fragmentary sandstone discoidal from the surface of Mound 11 or its immediate environs is contained in the Preston Holder collections at the Museum of Anthropology, University of Michigan (Table 5.3).

Saws and Chisels

A rare artifact form, the sandstone saw, and three examples of an almost unknown type of sandstone tool, a chisel-like implement, make up 73 percent of the sandstone tool assemblage by count. Sandstone saws were first identified at Cahokia by Titterington (1938:8). Other examples have been found at Cahokia, including a fragment from Mound 12, collected by University of Michigan personnel in 1948 (UMMA cat. no. 54679), one fragment from a refuse pit excavated by Preston Holder at the Groves Borrow Pit (11-Ms-75; UMMA cat. no. 55323), one from Griffin and Spaulding's test pit 3 of Mound 34 at Cahokia (3.5–4.0′; UMMA cat. no. 54513), others from the Powell Mound area (Ahler and DePuydt 1987:28–29), two from a burial excavated by Gregory Perino (1947, 1980), and another from a burial at the ICT-II, excavated by Southern Illinois University (Collins 1990: fig. 4.7). Of these, it is possible that Holder's Groves Borrow Pit specimen dates to the late Lohmann or early Stirling phase, while the Mound 34 example may derive from an early Moorehead phase context. From outside Cahokia, specimens have been reported from the domestic refuse at the Radic site (McElrath et al. 1987:198) and the Turner site (Milner 1983b:106–9), and from burial offerings at the East St. Louis Stone Quarry cemetery (Milner 1983a:63–66) and Schild cemetery in the lower Illinois River valley (Perino 1971a:110). The Radic and Turner site examples date to the Stirling phase, while the cemetery finds date as late as the Moorehead or Sand Prairie phase.

Sandstone saws are thin, elongate slabs with one or two honed edges. The 29 Kunnemann Mound specimens are all fragments representing an indeterminate number of tools (Plate 5.3). About 66 percent of these fragments were found in early Stirling phase deposits (Table 5.4). Three were associated with F73, perhaps placing the sawing activities on Mound 11 itself.

The Kunnemann Mound saw fragments range in thickness from 2.5–10.0 mm (mean = 4.9; s.d. = 2.2). Of twelve midsection or end fragments, eight are from tools with one honed edge, the opposing edge having been ground smooth or dulled. The widths of these specimens range from a modal value of 3.0 cm to 4.7 cm. The other five artifacts exhibit opposing honed edges. These range in width from a modal value of 3.0 cm to 4.5 cm. Other fragments exceed 4.5, 5.2, and 5.7 cm in width. On most fragments, the honed edge was convex, giving single-edged tools a crescent shape, and double-edged tools a lenticular shape (Plate 5.3). Single examples exist of a small saw (47 × 26 × 10 mm) with one honed edge, and a sandstone (palette?) spall and a fractured palette, both of which had sharp edges utilized as saws.

Perino (1971b: fig. 79e) reported an unusual tool from the Kunnemann Tract which he called a "reamer." Another example from the Kunnemann Tract is described by Holley (1990:133) as "a squared rod with a blunt distal end (10 mm in diameter)." These same tools were found in the early Stirling phase features beneath Mound 11. The function of these tools is not entirely clear. They appear to be special smoothing or filing tools with the added qualities of chisels. Two complete and one fragmentary sandstone chisels were found in F5 and F89 (Table 5.4; Plate 5.3). The one specimen from F5 has a burned appearance, placing it on the floor of the structure. These cylindrical early Stirling phase tools are 44 and 55 meters long. The apparent bit of the two complete specimens consists of a beveled end. The

TABLE 5.3
Miscellaneous Tools

Feature	Item Description	Wt.(g)
4 (Find 14)	paired "granite grinding stones"; flat sides fit together	missing/ISM
4+5 (Find 25)	Mill Creek hoe blade (15×10 cm), heavily used, resharpened	398
4+5 (Find 25)	igneous hammerstone; 2 battered ends (one with spall scars)	155
5 (Find 10)	chert triangular proj. point (23×15×3.1 mm) flake with marginal RT	1
35	a lump of corroded copper	-
40	broken igneous celt with distal end reworked into hammerstone	520
40	igneous celt with re-knapped/unpecked bit exhibiting use-wear	1145
89	tiny stone disc bead (4 mm in diameter)	0.1
89	finished celt butt fragment	109
92 postmold	limestone "ball"; spheroidal artifact	94
General	fragment of sandstone discoidal (5.5 cm in diameter)	46
TOTAL	12	2468.1

Plate 5.2. Mill Creek chert hoe blade from Feature 3–5.

beveled surface is rough and unsmoothed on the F5 item and smoothed on the F89 tool. The bit of the latter is blunted and exhibits hinged impact scars (Plate 5.3).

Abraders

Another unusual form of sandstone tool has been called an abrader (type 1) but is unlike common slotted tools. Five type 1 abraders from the Kunnemann Mound excavations comprise 9 percent of the tools by count. Other typical abraders (type 2) and palette fragments comprise the remaining forms of sandstone tools from the Kunnemann Mound excavations (Table 5.4).

The type 1 abraders are characterized by a shaped, quadrilateral and tabular appearance and by a single large elongate *u*-shaped concavity (or slot) along one edge. The shape of this slot in cross section, it should be noted, conforms well to the curvature of finished shell beads found during excavations (see Chapter 6). A large specimen from F46 (21 mm thick) has two flat sides and four flattened

TABLE 5.4
Sandstone Artifacts

Feature	Saw Frags.	Wt.(g)	Chisel	Wt.(g)	Abrader#1	Wt.(g)	Abrader#2	Wt.(g)	Palette Frags.	Wt.(g)	Notes
5	1	12.7	1	16							Find 32
13									1*	173	*1.2 cm thick
17	2*	53.8									*from same tool
40	3	14.9			2	97.3			1*	48	*heat altered, perhaps an abrader #1
46					1	251.5					
48	1	21.3									
73	3	46.2									
75	1	23.7					2**	59	1*	42	*palette frag. used as saw; **1 with u-shaped slot, 1 cube with 2 flat/striated surfaces
77	1	8.7							1	103	
78					1	37.8					
87	1	32.5									
89	18	236.2	2	24	1	5.9	1 (shallow)	37	2*	135	*flat surfaces reused as abraders?; also a spall used as saw (10.2g)
TOTAL	31	450.0	3	40	5	392.5	3	96	6	501	

Plate 5.3. Sandstone saws and chisels.

edges. Two of the edges are rough and unsmoothed, one is smooth with a narrow *u*-shaped slot, and one has a broad, deep, *u*-shaped slot or concavity (Plate 5.4). Two fragments of similar sized tools, with slightly less well-rounded edge concavities, were found in F40 and F78. Two small type 1 abraders, from F40 (16 mm thick) and F89 (12.5 mm thick) have the *u*-shaped concave edge opposite a slightly honed edge (Plate 5.4). Type 1 abraders share affinities with what have sometimes been called arrowshaft smoothers. However, the Kunnemann Mound tools are believed to have been hand-held bead shaping and smoothing tools (Perino 1971b:110).

Miscellaneous Artifacts

A series of other lithic artifacts were recovered from the Kunnemann Mound excavations. Among these were a pair of "grinding stones," a hammerstone, two reworked celts, a celt fragment, and a tiny stone bead. Additionally, a small lump of deteriorated copper was found associated with the clayey mound cap F35 (Table 5.3). A spheroidal limestone chunk was recovered from a postmold within wall trench F92 but may not represent a modified object. A larger and apparently unmodified (and uncollected?) limestone slab was found on the F4 surface adjacent to the F7 hearth.

The "grinding stones" (so labeled in the field) have not been relocated at the Illinois State Museum. These were described by Holder on an artifact check list as "gray granite" objects each about 6 cm in diameter: "One is flat on both sides and about 1.5 cm thick." The mate "is flattened only on one side and rounded on the other" having a maximum thickness of 2.5 cm. These were found on the F3–5 floor (Find 14) just below the burned structural elements.

Other igneous rock artifacts include two reworked celts, a celt fragment, and a hammerstone. The two celts were found in F40. One had been recycled into a hammerstone and the other had a reknapped but unpecked and unsmoothed bit which exhibited heavy wear from chopping (Plate 5.5). The celt butt fragment was found in F89 and the hammerstone was associated with the F3–5 burned structure floor (Find 25). Opposing ends of this tool had been battered.

Lastly, a tiny stone disk-shaped bead, only 4.8 mm in

Plate 5.4. Type 1 sandstone abrader from Feature 46.

diameter and 1.7 mm in thickness, was found in F89. This bead appears to be manufactured from sandstone. It is approximately the size of a fossil crinoid segment, but crinoid fossils seldom, if ever, are associated with sandstone deposits.

Discussion

The Kunnemann Mound lithic assemblage is distinct in its small size. This primarily seems to be due to the unimportance of expedient tool-making activities. Feature 3 shows a clear example of this paucity of materials. Basin fills of Lohmann and early Stirling phase structures at Tract 15A and the Dunham Tract typically contained dozens of flakes, flake-tools, and cores (see Pauketat 1991). The low density of expedient tool chert artifacts in the Kunnemann Mound sample also contrasts with analyzed domestic refuse from nearby contemporaneous sites (e.g., Emerson and Jackson 1984, 1987; Esarey and Pauketat 1992; Fortier 1985; Jackson and Hanenberger 1990; Milner 1983b, 1984a). Only five flakes were collected from the early Stirling phase structure basin under the Kunnemann Mound (F3–5), a surprisingly low density given that the Kunnemann Mound feature fills were screened; few of the aforementioned samples from Cahokia or outlying sites were screened.

Plate 5.5. Igneous rock celts from Feature 40.

On the other hand, there is a much higher density of microlithic artifacts in the Lohmann and early Stirling phase submound features than has been excavated at any other site in the American Bottom region. The density of microblades in F86 and F89 is 17.3 artifacts/m^3 or 30.3 grams/m^3. The density of microblade cores for these same two features is 40 artifacts/m^3 or 1030.8 grams/m^3. Although comparisons with other areas of Cahokia and other contemporaneous American Bottom sites is inhibited by the lack of volumetric data, it is clear from inspections of site reports that this density is far above anything recovered from excavated contexts in the American Bottom. For instance, of the hundreds of cubic meters of Lohmann and early Stirling phase feature fill excavated at Tract 15A and the Dunham Tract, only two microdrill-like tools, one microblade core, and no microblades were found (Pauketat 1991:271).[1] Table 5.5 compares the density of Kunnemann Mound microlithic items with those of other excavated assemblages using item/jar as a proxy density measure rather than item/m^3 (see Pauketat 1991: fig. 5.23). Using these indices, the density of microblade cores in the Kunnemann Mound early Stirling phase features is at least 68 times higher than their densities in Mississippian features at other sites.

The distribution of microliths in lithic assemblages from American Bottom sites makes it clear that microlith production and usage was not an everyday activity of most households (Koldehoff 1990a:179ff.; Pauketat 1987c:81; Prentice 1985; Yerkes 1989, 1991). The high densities of these artifacts under the Kunnemann Mound could be used to argue that the activities involving microliths here were far more labor intensive than anywhere else in the surrounding floodplain. The same could be said of the activities involving sandstone filing and smoothing tools. More fragments of sandstone saws were excavated from F89 beneath the Kunnemann Mound than previously have been reported from all other sites in the American Bottom combined, including other portions of the Cahokia site. The sandstone chisels and type 1 abraders seem almost unknown outside of the Kunnemann Tract (see Perino 1971b).

There can be no doubt that the lithic artifacts dating to the Lohmann and Stirling phases beneath the Kunnemann Mound include tool and debitage remains common to both central and rural Mississippian domestic refuse in the American Bottom. On the other hand, it seems likely that most of the lithic artifacts described above were used in specialized craft-production, such as the manufacture of shell, bone, antler, and possibly wood ornaments or sumptuary paraphernalia (see Chapter 10). At the same time,

TABLE 5.5
Microlith Assemblage Comparison

Site	Provenience	A	B	C	B/A	C/A	Phase	Reference
Kunnemann Md.	F86 and F89	22	52	120	2.36	5.45	early Stirling	-
Cahokia Palisade	F1797	30	2	0	0.07	0.00	Edelhardt	Koldehoff 1990b; Pauketat 1990
BBB Motor	Southern Unit	64	11	1	0.17	0.02	Stirling	Emerson and Jackson 1984
Lohmann	S5 and F35	72	11	0	0.15	0.00	Lohmann	Esarey and Pauketat 1992
Turner	Fea. Clusters 1-4	90	55	7	0.61	0.08	Lohmann-Stirling	Prentice 1985; Pauketat 1989
15A-DT	Lohmann features	208	2	1	0.01	0.01	Lohmann	Pauketat 1991:271

A = no. of undecorated jars; **B** = no. of microblades or microdrills; **C** = no. of microblade cores.

fewer expedient tools and debitage are associated with these same features than would be expected of a common rural homestead or even a central domestic zone.

The limited array of refuse becomes even more clear if the vertebrate, floral, and molluscan remains are taken into account. These artifact classes are analyzed in Chapters 6 through 8. A summary of all of these artifacts in terms of craft production is provided in Chapter 10.

CHAPTER 5 NOTE

1. It is conceivable that some microdrills were overlooked during the salvage operations at 15A; no screens were used during the 1961 excavations. Likewise, except for the flotation samples from each feature, fills from FAI-270 sites were not screened. Of course, screening through quarter-inch mesh would not ensure recovery of the tiny microdrills.

Chapter 6

Mollusc Shell Artifacts

Mollusc shell artifacts are a common component of late prehistoric refuse from American Bottom sites. Marine shell is prevelant at the Cahokia site proper and has been recovered from a number of contemporaneous sites throughout the American Bottom region. Unfortunately, few studies of sizable assemblages have been performed (Baker 1929, 1941; L. Kelly 1990; Parmalee 1957). It would appear that marine shell beads were manufactured at Cahokia and other sites during the Mississippi Period (Milner 1990:13). In fact, it has been proposed that during certain periods and in some contexts bead manufacture was the work of manufacturing specialists (Prentice 1983, 1985; Yerkes 1983, 1986, 1989, 1991). It would seem ironic, then, that bead-making specialists most often are identified by lithic tools and debitage rather than shell debris, but this is because shell does not always weather well the acidic soils of the American Bottom (see Woods and Holley 1989:229). Fortunately, this was not the case in Holder's Kunnemann Mound sample, in which mollusc shell was well preserved.

Marine and freshwater mollusc shell artifacts weighing about 3.5 kg were found in the excavated portions of the Kunnemann Mound (Table 6.1). The Kunnemann Mound artifacts include 313 ornaments, ornament fragments, or ornament-manufacturing scrap made from marine gastropod shells (*Busycon*, *Conus*, and *Marginella* spp.). Modified gastropod shell is difficult to identify at the species level. A comprehensive identification of species remains to be accomplished.

Marine pelecypod species are represented by six shells (Plate 6.1). Two of the largest marine bivalves have characteristics of the Veneridae family, similar to what Morris (1958:70) identifies as *Venus mercenaria* or what Perry and Schwengel (1955:69) and Dance (1974:270) identify as *Mercenaria* spp. The four smaller shells, possessing distinctive spoon-shaped fosse, appear to be *Mactra* spp. shells (Dance 1974:250–251; Perry and Schwengel 1955:88). All of these species probably originated from the waters of the Gulf of Mexico (see Dance 1974; Morris 1958; Perry and Schwengel 1955).

Freshwater naiades (specific taxa not identified) are represented by 91 artifacts. Freshwater gastropods (*Anculosa* spp.) are represented by five specimens. All mollusc shell appears to have been used in the manufacture of shell tools and ornaments (cf. Baker 1929, 1941; L. Kelly 1990; Parmalee 1958). The shell was well preserved and we can be certain that the recovered materials accurately mirror the deposited assemblage.

Marine Shell Ornaments and Manufacturing Debris

About 48 percent of the total molluscan shell assemblage by weight is comprised of whelk shell scrap fragments. These *Busycon* fragments, the bulk of which were found either in F3–5 or F89 (the uncertainty is due to lack of records at the ISM), appear to be amorphous-shaped periphery or whorl fragments and bits of columellae. This marine shell scrap appears to have resulted primarily from the reduction of whole whelk shells into beads and pendants. Saw marks are visible on at least 12 whelk shell fragments from Features 3, 5, 40, 48, 60, 79, 80, and 89 (Table 6.1). These saw marks appear to match the *v*-shaped honed edges of sandstone saws. In a number of cases, it is clear that sections of whorl and columellae were scribed by sawing (i.e., filing grooves) and were subsequently snapped into sections. A number of columellae exhibit other filing or smoothing marks (Plate 6.1), perhaps the initial stages of the production of columnar or barrel-shaped beads.

Marine shell beads or bead fragments found during the Holder excavations include two distinct types in four stages of manufacture. A minimum of 29 beads, 9 columnar or barrel-shaped specimens and 20 disk-shaped items, were recovered from the excavations (Table 6.1; Plate 6.2). The columnar beads and bead fragments—manufactured from whelk shell columellae—have lengths (mean = 18.3

TABLE 6.1
Mollusc Shell Artifacts

Feature	MARINE WHELK SHELL				FRESH-WATER MUSSEL SHELL				OTHER		Comments
	Beads	Wt.(g)	Scrap	Wt.(g)	Modified	Wt.(g)	Valve Frags.	Wt.(g)	Item	Wt.(g)	
3			1	0.2					1 pendant*	-	*Find 10, a columella pendant, missing at ISM
3 (Find 1–4)	2*	7.5	†3.8	38							*unfinished disk bead & one narrow-cylindrical bead blank; †saw marks
3+5	1*	0.4	†2	4.5			3 whole**	190.5			*finished disk frag., A3 B22; **1 modified; †saw marks
4 (Find 17, 24, 25)	6*	12.8					2	35.9	large shell disk**	-	*unfinished disk (4 undrilled, 1 partially drilled, 1 drilled); **gorget/pendant blank
									marine bivalve***	35.9	***fragment
4 or 5	1*	2.0			9+ hoes**	-	10***	695.9			*unfinished disk frags; **wt. combined with valves; ***1 has sawed & snapped edges
4/5 or 89?			220*	1337.0							*whorl & columellae frags., appear to be lot from F89?; at ISM
5? (C3 B22)			1	4.0	1 whole hoe	96.6					
8							1	1.0			
40			†12	78.7	1 pendant?*	22.8	2	25.3	4 snail shells**	8.1	*unfinished ?; **1 unworked conus, 3 anculosa beads; †one has sawed/snapped edge
46			5	6.6							
48	11*	10.5	2	1.8			1 whole	102.2			*7 finished disk, 1 unfinished disk, 2 narrow blanks, 1 broken columnar
60			1	1.9			3	1.0	3 snail shells*	1.3	*1 marginella bead, 2 unmodified marginella, & one unmodified conus
72			1	1.5			1	2.9			
73			3	16.9			2 frags, 1 whole	20.6	bead*, bivalve**	4.8	*anculosa; **1 whole marine bivalve shell
73A			2	26.6			2	10.2			
75			12	41.6			13*	68.2	2 marine bivalves	28.2	*one whole valve

TABLE 6.1
Continued

Feature	MARINE WHELK SHELL				FRESH-WATER MUSSEL SHELL				OTHER		Comments
	Beads	Wt.(g)	Scrap	Wt.(g)	Modified	Wt.(g)	Valve Frags.	Wt.(g)	Item	Wt.(g)	
77			1	2.9					marine bivalve	57.1	
78			1	5.1			3*	38.4			*2 whole valves
79			1	10.0			6 frags	113.0	marine bivalve*	9.2	*1 whole valve
80			†1	36.5							†saw marks
86							7	31.1			
89	8*	13.0			2 disks**	5.0	5 frags, 2 whole	71.7	4 snail shells***	1.2	*1 whole & 2 frag columnar, 1 undrilled/smoothed disk, 1 drilled unfinished disk, 1 whole & 1 frag finished disk, 1 smoothed narrow columnar; **undrilled; ***3 maginella beads, 1 unmodified conus
91							1	43.7			
92			2	5.3							
94							1	1.5			
95									anculosa bead	1.4	
101							1 whole	40.6			
BE			1	1.0							
BP			1	2.8			1	8.0	1 pendant	2.1	
MP1			1?	1.9			7	39.5			
MP2			†2	4.2							†saw marks
EA3			1	2.8			1	8.0			
TOTAL	29	46.2	277	1624.8	14	124.4	76	1541.2	19	149.3	Grand Total Wt. (g) = 3485.9

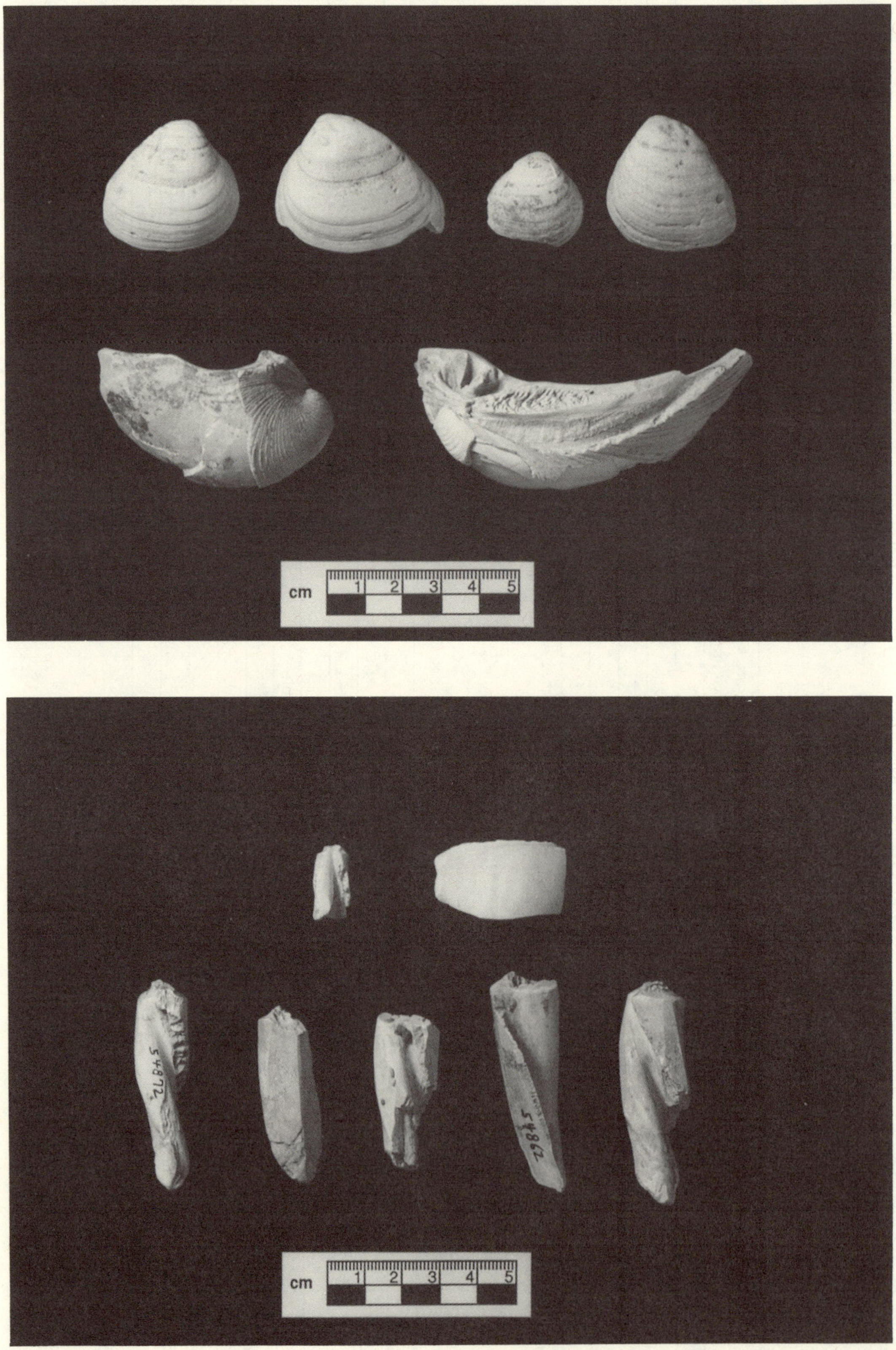

Plate 6.1. Marine shell artifacts: *top*, unmodified marine pelecypod valves; *bottom*, modified (sawed or filed) whelk shell and mussel shell.

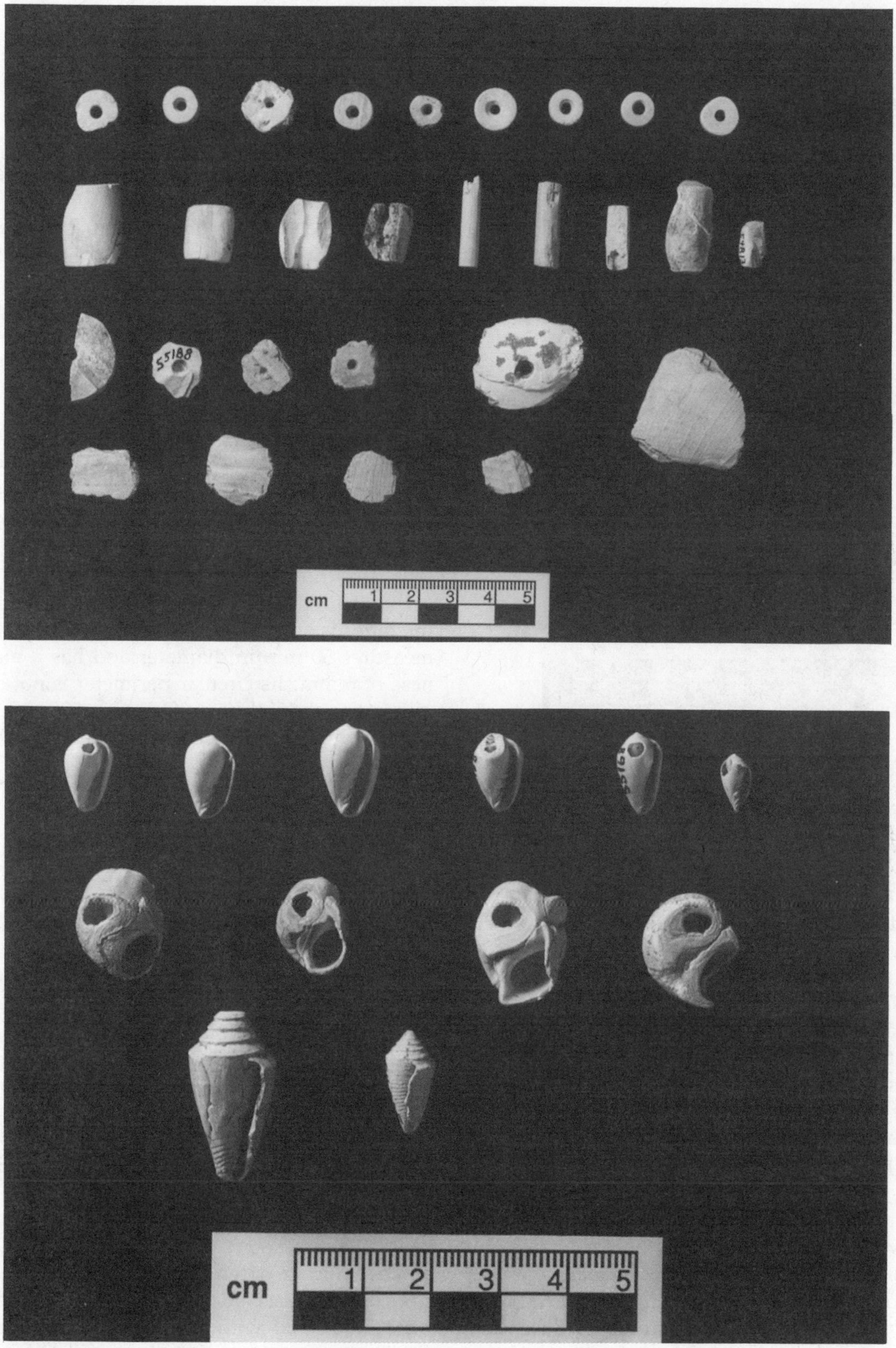

Plate 6.2. Mollusc shell beads: *top,* marine shell disk and columnar beads; *bottom,* marginella, conus, and anculosa beads and unmodified shells.

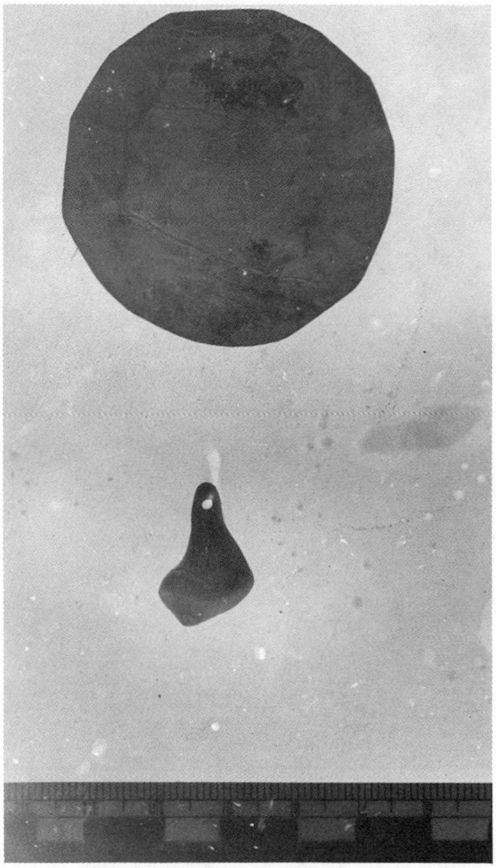

Plate 6.3. Mollusc shell ornaments from Feature 3–5: *top*, pendant or gorget blank; *bottom*, marine shell core pendant.

mm, s.d. = 4.4, n = 9) which exceed their diameters (mean = 9.6 mm, s.d. = 4.0, n = 8). Four narrow cylindrical bead blanks (mean length = 18.5 mm, mean diameter = 6.0 mm) appear to have been too narrow to perforate, although one specimen exhibits an unfinished attempt to drill a longitudinal hole. Four columnar beads appear to have been fractured during drilling; the exteriors of these are faceted as if final smoothing had not yet been performed. At least one had not been completely drilled. Only one finished and complete columnar or tubular bead was found (in F89).

The marine shell disk beads include five rough undrilled blanks, one partially drilled blank, four drilled unfinished specimens, two broken but apparently finished items, and eight whole finished beads (Table 6.2). The mean diameter of the latter group is 9.8 mm (s.d. = 1.0); their mean thickness is 2.9 mm (s.d. = 1.0). These groups of disk beads may represent three stages of bead manufacture during or subsequent to which the specimens in question were broken, discarded, or lost: bead blank production (from larger shell sections), blank drilling, and edge grinding.

Two finished and one unfinished marine shell pendants or gorgets were recovered from the Kunnemann Mound excavations. One columella pendant was found in F3. Only a poor quality photograph of this item exists; the artifact itself could not be relocated at the ISM. Based on the photograph, the pendant appears to be the core (columella and inner whorls) of a small marine shell whelk, approximately 21 mm in length and perforated for suspension at one end (Plate 6.3, bottom). Another tabular pendant, perforated for suspension at one end, was recovered from somewhere in the BP area (Plate 6.4, lower left). Given some initial confusion surrounding feature definition in the BP Area (in the vicinity of the burned structure) during the early part of the 1955 excavation, it is possible that this item came from F3–5 or F89.

One final shell pendant or gorget blank was found on the burned F3–5 surface. This circular disk was sent in 1957 by Holder to Thorne Deuel at the Illinois State Museum but could not be relocated for this study. Fortunately, it was described in Holder's Kunnemann Mound records and a single poor quality photograph of it exists (Plate 6.3, top). It is not known for certain whether this item was manufactured out of mussel shell or marine shell, although the latter is suspected. The disk pendant or gorget blank measures 50 mm in diameter and has a maximum thickness of 6 mm. Its circular perimeter is not smoothed, but rather, has about thirteen facets, making it a complex polygon. In cross-section, this artifact has one flat side and one humped side.

Mussel Shell Artifacts

Freshwater naiades exhibit a lower frequency of modification, probably due to the fact that individual mussel shell valves could be used as tools (e.g., spoons) with only limited modification to pseudocardinal and laterial teeth and the posterior margins (see L. Kelly 1990:259). It is certain, on the other hand, that some mussel shell was sawed and modified in a fashion similar to marine shell. Besides the ornaments described below, saw marks were observed on another fragment of a mussel shell valve.

Finished and unfinished mussel shell ornaments and tools in the shell artifact assemblage include an elongate ovoid valve segment with ground edges (a possible pendant blank; Plate 6.4, top), two small undrilled circular disks (0.8 mm and 5.3 mm thick; Plate 6.4, bottom right) and a minimum of ten large mussel shell valves which had been used as hoe blades (Tables 6.1–6.2). The hoe blades all were associated with the floor of the burned structure (F3–5) and many appear to have been burned as a consequence. Because of the burning, some have deteriorated and are missing their bits. Three whole specimens exhibit use-wear, presumably from digging activities.

TABLE 6.2
Mollusc-Shell Bead Metric Attributes

Provenience	No.	L × W Dimensions (mm)	Notes
MARINE-SHELL DISK BEADS			
F3 (find 1–4)	1	28.0×23.0	unfinished
F3–5	1	11.4	broken
F4 (find 24)	1	30.0×30.0	unfinished
	1	18.0×12.0	unfinished
	4	12.5–13.0	unfinished, diameter range
F48	7	9.8	average diameter
	1	13.7×14.0	unfinished
F89	1	18.5×16.5	unfinished
	1	13.0×13.0	unfinished
	1	23.0	broken
	1	10.1×10.1	whole/finished
MARINE-SHELL COLUMNAR BEADS			
F3	1	16.8×5.9	narrow cylinder, partially drilled
F4 or 5	1	17.4×13.4	unfinished fragment
F48	1	11.8×6.5	narrow cylinder
	1	23.5×5.0	narrow cylinder
	1	20.3×15.4	unfinished barrel fragment
F89	1	14.2×12.5	finished tubular
	1	24.3×?	unfinished fragment, width unknown
	1	14.6×11.6	unfinished fragment
	1	21.7×6.5	narrow cylinder
MUSSEL-SHELL DISKS (UNDRILLED)			
F89	1	6.8×5.5	–
	1	26.5×22.0	–
TOTAL	31		

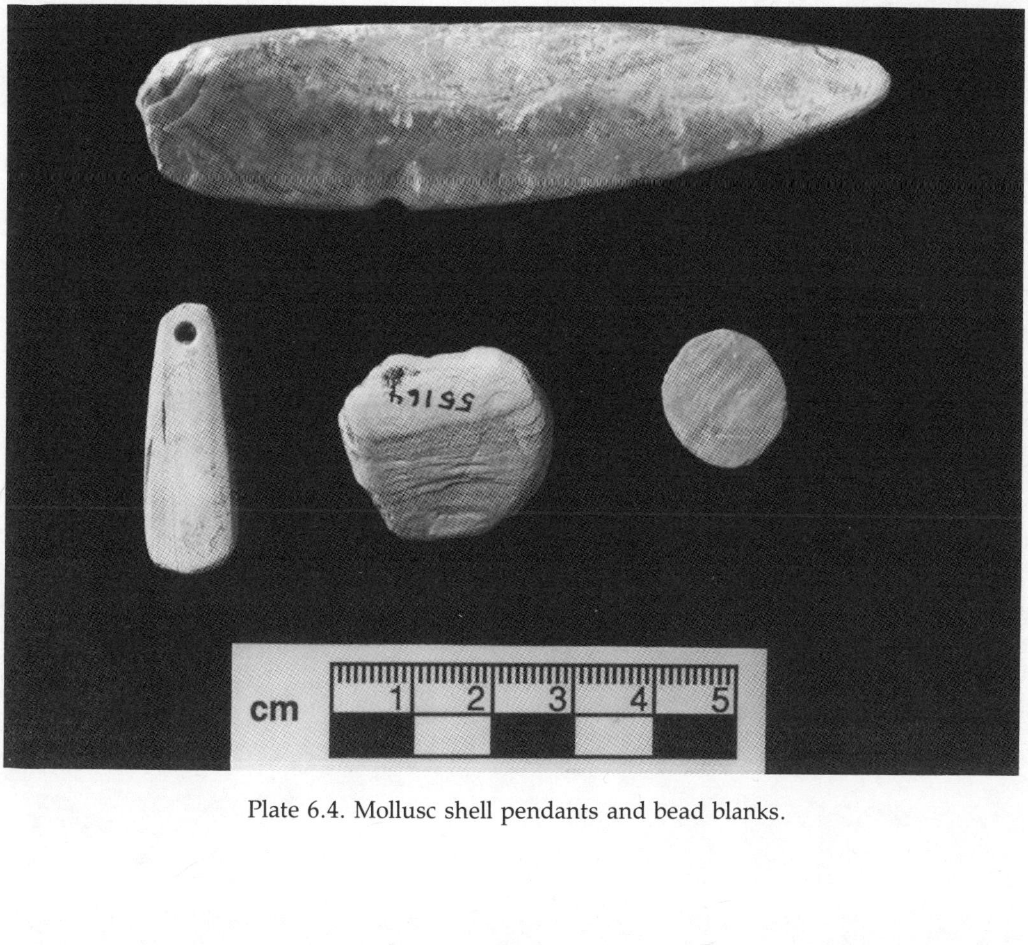

Plate 6.4. Mollusc shell pendants and bead blanks.

Small Snail Shells

Three other species of marine and freshwater gastropods are represented by fourteen conus, marginella, and anculosa items in the Kunnemann Mound mollusc shell assemblage (Table 6.1; Plate 6.2, bottom). Three apparently unmodified conus shells were associated with F40, F60, and F89. These measured 14.6, 18.5, and 24.8 mm in length. One marginella bead and two unmodified marginella shells were found in F60. These measured 10.7, 11.7, and 13.0 mm in length. Three more marginella shell beads were found in F89, measuring 8.0, 11.0, and 11.7 mm in length. These marginella beads each had a single exterior perforation created by grinding a flat surface on the outer whorl. Thread could have been passed through this hole and out the shell opening. Presumably, the conus shells would have been made into beads in the same manner.

Five anculosa beads were associated with F40, F73, and F95 (Table 6.1). All five were abraded on one side, exposing the interior chambers and forming two holes through which thread could have been passed (see L. Kelly 1990: fig. 6.5). These ranged from 13.9 to 21.5 mm long and 10.5 to 14.5 mm thick.

Discussion

There are two principal conclusions to be drawn from this analysis of the Kunnemann Mound mollusc shell artifacts. First, the shell artifacts stand out among a regional archaeological sample in quantitative terms and, second, the molluscan remains stand out in a qualitative sense.

Like the microlithic assemblage and the sandstone artifacts, the density of shell artifacts in the Lohmann and early Stirling phase submound deposits greatly exceeds other reported refuse in the American Bottom. The density of marine shell in the combined F3–5 and F89 fills is approximately 115 g/m^3. The density of all shell artifacts in these two features is about 270 g/m^3. Explained in part by poor preservational conditions, none of the Mississippian sites excavated to date in the American Bottom region have produced marine shell artifact densities higher than a few grams per cubic meter of feature fill (e.g., Emerson and Jackson 1984, 1987; Esarey and Pauketat 1992; Finney 1985, 1987; Fortier 1985; Jackson and Hanenberger 1990; McElrath and Finney 1987; McElrath et al. 1987; Milner 1983b, 1984a). The same is true of deposits from the large-scale excavations of Tract 15A, the Dunham Tract, and the ICT-II at Cahokia (L. Kelly 1991; Pauketat 1991). The only excavated high-density deposits of marine shell beads and refuse besides that found below the Kunnemann Mound are a number of cache pits at Cahokia (Pauketat 1987c:82). Most of these were excavated at the Ramey Tract (which flanks Monks Mound to the east).

It is likely that the end products of shell-working activities as represented in the Kunnemann Mound deposits are not entirely comparable to the Mississippian shell-craft production previously thought to exist at Cahokia and outlying sites. It seems reasonable to conclude, for instance, that Kunnemann Tract artisans, like those represented by F3–5 and F89 refuse, were not simply making shell beads but were fashioning whole necklaces. These would have included disk-bead and barrel-bead necklaces or some bead-combination necklaces. Individual pendants, such as those found during the Kunnemann Mound excavations (two finished and one or two unfinished), were likely components of these necklaces. Entire disk-bead and columnar-bead necklaces, one with a pendant, were recovered during the salvage inspections of the Powell Mound when it was razed in 1930–1931 (Titterington's collection, neg. #13, 184–186, UMMA files). The marginella, conus, and anculosa shell beads (and the sandstone bead) might have been spacer components of necklaces. The marginella and conus shell beads also might have been fastened to fabric as seems to have been the case with the quantities found in the Powell Mound mortuary (see Ahler and DePuydt 1987; Titterington 1938: fig. 50).

Based on these finds and in conjunction with lithic data (see Chapter 5), it is possible that necklace production was an ongoing activity on or around the Kunnemann Mound during its occupancy. This is certainly the case with the F3–5 and F89 features which, as argued in Chapter 10, may have occurred adjacent to the early south mound stage of the Kunnemann Mound. Minimal amounts of marine and freshwater mollusc shell artifacts were associated with the F72 floor and the F73 prepared surfaces. An anculosa bead was found in F95, a wall trench to one of the structures on the south mound (no. 11) and eleven finished and unfinished shell beads were associated with F48, the late Stirling phase wall trench on the summit of Mound 10 (see Chapter 4).

It also should be recalled that Moorehead (1929:36) reported finding "large flat, shell beads" in the mound as well and in at least one instance these seem to have been associated with a floor or prepared surface within the mound (Moorehead 1929:36). Fowke (1906:27), too, makes mention of "a few shell beads" among the "wigwam" refuse on one of the two mounds he excavated nearby. The distinctive quantitative and qualitative aspects of the Kunnemann Tract shell-working evidence will be explored more fully in Chapter 10.

CHAPTER 7

Vertebrate Faunal Remains

John R. Bozell, Nebraska State Historical Society

Introduction and Background

American Bottom zooarchaeology began with Frank Collins Baker (1930, 1941), who studied vertebrate exploitation with the remains excavated at Cahokia by Warren K. Moorehead. Paul Parmalee, in the 1950s through the 1970s, carried on the work, developing detailed and comprehensive overviews (Parmalee 1957, 1975; Chmurny 1973; Smith 1975, 1978). It was the construction of Federal Aid Interstate 270 (FAI-270) through the American Bottom, however, that sparked the flurry of faunal studies which would make the greatest contribution to American Bottom zooarchaeology, yielding new data, much of it acquired through the innovative technique of flotation sampling.

In fact, contemporary American Bottom zooarchaeology developed largely through the efforts of Lucretia Kelly and Paula Cross (L. Kelly 1979 and L. Kelly and Cross 1984). Mississippian animal procurement in the region is now seen as a system more complex than people simply feeding themselves. Redistribution and exchange of food apparently played a prominent role in Cahokian social networks. Also, the content of vertebrate assemblages in the locality is now thought to vary in response to seasonality, overhunting, and social stratification. In this chapter, the Kunnemann Mound vertebrate assemblage will be considered in the context of these new ways of looking at Mississippian animal procurement.

This chapter provides an analysis of vertebrate material recovered during the 1955 and 1956 excavations at the Kunnemann Mound.[1] Vertebrate remains may be modified and unmodified and are treated as separate data sets. *Unmodified* remains are bones that are food remains. The term is actually a misnomer, as they may be "modified" by gnawing, or even cut marks. These form the largest proportion of vertebrate remains. *Modified* remains are those that seem to be tools or ornaments. They are considered artifacts and may not be directly related to subsistence pursuits. They may have been "curated" by Kunnemann inhabitants for some time and cannot be clearly associated with obvious food remains.

The chapter has four sections. The first is a summary of laboratory methods. The second and third sections are descriptive treatments of unmodified and modified remains. These sections constitute the major portion of the chapter. The final segment is a discussion on environmental zones exploited, meat portions represented, and regional comparisons. These comments address issues raised by L. Kelly, Cross and others and contribute to the growing body of American Bottom zooarchaeological research.

All faunal remains were assigned to one of the five temporal analytic units used throughout the book. I collapsed specific catalog lots into analytic units based on provenience, catalog, and excavation information provided to me by Tim Pauketat. Analytic units include: the Lohmann phase, the early Stirling phase, the Stirling phase (F73), the late Stirling phase, and "unknown." Lohmann phase and most early Stirling phase faunal remains were derived from submound features. Late Stirling phase remains originated from features associated with the mound.

Faunal remains from the Kunnemann Mound contribute to understanding of Mississippian vertebrate resource use in the Cahokia locality; however, several limitations are noteworthy. Holder was extraordinarily cautious, and his field methods thorough and careful. Quarter-inch screens were used and there is no reason to suspect any materials were discarded in the field. However, excavation took place prior to the advent of fine-screen recovery techniques. Consequently, the present data are difficult to compare with FAI-270 assemblages which do include flotation samples. Small birds, small mammals and fish are underrepresented in the Kunnemann Mound collection, although the extent of the bias is unknown. Comparisons with FAI-270 samples must also be made with caution because the Kunnemann sample is from an administrative center. Most FAI-270 components are farmsteads and it is reasonable to assume the subsistence patterns responsible for vertebrate accumulations may have differed. Only the early Stirling phase sample is large enough for discussion beyond basic description.

Method of Analysis

The Kunnemann Mound vertebrate assemblage was washed and cataloged following the 1955 and 1956 excavations. At this time, specimens were labeled with a catalog number referencing a specific provenience. In the fall of 1990, the sample and all pertinent catalog material were submitted to me. I weighed and counted each catalog lot and noted the proportion of burned material. During this initial processing phase, post-excavation fractures were glued but no other stabilization measures taken. I examined each lot for potentially identifiable specimens which were taken aside for further consideration. Modified materials were also segregated at this time.

I considered a specimen identifiable if the element, side, and portion could be allocated to a taxonomic grouping at the family level or below. To facilitate identification, I consulted modern reference collections maintained by the Nebraska State Historical Society and the Midwest Archeological Center (National Park Service), both in Lincoln, Nebraska. I asked University of Tennessee zooarchaeologists to examine several specimens.

The data collected for each unmodified identified specimen include: catalog number, provenience, analytic unit, taxon, element, side/portion, and comment. Comment entries note modification by natural or cultural agents such as: burning, rodent gnawing, carnivore gnawing, cut marks, and pathological bone growth. Also noted were immature specimens. Identification data were placed in a computerized data base (program PC-File+, version 2.0) using a coding format designed by Falk et al. (1979), and are on file at the Nebraska State Historical Society and the University of Michigan.

The unmodified identified samples were quantified using number of identified specimen (NISP) and minimum number of individual (MNI) values for each taxon. MNI values were tabulated by the standard method of determining the element and portion which occurs in the greatest frequency for a taxon from a particular analytic unit—the component in this case (Chaplin 1971:62–75).

To describe the modified sample, length, width, thickness, and weight data were gathered. At the same time, each specimen was allocated to the most specific taxonomic and anatomical grouping possible by comparison with modern reference materials. All modifications such as grinding, striations, polish, and so forth, were carefully described, and the specimen was assigned to an artifact category. The categories I used are, wherever possible, based on function. Some items are functionally unknown, and in those cases I used a simple descriptive category. Artifact categories are consistent with those developed during prior American Bottom Mississippian research (e.g., Parmalee 1975).

Unmodified Remains

Two hundred and ninety-two pieces of bone or antler weighing 1375.5 g make up the unmodified vertebrate sample (Tables 7.1 and 7.2). By frequency, the majority (75.3%) was recovered from features and general fill associated with the early Stirling phase component. Over 60% of the elements were recovered from Feature 89—an early Stirling phase midden or pit. Lohmann phase proveniences contributed 9.6% of the sample, Stirling phase (Feature 73) 0.7%, late Stirling phase 4.5%, and nonspecific phase features and excavation units yielded 9.9%. Over 22% of the recovered specimens are burned and the majority of these burned bones (97.0%) are associated with the early Stirling phase.

The recovered sample is not large, but in general, it is well preserved. Few elements exhibit cracking, abrasion, or erosion as a result of adverse soil conditions. Rather, most alterations result from modifications made during carcass dismemberment and food preparation. Gnawing carnivores and rodents inflicted some minor bone damage.

The identified portion consists of 132 specimens (43.4% of the total sample), representing 19 taxonomic groupings. Nearly half of the identified fraction is *Odocoileus virginianus* (white-tailed deer). The rest are mostly small mammals and birds. Small amounts of fish and reptiles were also identified. The majority of remains are present as the result of human predation. Pocket gophers may represent recent intrusion into the deposit. Table 7.3 provides a summary of identified remains and the same data are subdivided by analytic unit in Table 7.4. A full inventory of the identified fraction is contained in Table 7.5. Brief taxon-specific descriptions are offered below which also include regional comparisons with select data compiled by Baker, Parmalee, L. Kelly, and other American Bottom investigators.

Catostomidae (sucker)

Single sucker skull elements were recovered from early Stirling and late Stirling proveniences and represent 1.5% of the identified sample. The sample is too small for confi-

TABLE 7.1
Frequency and Weight Data for Unmodified Fauna

Catalog Number	Feature	Grid Point	Other Proveniences	Number (Burned)	Grams (Burned)
54815	48		trench 3	9 (0)	0.1 (0)
54817	50		trench 3	1 (0)	0.2 (0)
54826	60		trench 4	1 (0)	0.2 (0)
54833			trench 1, sq. 8	2 (0)	23.4 (0)
54843		A32 B17	cut 1, sand	1 (0)	1.4 (0)
54846		A32 B19	cut 1	2 (0)	1.8 (0)
54867	03	A4–5 B22–23	borrow pit	1 (0)	8.8 (0)
54890	05	C3 B22	borrow pit	3 (0)	28.9 (0)
54925	40	A1–5 B35–37	F78, submound	1 (0)	7.2 (0)
54936	40	A3–6 B22–31	borrow pit ?	4 (0)	5.0 (0)
54941	40	A3–6 B30–33	above F89?	1 (0)	0.2 (0)
54943	40	A3–6 B35–37	borrow pit	2 (0)	0.8 (0)
54949	40	A6–8 B20–37	borrow pit ?	1 (0)	7.8 (0)
54950	40	A7–9 B15–19	borrow pit	18 (1)	53.3 (.7)
54965	46	A7–9 B16–19	borrow pit	1 (0)	0.7 (0)
54988	73	A7.5 B22.5		1 (0)	2.3 (0)
55001	73a	A4–8 B22–29	borrow pit	1 (0)	2.5 (0)
55027	75	A4–8 B21–28	borrow pit ?	1 (0)	0.4 (0)
55039	75	A6–8 B16–19	borrow pit	2 (0)	8.8 (0)
55045	75	A6–9 B19–20.5	borrow pit ?	1 (0)	2.1 (0)
55051	75	A7–8 B29–31	borrow pit ?	1 (0)	0.6 (0)
55075	75	A7–9 B16–19	borrow pit	1 (0)	1.1 (0)
55066	77	A3–5 B33–34	borrow pit ?	3 (0)	5.3 (0)
55070	77	A3–6 B30–33		1 (0)	0.2 (0)
55074	78			2 (0)	5.2 (0)
55085	78	A6–8 B35–37	borrow pit	4 (0)	13.6 (0)
55092	79	A3–6 B32–35		1 (0)	3.0 (0)
55113	83	A4 B25	borrow pit	23 (0)	6.1 (0)
55121	86			5 (0)	5.1 (0)
55154	87	A6–8 B35–37	borrow pit	1 (0)	4.7 (0)
55159	87	A7–8 B31–34	borrow pit	1 (0)	50.1 (0)
55166	89		find 36	1 (0)	0.2 (0)
55169	89	A3 B19	borrow pit	6 (1)	159.6 (10.9)
55175	89	A8–9 B15–17	in F40	43 (0)	226.6 (0)
55187	89		in F40	134 (63)	720.8 (346.2)
55232		C3 B22	find 18	4 (0)	0.8 (0)
55272			Bell's expl.	2 (1)	11.9 (.9)
55293				5 (0)	4.7 (0)
TOTAL				292 (66)	1375.5 (358.7)

TABLE 7.2
Frequency and Weight Data, Organized by Analytic Unit, of Unmodified Bone Debris

	Lohmann	Early Stirling	Stirling F73	Late Stirling	Unknown	Total
Number	28	220	2	13	29	292
% of row	(9.6)	(75.3)	(0.7)	(4.5)	(9.9)	(100.0)
Number burned	1	64	0	0	1	66
% of row	(1.5)	(97.0)	(0.0)	(0.0)	(1.5)	(100.0)
Grams	75.0	1156.9	4.8	55.3	83.5	1375.5
% of row	(5.9)	(83.7)	(0.3)	(4.0)	(6.0)	(100.0)
Grams burned	0.7	357.1	0.0	0.0	0.9	358.7
% of row	(0.2)	(99.5)	(0.0)	(0.0)	(0.3)	(100.0)

dent taxonomic assignment below the family level. However, at least ten species representing six genera formerly inhabited or presently inhabit waters of the American Bottom (Smith 1979:147). Sucker materials previously recovered from Lohmann phase and Stirling phase components in the American Bottom are limited to *Ictiobus* sp.—buffalo fish (Cross 1983:204, 1984:226; Finney 1985:84). *Carpiodes* sp. (carpsucker) elements have been retrieved from components representing other Mississippian phases in the locality (Baker 1930:54; L. Kelly 1979:5).

Ictalurus *sp. (catfish/bullhead)*

Five catfish or bullhead bones (3.8% of the identified fraction) were collected; included were one coracoid (Lohmann phase), one cleithrum (early Stirling phase), and three vertebrae (early Stirling phase, late Stirling

TABLE 7.3
Summary of Identified Unmodified Vertebrates

Taxon	Number	Percent of Class	Percent of Total
FISH			
Catostomidae (sucker)	2	25.0	1.5
Ictalurus sp. (catfish/bullhead)	5	62.5	3.8
Aplodinotus grunniens (freshwater drum)	1	12.5	0.8
Subtotal	8	100.0	6.1
REPTILE			
Testudines (turtle)	2	100.0	1.5
Subtotal	2	100.0	1.5
AVES			
Olor sp. (swan)	2	5.1	1.5
Chen caerulescens (snow/blue goose)	1	2.5	0.8
Anatidae (duck)	8	20.5	6.1
Anatinae (surface-feeding duck)	3	7.7	2.2
Anas cf.*platyrynchos* (mallard)	8	20.5	6.1
Anas discors/carolinensis (teal)	5	12.8	3.8
Tympanuchus cupido (prairie chicken)	6	15.4	4.5
Meleagris gallopavo (turkey)	4	10.2	3.0
Fulica americana (coot)	2	5.1	1.5
Subtotal	39	99.8	29.5
MAMMAL			
Sylvilagus floridanus (eastern cottontail)	6	7.2	4.5
Sciuridae (squirrel)	1	1.2	0.8
Sciurus sp. (tree squirrel)	10	12.0	7.6
Geomys bursarius (plains pocket gopher)	2	2.4	1.5
Canis sp. (dog/wolf/coyote)	1	1.2	0.8
Odocoileus virginianus	63	75.9	47.7
Subtotal	83	99.9	62.9
TOTAL	132		100.0

TABLE 7.4
Identified Unmodified Vertebrate Remains, Organized by Analytic Unit

Taxon	Lohmann	Early Stirling	Stirling F73	Late Stirling	Unknown	Total
Sucker	0 (0)	1 (1)	0 (0)	1 (1)	0 (0)	2 (2)
Catfish	1 (1)	2 (1)	0 (0)	1 (1)	1 (1)	5 (4)
Freshwater drum	0 (0)	1 (1)	0 (0)	0 (0)	0 (0)	1 (1)
Turtle	0 (0)	2 (1)	0 (0)	0 (0)	0 (0)	2 (1)
Swan	0 (0)	2 (1)	0 (0)	0 (0)	0 (0)	2 (1)
Snow/blue goose	0 (0)	1 (1)	0 (0)	0 (0)	0 (0)	1 (1)
Duck	0 (0)	5 (1)	0 (0)	0 (0)	3 (1)	8 (2)
Surface feeding duck	0 (0)	3 (1)	0 (0)	0 (0)	0 (0)	3 (1)
Mallard	1 (1)	7 (2)	0 (0)	0 (0)	0 (0)	8 (3)
Teal	1 (1)	4 (1)	0 (0)	0 (0)	0 (0)	5 (2)
Prairie chicken	0 (0)	6 (2)	0 (0)	0 (0)	0 (0)	6 (2)
Turkey	2 (1)	2 (1)	0 (0)	0 (0)	0 (0)	4 (2)
Coot	0 (0)	2 (1)	0 (0)	0 (0)	0 (0)	2 (1)
Eastern cottontail	1 (1)	5 (1)	0 (0)	0 (0)	0 (0)	6 (2)
Squirrel	0 (0)	1 (1)	0 (0)	0 (0)	0 (0)	1 (1)
Tree squirrel	0 (0)	10 (2)	0 (0)	0 (0)	0 (0)	10 (2)
Plains pocket gopher	0 (0)	2 (2)	0 (0)	0 (0)	0 (0)	2 (2)
Dog/wolf/cotyote	0 (0)	0 (0)	0 (0)	0 (0)	1 (1)	1 (1)
White-tailed deer	6 (1)	51 (4)	1 (1)	2 (1)	3 (1)	63 (8)
TOTAL	12 (6)	107 (25)	1 (1)	4 (3)	8 (4)	132 (39)

Minimum number of individuals indicated in parentheses.

phase, and unknown). Six species of this genus are known from the American Bottom region (Smith 1979:175–183). Those most common are *I. furcatus* (blue catfish), *I. melas* (black bullhead), *I. natalis* (yellow bullhead), and *I. punctatus* (channel catfish). Catfish and bullheads are regularly recovered from Mississippian settlements in the Cahokia region (e.g., L. Kelly 1979: 5; L. Kelly and Cross 1984: 231; Cross 1992).

Aplodinotus grunniens *(freshwater drum)*

A single drum pharyngeal was retrieved from an early Stirling phase provenience, and constitutes 0.8% of the identified remains. The element is quite robust and from a large fish. Smith (1979: 299) notes drums in the region can attain lengths of one meter. Parmalee (1975:146) reported the drum was "an important food fish" at Cahokia, yet ironically, the taxon was not recovered from Lohmann, Stirling, or later phases during the FAI-270 investigations. Drum does occur in Emergent Mississippian contexts (L. Kelly 1979:6; L. Kelly and Cross 1984: table 15). Baker (1930:54) also reported drum pharyngeals from Cahokia.

Testudines (turtle)

Two carapace fragments from an immature turtle(s), representing 1.5% of the sample, were recovered during excavation of the early Stirling phase component. The sample is too small and the elements too fragmentary to make a more specific taxonomic assignment; however, the remains are not *Trionyx* (soft-shelled turtle). Turtle remains are not particularly common from American Bottom Mississippian components. Genera previously identified include *Chelydra* (snapping turtle), *Graptemys* (map turtle), *Pseudemys* (pond terrapin), *Chrysemys* (painted turtle), and *Trionyx* (Parmalee 1975:140).

Olor *sp. (swan)*

A swan radius and a carpal were discovered among the early Stirling phase debris and represent 1.5% of the identified portion. Both elements have been burned and display cut marks. Parmalee reported swan bones abundant in Cahokia features, second only to mallard, and that they were a source of food as well as raw material for tools and ornaments (Parmalee 1975:152; 1957:238). He also observed that the majority of swan materials recovered are *O. buccinator* (trumpeter swan), a species now extirpated in Illinois, but once a common Mississippi-flyway migrant. During the FAI-270 investigations, swan remains were not recovered from Lohmann phase or Stirling phase components but did occur in low frequencies from late Mississippian contexts (Cross 1984:229).

TABLE 7.5
Inventory of Unmodified Identified Vertebrate Remains

Taxon	Element	Portion	Comment	Cat. No./AU[a]
Catostomidae (sucker)	subopercle	right complete		54826/04
	supracleithrum	left complete		55187/02
Ictalurus sp. (catfish/bullhead)	coracoid	left medial		54936/01
	cleithrum	right complete		55187/02
	non-specific vertebra	axial complete		55175/02
		axial complete		54817/04
		axial complete		55293/05
Aplodinotus grunniens (drum)	pharyngeal	indeterminate complete		54867/02
Testudines (turtle)	neural carapace	axial complete	immature	55121/02
	marginal carapace	indeterminate lateral	immature	55121/02
Olor sp. (swan)	radius	right proximal	burned cut marks	55187/02
	scapholunar	right complete	burned cut marks	55187/02
Chen caerulescens (snow/blue goose)	humerus	left proximal	burned	55175/02
Anatidae (duck)	non-specific lumbar	axial complete		55175/02
	scapula	left inferior		55187/02
	humerus	left proximal		55175/02
	coracoid	left distal		55027/05
	carpometacarpus	right complete		55066/05
	tarsometatarsus	right complete	rodent gnawing	55066/05
	non-specific vertebra	axial complete		55175/02
		axial complete		55175/02
Anatinae (surface-feeding duck)	ulna	left complete		55187/02
	femur	right proximal		55175/02
	coracoid	left complete		55175/02
Anas cf. platyrhynchos (mallard)	humerus	right proximal		55175/02
		left distal		55175/02
	ulna	right proximal	burned	55175/02
		right proximal		55175/02
		left complete	cut marks	55175/02
	coracoid	left complete		55175/02
		left complete		55175/02
	carpometacarpus	left proximal		54950/01
Anas discors/carolinensis (teal)	humerus	right proximal		55175/02
		right distal		55232/02
	femur	right distal	immature	55187/02
	coracoid	left complete		54950/01
	tibiotarsus	left distal	immature	55175/02
Tympanuchus cupido (prairie chicken)	scapula	left complete		55169/02
	humerus	right complete	cut marks	55187/02
	coracoid	right complete		55187/02
	carpometacarpus	right complete	burned	55187/02
		right distal		55175/02

Taxon	Element	Portion	Comment	No./AU[a]
(prairie chicken)	tarsometatarsus	right distal		55187/02
Meleagis gallopavo (turkey)	ulnar carpal	left complete	cut marks	55187/02
	carpometacarpus	right complete		55187/02
		left complete		54949/01
	digit 1, phalanx 1	indeterminate complete		54965/01
Fulica americana (coot)	humerus	right complete		55187/02
		left proximal		55175/02
Sylvilagus floridanus (eastern cottontail)	scapula	right inferior		54950/01
	humerus	left distal		55187/02
	ulna	right proximal	burned	55187/02
	femur	right proximal	burned	55187/02
		right distal	burned	55187/02
		left distal	burned	55187/02
Sciuridae (squirrel)	femur	left distal	immature	55175/02
Sciurus sp. (tree squirrel)	frontal	axial complete	pathological	55187/02
	mandible	right complete		55187/02
	incisor 1/	right complete		55187/02
	humerus	left proximal	burned	55187/02
		left distal	burned	55187/02
	femur	left proximal	immature	55187/02
		left proximal	burned	55187/02
		left distal		55187/02
	tibia	left complete	immature	55187/02
		left distal		55187/02
Geomys bursarius (plains pocket gopher)	mandible	right complete		55187/02
		right complete		55187/02
Canis sp. (dog/coyote)	incisor 1/	right complete		55045/05
Odocoileus virginianus (white-tailed deer)	incisor /?	right complete		54950/01
	molar ?/	left complete		55001/03
	non-specific cervical	axial inferior/ posterior	immature, burned	55187/02
		axial inferior posterior	immature	54950/01
	non-specific thoracic	axial complete	immature	55187/02
		axial superior	immature	54950/01
	non-specific lumbar	axial complete	cut marks immature	55187/02
		axial complete	cut marks immature	55187/02
		axial complete	cut marks	54890/02
		axial superior	cut marks	55187/02
	sternebra	axial complete	immature	55175/02
		axial complete		55154/04
	non-specific rib	right complete		55175/02

TABLE 7.5
Continued

Taxon	Element	Portion	Comment	Cat. No./AU[a]
(deer)		right medial	immature	55121/02
		right medial	cut marks	55175/02
		left medial	burned	55187/02
	scapula	right inferior	burned	55187/02
		left complete		55159/02
		left inferior	carnivore gnawing	55187/02
		left inferior	burned	55187/02
	humerus	right proximal	immature cut marks	55187/02
		right distal	immature, burned	55187/02
		left distal	cut marks, burned	55187/02
		left posterior diaphysis		55085/05
	ulna	right proximal	immature, burned	55187/02
		right proximal	burned	55187/02
		right diaphysis	cut marks	55169/02
		left proximal	burned	55169/02
		left proximal	carnivore gnawing	55187/02
	radius	right proximal	burned	55187/02
		right proximal	carnivore gnawing	55187/02
		right proximal		55169/02
		left proximal	immature	55187/02
		left proximal	immature, burned	55187/02
		left distal medial	burned	55187/02
		left posterior diaphysis		55169/02
		left posterior diaphysis		54950/01
	intermediate carpal	left complete		55187/02
	os coxae	right complete	immature	55169/02
	ilium	right anterior	burned	55187/02
		left anterior	cut marks	54950/01

Taxon	Element	Portion	Comment	No./AU[a]
(deer)	femur	right distal	cut marks	55187/02
		right distal	gnawing, cut marks	55187/02
		left proximal	immature	55187/02
		left proximal		55187/02
		left proximal medial	immature	55187/02
		left proximal medial	immature	55187/02
		left proximal lateral	immature	55187/02
		left distal	burned, cut marks	55187/02
		left distal	immature, cut marks, carnivore gnawing	55187/02
		left distal	immature, cut marks	55187/02
		left lateral diaphysis		55175/02
	patella	left complete	carnivore gnawing	55272/05
	tibia	right proximal	burned, immature	55187/02
		right distal	cut marks, immature	55187/02
		right distal	cut marks, immature	55175/02
		right distal	rodent gnawing, immature	54833/05
		left proximal		54936/01
		left proximal	burned, immature, cut marks	55187/02
		left proximal medial	immature, burned	55187/02
		left proximal anterior	immature	55187/02
		left distal	cut marks	55175/02
	tibial tarsal	left complete	burned	55187/02

[a] Analytic unit: **01** = Lohmann, **02** = early Stirling, **03** = Stirling (Feature 73), **04** = late Stirling, **05** = unknown.

Chen caerulescens (*snow/blue goose*)

A burned *Chen* humerus fragment was recovered from the early Stirling phase component. The species is well represented in the samples considered by Parmalee (1957:238, 1975:152) but not specifically present among the FAI-270 samples. Low frequencies of *Branta canadensis* (Canada goose) and nonspecific goose remains were reported from Emergent Mississippian components at the Merrell Tract (L. Kelly 1979: table 5) and along the FAI-270 corridor (Cross 1983:204, 1992).

Anatidae (*duck*)

Eight nonspecific duck bones (6.1%) were collected, including three vertebrae, a scapula, and a humerus from the early Stirling phase component, and a coracoid, a carpometacarpus, and a tarsometatarsus from proveniences not attributable to a specific component. Rodents have gnawed the tarsometatarsus. Ducks dominate the avian fractions of all identified Mississippian faunas in the American Bottom. Parmalee (1975:152) identified at least 16 species.

Anatinae (*surface-feeding duck*)

Three surface-feeding duck bones, representing 2.2% of the identified sample, were recovered during excavation of early Stirling phase features. Elements present include an ulna, a femur, and a coracoid. Parmalee (1957:238–39) reported numerous surface-feeding species. Only *Anas platyrhynchos* (mallard) and *Anas discors/carolinensis* (teal) remains are common from other early Mississippian contexts at FAI-270 communities (L. Kelly and Cross 1984:231).

Anas *cf.* platyrhynchos (*mallard*)

Eight mallard bones were identified (6.1%). A carpometacarpus is associated with the Lohmann phase. The remainder were recovered from the early Stirling phase deposit and include: humeri (n = 2), ulnae (n = 3), and coracoids (n = 2). One ulna is burned and another bears cut marks. A minimum of two individuals is represented from the early Stirling component.

Mallards were the most common bird in the samples identified by Parmalee (1957:238). This holds partially true for the FAI-270 investigation of Lohmann and Stirling communities (L. Kelly and Cross 1984:231). Mallards remain abundant migrants in this region of the Mississippi valley and are occasional summer residents and common winter residents (Bohlen 1978:26).

Anas discors/carolinensis (*blue- or green-winged teal*)

Five teal elements (3.8%) were retrieved. One coracoid was recovered from the Lohmann phase component and two humeri, a femur, and a tibiotarsus from the early Stirling phase deposit. Like mallard, teals were well represented in Parmalee's samples as well as in later investigations. Both species of teal are common migrants through the region and occasional summer and/or winter residents (Bohlen 1978:28).

Tympanuchus cupido (*prairie chicken*)

Six prairie chicken bones were recovered (4.5%). All are associated with the early Stirling phase occupation and include two carpometacarpi, a scapula, a humerus, a coracoid, and a tarsometatarsus. The humerus displays cut marks and one carpometacarpus is burned. A minimum of two individuals is represented.

Although not as frequently recovered as geese and ducks, prairie chickens are the most common nonmigratory species represented at American Bottom Mississippian sites. They were only associated with Emergent Mississippian and Lohmann phase contexts within the FAI-270 project area (L. Kelly 1979:12; Cross 1983:204, 1992; L. Kelly and Cross 1984: table 15). Prairie chickens were well represented in the samples identified by Parmalee (1957:238, 1975:152). Prairie chicken is the only member of the Tetraonidae family to inhabit west-central Illinois, strongly diminishing the possibility that the remains are grouse (Bohlen 1978:45).

Meleagris gallopavo (*turkey*)

Elements recovered representing this large bird include an ulnar carpal and a carpometacarpus (with cut marks) from the early Stirling phase component and a carpometacarpus and a digit associated with the Lohmann phase component. Turkey comprises 3.0% of the identified portion of the sample.

Turkey bones were not present in the FAI-270 Mississippian samples but were common among the collection considered by Parmalee (Parmalee 1957:238). Turkeys were once quite abundant in Illinois but were extirpated in the nineteenth century. They have recently been reintroduced (Bohlen 1978:46).

Fulica americana (*coot*)

Two coot humeri were recovered from the early Stirling phase component and represent 1.5% of the identified fraction. Coots are not a common taxon in American Bottom Mississippian faunas but have been reported by Parmalee (1957:238) and L. Kelly (1979:12). The coot is a common migrant and an occasional resident in southern Illinois (Bohlen 1978:49).

Sylvilagus floridanus (*eastern cottontail*)

Six cottontail bones were recovered (4.5%). The sample includes a scapula from the Lohmann phase occupation and a humerus, an ulna, and three femur fragments from early Stirling phase proveniences. The ulna and all femora are burned. Cottontails have not previously been reported specifically from Lohmann or Stirling phase components in the American Bottom. They did occur in the collection analyzed by Parmalee but were not abundant (Parmalee 1957:239).

Sciuridae (squirrels)

One immature femur fragment is allocated to the squirrel family. It represents either *Sciurus* (tree squirrel) or *Spermophilus* (ground squirrel). Tree squirrels are common to local Mississippian fauna but ground squirrels are rare. Only *S. franklinii* (Franklin's ground squirrel) has been reported (Parmalee 1957: 239) although *S. tridecemlineatus* (thirteen-lined ground squirrel) also occurs naturally in the region (Jones and Birney 1988:160–65).

Sciurus *sp.* (*tree squirrel*)

Ten tree squirrel bones, representing 7.6% of the identified fraction, were recovered from early Stirling phase proveniences. A minimum of two individuals is present. Elements identified include: frontal (n = 1), mandible (n = 1), incisor (n = 1), humerus (n = 2), femur (n = 3), and tibia (n = 2). Two elements are burned and three are from an immature animal. The frontal has a pronounced symmetrical pathological bone growth resulting from nonfatal trauma (L.M. Snyder and P. Parmalee: pers. comm.).

The sample is too small for separation of *S. niger* (fox squirrel) and *S. carolinensis* (gray squirrel) although both have been recovered from regional Mississippian sites. Tree squirrels were reported from the Lohmann site (Cross 1992) and the Julien site (Cross 1984:228) during FAI-270 research as well as at Cahokia by Parmalee (1957:239). Parmalee (1975:154) noted "other than deer only the gray and fox squirrels (*Sciurus*) appear to have been taken consistently and in appreciable numbers."

Geomys bursarius (*plains pocket gopher*)

Two gopher mandibles (1.5%), representing two individuals, were recovered from the early Stirling phase component. Gophers were also present at the Julien site Stirling component (Cross 1984:227) as well as from Cahokia proper (Parmalee 1957:239). The origin of the species in the Kunnemann deposit is unclear.

Canis *sp.* (*dog/wolf/coyote*)

A canid incisor was recovered from a Kunnemann Mound provenience not attributable to a specific phase. Domestic dog remains are relatively common at Cahokia; however, wolf and coyote occur in only trace amounts (Parmalee 1957:239). Early Mississippian dog or coyote remains are also reported from the Lohmann site (Cross 1992), the Merrell Tract (L. Kelly 1979:16), and the Range site (L. Kelly and Cross 1984: table 15).

Odocoileus virginianus *(white-tailed deer)*

Sixty-three deer elements were identified, constituting nearly half of the Kunnemann assemblage. All major analytic units are represented, including: Lohmann (n = 6, MNI = 1), early Stirling (n = 51, MNI = 4), Stirling, Feature 73 (n = 1, MNI = 1), late Stirling (n = 2, MNI = 1), and unknown (n = 3, MNI = 1). Seventeen elements are completely or partially burned and 18 display butchering marks. Gnawing by carnivores (n = 6) and rodents (n = 1) was also observed. Twenty-seven elements are from immature animals. Deer was the most important animal food resource available to local Mississippian populations (Parmalee 1975: 154; Smith 1975; L. Kelly and Cross 1984).

Modified Remains

Twenty-three pieces of bone or antler intentionally fashioned into tools or ornaments, as well as manufacturing debris, are included in the Kunnemann Mound sample. Twenty additional modified items are housed at the Illinois State Museum (ISM) or are on display at the Cahokia Mounds Interpretive Center. The ISM and Cahokia materials were not available to me for examination but Tim Pauketat provided notes on the specimens.

The modified sample is summarized by analytic unit in Table 7.6 and described below. The modified fraction is consistent with other Mississippian samples. The most common categories such as cut swan and turkey long bones, deer long bone awls, beads, and cut antlers, are well documented from previous samples (Baker 1930:43–46; L. Kelly 1979:18–19; Parmalee 1975). Kunnemann Mound items not well documented in the American Bottom include a projectile point and two fish hook blanks.

Specimen Descriptions

Descriptive Category: bone/antler projectile point (Fig. 7.1)

TABLE 7.6
Frequency of Modified Bone and Antler, by Analytic Unit

Item	Lohmann	Early Stirling	Stirling F73	Late Stirling	Unknown	Total
Projectile point	0	0	0	0	1	1
Deer scapula hoe	0	1	0	0	0	1
Deer ulna awl	0	3	0	0	0	3
Cut deer ulna	0	1	0	0	0	1
Splinter awl	1	0	0	0	1	2
Awl—unknown type	0	1	0	0	1	2
Perforated turtle shell	0	0	0	1	0	1
Cut turtle shell	0	0	0	0	1	1
Fish hook blank	0	1	0	0	1	2
Cut bird bone	1	0	0	0	0	1
Cut turkey bone	0	2	0	1	0	3
Cut swan bone	0	4	0	0	0	4
Cut mammal bone	0	0	0	0	1	1
Bone bead	0	0	0	0	9	9
Cut deer/elk antler	0	7	0	0	4	11
TOTAL	2	20	0	2	19	43

Figure 7.1. Polished bone or antler projectile point from borrow pit area.

Catalog No.: unknown
Provenience: BP, unknown feature association

This specimen is on display at the Cahokia Mounds Interpretive Center. It is 34 mm long, 14.5 mm wide, and is triangular with *u*-shaped side notches. The specimen has a slightly concave base and serrated lateral margins. Notches and serrations have been cut into the bone or antler.

Descriptive Category: deer scapula hoe
Catalog No.: unknown
Provenience: Feature 5; submound, early Stirling

This tool is curated by the ISM but could not be located. Further information is not available.

Descriptive Category: deer ulna awl (Plate 7.1a)
Catalog No.: 55166
Provenience: Feature 89 (find 36); submound, early Stirling

This specimen is a complete awl manufactured from a right proximal adult deer ulna and is 151.8 mm long, 34.3 mm wide, 19.6 mm thick and weighs 16.8 g. The lower diaphysis has been removed and the remaining segment ground and tapered to a sharp point. The point is heavily polished and the diaphysis exhibits numerous striations. The proximal epiphysis displays slight polish but is otherwise unmodified.

Descriptive Category: deer ulna awl (n = 2) (Plate 7.1b, c)
Cat. No.: 55187
Provenience: Feature 89; submound, early Stirling

Two right deer ulna awls were recovered from Feature 89. One weighs 32.0 g and is 182.8 mm long, 41.6 mm wide, and 22.6 mm thick. The bottom portion of the diaphysis has been cut away at an oblique angle. The tip was then ground to a blunt point. A limited amount of polish and striations are evident near the point but the item is otherwise unmodified. The other artifact weighs 20.1 g and is 131.2 mm long, 33.5 mm wide, and 23.0 mm thick. The distal one-half of the diaphysis has been broken off. Traces of polish and striations are evident along the remaining portion of the diaphysis suggesting this item is a broken awl.

Descriptive Category: cut deer ulna (Plate 7.1d)
Cat. No.: 55191
Provenience: Feature 89; submound, early Stirling

This specimen is an immature left proximal deer ulna weighing 13.7 g. The length is 69.5 mm, the width 38.7 mm, and the thickness 22.3 mm. The diaphysis has been grooved and snapped off immediately below the semilunar notch. The item is probably debris from manufacture of a punch or an awl.

Descriptive Category: splinter awl (Plate 7.1e)
Cat. No.: 54950
Provenience: Feature 40; submound, Lohmann

Manufactured from a large mammal (deer?) unidentified long bone diaphysis fragment, this artifact weighs 2.5 g and is 68.2 mm long, 12.9 mm wide and 4.5 mm thick. The splinter tip has been ground to a sharp point. Striations and polish are evident along all margins.

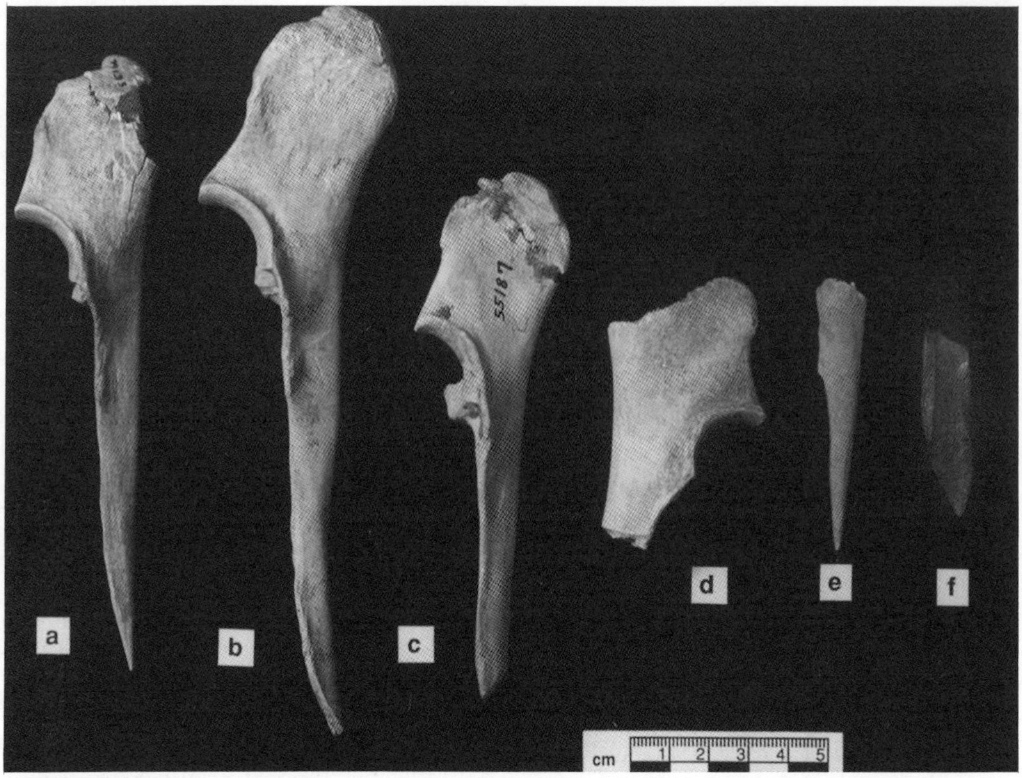

Plate 7.1. Bone awls. See Specimen Descriptions.

Descriptive Category: splinter awl (Plate 7.1f)
Cat. No.: 55273
Provenience: unknown mound fill
This awl fragment was fashioned from a large mammal long bone diaphysis splinter. The tool weighs 2.7 g, measures 47.0 mm by 13.3 mm by 4.9 mm, and is burned on all surfaces. One tip has been ground and tapered to a short sharp point. Striations and polish are common on the working point.

Descriptive Category: awl
Cat. No.: unknown
Provenience: Feature 3–5; submound, early Stirling
This awl is in the ISM collections; data regarding form or taxonomic identification are not available.

Descriptive Category: awl
Cat. No.: unknown
Provenience: unknown
A 35 mm-long portion of an awl is in the ISM collections; additional information is not available.

Descriptive Category: perforated turtle carapace (Plate 7.2a)
Cat. No.: 54824
Provenience: Feature 60; late Stirling
This specimen is a small marginal fragment of a turtle carapace identified to the genus *Terrapene* (box turtle) or the genus *Pseudemys* (map turtle). A small hole, 2.1 mm in diameter, has been drilled through the specimen and faint traces of red pigment are evident on the interior. The specimen is 32.4 mm long, 27.3 mm wide, 5.6 mm thick, and it weighs 2.7 g.

Descriptive Category: modified turtle carapace
Cat. No.: unknown
Provenience: unknown
A cut and ground turtle carapace or plastron is in the ISM collections. Additional information is not available.

Descriptive Category: fish hook blank (Plate 7.2b)
Cat. No.: 55191
Provenience: Feature 89; submound, early Stirling
An unfinished fish hook fashioned from a bird long bone diaphysis fragment was discovered in Feature 89. The hook weighs 0.6 g and is 34.3 mm long, 11.6 mm wide, and 3.9 mm thick. The specimen is now *J*-shaped with straight lateral and basal margins. The specimen was originally a rectangular segment with a *u*-shaped perforation in the center forming a blank for two hooks. One hook is now missing. The specimen exhibits striations and polish on all exterior and lateral margins.

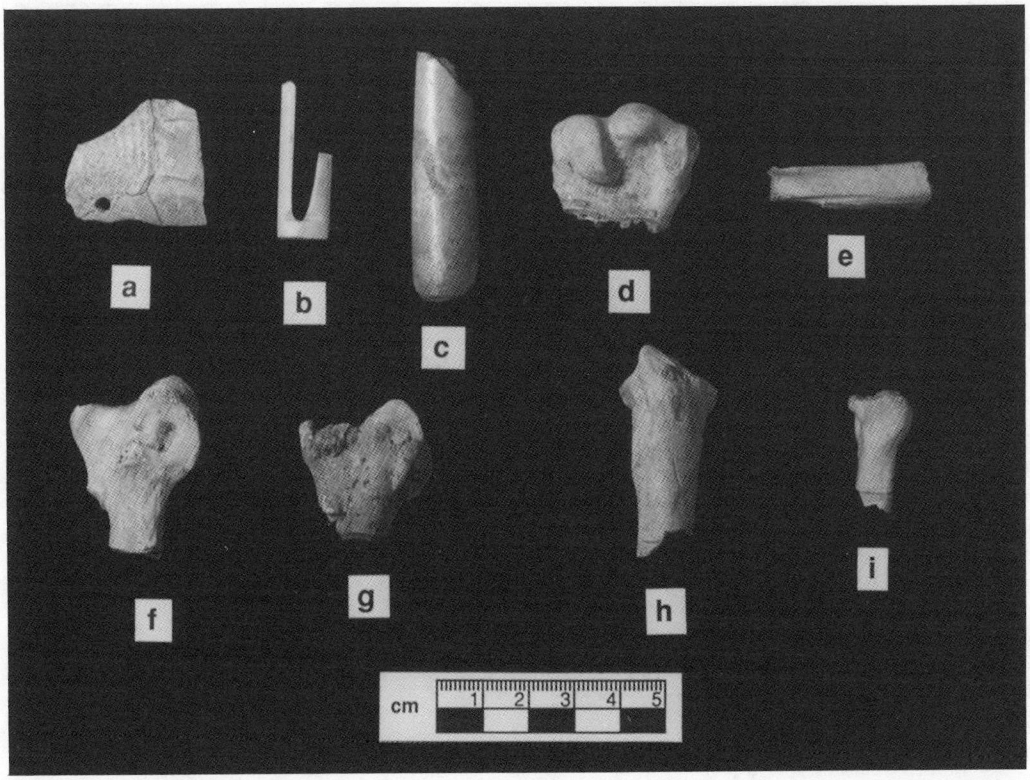

Plate 7.2. a, turtle carapace; b, fish hook blank; c, bird bone diaphysis; d, e, modified turkey bone; f, g, modified swan bone. See Specimen Descriptions.

Descriptive Category: fish hook blank (?)
Cat. No.: unknown
Provenience: unknown

A cut and ground piece of mammal long bone weighing 2.6 g is housed at the ISM. Pauketat's notes indicate the item may be a fragment of a spatulate awl or the residual element from the manufacture of a fish hook (sensu L. Kelly 1987:378–79).

Descriptive Category: cut bird bone diaphysis (Plate 7.2c)
Cat. No.: 54874
Provenience: Features 3 and 5; Lohmann

This specimen is a cut and highly polished diaphysis fragment of an unidentified large bird long bone. The lateral margins and one end have been cut and extensively ground and are semi-rounded with numerous small striations. The specimen was cataloged as an awl fragment; however, the other tip has been broken away, precluding positive functional designation. The object weighs 3.1 g and is 54.4 mm long, 14.5 mm wide, and 5.6 mm thick.

Descriptive Category: cut turkey humerus (Plate 7.2d)
Cat. No.: 55175
Provenience: Feature 89; submound, early Stirling

This artifact is a left distal turkey humerus which has been grooved around the entire width of the diaphysis and snapped off. The specimen is 36.5 mm long, 32.2 mm wide, 17.3 mm thick, and weighs 4.0 g. It is debris left from manufacture of a tubular diaphysis artifact.

Descriptive Category: cut turkey (?) bone
Cat. No.: unknown
Provenience: Feature 4/5; submound, early Stirling

This cut diaphysis is housed at the ISM. Pauketat's notes indicate that the artifact weighs 4.5 g and is highly polished.

Descriptive Category: cut turkey carpometacarpus (Plate 7.2e)
Cat. No.: 54814
Provenience: Feature 48; late Stirling

This left turkey carpometacarpus diaphysis segment weighs 1.8 g and measures 35.7 mm by 9.5 mm by 8.2 mm. The specimen has been grooved on both ends and the epiphyses snapped off. A deep longitudinal groove runs the full length of the specimen. The function is uncertain.

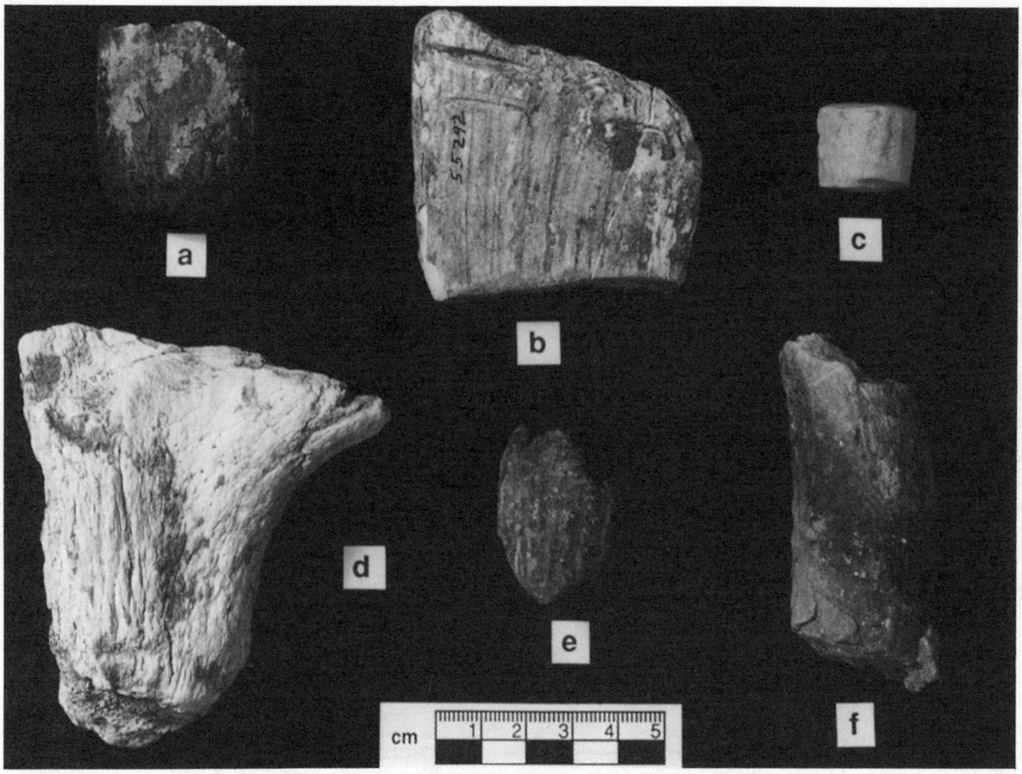

Plate 7.3. Cut elk or deer antler. See Specimen Descriptions.

Descriptive Category: cut swan carpometacarpus (n = 2) (Plate 7.2f, g)
Cat. No.: 55187
Provenience: Feature 89; submound, early Stirling
Two proximal swan carpometacarpi were recovered from Feature 89. Both have been grooved around the diameter of the diaphyses and snapped off. They may be manufacturing debris from making tubular diaphysis artifacts. One specimen is from the right side of the body; it is 38.3 mm long, 30.3 mm wide, 13.2 mm thick, and weighs 3.7 g. The other example is a left and weighs 2.9 g. This specimen is 31.0 mm long, 28.0 mm wide, and 11.6 mm thick.

Descriptive Category: cut swan ulna (Plate 7.2h)
Cat. No.: 55121
Provenience: Feature 86; submound, early Stirling
This item is a right proximal swan ulna which has been grooved and snapped. Several longitudinal grooves and striations are evident. The specimen weighs 3.5 g, measures 45.7 mm by 23.1 mm by 21.9 mm, and is related to bone tube manufacture.

Descriptive Category: cut swan radius (Plate 7.2i)
Cat. No.: 55121
Provenience: Feature 86; submound, early Stirling
Also apparently related to fabrication of diaphysis tubular items, this specimen is a right proximal swan radius weighing 1.7 g. The artifact is 26.2 mm long, 13.9 mm wide, 12.1 mm thick, and has been grooved and snapped.

Descriptive Category: cut mammal bone
Cat. No.: unknown
Provenience: unknown
One grooved and snapped articular end of a mammal bone, weighing 3.5 g, was recovered. The item is stored at the ISM and other data are not available.

Descriptive Category: tubular beads (n = 9)
Cat. No.: unknown
Provenience: unknown
Nine tubular bone beads are curated by the ISM; other data are unavailable.

Descriptive Category: cut elk or deer antler (Plate 7.3a)
Cat. No.: 54882
Provenience: Feature 5; submound, early Stirling
This item is a cut and burned antler fragment. The specimen weighs 18.6 g and measures 41.7 mm by 39.7 mm by 21.3 mm. One basal margin has been cut and the resulting surface is smooth with numerous multidirectional striations. The antler has been split or cut longitudinally. One lateral margin has been ground into a blunt *v*-shaped edge.

The opposing edge exhibits some modification but breakage precludes further description.

Descriptive Category: cut elk or deer antler (Plate 7.3b)
Cat. No.: 55292
Provenience: surface
A modified elk or deer antler fragment was collected from the surface. The specimen appears to be from the lower portion of the main beam although the precise location and side could not be determined. The artifact weighs 60.8 g and is 61.2 mm long, 62.6 mm wide, and 21.5 mm thick. Both ends have been cut although the lateral margins are eroded and gnawed by rodents and it is difficult to determine if they also are modified. The cut on one end is highly polished and displays small striations. The specimen has been cataloged as an "elk antler scraper."

Descriptive Category: cut elk or deer antler (Plate 7.3c)
Cat. No.: 55190
Provenience: Feature 89; submound, early Stirling
This artifact is a short cut cube-shaped antler tine segment weighing 8.8 g and measuring 18.4 mm by 21.0 mm by 20.5 mm. The specimen was cut on both ends, extensively ground and polished. The function is uncertain.

Descriptive Category: cut elk or deer antler (*n* = 12) (Plate 7.3d, e, f)
Cat. No.: 55192
Provenience: Feature 89; submound, early Stirling
Twelve antler fragments are included in this lot. Seven are unmodified except for two burned pieces. The remaining five examples have all been cut on one end. Due to extensive erosion and fragmentation, none can be assigned any specific function such as flaking tools. All exhibit striations and some degree of polish on the cut margins. Descriptive data are inventoried in Table 7.7. The seven unmodified specimens are likely broken off of cut items.

Descriptive Category: cut elk or deer antler (*n* = 3)
Cat. No.: unknown
Provenience: unknown
Three cut deer or elk antler segments are in the ISM collections. One item weighs 76 g. Other data are not available.

TABLE 7.7
Modified Elk or Deer Antler Data (Cat. No. 55192)

Length	Width	Thickness	Weight	Comment
72.6 mm	33.3 mm	29.2 mm	53.3 g	burned/cut
37.9 mm	29.3 mm	26.7 mm	18.4 g	burned/cut
48.8 mm	48.2 mm	24.1 mm	30.4 g	cut
82.2 mm	35.6 mm	20.4 mm	31.8 g	cut
87.3 mm	79.2 mm	35.7 mm	96.2 g	cut

Discussion

Over 80 percent of the fauna was recovered from early Stirling phase proveniences. Consequently, the bulk of the following discussion addresses remains from this component. This occupation, and the Lohmann phase use of the area, occurred before or during the early stages of mound construction. These components may represent domestic (not strictly ceremonial) use of the tract. Apparently the sites's later use as a platform mound did not involve much food consumption or, if so, the refuse was regularly cleared and deposited elsewhere.

I tabulated the early Stirling phase environmental zones represented as a function of the percentage of MNI which prefer specific habitats (Fig. 7.2). Four percent is represented by species which occupy widespread habitats. The majority reflects species likely taken in riparian (32%) or forest/forest edge (36%) habitats. About 12% were taken from aquatic habitats, and the rest from upland prairies (16%).

Riparian habitats are represented primarily by the diverse waterfowl assemblage. Most mammals in the collection, as well as turkey, are typical forest and forest-edge dwellers. Prairie species include prairie chicken and pocket gopher. Except for the upland prairie, this configuration closely mirrors habitats within about 10 km of Cahokia, suggesting most meat was obtained within the general area and hunters were exploiting game in proportions consistent with available resources.

Only deer remains occur in sufficient abundance to further explore procurement strategies. I extended the MNI value (4) for early Stirling phase deer to major skeletal portions and calculated the difference between observed (*fo*) and expected (*fe*) frequencies (Fig. 7.3). Expected frequency is the value that would be obtained if all elements from the minimum of four deer were returned to Kunnemann and recovered archaeologically. This index approximates carcass portions present and absent, similar to Binford's "minimal animal units" (Binford 1978; Lyman 1985). Skeletal portions depicted in Figure 7.3 include skull, vertebra/ribs, upper forelimb, lower forelimb, upper hindlimb, lower hindlimb, and feet.

The *fo*/*fe* values are predictable and easy to interpret. Skulls and feet are absent and vertebrae and ribs have values of less than 10. Similarly, lower forelimb and lower hindlimb portions are not particularly well represented. The most common carcass portions are upper fore- and hindlimbs. These segments have high nutritional value.

It appears that early Stirling phase Kunnemann inhabitants obtained deer meat at such a distance from the site that a certain degree of in-field carcass reduction was re-

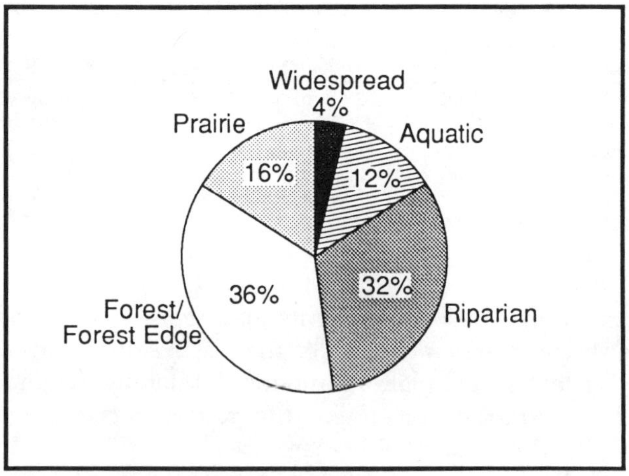

Figure 7.2. Habitats represented by MNI of vertebrates recovered from the early Stirling phase component.

quired. This entailed separating and discarding the head and feet at the kill locations. Meat from the lower limbs, ribs and vertebrae was often stripped from the bone and packaged for transport to the Kunnemann Tract. The meaty upper limbs were removed from kill sites intact and delivered to the site for more thorough processing. Cahokia residents were not acquiring their own food but were supplied through gift-giving or tribute from rural components (L. Kelly 1979, 1990a, 1991; see also Pauketat 1991: chaps. 2, 6). If this pattern intensified during the Cahokian climax of A.D. 1100–1300, meat was often supplied to Cahokia fully processed and relatively free of bone. This may explain the general paucity of faunal remains from late Stirling phase Kunnemann Mound proveniences.

Finer-grained examination of the *fo/fe* values was accomplished by plotting these data against nutritional ranking values generated by Binford for arctic caribou (Binford 1978: table 2.7; also see Metcalfe and Jones 1988 for a proposed modification of Binford's approach). This measure is referred to as the Modified General Utility Index (MGUI) and approximates the combined value of grease, marrow,

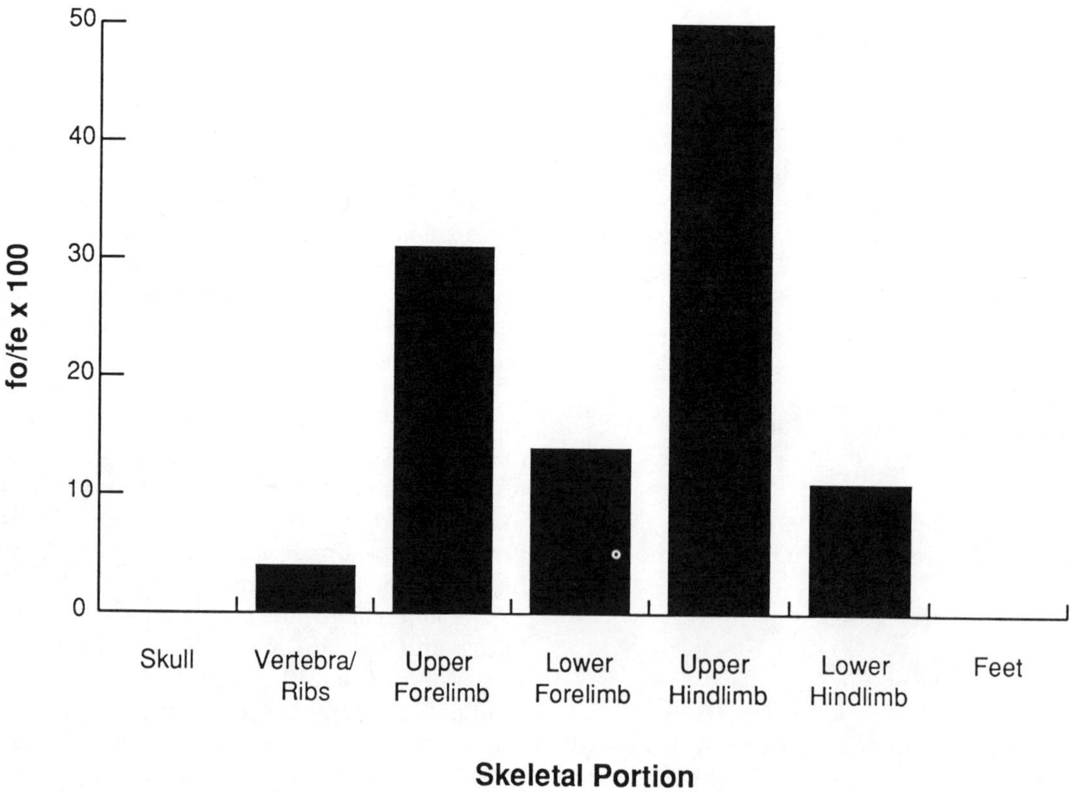

Figure 7.3. Deer skeletal portions represented from the early Stirling phase component.

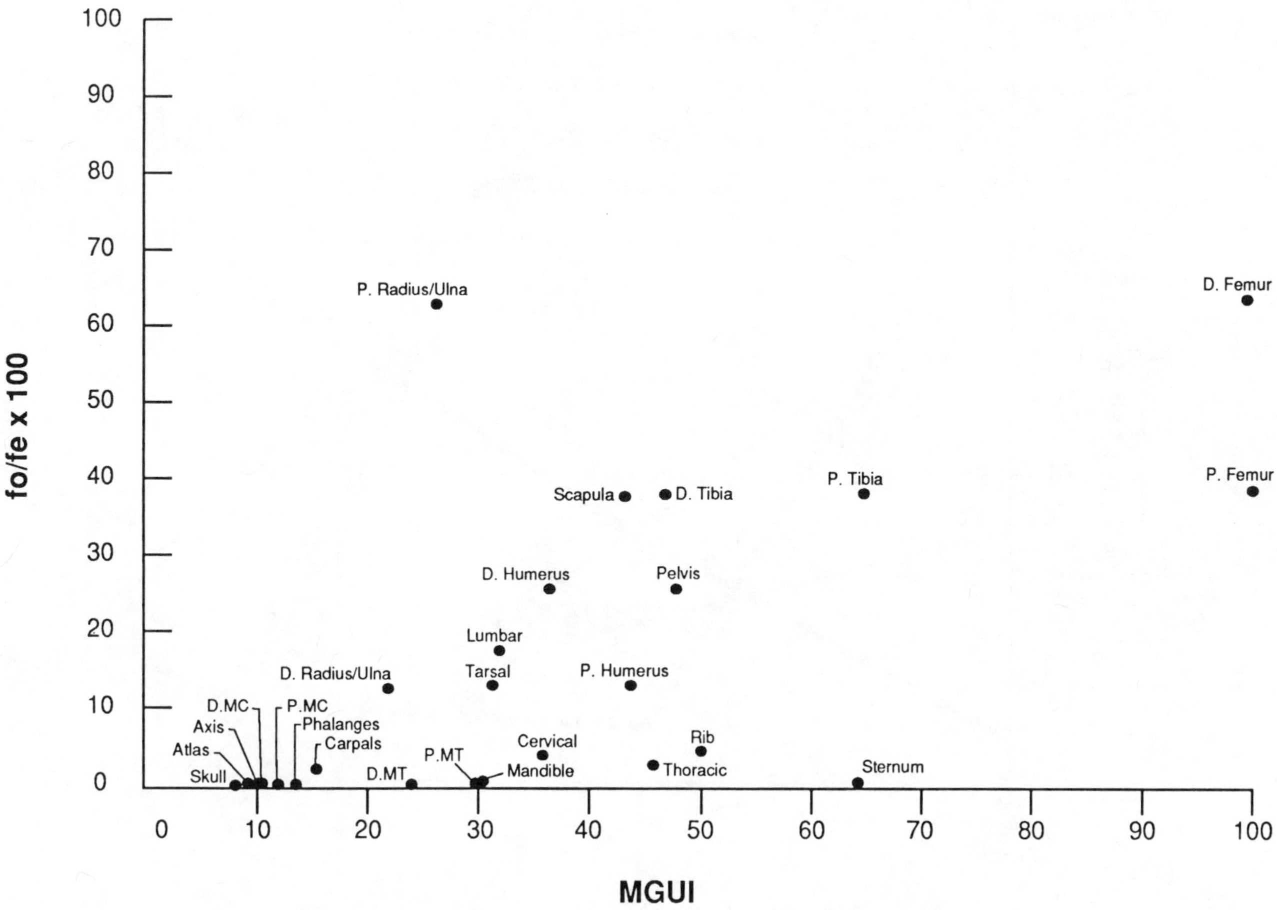

Figure 7.4. Modified General Utility Index (MGUI) values for deer remains recovered from the early Stirling phase component.

and meat for each element. The pattern illustrated in Figure 7.4, with several exceptions, indicates that the higher-rated MGUI elements are more likely to be present in greater quantities in the early Stirling phase fauna. The pattern reflects what Binford refers to as an "unbiased" strategy which is neither a "bulk" or a "gourmet" pattern. That is, hunters supplying Cahokia practiced a strategy "requiring equal knowledge and understanding of the actual differences between anatomical parts in terms of their overall utility" (Binford 1978:81).

The several outliers in Figure 7.4 include proximal radius/ulna, rib, thoracic vertebra, and sternum. The high proportion of proximal radius/ulna (*fo*/*fe* × 100 = 62) in the early Stirling sample is not consistent with the portion's relatively low MGUI rating. This pattern is a signature of frequent Mississippian proximal deer ulnae selection for awl manufacture. The unmodified ulnae from the Kunnemann Mound sample may ultimately have been intended for use as awls. Other outliers have relatively high MGUI values but are poorly represented. For whatever reason, meat appears to have been stripped from these bones at kill sites and the bones not returned to Kunnemann.

Review of prior analyses of Cahokia-region fauna sheds a little light on why some high-value elements are poorly represented in the Kunnemann deposits. L. Kelly (1979) noted that aquatic and semiaquatic fauna such as migratory waterfowl and fish supplied the majority of meat to Emergent Mississippian phases in the American Bottom. As the local human population grew, these resources became scarce and attention turned to deer, squirrel, turkey and other dwellers of the more distant forests and uplands. L. Kelly (1979:19–20) proposed that some deer meat may have arrived at Cahokia through social networking with rural communities. Deer hunted in the forests and uplands may have had meat stripped entirely from bulky portions such as ribs and vertebrae in anticipation of transport to Cahokia. Limbs are less bulky and could have been more easily moved intact.

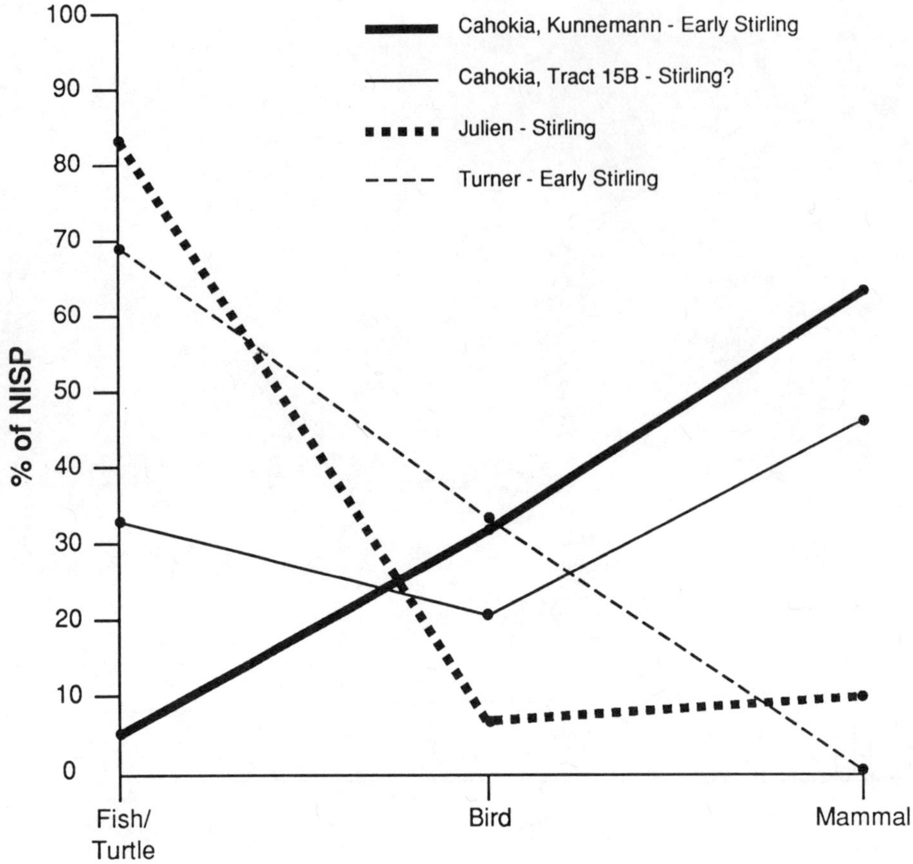

Figure 7.5. Comparison of identified unmodified vertebrates from select early Stirling phase components.

Similarly, L. Kelly and Cross (1984) noted a distinction between Late Woodland/Emergent Mississippian and Mississippian faunas. The earlier samples display a greater abundance of fish and less diversity in the use of some birds and mammals (see L. Kelly and Cross 1984: fig. 80). Also, fauna from the early Mississippian Lohmann site indicates a heavy reliance on aquatic fauna, rather than deer or other upland and forest species (Cross 1992).

In broad terms, the Kunnemann Tract early Stirling phase component conforms to elements of the temporally later aspects described by L. Kelly and Cross (1984). The fauna includes few fish and a low diversity of waterfowl. Deer is by far the most common taxon and the elements represented suggest distant processing and transport. Apparently, the proposed shift in emphasis from local aquatic resources to deer and other mammals began as early as A.D. 1100. Temporal and spatial variation as a function of the social hierarchy also may have come into play.

As noted above, comparisons between the Kunnemann Mound collection and other samples are hampered by the lack of control over bias introduced by varying recovery strategies. Figure 7.5 illustrates the proportion of identified specimens of fish/turtle, bird, and mammal for four Stirling phase components. These include Holder's Kunnemann Mound sample, the Tract 15B remains (Parmalee 1975), and the Julien and Turner site remains (Cross 1983, 1984). The latter two samples, derived from the FAI-270 Project, were recovered partially in flotation samples. The sites are located several miles south of Cahokia proper.

The Kunnemann Mound and Tract 15B faunal assemblages are similar to one another, both having higher proportions of mammal relative to fish or reptile. Inversely, the Julien and Turner samples share substantially higher numbers of fish and reptile bones relative to mammal remains. The distinction between Cahokia and non-Cahokia samples must be due in part to recovery measures. The possibility exists, however, that the shift from local aquatic resources to forest and upland taxa occurred somewhat later at the non-Cahokia communities. Again, this may relate to social status variability. Nevertheless, the Stirling phase is a critical temporal unit in understanding Mississippian subsistence change in the American Bottom.

CHAPTER 7 NOTE

1. I would like to express my appreciation in particular to Tim Pauketat for providing all necessary background information on the American Bottom and the Kunnemann Mound excavations. Tim as well as John Ludwickson, Ken Cannon, and Sally Horvath provided comments on the draft manuscript. Paul Parmalee and Lynn Snyder assisted by cross-checking several identifications. Artifact photographs were prepared by Roger Bruhn, and other illustrations by Curt Peacock.

CHAPTER 8

Plant Remains

Sandra L. Dunavan, University of Michigan

The botanical remains described here are relatively large hand collected carbonized specimens recovered during Preston Holder's excavations at Kunnemann Mound (11-Ms-11) in 1955–1956. Some botanical specimens excavated from Kunnemann Mound (mostly wood fragments) were sent to the University of Michigan Museum of Anthropology in 1957, but another sample of botanical remains (mainly corn and seeds) was sent to Hugh C. Cutler and Leonard W. Blake at the Missouri Botanical Garden for analysis. Cutler and Blake (1973) provide a list of the species identified from the Missouri Botanical Garden collection as well as an analysis of the maize cob morphology from Kunnemann Mound (1969, 1973:24), but the plant remains in the University of Michigan, Museum of Anthropology collection have never been described. In the following report, I use Cutler and Blake's notes on the seeds and maize which they identified (1969; 1973:24; Terrance J. Martin, pers. comm.). This collection is now curated in the Illinois State Museum.

Methods

Most of the specimens in the UMMA collection consist of well-preserved chunks of carbonized wood, some with associated soil, fibers, seeds, or carbonized thatch. Each specimen received from Holder was assigned a UMMA catalog number, which was sometimes divided into several boxes for storage (as in UMMA 54902/1-21). Not all of these specimens were analyzed, since the collection is large and probably contains a great deal of redundant information. A sample of 27 of the total 40 specimens (and UMMA catalog numbers) was analyzed. In a few cases, where several boxes constitute a catalog number, only a few of the boxes were analyzed (as in the analysis of UMMA 54902/1, /6, etc.).

Specimens consisting mainly of wood were weighed and then gently screened using a 2 mm sieve if the initial inspection indicated that the sample would not be destroyed by this process. After recording the sample weight of the >2 mm fraction, 10 percent or more of this wood (by weight) was inspected and identified to species, genera, or anatomical type such as ring porous, diffuse porous, or bark. A binocular microscope with magnifications from 0.7–30× was used for most identifications. In a few cases, such as differentiating between *Juniperus virginiana* (red cedar) and *Taxodium distichum* (bald cypress), higher magnifications (from 100× to 400×) were necessary. Identifications of wood and other plant remains were facilitated by the comparative collection of modern and archaeological species in the UMMA Ethnobotanical Laboratory and the use of a few descriptive texts (Core et al. 1979; Martin and Barkley 1961; Record 1934).

Results

Wood

All of the plant remains analyzed are listed by UMMA catalog number, grouped by provenience, in Table 8.1. Clearly, wood constitutes more than half of the plant remains identified (by weight), and although fragment counts were not recorded, wood is also the most abundant type of plant remain present. This is not too surprising, since wood (especially timber from burned structures, as found in Features 5 and 89) is clearly recognizable as such during excavation, and is more likely to be recovered than small carbonized fragments of nutshell or seeds which are

TABLE 8.1
Plant Remains from Kunnemann Mound

UMMA Cat. No.	Provenience	Specimen Wt. (g)	>2mm Specimen Wt. (g)	Identification	Wt (g)	Count
55261	A10.50 B23	8.4	2.9	**wood identified**		
				Carya spp. (hickories)	0.04	
				Quercus spp. (oaks)	0.09	
				bark	0.16	
				unidentified ring porous	0.03	
				total wood identified	0.32	
				Diospyros virginiana (persimmon) seed	–	1
				Zea mays (maize) kernel fragments	0.1	7
				unidentifiable fragments	0.1	2
				fish bones	0.1	
55281	F5, Pit 1	7.8	5.5	*Arundinaria gigantea* (cane)	5.5	
54860/1	A0 B22 below F3, sw corner housefall (F5)	190.7	90.1	**wood identified**		
				Salix spp. (willows)	17.1	
				bark	0.3	
				total wood identified	17.4	
			29.3	monocot stems and leaves (thatch)	29.3	
54860/2	A0 B22 below F3, sw corner housefall (F5)	124.7	72.6	**wood identified**		
				Salix spp. (willows)	15.7	
				total wood identified	15.7	
55239	A0 B22 F5	675.5	419.5	**wood identified**		
				Acer spp. (maples)	3.2	
				Quercus (red subfamily) sp. (red oaks)	10.6	
				Salix spp. (willows)	23.4	
				Ulmaceae (hackberries/elms)	9.4	
				total wood identified	46.6	
55252	A3 B22 F5	143.5	89.0	**wood identified**		
				Salix spp. (willows)	8.5	
				Ulmaceae (hackberries/elms)	1.8	
				(carved wood 40% of Ulmaceae identified)		
				total wood identified	10.3	
54900	A3 B22 F5	157.5	84.2	**wood identified**		
				Salix spp. (willows)	5.1	
				Ulmaceae (hackberries/elms)	4.3	
				total wood identified	9.4	
54905	F5, associated with Find 15	65.6	56.5	**wood identified**		
				Salix spp. (willows)	7.4	
				total wood identified	7.4	
54893	C60 B21.5 F5	8.6	8.6	large chunk of monocot leaves and stems (thatch)	8.6	
54902/1	F5	1315.8	489.4	**wood identified**		
				Quercus spp. (red oaks)	3.2	
				Salix spp. (willows)	15.6	
				Ulmaceae (hackberries/elms)	28.8	
				(carved wood 98% of Ulmaceae identified)		
				unidentified ring porous	1.7	
				unidentifiable wood	2.5	
				total wood identified	51.8	

TABLE 8.1
Continued

UMMA Cat. No.	Provenience	Specimen Wt. (g)	>2mm Specimen Wt. (g)	Identification	Wt (g)	Count
				woven mat fragment (monocot stem or leaf)	3.7	
54902/2	F5	384.1	161.0	**wood identified**		
				Salix spp. (willows)	21.8	
				total wood identified	21.8	
				Zea mays (maize) kernel	0.1	1
54902/3	F5	85.6	85.6	**wood identified**		
				Carya spp. (hickories)	77.1	
				total wood identified	77.1	
54902/6	F5	72.3	28.5	monocot stems and leaves (thatch)	>15.0	
				wood identified		
				Salix spp. (willows)	2.4	
				total wood identified	2.4	
54902/11	F5	67.2	67.2	**wood identified**		
				Carya spp. (hickories)	47.3	
				total wood identified	47.3	
54909	C3 B22 F8 (in F5)	90.9	59.0	**wood identified**		
				Carya spp. (hickories)	10.2	
				Quercus spp. (red oaks)	9.7	
				Salix spp. (willows)	2.3	
				total wood identified	22.2	
54912	C3 B22 F8 (in F5)	3.1	3.1	**wood identified**		
				carved piece of *Juglans* sp. (walnut)	3.1	
				total wood identified	3.1	
54913	C3 B22 F8 (in F5)	3.5	3.5	fiber fragments (10 are braided)	3.5	10
54914	C3 B22 F8 (in F5)	1.2	1.2	fiber fragments (2 are braided)	1.2	5
54915	C3 B22 F8 (in F5)	760.5	455.0	**wood identified**		
				Carya spp. (hickories)	1.5	
				Quercus ssp. (red oaks)	26.4	
				Salix spp. (willows)	13.0	
				Ulmaceae (hackberries/elms)	5.4	
				(carved wood 54% of Ulmaceae identified)		
				total wood identified	46.3	
54957	A7–9 B16–19 F40	2.9	2.9	**wood identified**		
				bark	2.8	
				total wood identified	2.8	
				Zea mays (maize) kernel fragment	0.1	1
54959	A7–9 B16–19 F40	23.5	12.3	**wood identified**		
				Quercus spp. (oaks)	0.2	
				Salix spp. (willows)	0.4	
				Taxodium distichum (bald cypress)	1.0	
				total wood identified	1.6	
				nutshell		
				Carya spp. (hickories)	0.1	1
				Quercus spp. (acorns)	<0.1	1

TABLE 8.1
Continued

UMMA Cat. No.	Provenience	Specimen Wt. (g)	>2mm Specimen Wt. (g)	Identification	Wt (g)	Count
				other		
				Polygonum erectum (erect knotweed)	–	1
				Strophostyles sp. (wild bean)	–	3
				Zea mays (maize) kernels	0.1	1
				kernel fragments	0.2	15
				cupule fragments	0.1	3
				unidentifiable seed or maize fragments	0.2	16
55008	A7–9 B16–19 F73 floor surface	7.8	1.8	**wood identified**		
				Quercus spp. (red oaks)	1.1	
				total wood identified	1.1	
55129	F86 (in F40)	0.4	0.3	**wood identified**		
				Juniperus virginiana (red cedar)	0.1	
				diffuse porous	<0.1	
				total wood identified	0.1	
				other		
				Diospyros virginiana (persimmon) seed	–	1
				Zea mays (maize) kernel	0.1	1
				kernel fragments	0.1	4
55128	F86 (in F40)	19.5	15.5	**wood identified**		
				Carya spp. (hickories)	1.1	
				Gymnocladus/Gleditsia sp. (Kentucky coffee tree/locust)	0.1	
				Juglans sp. (walnut)	0.2	
				Juniperus virginiana (red cedar)	0.4	
				total wood identified	1.8	
				Arundinaria gigantea (cane)	0.1	
55134	F87 profile trimmings	4.0	1.1	**wood identified**		
				Juniperus virginiana (red cedar)	0.3	
				total wood identified	0.3	
55156	A7.5 B34.5 F87 bottom of fill	5.0	3.7	**wood identified**		
				Salix spp. (willows)	0.4	
				total wood identified	0.4	
				other		
				fish bones	0.1	
55193/1	F89 (in F40)	6.3	4.9	**wood identified**		
				Quercus spp. (oaks)	0.2	
				Salix spp. (willows)	0.1	
				bark	0.1	
				ring porous	0.1	
				total wood identified	0.5	
55165/1	F89 (in F40)	43.8	23.8	8.5 g sampled		
				wood identified		
				Quercus spp. (red oaks)	0.8	
				Salix spp. (willows)	0.1	
				diffuse porous	0.1	
				total wood identified	1.0	

TABLE 8.1
Continued

UMMA Cat. No.	Provenience	Specimen Wt. (g)	>2mm Specimen Wt. (g)	Identification	Wt (g)	Count
				nutshell		
				Carya spp. (hickories)	0.1	2
				other		
				Arundinaria gigantea (cane)	0.1	1
				Diospyros virginiana (persimmon) seed	–	1
				Gramineae (grass family) seeds	–	1
				Zea mays (maize) kernel fragments	0.1	3
				cupule fragments	0.2	7
				glumes	<0.1	2
				monocot stems (thatch fragments)	0.1	12
				unidentified crust with seeds/maize	6.8	
				2 mm sample (3.45 g out of 20.0g)		
				Chenopodium berlandieri (chenopod)	–	33
				Phalaris caroliniana (maygrass)	–	2
				Polygonum sp. (smartweed)	–	2
				Rosaceae (crabapple family)	–	2
				unidentifiable seed fragments	–	13
55165/3	F89 (in F40)	2.1	1.3	**wood identified**		
				Quercus spp. (oaks)	0.3	
				Salix spp. (willows)	0.5	
				total wood identified	0.8	
55212	F103	1.3	0.6	**wood identified**		
				Salix spp. (willows)	0.1	
				total wood identified	0.1	
55227	F118 (hearth)	0.5	0.2	**wood identified**		
				diffuse porous	0.1	
				total wood identified	0.1	

not easily seen and not commonly collected from this type of site without flotation processing.

Wood from the burned structure (F3–5) or from other features associated with this structure (F8 and an unnumbered "Pit 1," probably part of the F5 basin fill) makes up over 97 percent of the wood analyzed here, in spite of the fact that these specimens only constitute about 66 percent of the total specimens with wood analyzed. As shown in Table 8.1, many of the specimens from F5 are large samples, mostly composed of structural wood, clumps of carbonized thatch, or other building materials.

Table 8.2 lists the total weights, percentages, and ubiquity (percent of the samples with wood of a particular type present, followed by the number of samples with presence) of species, genera, family, or anatomical type of wood identified. Four genera or families of wood make up almost 96 percent of the wood identified, and these four—oaks, hickories, willows, and the elms and hackberries—also constitute most (about 88%) of the wood identified from Feature 5. Although the two most abudant genera, the willows and the hickories, were found in similar quantities (both overall and in F5), in this structure much of the willow wood was in the form of young saplings or branches with a complete diameter (varying from 1 to 4 cm), while the hickory (like the oak from this feature) seemed to consist mainly of chunks broken off larger timbers with larger (and more) annual rings. Interestingly, much of the wood identified as belonging to the elm/hackberry family, or Ulmaceae, was shaped or planed, with rounded surfaces clearly at angles with the annual rings or other natural structures in the wood. One large piece of walnut (*Juglans* sp.) from F8, an internal pit, was also carved in this way. All of the worked wood identified from this collection was recovered from the F3–5 structure. The only other type of wood recovered from this structure was a large chunk of maple (*Acer* sp.), which also may have been a structural timber fragment. In contrast, no seeds, maize, or nutshell fragments were identified from F5.

Three other genera of wood were identified from other features or midden contexts, but in minor amounts, as shown in Table 8.2. Kentucky coffee tree or honey locust (*Gymnocladus* sp. or *Gleditsia* sp.) was found only in F86 fill,

TABLE 8.2
Kunnemann Mound Wood

Species	Weight (g)	%	% samples with wood with sp. (*n*)
Acer spp. (maples)	3.2	0.8	3.7 (1)
Carya spp. (hickories)	137.1	35.2	22.2 (6)
Gymnocladus/Gleditsia spp. (Kentucky coffee tree/locust)	0.1	<0.1	3.7 (1)
Juglans sp. (walnut)	3.3	0.8	7.4 (2)
carved wood 94% of *Juglans* sp. identified			
Juniperus virginiana (red cedar)	0.8	0.2	11.1 (3)
Quercus spp. (oaks)	0.8	0.2	14.8 (4)
Erythrobalanus (red oak subfamily)	51.8	13.3	22.2 (6)
Salix spp. (willows)	133.9	34.4	63.0 (17)
Taxodium distichum (bald cypress)	1.0	0.3	3.7 (1)
Ulmaceae (hackberries/elms)	49.7	12.8	18.5 (5)
carved wood 64% of Ulmaceae identified			
Bark	3.4	0.9	14.8 (4)
Diffuse porous	0.3	<0.1	11.1 (3)
Ring porous	1.9	0.5	11.1 (3)
Unidentifiable	2.5	0.6	3.7 (1)
Total wood analyzed	389.8	100.0	100.0 (27)

along with cedar (*Juniperus virginiana*), which was also identified from F87. Bald cypress (*Taxodium distichum*) was identified only from the general F40 midden.

Nutshell, Seeds, Maize, and Other Botanical Remains

The minor amounts of nonwoody botanical remains identified from the UMMA collection are summarized in Table 8.3, and the species reported by Cutler and Blake (1973:24), with proveniences and quantities from their notes (Terrance J. Martin, pers. comm.), are listed in Table 8.4. Given the dry-screening recovery techniques available, it is perhaps unusual that so much of this smaller, more fragile material was recovered from the F40 midden, F86 and F89.

Most of the smaller seeds, however, (such as chenopod and maygrass) were found in one remarkable specimen (UMMA cat. no. 55165/1) from F89. Much of this specimen consisted of a carbonized "unidentified crust with seeds and maize" that may represent some kind of burned food residue. Out of the 8.5 g sampled (from the 23.8 g >2 mm in size), 6.8 g consisted of pieces of this flaky, fragile mass, and a large part of the <2 mm fraction analyzed also consisted of smaller pieces of this material. A few of the larger pieces of this material had perpendicular monocot leaf or stem impressions, as if it had been burned while adhering to some sort of basket or mat with a loose weave. A few maize cupules and glumes and several "popped" chenopod seeds were found embedded in this material, but most of the identified seeds were found loose in the <2 mm fraction sampled. The chenopodium and other seeds were in very poor condition, making identification difficult, and producing a relatively large unidentifiable seed count. Two seeds identified to the Rosaceae or crabapple family may be hawthorn (*Crataegus* spp.) or serviceberry (*Amelanchier*

TABLE 8.3
Kunnemann Mound Non-Wood Materials Identified

	n	g
SEEDS		
Chenopodium berlandieri (chenopod)	34	–
Diospyros virginiana (persimmon)	3	–
Gramineae (grass family)	2	–
Phalaris caroliniana (maygrass)	2	–
Polygonum erectum (knotweed)	1	–
Polygonum sp. (smartweed type)	2	–
Rosaceae (crabapple family)	2	–
Strophostyles sp. (wild bean)	3	–
Unidentifiable seed fragments	13	–
TOTAL SEEDS	59	–
ZEA MAYS (maize)		
Kernels	3	0.3
Kernel fragments	30	0.6
Cupule fragments	7	0.2
Glumes	2	<0.1
TOTAL	42	1.1
NUTSHELL		
Carya sp. (hickory)	3	0.2
Quercus sp. (acorn)	1	<0.1
TOTAL	4	0.2
FIBER AND BUILDING MATERIAL		
Arundinaria gigantea (cane)	–	5.7
Unidentified monocot stems/leaves (thatch)	–	>53.0
Unidentified monocot stems/leaves (woven mat)	1	3.7
Twisted cordage fragments (12 braided)	15	4.7

TABLE 8.4
Kunnemann Mound Botanical Remains in the Illinois State Museum Collections

	Feat. (n)	Feat. (n)	Feat. (n)
SEEDS			
Asimina triloba (paw paw)	?		
Diospyros virginiana (persimmon)	F 89	F 114 (1)	F 116 (36)
Strophostyles helvola (wild bean)	?		
ZEA MAYS (MAIZE)			
Kernels	F 5		
Cob fragments	F 5 (40)	F 40 (1)	F 89 (5)
NUTSHELL			
Carya spp. (hickory)	F 89	?	
WOOD			
Juniperus virginiana (red cedar)	?		
FIBER AND BUILDING MATERIALS			
Cordage	F 5		
"Grass and reed fragments"	probably F 5		

spp.). The two *Polygonum* sp. achenes identified, unlike the single *Polygonum erectum* achene identified from F40, are most like *Polygonum pennsylvanicum* or *P. lapathifolium* (pinkweed or smartweed), which were common weeds in wet areas in the American Bottom.

Although most of chenopod identified was quite distorted (many lacking embryos and/or seed coats), one specimen with a testa or seed coat did have the truncate margin that characterized *C. berlandieri* var. *jonesianum*, a prehistoric domesticated variety of chenopod found in this area. A few of the eroded unidentifiable fragments in this specimen may also be maygrass (*Phalaris caroliniana*), another local cultigen, which was found in low quantities in the sample analyzed.

Interpretations

Although this collection from Kunnemann Mound cannot be expected to provide the detailed information on prehistoric ethnobotany that has been provided for Mississippian sites in this area by flotation sampling, such as that done by Johannessen (1984a) and Lopinot and Woods (1988), these specimens can provide some interesting and useful information that complements more systematic analyses.

In fact, the seeds identified in both the UMMA and the ISM collections from the Kunnemann Mound fit very well into recent models of Mississippian subsistence in the American Bottom. The three most important native starchy seed cultigens are present—chenopodium, maygrass, and erect knotweed. Maize, wild beans, persimmon, paw paw, hickory nuts, acorns, and a few other minor seed types are also well known from other analyses of plant remains in the American Bottom. The recovery of any of the native starchy seeds and acorn shell is unexpected in hand-collected samples like these, but the recovery of wood, some maize, persimmon seeds, and hickory nutshells from a burned structure is not unduly surprising, given the careful excavation that apparently took place at the Kunnemann excavations.

Hally (1981) suggests that structures burned with a full complement of household artifacts, furnishings, food, and debris ("catastrophically" or deliberately burned) will have paleoethnobotanical assemblages different from those of abandoned structures. He specifically hypothesizes that there may be relatively high numbers of persimmon seeds and large hickory nutshell fragments (especially if the structure was burned in late fall), both of which are present in the Kunnemann Mound assemblage and in several other burned Mississippian structures in the American Bottom (DeMott et al. 1989; Dunavan 1989; Pauketat 1987a). Furthermore, the presence of several pieces of carved wood supports the notion that this house burned with artifacts, furnishings, or carved timbers intact.

The wood identified, particularly in the F3–5 structure, is also interesting since comparisons with several other Mississippian houses can be made. It is clear that most if not all of the F3–5 wood identified is structural. Some of the wood in the other features may represent a mixture of structural wood and firewood, but the size of the timbers, the cordage, and the thatch (all found in close association) in F5 confirms that we are dealing with carbonized building materials and not firewood or hearth debris.

Harvey notes that oak and hickory, which are hard, durable woods, seemed to be preferred building materials in areas where "hardwoods were readily available" (1977:280). Oak and hickory have certainly been identified as the major construction elements of many late prehistoric houses in the Southeast and Midwest (Asch and Asch 1985; Cowan et al. 1990; Harvey 1977; Pauketat and Woods 1986; Riley and Lorenz 1989). Lopinot and Woods (1988), however, suggest that hickory (a predominately xeric upland species) was not available in the immediate vicinity of Cahokia, although red oaks (another important timber element in F5) may have been present on the floodplain. Lopinot and Woods go on to postulate "considerable use of nonlocal woods during Lohmann and Early Stirling phases" (1988:23–24), especially hickory and white oak from the uplands, while they suggest that the use of locally available floodplain species, such as red oak, maple, hackberry/elm, Kentucky coffee tree/honey locust, sycamore, and cottonwood/willow probably increased after the end of Stirling phase (A.D. 1150).

Other burned Mississippian structures in the American Bottom containing identifiable wood have been summarized by DeMott et al. (1989), Johannessen (1984b), Pauketat (1987a), and Pauketat and Woods (1986). Two struc-

Plate 8.1. Maize cobs from early Stirling phase Feature 3–5 or Feature 89.

tures from Cahokia itself date to the latter part of the Stirling phase and contain a diverse assortment of wood types, including bald cypress, cottonwood/willow, cedar, Kentucky coffee tree/locust, oak, and hickory (DeMott et al. 1989; Pauketat 1987a). Cypress is said to be the most common timber in the ICT-II Feature 178 (DeMott et al. 1989), but no quantities of different wood types are specified for House 4 (Pauketat 1987a).

The F3–5 structure contains a higher percentage of local floodplain woods (red oaks, willows, and elms and/or hackberries) than upland woods (hickory), although the proportion of hickory in F3–5 is still quite considerable. Thus, this neither refutes nor supports Lopinot and Wood's (1988) hypothesis of local/nonlocal wood use during the different Mississippian phases. Perhaps even more interesting is the pattern of wood use in F3–5. Hickory seems to have been used mainly as large timbers, probably as structural supports, while smaller (and more flexible) willow saplings or branches were used for other construction purposes. Elm or hackberry and walnut were carved. Chmurney (1973:150) describes "partially squared and planed specimens of red cedar" among the refuse from a large pit under Mound 51 at Cahokia, but the elm and walnut from F5 is the first record of carved wood in a structure, a hint of some of the perishable material wealth that filled at least some of the houses at Cahokia.

One very large piece of cane (*Arundinaria gigantea*), about 1.5 cm in diameter, was also found in Feature 5 (in what was first called Pit 1 but probably part of the F5 basin fill) along with woven matting (see Chapter 9), several chunks of monocot leaves and stems that are undoubtedly thatch, and twisted and braided cordage which may have been used as lashings for thatch or beams (see Chapter 3). Similar twined and braided lashings have been reported from a structure on the first terrace of Monks Mound at Cahokia (Benchley 1975) and from Mississippian structures at Hiwassee Island (Lewis and Kneberg 1946:48) and Kincaid (Cole et al. 1951:91, plate XIIc).

The maize recovered from Kunnemann Mound is also worth close examination. Cutler and Blake (1969:126), believing the maize from Kunnemann Mound dated between A.D. 800–1100, suggested that this was some of "the oldest corn" from Cahokia (Plate 8.1). Based largely on the scarcity of eight row cobs and the relatively high mean row number (12.3) for the 45 cobs they measured (over half of the Kunnemann cobs have 12 rows, about 20% have 10 rows, and almost 25% have 14 or more rows), they postulated that this (now known to be not so very old) Cahokian corn was "a very hard flint or pop similar to the Mexican races . . . Chapalote, Reventador, and Nal-Tel," which was believed to have a more primitive or ancestral morphology. Cutler and Blake's mean cupule width for the Kunnemann

Mound cobs is 6.5 mm, with cupule widths ranging from 4.8 mm to 8.3 mm.

Most of the Kunnemann Mound cupules, however, are between 5.5 mm and 7.5 mm in width (Terrance J. Martin, pers. comm.), much like the cupules measured from the Lohmann phase features at Tract 15A, Cahokia (where cupule width averaged 6.7 mm—Dunavan 1989). The single cupules identified from the analyzed features were too distorted for analysis. The three complete kernels identified in the UMMA specimens do little to resolve the issue of what type of corn was being grown at Cahokia (Table 8.5).

This maize is clearly quite different from the "Northern Flint" or "Eastern Eight Row" varieties grown by the Fort Ancient peoples of Ohio and by many historic farmers in the following centuries, since Northern Flint is characterized by high percentages (85–90%) of eight-rowed cobs and cupule widths between 8 and 11 mm (Wagner 1987).

TABLE 8.5
Maize Kernels from Kunnemann Mound

Provenience	Width (mm)	Thickness (mm)	Height (mm)
F40	6.8	4.6	5.3
F86	6.7	4.9	6.8
F5	9.0	6.1	6.98

Whether or not this "Midwestern Twelve Row," as the Kunnemann Mound type of corn at Cahokia has been called, is really that similar to Chapalote or other "ancestral" or "transitional" types remains to be seen. Fritz (1990:409) suggests that maize from this period in the Central Mississippi Valley is "probably typical of most of the Eastern Woodlands outside of the Fort Ancient and Owasco regions."

CHAPTER 9

Woven Material

Two pieces of evidence of prehistoric woven matting, or fabric, survive. These came from two distinct contexts within the Kunnemann Mound. One of these cases involves the charred remains from the floor of the structure F3–5. The other involves the negative impressions left behind by floor or wall mats within the rotunda F74. In neither case can the raw material used to make the fabric or mat be identified, except to say that in both cases it probably was processed plant fibers. A third possible instance consists of impressions, possibly made by a basket, left on a mass of charred food residue from F89 (see Chapter 8). No further information is obtainable from this F89 instance.

The Feature 5 Fabric

A charred fragment of textile was found between the floor of the structure F3–5 and the fallen roof and wall timbers (Fig. 3.19). This fragment measures about 30 cm by 30 cm (Plate 9.1). It seems to have a twined structure consisting of a series of two-strand twisted warp elements about 6 mm in width woven together using three-strand weft elements (see Drooker 1990, 1992). It's unlikely that a floor covering would be so finely woven, so the F5 fabric remnant may have been from an inner wall covering.

The Feature 74 Impressions

As noted in the Chapter 3 description of the F74 circular structure, the distinct black "plate" floor of the rotunda revealed the negative impressions of a loosely woven mat sunk into the surface of F74 to a depth of a millimeter or so. These imprints showed up clearly because they were filled with light-colored sand (Fig. 3.24). The warps of this plain twined mat are about 2 mm wide and spaced about 10 mm apart. The stiff warp elements responsible for these imprints may have been strips of reeds or cane. Weft elements (cords?) were woven into this fabric about every 50 mm, but in some cases every 100 mm (Fig. 9.1).

It is not certain whether these mats represent wall hangings or floor mats. Given the orientation of the warp impressions relative to the circular structure's perimeter, floor mats seem most plausible. Perhaps they were temple "mattresses" of "fine splinters of long canes, tied together" like those described by Adair (1775:100) used as seats in a Creek temple (see Drooker 1990:169).

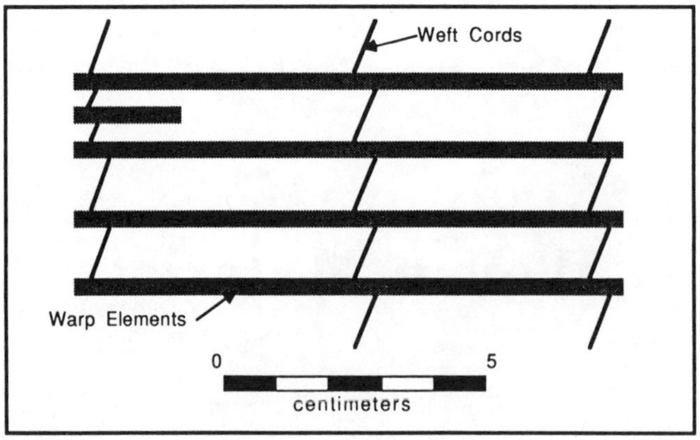

Figure 9.1. Sketch of the Feature 74 mat impressions.

Plate 9.1. The charred fabric on the Feature 3–5 floor.

CHAPTER 10

Sacred Rhythms and Monumental Changes

Interpreting Craft, Temple, and Mound

Behold the wonderful work of our hands; and let us be glad. Look upon the great mound; its top is above the trees, and its black shadow lies on the ground, a bowshot. It is surmounted by the golden emblem of the sun; its glitter (tohpakali) dazzles the eyes of the multitude.

Choctaw song (in Lincecum 1904:532)

Mounds, and the temples and houses on their summits, were the central sacred features of the world of the late prehistoric midcontinent and southeastern Native American. They were the wonderment of the community. They dazzled the eyes of the multitudes. It follows, then, that we must appreciate the place of these sacred monuments within the community and through time if we hope to comprehend the late prehistoric Cahokia-Mississippian world, the dynamics of the community, and—following Holder—the "basic patterns of thinking" of the multitudes.

Preston Holder's excavation of the Kunnemann Mound has provided details on sacred temples, mound-building, and craft production at Cahokia which elucidated what was before only vaguely comprehended. A summary of these details, along with an elaboration of their sociological significance in the larger context of Cahokia and Mississippian culture, follows. This discussion will focus on nonmound domiciles and activities on the Kunnemann Tract (particularly the production of craft goods), mound-top buildings and associated features, and the mound itself.

The Kunnemann Tract Residential Occupation and Craft Production

As documented in the 1955–1956 excavations, the earliest Mississippian occupation of the Kunnemann Tract dates to the Lohmann phase (A.D. 1000–1050). Holley (1990) also notes the prevalence of Lohmann (and Stirling) phase ceramics from the surface of the Kunnemann Tract. A middenlike soil (F40) is found everywhere under the Kunnemann Mound. The materials recovered from this occupation layer appear to include typical domestic garbage, with three notable exceptions.

First, and perhaps a result of sampling error, are the numerous ceramic jugs in the refuse. They make up 18 percent (n = 6) of the Lohmann phase vessel assemblage, and are more than twice as prevalent here as in other Lohmann phase assemblages at Cahokia or elsewhere in the Bottom (Pauketat 1989: table 3). Presumably, these containers would have served in the storage of liquids (Pauketat 1987b:5), a function which might have been more important to some segments of the Cahokian community than others.

The other two exceptions to the typical American Bottom early Mississippian domestic pattern include the presence of submound human remains and craft-production refuse. Each of these has important interpretive potential and will be explored in some depth in the following paragraphs.

Human Remains

An anomalous feature of the Kunnemann Tract occupation, at least compared to rural outlying settlements, is the interment of human remains in what otherwise appear to be domestic zones. These human remains appear to date to the Lohmann and early Stirling phases. The existence of human burials in, or superimposed on, the submound Lohmann phase occupation surface was noted during three independent research programs at the Kunnemann Tract. Fowke (1906) reported finding skeletons during the excavation of one of the low mounds east of tumulus 10/11. A 1985 controlled surface collection of the Kunnemann Tract, supervised by James Collins, recovered occasional human skeletal elements from the surface of the Kunnemann Tract (Holley 1990). Lastly, Holder recovered four discrete instances of human remains from three submound features.

Fowke found extended human burials on the "original surface," both laying east-west, but with heads in opposite directions. Holder partially excavated one skeleton which may have been an extended adult, but the other three (in two pits) include a fetal skeleton, a jumble of bones from more than one individual (both in F83), and a single cranial fragment (from F89). It is important to highlight what seems to be the occurrence of articulated and disarticulated human remains (seemingly adults mixed with infants) in the midst of what appears to be an extensive residential tract during the Lohmann and early Stirling phases (A.D. 1000–1100). The human remains may indicate a sort of mortuary behavior, the social significance of which heretofore has not been given much attention (see Milner 1984:478; Milner and Paine 1991). That is, a segment of the population may have been buried in the midst of the habitation area. Some burials may have included the odd bones of a number of individuals, which Holder thought was apparent in F83. While far from clear, these remains are probably not part of a cemetery—like those at a number of locations at Cahokia (Milner 1984:478)—but of a living community disposing of some dead in convenient ways (Milner and Paine 1991:2) or, perhaps, in ways designed to retain the linkage between the dead and the living. I doubt that such burial is indicative of "the low social position of these people" (Milner and Paine 1982:2). This was probably a relatively high-status community, or one attached to Cahokia's social elite.

It is perhaps of some relevance that Fowler (1989) has identified the mounds on the Kunnemann Tract as paired structures—flat-topped and conical mounds. One explanation is that the rectangular mound would have been the substructure of a mortuary temple and the other conical mound a place of final interment (see also Fowler 1975:96, 1989:194; Holley 1990:30; Reed 1977:39–40). Of course, the proposed burial function of conical mounds is not supported in the Kunnemann Tract excavations of Holder or Fowke (or other conical Cahokia mounds; see Mound Structure and Function, below). The Kunnemann Tract burials all derive from the occupation zone, not the mounds themselves. Nonetheless, the potential importance of these Lohmann and early Stirling human remains (as precursors to, or deriving from, the earliest temples on the Kunnemann Tract) may be an important clue to the social configuration of this northern segment of the Cahokia site.

Craft Production

It has been speculated that the lack of mollusc shell on the surface of the Kunnemann Tract and the Powell Tract might be due to the manufacture of microdrills but not actual shell beads (Ahler and DePuydt 1987:27–28; Mason and Perino 1961:554; Yerkes 1983:500). The absence of mollusc shell on the surface of the Kunnemann Tract has colored the entire discussion of the microlithic and shell-working industries in the American Bottom. Archaeologists have treated the microlithic tools themselves as if they might provide insights into specialized production (Holley 1990:75–77; Yerkes 1983, 1991). However, evaluating the microlithic industry in a technological sense, as a means of assessing the problem of specialization, is probably a poor substitute for understanding the entire craft production sequence and its social context at Cahokia.

While some speculation on the Powell Tract might be in order, the absence of shell from the Kunnemann Tract is explained in Holder's subsurface sample. Here mollusc shell simply disintegrated in the plow zone. There is solid evidence from the 1955 and 1956 excavations that mollusc shell, bone, and antler (and possibly wood) ornaments were produced during the Lohmann and early Stirling phases. At a minimum, this consists of the chert and sandstone components—and their by-products—of shell, bone, and antler, (and possibly wood) -working tool kits along with the residue of worked shell, and incomplete or broken shell and bone beads and pendants, all in association with domestic features or refuse. The Lohmann (and early Stirling) phase F40 and F46 sandstone artifacts included three saw fragments, three type 1 abraders, and a broken palette or type 1 abrader. These same two features contained marine-shell scrap, a possible mussel-shell pendant, three anculosa beads, an unworked conus shell, a chert microblade, and four microblade cores. The early Stirling phase features produced 121 microblade cores, 57 microblades (3 of which are gravers), 19 fragmentary sandstone saws, 2 palettes, a type 1 abrader, 19 finished and unfinished busycon disk and barrel beads, other apparent shell-bead preforms, a pendant and a pendant/gorget blank, 1.3 kg of marine-shell whelk fragments, 3 marginella beads, a conus shell, a shaped mussel shell, cut deer or elk antler, cut swan and mammal bones, and a number of bone beads.

The density of these artifacts in the early Stirling phase features is one or more orders of magnitude greater than any other previous excavated refuse sample of any phase, especially rural site samples. The exceptions may be the occasional cache pit at the Cahokia site, full of marine-shell residue and beads.[1] It is anticipated that, besides the Kunnemann Tract, similar densities of shell-working tools or shell refuse exist in the Powell Tract and to a more limited extent in the Dunham and Ramey Tracts and the Groves Borrow Pit Area (Ahler and DePuydt 1987:24–27; Gums et al. 1989; Jensen 1963; Pauketat 1987a, 1987c; Vanderleest 1980:254; Winston 1963). Other excavated areas of Cahokia, like Tract 15A or the ICT-II, contained very little in the way of marine shell or shell-working tools. Thus, there is reason to doubt that every Cahokia household dabbled in shell-working (cf. Muller 1987:17).

Moreover, Tract-15A and ICT-II domestic refuse, along with that found at rural homesteads, contained high densities of expedient chert tools and debitage. In contrast, the density of expedient chert tools and debitage found in the domestic refuse of the Lohmann and early Stirling phase features below Mound 11 was quite low. Consequently, using the sub–Kunnemann Mound features as a guide, it may be tentatively asserted that Kunnemann Tract shell workers probably did not perform domestic tasks with expedient tools to the same degree that other American Bottom Mississippians did. This would certainly qualify the Kunnemann Tract artisans as "specialists" no matter whose definition is used.

In addition to the abundance of the tools and residues of shell working in Holder's excavated sample, two other important aspects of the Kunnemann Mound data shed new light on craft production at Cahokia. The first is the composition of the craft output.

To begin with, it is fairly clear that Kunnemann saws, drills, and abraders were not used only to manufacture shell beads. Holder's sample shows that carved walnut wood, cut and smoothed antler, bone beads, and perhaps even sandstone beads were also made there. It is not clear whether these were produced in the same manner as mollusc-shell ornaments, but their co-occurrence with shell items, and the clustering of cut and shaped wood, bone, and antler in one part of the structure floor hints of a craft industry which involved multiple media.

The second notable contribution of these data is the light it sheds on the context of production. As alluded to in Chapter 6, these craft-production activities stand in contrast to past characterizations by archaeologists and to the evidence from contemporaneous rural Mississippian sites. To archaeologists on both sides of the 1980s craft-specialization debate, Mississippian shell-working activities in the American Bottom seem to have included little besides the manufacture of disk beads (cf. Holley 1990; Koldehoff 1987, 1990; Muller 1984, 1986, 1987; Prentice 1983, 1987; Yerkes 1983, 1989, 1991; see also Brown et al. 1990). Indeed, at rural Mississippian sites in the Richland Creek drainage and the American Bottom proper (e.g., Milner 1983b; Koldehoff 1989; Prentice and Mehrer 1981; Yerkes 1987), the Lohmann and Stirling phase shell-working evidence is restricted to scattered microlithic artifacts, a few shell disk beads and, in one case, sandstone saws (not presented in Milner 1983b as shell-working tools). These data were the guides used by various archaeologists to argue about what Cahokia shell-craft production must have or have not involved.

However, it may be inappropriate to compare the small-scale shell-working or bead-manufacturing activities at rural sites to the shell-craft production of Cahokia. There appear to be both qualitative and quantitative distinctions between central and rural craft production. The Kunnemann Mound artifacts seem to be the remains of a much more complex and diverse production process than most archaeological characterizations indicate. It would appear that at least four kinds of mollusc-shell beads and a variety of pendant forms were manufactured under one roof. In short, this shell-artifact diversity warrants the suspicion that whole necklaces, perhaps along with other ornamental items, and not simply shell disk beads, were the product of the Kunnemann Tract household activities. And as stated above, it is possible that mollusc shell was only one of a number of media in which these same Kunnemann Tract artisans might have worked.

It is all the more significant to understand the immediate feature contexts from which the bulk of the craft-goods residue was recovered in 1955 and 1956. The large wall trench structure F3–5 had burned, resulting in the deposition of craft-production items *in situ* on its floor. Enough domestic garbage and still-usable implements—pots, filing and smoothing tools, and hoe blades made from mussel-shell, deer scapula, and chert—were found on this same floor to confirm its suspected domiciliary role. Within three meters of this structure was the amorphous Feature 89 which contained the same sorts of craft-production debris and domestic garbage, only in much greater densities. Both date to the early Stirling phase; both superimposed the F40 occupation zone; both contained burned debris. It is possible that F89 was a garbage receptacle for the occupants of F3–5 or another nearby household. In any case, it is a short step from here to suggest that the F3–5 building housed an artisan, or task specialist (cf. Muller 1984).[2]

The F3–5 Household

As Bozell's Chapter 7 analysis indicates, the diet of at least some of these early Stirling phase households was probably rich in the red meat of white-tailed deer. Presumably, this was obtained from outside the immediate Bottom area, perhaps through a centripetal social network (see L. Kelly 1979, 1990, 1991). While no other independent confirmation is available, the presence of imported deer meat and other subsistence goods would be expected where the production of craft goods was subsidized by elite patrons for display or use in social transactions (see Brumfiel and Earle 1987; Friedman and Rowlands 1978).

Given this, it is reasonable to suggest that this F3–5 household, and probably others like it on the Tract, was in some way related or attached to an elite group at Cahokia. As likely as not, this large structure was standing at the same time as an early stage of the south mound (no. 11, see Chapter 3). The F3–5 structure had an unusual *L*-shaped extension and a textile covering on the interior walls. It featured a large puddled central hearth, rare in Lohmann and Stirling phase structures in the American Bottom (see Collins 1990; Mehrer 1988; Milner et al. 1984). The hearth had been cleaned out and relined three times, a feature common to mound-top buildings like those of the later temples atop the Kunnemann Mound. It is reasonable to conclude that this large early Stirling phase building, with certain templelike qualities (i.e., large size, renewed hearth, interior tapestry), was a domicile situated adjacent to a platform mound. These things make it a likely candidate for the residence of an elite person or the residence of someone closely linked to an elite person.

In the accounts of Europeans who observed native Southeastern groups, there are a number of recorded instances of the death of chiefs or socially prominent individuals accompanied by the burning of the individual's home and possessions (e.g., DeBry's engraving of a Le Moyne drawing in Lorant 1946:115; Le Page Du Pratz 1763, Vol. II:221; Swanton 1946:811).[3]

> When the great chief dies they demolish his cabin and then raise a new mound, on which they build the cabin of him who is to replace him in this dignity, for he never lodges in that of his predecessor. [LePetit in Swanton 1911:103]

There is a considerable body of archaeological data to demonstrate that the incineration of structures on the tops of mounds was a common practice prior to the next stage of mound construction (e.g., Lewis and Kneberg 1946: chap. 5). From the first terrace of the largest earthen platform at Cahokia, Monks Mound, there is evidence of a series of burned structures and mound mantles (Benchley 1975). Buildings atop the Murdock Mound also were burned (H. Smith 1977).

In fact, it would seem that the Kunnemann Mound Feature 3–5 is one of at least three known Stirling phase buildings at Cahokia which were located adjacent to mounds and were burned with still-usable household items inside (Collins 1990:150; Pauketat 1987a, 1987b, 1987c, 1989:299–300). In light of the fact that the burning of one such building, Feature 178 at the ICT-II, was the final act in a long series of structure rebuildings on the exact same spot, the best guess now is that these Cahokia dwellings were residences of prominent community members, burned at the time of a resident's death (Collins 1990:150). With the incineration of the F3–5 structure on the Kunnemann Tract, the structure basin was filled in and a new temple structure (F72) erected where the F3–5 building had stood.

The Kunnemann Mound Temples

Nineteen separate structures, including the submound F3–5 building, were at least partially uncovered by Preston Holder during his 1955–1956 investigations. Excluding the F3–5 building and another unnumbered and ill-defined submound building and with the possible exception of F106/107, all of these buildings (n = 17) were situated on prepared earthen mounds or (in the case of F72) mantles. It is uncertain whether the F106/107 building, probably similar in size to F3–5, was on or beneath the earliest (unnumbered) south mound.

The Formal Qualities of Kunnemann Mound Temples

An outstanding trait of the 17 or so mound- or mantle-top buildings is their large size. While the areal dimensions of most structures remain unknown due to partial excavation, those buildings with most or all of their floors exposed—features 72, 74 (rotunda), 94, and 95—have floor areas of 40 to 90 m^2. These areas are much larger than the mean size of Lohmann and Stirling phase domestic structures at the ICT-II, Tract 15A, and the Powell Tract (Collins 1990; O'Brien 1972; Pauketat 1991). No building at any rural American Bottom Mississippian site even approaches the size of these Kunnemann Mound structures (Emerson and Jackson 1984, 1987; Finney 1985; Fortier 1985; Jackson and Hanenberger 1990; McElrath and Finney 1987; Mehrer 1982, 1988; Milner 1983b, 1984a; Yerkes 1987).

The floors of the Kunnemann Mound structures are specially prepared, unlike domestic buildings at Cahokia or outlying rural sites. In most cases, the structures were either located on mantles or contained floors consisting of black gumbo, an organic-rich, montmorillinitic, backswamp silty clay. The F72 floor, for instance, seems to have been made of a thin mantle of this black substance laid down over the old F3–5. In at least three and perhaps more of the 17 buildings under discussion, the floors and hearths were covered with a thin (<0.5 mm) red plaster or paint which appeared as if it had been splashed or brushed onto the surfaces. In the case of the F74 rotunda, not only red, but white, yellow, and black plaster or paint were observed on the floor along with the impressions of mats and unusual linear grooves (cf. Adair 1775:100–101).

In every case where sufficient floor area was exposed, the mound-top and submound buildings contained a formal circular hearth. These features were formal in the sense that they possessed paradigmatic qualities – puddled construction, radial symmetry, regular positioning within the structures, and regular maintenance. Most of the 16 hearths on more than one occasion had been cleaned out or relined. At least three sets of hearths indicate the complete reestablishment of the hearth somewhere else on the structure floor. A number were lined with the same red plaster found on the structure floors.

A few potsherds and persimmon seeds were found inside a few of the hearths.[4] Otherwise, the floors of the Kunnemann Mound structures were largely free of refuse. There is a case to be made that certain vessels and other artifacts found on structure floors or in hearth fill were related to daily tasks. The F73 artifacts and some artifacts associated with F48 (i.e., Ramey Incised pots, a funnel, shell beads, etc.) are likely candidates for mound-top debris. Feature 72 contained some microlithic artifacts which might have been primary refuse. Certainly, finely made ceramics were used and broken in a number of these buildings (e.g., F72, F74, F84). Leighton (1929:133) reported that Moorehead found a vessel associated with a Kunnemann Mound surface. Decorated beakers and bowls, sampling problems aside, seem prevalent in the collections from the 1955–1956 excavations.

The plastered floors, formal puddled (and cleaned-out) circular hearths (including an elaborate hearth-in-square-box example), and the large size and clean interiors of these Kunnemann Mound buildings warrant their being called temples in the sense of the native Southeastern sacred buildings encountered by European and Euroamerican observers after A.D. 1500. The temples of the Kunnemann Mound stand out as a group from the ordinary domiciliary architecture of the region. At the same time, these temples diverge from one another in some ways.

Architectural Form and Function

Architectural form is the primary point of divergence. Most Kunnemann Mound temples are large and rectangular in plan. Feature 94, however, apparently was *T*-shaped, or cruciform, like other Mississippian structures excavated at Cahokia (Gergen and Iseminger 1987; Kelly 1980: map 7; Pauketat 1991: fig. 3.12) and Mitchell (Porter 1974: map 8). Another structure on the F74 prepared surface was circular. This rotunda covers 58.1 m^2 and was larger than any other Lohmann and Stirling phase circular structures at Cahokia or other sites (see Mehrer 1988:156) with the exception of the truly monumental circular buildings which existed on Tract 15B. One of these Tract 15B buildings had a floor area covering 450 m^2 (Pauketat 1991:96; Kelly 1990b).

In other parts of southeastern North America, circular buildings were used as sweat houses or winter dwellings (Faulkner 1977). They often served communal purposes, reserved for an elite or male segment of the community (see Swanton 1979[1946]:386ff.; Willoughby 1932:21). In the rural American Bottom during the Mississippi Period, these circular buildings were usually small and contained a central hearth, thus the designation sweat lodge. The floor areas of rural circular sweat lodges cover between 0.8 and 10.0 m^2 (see Emerson 1992; Mehrer 1988: table 26). At Cahokia and Mitchell, the range is 3.0 to 38.0 m^2 (Mehrer 1988: table 26; Moorehead 1929; O'Brien 1972; Pauketat 1991; Porter 1974; H. Smith 1977).

The extraordinary Tract 15B circular buildings, strictly speaking, may not be comparable in functional terms. However, the Kunnemann Mound F74 circular structure does share all the characteristics of a Mississippian sweat lodge. It possessed four sequential hearths. There may even be some hint that the roof was covered with a clayey earth, possibly for heat retention, also a feature of a circular building on the Murdock Mound. The presence of a large sweat lodge atop a Mississippian mound is not surprising but it does suggest that elite-ritual activities other than the maintenance of a rectangular sacred temple may have been located on the summit. In fact, a number of different activities or facility types may have been located on the platform through time or even at the same time.

It should be recalled that only a portion of the total platform was uncovered by Holder in 1955 and 1956. Even so, almost every exposed prepared surface or mantle (both in the BP area and in Exploration Area 1) revealed the presence of a structure. It is reasonable to wonder just how many buildings might have been located on the Mound 10/11 tumulus and its associated terraces at any one point in time. The structure-form diversity evident in the Kunnemann Mound sample may be a valid representation of the array of building forms which could have coexisted on the mound, particularly after the large F73 surface had been established. Rectangular buildings – temples, residences, store houses – and sweat houses might have made up an elite-sacred set of buildings (Waring 1968:54). This set might have constituted an elite sacred or domestic zone not unlike the sorts of multiple-building domestic zones identified at certain rural Stirling phase locations (Emerson 1992; Mehrer 1988).

The latter often have two or three rectangular structures and one or two circular sweat lodges.

Garcilaso de la Vega notes of the "Indians of Florida":

> [O]n the top of these [platform mounds] they construct flat surfaces which are capable of holding the ten, twelve, fifteen or twenty dwellings of the lord and his family and the people of his service . . . [Varner and Varner 1988:171]

The only known examples of multiple structures atop Cahokia mounds would seem to be those on the fourth terrace of Monks Mound (Fischer 1972; Fowler 1975: fig. 31) and those on stages of the Murdock Mound (H. Smith 1977). The latter appears to include the co-occurrence of a rectangular and a circular structure as elsewhere encountered at places like Hiwassee Island in Tennessee (Lewis and Kneberg 1946).

The only other notable feature that occurs on the mounds are post pits. As at Cahokia and Mitchell (Gergen and Iseminger 1987; Pauketat 1991; Porter 1974; Smith 1977), the Kunnemann Mound post pits—F46, F60, and perhaps F104—have elongate oval-shaped plans. As it turns out, Holder was one of the earliest Cahokia researchers to define these features. Harriet Smith (1977) had correctly identified the example in her 1941 excavation of the Murdock Mound (no. 55) as a post pit, perhaps subsequent to her 1966 presentation of the Murdock Mound data in a symposium at the Central States Anthropological Society meeting; she does not mention this feature in her 1942 summary. Holder described them in 1955 as "bathtubs," just as they were called six years later by the baffled archaeologists who excavated Tract 15A (see Porter 1974:100, 1977:143; Wittry 1977).

The elongate plan shapes of post pits are the result of a ramp beginning at one end and leading down into a deep pit at the opposite end. As evidenced by the immense cypress log from just such a post pit at the Mitchell site, these post pits were used to insert, hold and remove large posts which probably served as marker poles (see Porter 1974:100–111, 1977: figs. 59 and 60; Kelly et al. 1990:349–53) or as internal roof supports to massive buildings (e.g., H. Smith 1977). Similar features are found all around Cahokia and at other southeastern Mississippian sites (Porter 1974:100–111). The posts in F46 and F60 seem to have been about 20 and 60 cm in diameter, respectively.

In summary, it would appear that a number of elaborate buildings with plastered floors and puddled hearths were situated on the various stages of the Kunnemann Mound. It is suspected that multiple buildings occupied the mound summit at any one time. All are suspected to have been sacred buildings of one kind or another, although a variety of elite-related facilities are possible.

The Rhythm of Mound Construction

The strata of the Kunnemann Mound, along with the numerous structures and hearths surmounting the platform stages, have all the hallmarks of a Southeastern temple mound that involved a regular construction cycle. In the profile walls which Preston Holder cut in Mound 11 alone, a minimum of 44 distinct platform enlargements and mantles may be tabulated; these numbers vary depending upon the significance attached to certain strata. Of these 44 fill components, about 33 of them are found in the lower one-third of the tumulus. These include roughly 13 horizontal enlargements (i.e., fill which did not increase the height of the platform) and 20 vertical enlargements, including thin mantles or prepared surfaces related to occupation or structure floors. Approximately 11 of the 44 platform enlargements are in the upper two-thirds of the mound.

It is undeniable that the lower Kunnemann Mound strata are the result of many relatively small-scale construction episodes which I have dated to the early Stirling phase. The later mound-construction episodes (i.e., after F81/87) were of a substantially greater magnitude. Holder recognized this early-late mound shift in the rhythm of construction. In an undated note to the Kunnemann Mound files, Holder records the following (edited slightly for clarity):

> The abrupt change in amount of loading and the frequency with which things are done to the mound surface which appears in the BP Profile above F74 (rotunda and related surface) is a large-scale change in building practices. Before this, little increments of fill and surfaces are continually being diddled with—put it up, take it down, clear it off, build something else, put in posts, take them out, dig trenches, and then refill them—all over the place. My bet is that any given surface will be this way all the way through the [lower] mound. Then abruptly begin big fills with little done to the surface. . . . [I]t is certain that the fill increments are BIG.

It is likely that this big shift occurred sometime during the late Stirling phase.

The question then becomes: is this mound construction pattern—the apparent shift in the size or structure of mound stages—unique to the Kunnemann Mound or common to other Cahokia earthworks? Assuming similar strata in other Cahokia mounds, might a shift in the size of mound mantles reflect some pan-Cahokia phenomenon, and if so, what would such changes signify? These questions are posed here to show the direction of inquiry followed below, a direction which begins to reach beyond the synchronic interpretation of Mississippian mounds enabled by comparative studies (e.g., Knight 1989). Concrete answers to these questions must await future archaeological study.

Mound Comparisons

The data from excavated mounds at Cahokia and two other Mississippian centers in the region suggest mounds were constructed in several stages. Large-scale land modification–leveling the principal plaza and establishing a number of mounds–probably took place early in the Mississippian (Holley et al. 1989; Holley and Woods 1989), though mound excavations have given us little detailed information on Lohmann phase construction. More can be gleaned on the later stages of mound construction. At Cahokia, we will briefly review Mounds 31, 33, 34, 38, 39, 50, 51, 55, 72, and 86. Other mounds at Mitchell (B, H, I, and J) and Emerald (Mound 2) also provide limited additional information.

Mounds 72, 38

Only two mounds provide any evidence at all of Lohmann phase construction. Mound 72 appears to have started out as "a series of smaller mounds" (Fowler 1989:148) later covered over by a ridge-top mound (see Fowler 1991). At least one of these early smaller mounds was a truncated platform (Fowler 1977: plate 17).

It has been said that Monks Mound (no. 38) consists of fourteen major stages (Reed et al. 1968; Porter 1977:152), although excavations on the first and fourth terrace show numerous minor mantles, or stages, within these fourteen putative principal stages (Benchley 1975:17–20; Reed et al. 1968: figs. 4, 5). The strata exposed in the first terrace are reminiscent of the lower strata of the Kunnemann Mound. They consist of "thin grey clay bands about 1 cm thick . . . interlain and interspersed with silt and fill layers" (Benchley 1975:18). Buildings had been constructed, sometimes burned, and reconstructed there in accordance with the relayering of the mound. Though the Monks Mound coring evidence fails to shed much light on the mechanism of Lohmann phase mound construction (Reed, Bennett, and Porter 1968), it does appear that an early-stage Monks Mound was standing during the Lohmann phase. This assertion is based on the coring evidence and the mound wash exposed along the eastern margins of the mound (Williams 1975:22).

It is not clear whether the Ramey Incised pots from the second-to-last major stage date to the Stirling phase or the early Moorehead phase (Reed et al. 1968:148). The uppermost zone or zones of Monks Mound contained Moorehead phase sherds. In any case, the final construction episode reportedly was a gumbo-clay cap which may not have supported any structures (Reed 1977:33).

Mounds 50, 51, 55

Other evidence for distinct mound stages derives from Mounds 50 and 51. William Iseminger's 1987 excavations into the basal remnants of Mound 50 at Cahokia demonstrated a "complex of activity" unexpected by the excavators in this formerly conical mound (Gergen and Iseminger 1987:31). At least four mantles were in evidence at the mound base, of a combined thickness of about 1 meter. Post pits and structures were erected on these individual stages. Likewise, Charles Bareis's 1961 salvage trenching of the basal remnants of the truncated pyramid Mound 51 revealed "at least two sand-filled stages" and "two large fireplaces" (Bareis and Lathrap 1962:8). Unfortunately, the temporal affiliation of these two mounds is uncertain, except that Mound 51 necessarily postdates the Lohmann phase remains beneath it (see Chmurny 1973).

One of the best documented studies of the internal structure of a Cahokia mound (besides Mound 10/11) was Harriet Smith's excavation of the Murdock Mound (no. 55). As it was being leveled to make way for a housing development, Smith directed a WPA crew for a period of four months in 1941. Her excavations revealed "16 successive ground surfaces, 13 of which had structures on them" (H. Smith 1977:50).

While Smith (1977:50–63) believed that the lowest sequence of five occupation surfaces and structures all predated the mound construction, it seems likely–given the 60 cm thickness of this layer–that most of the structures in her "premound" sample in fact surmounted a low earthen platform. An Emergent Mississippian structure (V-1) was found at the base of the mound. However, the next building, an unusual cross-shaped structure, was erected on top of a "mica floodline" (a fill zone several centimeters thick that contained flecks of mica). It is possible that this mica-laden zone constitutes the earliest mound surface that was subsequently enlarged in successive stages. Structures on this early Murdock Mound contained hearths. A pair of buildings–Smith's "latest village occupation, V-5"–includes two adjacent incinerated structures. A circular building, having a floor area of about 20 m² and a centrally situated puddled hearth, was adjacent to a rectangular building featuring a central hearth. Near the hearth of the latter was a smashed Ramey Incised jar (H. Smith 1977: fig. 33).

A "submound platform" or "Layer III," approximately one meter thick, was identified above these earliest structures (H. Smith 1977:62–70). Importantly, this platform mound "was *built up piecemeal* both vertically and horizontally over an indefinite time period" (H. Smith 1977:62, emphasis original). This piecemeal construction, not counting the lower ("village occupation") levels, included at least seven discrete stages (in addition to the four or more earlier stages), each of which was probably topped by a wall-trench structure with a central hearth. This would bring the total number of mound strata up to that point at about eleven.

One Murdock Mound structure (P-8, which Smith calls a "fence" apparently due to its large size) was rectangular and measured about 10 by 15 meters. One of probably three or four large roof support posts was located on the floor along the long axis of the building (H. Smith 1977: figs. 34–37). Like some structures on the Kunnemann Mound, this large Murdock Mound structure covered the entire flat top of the earthen platform, or substage, on which it was located. The excavated eastern and southern walls of the building stood at the very edge of the elevated platform.

Also comparable to the Kunnemann Mound are the final layers of the Murdock Mound what Smith (1977:52, 70) called the "Murdock Temple Mound." These layers, IV-VI, consisted of one or more massive fill additions. Layer IV was a "relatively sterile gumbo" that Smith contends raised the mound to a height of ten meters and expanded the horizontal limits as well. Smith's illustration (1977: fig. 34) of layer IV shows it to be about 2.5 m thick. Layer V was a 120 cm-thick loess lower terrace or "apron" to one side of the gumbo mound; layer VI appeared on the sides of the mound to be an eroded upper layer, its significance unclear (H. Smith 1977:52). Given the probable Stirling phase date of the V-5 layer, it is likely that these upper layers date no earlier than the middle Stirling phase.

Mound 86

The Powell Mound (no. 86), perhaps not unlike the Murdock and Kunnemann Mounds, is known to have consisted of a least four lower platform stages and an enormous upper mound addition (Ahler and DePuydt 1987; Titterington 1938). In this case, of course, the largest of mantles was not a platform stage but a ridge-top mound covering a large elite mortuary tomb. The sub-Powell Mound occupational residue appears to date to the Lohmann and Stirling phases. The date of the ridge-top mantle is uncertain.

Other Mounds for Comparison

Mounds 31, 33, 34, 39, and the first terrace of Mound 38 at Cahokia, Mound H at Mitchell, and Emerald Mound 2 probably date to the late Stirling and Moorehead phases. Mound 31 was a rectangular platform which consisted of a series of strikingly uniform layers (see Fowler 1989: fig. 4.15). Layers 1 through 8 ranged from 25 to 60 cm in thickness without any hint of associated structures (Birong et al. 1980). These may date to the late Stirling or Moorehead phases. At least one of the last two stages (layer 9) was massive, measuring 120 cm in thickness. Both layers 9 and 10 are affiliated with the Moorehead or Sand Prairie phase by virtue of the abundance of Cahokia Cordmarked in these thick mound fills (Birong et al. 1980).

Moorehead's excavation of the James Ramey Mound (no. 33) revealed what primarily seems to have been a Moorehead phase tumulus, based on the excavated material from the mound itself (Moorehead 1929: plates 21, 22, 35; Wagner 1959); it is possible that the ill-defined earlier stages of this mound predate the Moorehead phase. The earliest structures below this "conical" mound are circular sweat lodges which have formal hearths (Fowler 1989:88; Moorehead 1929: pl. 30). Other burned floors were isolated in the mound (Leighton 1929:125–27; Moorehead 1929:50) and, based on Leighton's profile, it would appear as if at least six primary mound strata and four occupation surfaces were defined within the three to four meters of the profile.

About 45 years ago, Albert Spaulding exposed a stratified sequence of up to five mound fill elements in Mound 34, a supposed conical mound with a lower terrace/apron to one side (notes and manuscript on file in the North American Range, UMMA). In his test trench 3, one mound fill element was found to have a thickness of at least 86 cm. The truncated pyramid Mound 39 (i.e., the Sawmill Mound) was found to have been constructed in at least nine stages (Moorehead 1929:40). These consisted of "yellow earth" or "mixed earth" mound fill separated by "dark earth" or a "dark streak" (perhaps gumbo caps or prepared surfaces). A few burials were located along the mound's fringe (Fowler 1989:110). The small Moorehead phase pyramid on the southwest corner of the first terrace of Monks Mound was initially built one-meter high; eight additional mantles were laid down on it, adding a total of 40 cm to its height (Benchley 1975:19).

Evidence of multiple platform stages and associated structures and hearths was recovered in the salvage excavations of Mounds B, H, I, and J at the Mitchell site (Porter 1974:120–24) and Mound 2 at the Emerald site (Illinois). Mound H, which probably dates to the Moorehead phase, had prepared "yellow-orange" or "yellow brown sandy silt" prepared surfaces. Emerald Mound 2, which dates to the Moorehead (or possibly Sand Prairie) phase, showed evidence of having been "enlarged two or three times. . . . The earliest truncated pyramid had been constructed of very dark soil, with a sharply contrasting yellow clay used in the building of the later stages" (Winters and Struever 1962:87).

Mound Structure and Function

With the exception of the Kunnemann Mound, the excavated sample of Cahokia, Mitchell, and Emerald site mounds leaves much to be desired both in terms of the delineation of mound structure and mound-top usage. Thus, it is with difficulty that three issues surrounding mound structure and function may be addressed—overall mound form, the rhythm of construction, and the construction of gumbo caps. This discussion is directed toward the desired expansion of our understanding of diachronic mound-construction patterns and changing meanings of mounds.

As noted earlier, a primary distinction has been made in the past between platform and conical mounds at Cahokia. Most often, the platform mounds are rectangular in plan while the conical mounds are, of course, circular in plan (see Fowler 1989:192–94; Reed 1977). The rectangular platform mounds, it has been demonstrated, were primarily substructures for buildings. Knight (1986, 1989) has delved into the symbolism of these quadrilateral tumuli.

The conical mounds at Cahokia, most often paired with rectangular platforms, were thought to be the burial-mound counterpart to the rectangular temple mound which supported the mortuary temple or charnel house (Fowler 1975, 1977, 1989; Reed 1977:39–40). It will be recalled Fowke, Moorehead and Holder claimed that the Mound 11 portion of the Kunnemann tumulus was "conical," based on the testimony of local residents. Yet, on the oldest map of the site known to exist (the Patrick Map), the round Mound 11 was depicted as a tall but truncated cone (i.e., frustum). As demonstrated both by Moorehead and Holder, no burials were interred in this particular truncated-conical mound. Nor were burials found in the conical Mounds 33, 34, or 50. If Fowke did excavate Mound 9 as suspected (see Chapter 1), then no burials were found in this conical tumulus either.

It seems, in fact, that so far there is only one possible candidate for a "conical" burial mound, Mound 78 (the Jondro Mound) near the western edge of the Cahokia site (Fowler 1989:156). Mound 78 consisted of at least four stages containing more than two dozen extended human interments apparently in the middle to lower strata. However, it must be noted that Moorehead (1929:51) also wrote that Mound 78 "might have served a double purpose, that is, for burials and later as an elevation on which wigwams were set." Even this conical mound does not seem to have always been a burial mound.

Burials seem to occur associated with, or superimposing, other (non-ridge-top) mounds at Cahokia, such as Mounds 17 through 21 (Fowler 1989:75–80; Moorehead 1929:41–44). Perhaps two of these tumuli, Mounds 19 and 21, were "conical" (see Fowler 1989:79–80); certainly they were circular. In any case, the provenience of burials relative to the internal structure of these mounds is unknown. Moreover, it is fairly obvious—based on the descriptions of artifacts (see Fowler 1989; Moorehead 1929)—that these tumuli postdate the Stirling phase. That is, even if burials could be associated with a particular kind of conical mound deposit (and they cannot), this association would exist only during the Moorehead or Sand Prairie phases.

Additionally, it is widely known that the area due east of Monks Mound contained occupational remains, mounds, and a cemetery dating to the Moorehead and Sand Prairie phases (Milner 1984c; Perino 1947, 1971a, 1980). The burials supposedly associated with or located near Mounds 17–21 may be nothing more than a portion of this late Mississippian occupation/cemetery rather than being indicative of a pan-Cahokia relationship between mound form and function. The same may be true of the Jondro Mound (no. 78) mentioned above, which, as it turns out, is near the so-called Fingerhut cemetery on the western fringe of the Cahokia site (see Milner 1984c).

Certainly the Moorehead or Sand Prairie phase Mound 2 at the Emerald site, and its counterpart Mound 1, were flat-topped circular platforms. This conclusion is based on the account of John Francis Snyder (1909) who describes them as "true circles, both at their bases and flat summits." As earlier mentioned, Mound 2 was found to consist of multiple strata (Winters and Struever 1962:87). No burials were found in association.

The massive elite mortuaries at Cahokia are often associated not with conical mounds but with ridge-top mounds (Ahler and DePuydt 1987; Fowler and Anderson 1975; Milner 1984c; Moorehead 1929:71–74). Similar mortuaries at the Mississippian centers in St. Louis, East St. Louis, and Mitchell were found either in platform or ridge-top mounds.[5] We are left, hence, with putative conical mounds which usually seem to have served as substructural platforms, not tombs. These circular mounds often are paired—as exemplified by the Kunnemann or James Ramey Mounds—with rectangular platforms.

This paired rectangular and circular mound arrangement certainly is not surprising to those familiar with Native American architecture of the Southeast. Bartram (cited in Knight 1989:285; Swanton 1979) observed a similar pairing of rectangular and round mounds among the early historic period Creek. In that case, the rectangular truncated pyramid was surmounted by the rectangular temple, while the circular truncated mound was the substructure of a circular town house. As noted earlier in this chapter, circular and rectangular structures have been found paired in the Murdock Mound and, arguably, at smaller outlying sites in the American Bottom. Other cases of circular and rectangular buildings atop earthen platforms are known at Cahokia.

In favor of the circular platform-mound idea are the irrefutable indications that the horizontal dimensions of at least some of the Kunnemann Mound and Murdock Mound structures were the same as the horizontal dimensions of the substructural platforms. That is, if the shapes of structures and mounds matched, then rectangular buildings would have been elevated by four-sided substructural platforms while circular structures would have rested atop circular flat-topped platforms. While little concrete evidence is available to add credence to this proposition, it is worthy of note that this close structure-mound fit also was common for platforms elsewhere in the Southeast (e.g., I. Brown 1985; Lewis and Kneberg 1946; Rudolph 1984; Schnell et al. 1981; Williams and Brain 1983).[6] Again, if a close structure-mound fit did characterize monumental architecture at Cahokia, then we should expect that rectangular buildings would have been built upon rectangular mounds and circular buildings would have had circular earthen substructures. In this light, the so-called conical mounds of Cahokia (with perhaps one or two exceptions) may be nothing more than circular flat-topped mounds, substructures for circular rotundas. Their conical appearance might be the result of years of cultivation and erosion.

The Meanings of Mounds

The close correspondence between the horizontal dimensions of the early Kunnemann and Murdock Mounds and the buildings on their summits, along with their small-scale stage enlargements and mantles, suggests we should separate mound from mound-top usage (cf. Knight 1989). The structures on the summits of the early mound stages probably would have dwarfed the low substructural platforms. If the Kunnemann and Murdock Mounds, and other tumuli with thin but complex stratigraphy at Cahokia, were all built during roughly the same period of time, then this disproportionate structure–substructure size relationship suggests the relative insignificance of the mound itself as an "earth icon" during the early Mississippi Period Lohmann and early Stirling phases. More significant, perhaps, was the process of mound construction, and the mound-top facility.

As Waring (1968:57–58) observed in other Southeastern archaeological cases, the layers of the Kunnemann Mound—particularly its lower portions—suggest that "the sealing off of the old structure was more important than the purely architectural consideration of creating an imposing temple foundation." This may best be exemplified by F72, a thin "blanket mantle" of earth laid down on the premound surface where a previous structure of some importance had stood (see Schnell et al. 1981:132; Blitz 1983:251–52). The Kunnemann Mound was raised in several larger increments during the early to middle Stirling phase (i.e., F75/77, F79/131) but each of these actually amounts to several distinct horizontal enlargements and each seems to have had relatively stable surfaces which witnessed the deposition of multiple thin mantles (probably as a result of reconstructions of buildings or regular renewals of mound-top facilities; see Blitz 1983; Knight 1986:683; Rogers et al. 1989; Waring 1968).

Between the base of the mound and F81/87, less than 2 meters in height, the rhythm of mound construction seems to have consisted of small-scale, but elaborate, incremental construction episodes, including blanket mantles and stage enlargements. We may surmise that the elevation of the mound had little meaning, or at least what meaning there was was secondary to the act of construction itself, which was seen as a renewal of the purity of the location (see Blitz 1983; Payne cited in Knight 1989:285; Schnell et al. 1981: 143–45; Waring 1968:57–58). The importance of mound renewal is recounted in a Choctaw legend of the nineteenth century:

> [I]t became an honorable thing to carry and deposit earth on the mound at any time they were not engaged at work in their domestic vocations. . . . [Y]ears rolled round; the work on the mound was regularly prosecuted . . . [Lincecum 1904:531]

What then, might be the significance of the shift in the size of fill units in the Kunnemann tumulus subsequent to F81/87? As apparent both in the Moorehead Profile and the borrow pit area profiles, each of the successive construction stages in the upper two-thirds of Mound 11 consist of thick mound-fill elements surmounted by a number of sandy prepared floors and, sometimes, by a moderately thick layer of gumbo. Feature 17, for instance (as documented in the eastern arm of the BP area/MP2), was measured three meters thick.

While the temporal affiliation of the later strata of the Murdock Mound is uncertain, it is obvious that a dramatic change in mound construction took place after the early Stirling phase here, as well. There is reason to suspect, although not enough to conclude, that other mound construction postdating the early Stirling phase did not follow the "piddling-about" or "piecemeal" modes identified by Preston Holder and Harriet Smith, respectively. Certainly, it has not yet been demonstrated that Lohmann and early Stirling phase mounds were erected in massive stages. And where relatively thin Moorehead phase mantles have been identified, they appear rather consistent in form, covering the entire mound, as on the first terrace of Mound 38 or in Mound 31.

Unfortunately, the Cahokia site mound data are not yet definitive on this issue of construction trajectories. Clearly, mounds had different histories. The construction history (although perhaps not the internal structure) of Monks Mound, for instance, was unique. Nonetheless, the possibility remains that a major structural change of some kind occurred around the late Stirling phase and is reflected in the rhythmic shift documented in Kunnemann Mound and perhaps other mounds at Cahokia. It is not necessary to view this tentatively identified change as involving a changed construction cycle or a de-emphasis on the sacred rhythms of mound renewal or purification. Rather, some other phenomenon aside from traditional world-renewal and purification rites might have been expressed in the size of the mound increments. What this phenomenon might have been is still a mystery.

The Potential Implications of Gumbo Caps

In light of the changes tentatively identified above, the use of gumbo clay versus sandy loam in mounds is of special interest. Moorehead pondered this matter:

> Tumuli of gumbo contain a minimum of cabin or camp-fire refuse, whereas, the loam mounds contain much. . . . Why were so many mounds built of gumbo? It was difficult to handle–even our own men using modern steel shovels find it heavy and wearisome to remove. [Moorehead 1929:104–5]

The functional explanation for the use of gumbo is easy enough to derive from Holder's Kunnemann Mound profiles. Sand or loam erodes easily and looses its shape. Gumbo, although possessing a high shrink-swell ratio unsuitable for many modern purposes, would have been less susceptible to splash erosion. It would have held its shape on a mound.

Perhaps the black color of gumbo also might have had desirable symbolic overtones. It was used on the floors of temples in the lower portions of the Kunnemann Mound, perhaps adding some credence to this symbolic explanation. In the upper layers of the Kunnemann Mound, gumbo "caps" or mantles are apparent on which no evidence of buildings has been found. One such gumbo cap, perhaps the final layer of the Kunnemann Mound, was over 110 cm thick.

Similar gumbo caps are found on other Cahokia mounds. The Mound 10 terrace was capped by up to 90 cm of gumbo. Fowke (1906:26) excavated one mound on the Kunnemann Tract with a "capping" of gumbo which originally was over 120 cm thick. The massive upper layer of the Murdock Mound was all gumbo (H. Smith 1977). The uppermost layer of Monks Mound is a gumbo matrix in which no structural features were observed by its excavators (Reed 1977; Reed et al. 1968).

Given what Moorehead noted as the "minimum of cabin or camp-fire refuse" on gumbo-based surfaces, and the structural qualities of gumbo clay, it is reasonable to assert that the gumbo caps in the above cases may have been ritual seals. Such ritual seals could mark periods during which the flat mound summits were not used. If this is the case, then such gumbo caps denote not the renewal of the sacred location, as I believe to be the meaning of other blanket mantles, but the closure of a sacred location. Restated, gumbo caps would seem to be quite different from the sorts of mantles found in the lower levels of the Kunnemann Mound, in the first terrace of Monks Mound, and in Mounds 50, 51, and 55, among others. Where such substantial labor efforts were put into the closure of a mound and the perpetuation of its size and shape, it would seem that the mound itself had become an icon (sensu Knight 1989). Here, the mound cannot be considered the lesser of the two principal components–building and mound–of a monument.

Here, then, may be part of the explanation of the rhythmic shift observed by Holder in the Kunnemann Mound at the juncture of its lower and upper fill stages. This change may have been related to a thematic shift in the meanings attached to a monument. Whereas the meanings of the early monument could be interpreted to have been dominated by the symbolism of the mound-top building or activity, later on, the dominant symbolic meaning was found in the mound itself. Whether this might have been a pan-Cahokia phenomenon is unknown. Whether such a symbolic transformation might have been isomorphic with a political-religious transformation likewise is speculative. At present, answers to the questions posed earlier in this chapter concerning the mound construction patterns of the Kunnemann and other Cahokia monuments are beyond the reach of modern hands.

Conclusion: The Hands of Time

> It is my feeling that the most minor authenticated substantive data from the Cahokia group are of value in trying to reconstruct the details of the way of life of these peoples. This report is presented in this spirit. It leaves more questions unanswered than it is able to answer. There are many lacunae in such facts as are presented. [Holder 1980]

To be sure, we have only begun to recognize the complexity of the Cahokia monuments–how the construction, and hence the meaning changed over the years–and how the monuments relate to Cahokia-Mississippian culture and the political-religious developments of the late prehistoric American Bottom. Given the formative condition of our present understanding of Cahokia monuments, we are fortunate that Preston Holder recognized the worth of minute details from a Mississippian mound. Lacunae exist in the Kunnemann Mound data, but the fragments of solutions and pieces of puzzles offered here as a result of Holder's meticulous excavations in 1955 and 1956 are perhaps the most thought-provoking details yet from a Cahokia platform mound.

Holder's data provide a series of tantalizing glimpses into the relationship between craft production and social reproduction, between the secular and the sacred, the political and the religious. Specifically, this analysis has provided insights into the final disposition of some Cahokia dead, the relationship of craft production to elite-sacred remains, the uses of mound summits, the architectural qualities of sacred buildings, the size, shape, and possible meanings of mounds, and the periodicity of enlargements over about a century. Most of these data contribute to a broadened understanding of the sacred-temple and mound themes, part and parcel of what Holder called the Cahokians' "basic patterns of thinking."

The basic patterns of thinking of these Mississippians merged a concern for cosmological order with a hierarchical social order. That is, the order of the Mississippian cosmos was vested in an elite class (Pauketat 1991; Pauketat and Emerson 1991). The sacred temple and the platform mound were shrines to this authority, nodal points of articulation between the community and the cosmos. Building or rebuilding mound and temple undoubtedly would have been a regularly performed, honorable endeavor–the "wonderful work" of communal hands (see Lincecum 1904:532). However, performing the ceremonies associated with the monument and curating the community symbols therein would have been placed in elite hands. The "eyes of the multitude," as the Choctaw song goes, were in some sense being dazzled by an elite sleight of hand.

To a large extent, the cultural-historical development of the Cahokia-Mississippian phenomenon depended on maintaining the dazzled masses and the elite dazzlers as a community. It involved a perpetuation of order. That is, political and religious order mediated social order and social change. The sacred temple, mound-building, and even the production, display, and distribution of valuables were all components of this maintenance of the social order which was at the same time the reproduction of elite power and religious authority.

In the Cahokia monuments, the hands and minds of the elites and the nonelites were joined as community, class, and power were symbolically merged and maintained. The Kunnemann monument was a symbol of the order that was the cultural basis for the events–the work of both elite and nonelite hands–that make up the diachronic phenomenon called Cahokia-Mississippian. The sacred rhythms and monumental changes seen in the Kunnemann Mound are a means to understand the basic themes which gave meaning to life in the Mississippian world and which are at the same time an essential part of any fuller understanding of the development and decline of Cahokia. In a sense then, the Kunnemann Mound excavations have provided us with a set of handprints. From these handprints, we have moved toward a diachronic delineation of the Cahokians' basic patterns of thinking and, in a way, a better comprehension of the hands of time.

CHAPTER 10 NOTES

1. A note on the potential diachronic trends in shell-working might be useful here. An inspection of ceramic contents of Perino's Ramey Tract pit (described in Pauketat 1987c:82) by John E. Kelly and myself in 1991 revealed that it dates to the Moorehead phase. The finished and unfinished beads and scrap whelk in that pit suggests to us that Moorehead phase shell working may have involved (1) less use of sandstone saws in the reduction of whelk shell into bead blanks (instead the shells being smashed or fractured into bead blanks), (2) the use of the crown elements of the whelk shell for beads (not seen in the Kunnemann Mound assemblage), and (3) the reduced manufacture of barrel-shaped beads out of whelk columellae, a highly labor-intensive process.

2. The problem of specialization received much attention through the 1980s. Those uninitiated readers wishing to jump into this literature might find it useful to first consult the works of Brown, Winters, and Kerber (1990), Cobb (1989), and Welch (1991) in order to orient the problem within a political-economic framework.

3. This is a practice found throughout the native New World, even in contemporary contexts (e.g., Kent 1984:153–54; Deal 1985:269).

4. A Moorehead or Sand Prairie phase hearth in Mound 2 of the Emerald site (of Illinois, just east of the American Bottom) contained ash, sherds of a pot, the bones of a young white-tailed deer fawn, and the carapace of young turtles (Winters and Struever 1962:87).

5. I elsewhere have speculated that rather than being markers of the limits of Cahokia (Fowler 1989:194–95), these may have been earthen versions of hipped roofs, symbolic "houses of the elite dead" (Pauketat 1991:88).

6. Additional comparative information on late prehistoric mounds and sacred-elite buildings may be obtained from Blitz 1983; Brown 1971, 1990; Fairbanks 1956; DeJarnette and Wimberly 1941; Larson 1971; Quimby 1957; Neitzel 1965; Rogers et al. 1989; Schnell et al. 1981; and Webb and DeJarnette 1942.

References Cited

Adair, James
1775 The History of the American Indians; Particularly Those Nations Adjoining to the Mississippi, East and West Florida, Georgia, South and North Carolina, and Virginia. London: Edward and Charles Dilly.

Ahler, Steven R., and Peter J. DePuydt
1987 A Report on the 1931 Powell Mound Excavations, Madison County, Illinois. Illinois State Museum Reports of Investigations 43. Springfield.

Anderson, James
1977 A Cahokia palisade sequence. In: Explorations into Cahokia Archaeology, edited by M.L. Fowler, pp. 89–99. Illinois Archaeological Survey, Bulletin 7. Urbana.

Asch, Nancy B., and David L. Asch
1985 Archeobotany. In: The Hill Creek Homestead and Late Mississippian Settlement in the Lower Illinois Valley, edited by M.D. Connor, pp. 130–65. Kampsville Archeological Center Research Series 1. Kampsville, IL: Center for American Archeology.

Baker, Frank C.
1929 The use of molluscan shells by the Cahokia Mound builders. Appendix A. In: The Cahokia Mounds, by W.K. Moorehead, University of Illinois, Bulletin 26(4):147–54. Urbana.
1930 The use of animal life by the mound-building Indians of Illinois. Transactions of the Illinois State Academy of Science 22:41–64.
1941 A study of ethnozoology of the Indians of Illinois. Transactions of the American Philosophical Society 32:51–57.

Bareis, Charles J.
1975 Report of 1972 University of Illinois-Urbana excavations at the Cahokia site. In: Cahokia Archaeology: Field Reports, edited by M.L. Fowler, pp. 12–15. Illinois State Museum Research Series, Papers in Anthropology, 3. Springfield.

Bareis, Charles J., and Donald Lathrap
1962 University of Illinois projects. In: First Annual Report: American Bottoms Archaeology, July 1, 1961–June 30, 1962, pp. 3–9. Urbana: Illinois Archaeological Survey.

Bareis, Charles J., and James W. Porter (editors)
1984 American Bottom Archaeology. Urbana: University of Illinois Press.

Barker, Alex W., and Timothy R. Pauketat (editors)
1992 Lords of the Southeast: Social Inequality and the Native Elites of Southeastern North America. American Anthropological Association, Archeological Paper 3. Washington, D.C.

Benchley, Elizabeth
1975 Summary field report of excavations on the southwest corner of the first terrace of Monks Mound: 1968, 1969, 1971. In: Cahokia Archaeology: Field Reports, edited by M.L. Fowler, pp. 16–24. Illinois State Museum Research Series, Papers in Anthropology 3. Springfield.

Binford, Lewis R.
1978 Nunamiut Ethnoarchaeology. New York: Academic Press.

Birong, Marcia, Connie Horstman, Gregory James, and Lynne Peters
1980 An Analysis of Ceramics from Mound 31, Cahokia. Manuscript on file, Department of Anthropology, University of Wisconsin, Milwaukee.

Black, Glenn A.
1967 Angel Site: An Archaeological, Historical, and Ethnological Study. Indianapolis: Indiana Historical Society.

Blitz, John H.
1983 The Summerville mound. In: Excavations in the Lubbub Creek Archaeological Locality. Volume 1 of Prehistoric Agricultural Communities in West Central Alabama, edited by C.S. Peebles, pp. 198–253. Mobile: U.S. Army Corps of Engineers.

Bohlen, H.D.
1978 An Annotated Check-List of the Birds of Illinois. Illinois State Museum, Popular Science Series 9. Springfield.

Bourne, Edward G. (editor)
1904 Narratives of the Career of Hernando De Soto. New York: A.S. Barnes and Company.

Brackenridge, Henry M.
1814 Views of Louisiana (1962 edition). Chicago: Quadrangle Books.

Browman, David L.
1978 The "Knockers": St. Louis archaeologists from 1904–1921. Missouri Archaeological Society Newsletter 319:1–6.

Brown, Ian W.
1985 Plaquemine architectural patterns in the Natchez Bluffs and surrounding regions of the lower Mississippi valley. Midcontinental Journal of Archaeology 10:251–305.

Brown, James A.
1971 The dimensions of status in the burials at Spiro. In: Approaches to the Social Dimensions of Mortuary Practices, edited by J.A. Brown, pp. 92–112. Memoirs of the Society for American Archaeology 25.
1975 Spiro art and its mortuary contexts. In: Death and the Afterlife in Pre-Columbian America, edited by E.P. Benson, pp. 1–32. Dumbarton Oaks Research Library and Collections, Washington, D.C.
1976 The Southern Cult reconsidered. Midcontinental Journal of Archaeology 1:115–35.
1985 The Mississippian period. In: Ancient Art of the American Woodland Indians, pp. 92–145. New York: Harry N. Abrams.
1990 Archaeology confronts history at the Natchez temple. Southeastern Archaeology 9:1–10.

Brown, James A., Richard A. Kerber, and Howard D. Winters
1990 Trade and the evolution of exchange relations at the beginning of the Mississippian period. In: The Mississippian Emergence, edited by B.D. Smith, pp. 251–80. Washington, D.C.: Smithsonian Institution Press.

Brumfiel, Elizabeth M., and Timothy K. Earle
1987 Specialization, exchange, and complex societies: an introduction. In: Specialization, Exchange, and Complex Societies, edited by E.M. Brumfiel and T.K. Earle, pp. 1–9. Cambridge: Cambridge University Press.

Bushnell, David I., Jr.
1904 The Cahokia and Surrounding Mound Groups. Papers of the Peabody Museum of American Archaeology and Ethnology 3. Harvard University.

Chaplin, R.E.
1971 The Study of Animal Bones from Archaeological Sites. New York: Seminar Press.

Chmurny, William W.
1973 The Ecology of the Middle Mississippian Occupation of the American Bottom. Ph.D. dissertation, Department of Anthropology, University of Illinois at Urbana.

Cobb, Charles R.
1989 An appraisal of the role of Mill Creek chert hoes in Mississippian exchange systems. Southeastern Archaeology 8:79–92.

Cole, Fay-Cooper, Robert Bell, John Bennett, Joseph Caldwell, Norman Emerson, Richard MacNeish, Kenneth Orr, and Roger Willis
1951 Kincaid: A Prehistoric Illinois Metropolis. University of Chicago Press.

Collins, James M.
1990 The Archaeology of the Cahokia Mounds ICT-II: Site Structure. Illinois Cultural Resources Study 10. Springfield: Illinois Historic Preservation Agency.

Core, Harold A., Wilfred A. Cote, and Arnold C. Day
1979 Wood Structure and Identification. Syracuse Wood Science Series 8. Syracuse, NY: Syracuse University Press.

Cowan, C. Wesley, Sandra Dunavan, John P. Nass, Jr., and Susan Scott
1990 The Schomaker site: a middle period Fort Ancient town on the Great Miami River, Hamilton County, Ohio. West Virginia Archaeologist 42(1):11–35.

Cross, Paula G.
1983 Vertebrate faunal remains from the Turner and DeMange sites. In: The Turner and DeMange Sites, by G.R. Milner, pp. 201–12. Urbana: University of Illinois Press.
1984 Vertebrate faunal remains from the Julien site. In: The Julien Site, by G.R. Milner. Urbana: University of Illinois Press.
1992 Animal remains. In: The Lohmann Site: An Early Mississippian Center in the American Bottom, by D. Esarey and T.R. Pauketat. American Bottom Archaeology, FAI-270 Site Reports 25. Urbana: University of Illinois Press.

Cutler, Hugh C., and Leonard W. Blake
1973 Plants from Archaeological Sites East of the Rockies. St. Louis: Missouri Botanical Garden.
1977 Corn from Cahokia sites. In: Explorations into Cahokia Archaeology (second revised edition), pp. 123–36. Illinois Archaeological Survey, Bulletin 7. Urbana.

Dance, S. Peter
1974 The Collector's Encyclopedia of Shells. New York: McGraw-Hill.

Deal, Michael
1985 Household pottery disposal in the Maya Highlands: an ethnoarchaeological interpretation. Journal of Anthropological Archaeology 4:243–91.

DeBoer, Warren R.
1983 The archaeological record as preserved death assemblage. In: Archaeological Hammers and Theories, edited by J.A. Moore and A.S. Keene, pp. 19–36. New York: Academic Press.

DeJarnette, David L., and S.B. Wimberly
1941 The Bessemer Site. Alabama Museum of Natural History, Museum Paper 17. University of Alabama.

DeMott, Carol A., Neal H. Lopinot, and Rodney C. DeMott
1989 Archaeobotanical analysis of a burned Mississippian structure at Cahokia. Paper presented at the 54th Annual Meeting of the Society for American Archaeology, Atlanta.

DePratter, Chester B.
1983 Late Prehistoric and Early Historic Chiefdoms in the Southeastern United States. Ph.D. dissertation, University of Georgia, Athens.

Drooker, Penelope B.
1990 Textile production and use at Wickliffe Mounds (15BA4), Kentucky. Midcontinental Journal of Archaeology 15:163–220.
1992 Mississippian Village Textiles at Wickliffe. Tuscaloosa: University of Alabama Press.

Dunavan, Sandra L.
1989 Persimmons and maize: plant remains from Tract 15A, Cahokia. University of Michigan, Museum of Anthropology, Ethnobotanical Laboratory Report 573. Ann Arbor.

Earle, Timothy K.
1987 Chiefdoms in archaeological and ethnohistorical perspective. Annual Review of Anthropology 16:279–308.

Emerson, Thomas E.
1989 Water, serpents, and the underworld: an exploration into Cahokia symbolism. In: The Southeastern Ceremonial Complex: Artifacts and Analysis, edited by P. Galloway, pp. 45–92. Lincoln: University of Nebraska Press.
1991 Some perspectives on Cahokia and the northern Mississippian expansion. In: Cahokia and the Hinterlands: Middle Mississippian Cultures of the Midwest, edited by T.E. Emerson and R.B. Lewis, pp. 221–36. Urbana: University of Illinois Press.
1992 The Mississippian dispersed village as a social and environmental strategy. In: Late Prehistoric Agriculture: Observations from the Midwest, edited by W.I. Woods, pp 198–213. Studies in Illinois Archaeology 8. Springfield: Illinois Historic Preservation Agency.

Emerson, Thomas E., and Douglas K. Jackson
1984 The BBB Motor Site. American Bottom Archaeology, FAI-270 Site Reports 6. Urbana: University of Illinois Press.
1987 The Marcus Site. American Bottom Archaeology, FAI-270 Site Reports 17, Part 2. Urbana: University of Illinois Press.

Emerson, Thomas E., and R. Barry Lewis (editors)
1991 Cahokia and the Hinterlands: Middle Mississippian Cultures of the Midwest. Urbana: University of Illinois Press.

Esarey, Duane, and Timothy R. Pauketat
1992 The Lohmann Site: An Early Mississippian Center in the American Bottom. American Bottom Archaeology, FAI-270 Site Reports 25. Urbana: University of Illinois Press.

Fairbanks, Charles H.
1956 Archaeology of the Funeral Mound, Ockmulgee National Monument, Georgia. National Park Service, Anthropology Research Series 3.

Falk, C.R., C.A. Angus, D.F. Morey, and D. Meyers
1979 CODEX: A Simplified Numerical Coding System to Facilitate the Descriptive Analysis of Large Vertebrate Assemblages. Division of Archeological Research, Technical Report 79–15. Lincoln: University of Nebraska.

Faulkner, Charles H.
1977 The winter house: an early Southeast tradition. Midcontinental Journal of Archaeology 2:141–59.

Finney, Fred A.
1985 The Carbon Dioxide Site. American Bottom Archaeology, FAI-270 Site Reports 11, Part 1. Urbana: University of Illinois Press.
1987 Ceramics. In: The George Reeves Site, by D.L. McElrath and F.A. Finney, pp. 222–59, 276–81, 340–46. American Bottom Archaeology, FAI-270 Site Reports 15. Urbana: University of Illinois Press.

Fischer, Fred W.
1972 Recent Archeological Investigations on the Fourth Elevation of Monks Mound, Madison County, Illinois. Unpublished manuscript, Washington University, St. Louis.

Fortier, Andrew C.
1985 The Robert Schneider Site. American Bottom Archaeology, FAI-270 Site Reports 11, Part 2. Urbana: University of Illinois Press.

Fortier, Andrew C., Fred A. Finney, and Richard B. Lacampagne
1983 The Mund Site. American Bottom Archaeology, FAI-270 Site Reports 5. Urbana: University of Illinois Press.

Fortier, Andrew C., Thomas O. Maher, Joyce A. Williams, Michael C. Meinkoth, Kathryn E. Parker, and Lucretia S. Kelly
1989 The Holding Site: A Hopewell Community in the American Bottom. American Bottom Archaeology, FAI-270 Site Reports 19. Urbana: University of Illinois Press.

Fowke, Gerard
1906 Illinois mounds. The Commerce Monthly: 26–27.

Fowler, Melvin L.
1975 A pre-Columbian urban center on the Mississippi. Scientific American 233(2):92–101.
1977 The Cahokia site. In: Explorations into Cahokia Archaeology (second revised edition), edited by M.L. Fowler, pp. 1–42. Illinois Archaeological Survey, Bulletin 7. Urbana.
1989 The Cahokia Atlas: A Historical Atlas of Cahokia Archaeology. Studies in Illinois Archaeology 6. Springfield: Illinois Historic Preservation Agency.
1991 Mound 72 and Early Mississippian at Cahokia. A New Perspective on Cahokia: Views from the Periphery, edited by J.B. Stoltman, pp. 1–28. Madison, WI: Prehistory Press.

Fowler, Melvin L., and James Anderson
1975 Report of 1971 excavations at Mound 72, Cahokia Mounds State Park. In: Cahokia Archaeology: Field Reports, edited by M.L. Fowler, pp. 25–27. Illinois State Museum Papers in Anthropology 3. Springfield.

Fowler, Melvin L., and Robert L. Hall
1975 Archaeological phases at Cahokia. In: Perspectives in Cahokia Archaeology, pp. 1–14. Illinois Archaeological Survey, Bulletin 10. Urbana.
1978 Late prehistory of the Illinois area. In: Handbook of North American Indians 15:560–68. Washington, D.C.: Smithsonian Institution Press.

Friedman, Jonathan A., and Michael Rowlands
1978 Notes towards an epigenetic model of the evolution of "civilisation." In: The Evolution of Social Systems, edited by J. Friedman and M. Rowlands, pp. 201–76. Philadelphia: University of Pittsburgh Press.

Fritz, Gayle J.
1990 Multiple pathways to farming in precontact eastern North America. Journal of World Prehistory 4(4):387–435.

Galloway, Patricia (editor)
1989 The Southeastern Ceremonial Complex: Artifacts and Analysis. Lincoln: University of Nebraska Press.

Gergen, Robert D., and William R. Iseminger
1987 Testing of Mound 50 at Cahokia Mounds State Historic Site. Cahokia Mounds Museum Society, Collinsville, Illinois.

Griffin, James B.
1941 Report on pottery from the St. Louis area. The Missouri Archaeologist 7(2):1–17.
1949 The Cahokia ceramic complexes. In: Proceedings of the Fifth Plains Conference for Archaeology, edited by J. L. Champe, pp. 44–58. Lincoln: University of Nebraska.
1985 Changing concepts of the prehistoric Mississippian cultures of the eastern United States. In: Alabama and the Borderlands: From Prehistory to Statehood, edited by R. Reid Badger and L.A. Clayton, pp. 40–63. Tuscaloosa: University of Alabama Press.

Griffin, James B., and Albert C. Spaulding
1951 The Central Mississippi Valley Archaeological Survey, season 1950 – a preliminary report. Journal of the Illinois State Archaeological Society 1(3):74–81.

Gums, Bonnie L., Rodney C. DeMott, Neal H. Lopinot, George R. Holley, and Lucretia S. Kelly
1989 Archaeological Investigations for the Mississippi River Transmission Corporation Alton Line in Madison and St. Clair Counties, Illinois. Archaeology Program Research Report 3. Southern Illinois University at Edwardsville.

Hall, Robert L.
1966 Cahokia chronology. Paper presented at the Central States Anthropological Society meeting, St. Louis, Missouri.
1980 Ceramics. In: Investigations at the Labras Lake Site, Volume 1, Archaeology, by J.L. Phillips, R.L. Hall, and R.W. Yerkes, pp. 366–406. Department of Anthropology, University of Illinois at Chicago Circle, Reports of Investigations 1.

Hally, David J.
1981 Plant preservation and the content of paleobotanical samples: a case study. American Antiquity 46(4):723–42.

Harvey, Dennis E.
1977 Preliminary analysis of wood utilization at two Mississippian sites. Missouri Archaeologist 38:272–80.

Hayden, Brian, and Aubrey Cannon
1983 Where the garbage goes: refuse disposal in the Maya Highlands. Journal of Anthropological Archaeology 2:117–63.

Helms, Mary W.
1979 Ancient Panama: Chiefs in Search of Power. Austin: University of Texas Press.
1988 Ulysses' Sail: An Ethnographic Odyssey of Power, Knowledge, and Geographical Distance. Princeton, NJ: Princeton University Press.
1992 Political lords and political ideology in Southeastern chiefdoms: comments and observations. In: Lords of the Southeast: Social Inequality and the Native Elites of Southeastern North America, edited by A.W. Barker and T.R. Pauketat, pp. 185–94. American Anthropological Association, Archeological Paper 3. Washington, D.C.

Holder, Preston
1955 A disaster program for the salvage of archeological data from a mound and village complex in the heart of the Cahokia Mound group scheduled for immediate destruction in connection with highway improvement. Application to the American Philosophical Society, on file at the University of Michigan, Museum of Anthropology, Ann Arbor.
1958 Archaeological study of Kunneman Mound, central Cahokia group of Illinois, threatened by destruction. Year Book of the American Philosophical Society, 1957:384–85.
1966 Test excavations at the Kunneman Mound #11 (11 Ms 11): A brief review. Paper presented at the Central States Archaeological Society meeting, St. Louis, Missouri (read by Wike for Holder).
1968 Comment in "Brief of symposium on the 'Southern Cult'." In: The Waring Papers: The Collected Works of Antonio J. Waring, edited by S. Williams, pp. 72–77. Cambridge, Massachusetts: Peabody Museum.
1970 The Hoe and the Horse on the Plains. Lincoln: University of Nebraska Press.
1980 Write up, dictated by Holder to Wike (6/80). Manuscript on file at the University of Michigan, Museum of Anthropology, Ann Arbor.

Holder, Preston, and T.D. Stewart
1958 A complete find of filed teeth from the Cahokia Mounds in Illinois. Journal of the Washington Academy of Sciences 48(1):349–57.

Holley, George R.
1989 The Archaeology of the Cahokia Mounds ICT-II: Ceramics. Illinois Cultural Resources Study 11. Springfield: Illinois Historic Preservation Agency.
1990 Investigations at the Kunnemann Tract, Cahokia Mounds Historic Site, Madison County, Illinois. Unpublished report submitted to the Illinois Historic Preservation Agency, Springfield.

Holley, George R., Rinita A. Dalan, Neal H. Lopinot, and Philip A. Smith
1990 Investigations in the Grand Plaza, Cahokia Mounds Historic Site, St. Clair County, Illinois. Unpublished report submitted to the Illinois Historic Preservation Agency, Springfield.

Holley, George R., Neal H. Lopinot, William I. Woods, and John E. Kelly
1989 Dynamics of community organization at prehistoric Cahokia. In: Households and Communities. Proceedings of the 21st Annual Chacmool Conference, edited by S. MacEachern, D.J.W. Archer, and R.D. Garvin, pp. 339–49. University of Calgary.

Iseminger, William, Timothy R. Pauketat, Brad Koldehoff, Lucretia S. Kelly, and Leonard Blake
1990 East Palisade investigations. In: The Archaeology of the Cahokia Palisade. Illinois Cultural Resources Study 14. Springfield: Illinois Historic Preservation Agency.

Jackson, Douglas K.
1992 Oneota in the American Bottom. In: The Sponemann Site 2: The Mississippian and Oneota Occupations, by D.K. Jackson, A.C. Fortier, and J.A. Williams, pp. 383–91. American Bottom Archaeology, FAI-270 Site Reports 24. Urbana: University of Illinois Press.

Jackson, Douglas K., and Ned H. Hanenberger
1990 Selected Early Mississippian Household Sites in the American Bottom. American Bottom Archaeology, FAI-270 Site Reports 22. Urbana: University of Illinois Press.

Jensen, Harold P., Jr.
1963 Lithic analysis I. In: Second Annual Report: American Bottoms Archaeology, July 1, 1962–June 30, 1963, pp. 11–12. Urbana: Illinois Archaeological Survey.

Johannessen, Sissel
1984a Paleoethnobotany. In: American Bottom Archaeology, edited by C.J. Bareis and J.W. Porter, pp. 197–214. Urbana: University of Illinois Press.
1984b Plant remains from the Julien site. In: The Julien Site, by G.R. Milner, pp. 244–73. Urbana: University of Illinois Press.

Jones, J.K., and E.C. Birney
1988 Handbook of Mammals of the North Central States. Minneapolis: University of Minnesota Press.

Kelly, Arthur R.
1933 Some problems of recent Cahokia archaeology. Transactions of the Illinois State Academy of Science 25(4):101–3.

Kelly, John E.
1980 Formative Developments at Cahokia and the Adjacent American Bottom: A Merrell Tract Perspective. Unpublished Ph.D. dissertation, Department of Anthropology, University of Wisconsin at Madison.
1984 Late Bluff chert utilization on the Merrell Tract, Cahokia. In: Prehistoric Chert Exploitation: Studies from the Midcontinent, edited by B.M. Butler and E.E. May, pp. 23–44. Center for Archaeological Investigations, Occasional Paper 2. Carbondale.
1990a The emergence of Mississippian culture in the American Bottom region. In: The Mississippian Emergence, edited by B. Smith, pp. 113–52. Washington, D.C.: Smithsonian Institution Press.
1990b The realm of public architecture at Cahokia. Paper presented at the 47th Annual Meeting of the Southeastern Archaeological Conference, Mobile, Alabama.
1991a Cahokia and its role as a gateway center in interregional exchange. In: Cahokia and the Hinterlands: Middle Mississippian Cultures of the Midwest, edited by T.E. Emerson and R.B. Lewis, pp. 61–80. Urbana: University of Illinois Press.
1991b The evidence for prehistoric exchange and its implications for the development of Cahokia. In: New Perspectives on Cahokia: Views from the Periphery, edited by J.B. Stoltman, pp. 65–92. Madison, WI: Prehistory Press.
n.d. Archaeological investigations of the East St. Louis mound center: past and present. Draft manuscript on file, Contract Archaeology Program, Southern Illinois University at Edwardsville.

Kelly, John E., Steven J. Ozuk, Douglas K. Jackson, Dale L. McElrath, Fred A. Finney, and Duane Esarey
1984 Emergent Mississippian period. In: American Bottom Archaeology, edited by C.J. Bareis and J.W. Porter, pp. 128–57. Urbana: University of Illinois Press.

Kelly, John E., Andrew C. Fortier, Steven J. Ozuk, and Joyce A. Williams
1987 The Range Site: Archaic through Late Woodland Occupations. American Bottom Archaeology, FAI-270 Site Reports 16. Urbana: University of Illinois Press.

Kelly, John E., Steven J. Ozuk, and Joyce Williams
1990 The Range Site 2: The Emergent Mississippian Dohack and Range Phase Occupations. American Bottom Archaeology, FAI-270 Site Reports 20. Urbana: University of Illinois Press.

Kelly, Lucretia S.
1979 Animal Resource Exploitation by Early Cahokia Populations on the Merrell Tract. Illinois Archaeological Survey Circular 4. Urbana.
1990 Faunal remains. In: The Archaeology of the Cahokia Palisade: The East Palisade Investigations, by W.R. Iseminger et al., pp. 109–34. Illinois Cultural Resources Study No. 14. Springfield: Illinois Historic Preservation Agency.
1991 Zooarchaeological remains. In: The Archaeology of the Cahokia Mounds ICT-II: Biological Remains, Part II. Illinois Cultural Resources Study 13. Springfield: Illinois Historic Preservation Agency.

Kelly, Lucretia S., and Paula G. Cross
1984 Zooarchaeology. In: American Bottom Archaeology, edited by C.J. Bareis and J.W. Porter, pp. 197–214. Urbana: University of Illinois Press.

Kent, Susan
1984 Analyzing Activity Areas: An Ethnoarchaeological Study of the Use of Space. Albuquerque: University of New Mexico Press.

Kertzer, David I.
1988 Ritual, Politics and Power. New Haven: Yale University Press.

Knight, Vernon James, Jr.
1986 The institutional organization of Mississippian religion. American Antiquity 51:675–87.
1989 Symbolism of Mississippian mounds. In: Powhatan's Mantle: Indians in the Colonial Southeast, edited by P. H. Wood, G.A. Waselkov, and M.T. Hatley, pp. 279–91. Lincoln: University of Nebraska Press.

Koldehoff, Brad
1987 The Cahokia flake tool industry: socioeconomic implications for late prehistory in the central Mississippi valley. In: The Organization of Core Technology, edited by J. Johnson and C. Morrow, pp. 151–86. Boulder, CO: Westview Press.
1990a Household Specialization: The Organization of Mississippian Chipped-Stone-Tool Production. Unpublished M.A. thesis, Department of Anthropology, Southern Illinois University, Carbondale.
1990b Lithics. In: The Archaeology of the Cahokia Palisade: The East Palisade Investigations, by W.R. Iseminger et al. pp. 77–108. Illinois Cultural Resources Study 14. Springfield: Illinois Historic Preservation Agency.

Larson, Lewis H., Jr.
1971 Archaeological implications of social stratification at the Etowah site, Georgia. In: Approaches to the Social Dimensions of Mortuary Practices, edited by J.A. Brown. Memoirs of the Society for American Archaeology 25:52–67.

Leighton, Morris M.
1923 The geological aspects of some of the Cahokia (Illinois) Mounds. In: The Cahokia Mounds, by W.K. Moorehead. University of Illinois, Bulletin 21(6):57–97. Urbana.
1929 The geological aspects of some of the Cahokia (Illinois) Mounds. In: The Cahokia Mounds, by W.K. Moorehead, University of Illinois, Bulletin 26(4):107–43. Urbana.

Le Page Du Pratz, M.
1963 The History of Louisiana, or of the Western Parts of Virginia and Carolina (2 Vols.). T. Becket and P.A. DeHondt.

Lewis, Thomas M. N., and Madeline Kneberg
1946 Hiwassee Island: An Archaeological Account of Four Tennessee Indian Peoples. Knoxville: University of Tennessee Press.

Lincecum, Gideon
1904 Choctaw traditions about their settlement in Mississippi and the origin of their mounds. Publications of the Mississippi Historical Society 8:521–42.

Lopinot, Neal H.
1988 Archaeobotany, environmental degradation, and the collapse of Cahokia. Paper presented at the 53rd Annual Meeting of the Society for American Archaeology, Phoenix.

Lopinot, Neal H., Lucretia S. Kelly, George R. Milner and Richard Paine
1991 The Archaeology of the Cahokia Mounds ICT-II: Biological Remains. Illinois Cultural Resources Study 13. Springfield: Illinois Historic Preservation Agency.

Lorant, Stefan
1946 The New World: The First Pictures of America. New York: Duell, Sloan, and Pearce.

Lyman, R.L.
1985 Bone frequencies: differential transport, *in situ* destruction and the MGUI. Journal of Archaeological Science 12(3): 221–36.

Martin, Alexander C., and William D. Barkley
1961 Seed Identification Manual. Berkeley: University of California Press.

Mason, Ronald J., and Gregory Perino
1961 Microblades at Cahokia, Illinois. American Antiquity 26:553–57.

McElrath, Dale L., and Fred A. Finney
1987 The George Reeves Site. American Bottom Archaeology, FAI-270 Site Reports 15. Urbana: University of Illinois Press.

McElrath, Dale L., Thomas O. Maher, and Michael C. Meinkoth
1987 Emergent Mississippian and Mississippian Communities at the Radic Site. American Bottom Archaeology, FAI-270 Site Reports 17, Part 1. Urbana: University of Illinois Press.

Mehrer, Mark W.
1982 A Mississippian Community at the Range Site (11-S-47), St. Clair County, Illinois. M.A. Thesis, Department of Anthropology, University of Illinois, Urbana.
1988 The Settlement Patterns and Social Power of Cahokia's Hinterland Households. Unpublished Ph.D. dissertation, Department of Anthropology, University of Illinois, Urbana.

Mehrer, Mark W., and James M. Collins
1989 Household archaeology at Cahokia and its hinterlands. Paper presented in the symposium "Households and Settlements in the Mississippian Period" at the 54th annual meeting of the SAA, Atlanta, Georgia.

Metcalfe, D., and K.T. Jones
1988 A reconsideration of animal body-part utility indices. American Antiquity 53(3): 486–504.

Milner, George R.
1983a The East St. Louis Stone Quarry Site Cemetery. American Bottom Archaeology, FAI-270 Site Reports 1. Urbana: University of Illinois Press.
1983b The Turner and DeMange Sites. American Bottom Archaeology, FAI-270 Site Reports 4. Urbana: University of Illinois Press.
1984a The Julien Site. American Bottom Archaeology, FAI-270 Site Reports 7. Urbana: University of Illinois Press.
1984b The Robinsons Lake Site. American Bottom Archaeology, FAI-270 Site Reports 10. Urbana: University of Illinois Press.
1984c Social and temporal implications of variation among American Bottom Mississippian cemeteries. American Antiquity 49:468–88.
1986 Mississippian period population density in a segment of the central Mississippi valley. American Antiquity 51:227–38.
1990 The late prehistoric Cahokia cultural system of the Mississippi River valley: foundations, florescence, and fragmentation. Journal of World Prehistory 4 (1):1–43.

Milner, George R., Thomas E. Emerson, Mark W. Mehrer, Joyce A. Williams, and Duane Esarey
1984 Mississippian and Oneota period. In: American Bottom Archaeology, edited by C.J. Bareis and J.W. Porter, pp. 158–86. Urbana: University of Illinois Press.

Milner, George R., and Richard Paine
1991 Human skeletal remains. In: The Archaeology of the Cahokia Mounds ICT-II: Biological Remains, by N.H. Lopinot, L.S. Kelly, G.R. Milner, and R. Paine, Part III. Illinois Cultural Resources Study 13. Springfield: Illinois Historic Preservation Agency.

Moorehead, Warren K.
1922 The Cahokia Mounds: A Preliminary Paper. Urbana: University of Illinois.
1923 The Cahokia Mounds. University of Illinois, Bulletin 21(6). Urbana.
1929 The Cahokia Mounds. University of Illinois, Bulletin 26(4). Urbana.

Morris, Percy A.
1951 A Field Guide to the Shells of Our Atlantic and Gulf Coasts. Boston: Houghton Mifflin.

Morse, Dan F.
1974 The Cahokia microlith industry. Newsletter of Lithic Technology 3:15–19.

Muller, Jon
1984 Mississippian specialization and salt. American Antiquity 49:489–507.
1986 Pans and a grain of salt: Mississippian specialization revisited. American Antiquity 51:405–9.
1987 Salt, chert, and shell: Mississippian exchange and economy. In: Specialization, Exchange, and Complex Societies, edited by E. Brumfiel and T. Earle, pp. 10–21. Cambridge: Cambridge University Press.

Neitzel, Robert S.
1965 Archaeology of the Fatherland Site: The Grand Village of the Natchez. American Museum of Natural History, Anthropological Papers 51 (part 1).

O'Brien, Patricia J.
1972 A Formal Analysis of Cahokia Ceramics From the Powell Tract. Illinois Archaeological Survey, Monograph 3. Urbana.
1977 Some ceramic periods and their implications at Cahokia. In: Explorations into Cahokia Archaeology (second revised edition), edited by M.L. Fowler, pp. 100–120. Illinois Archaeological Survey, Bulletin 7. Urbana.

Parmalee, Paul W.
1957 Vertebrate remains from the Cahokia site, Illinois. Transactions of the Illinois Academy of Science 50: 235–42.
1975 A general survey of the vertebrate fauna from Cahokia. In: Perspectives in Cahokia Archaeology. Illinois Archaeological Survey, Bulletin 10: 137–55.

Pauketat, Timothy R.
1984 Notes on some non-local ceramics from an American Bottom collection. Illinois Antiquity 16 (1):4–6. Newsletter of the Illinois Association for Advancement of Archaeology.
1987a A burned domestic dwelling at Cahokia. Wisconsin Archeologist 68(3):212–37.
1987b A functional consideration of a Mississippian domestic vessel assemblage. Southeastern Archaeology 6:1–15.
1987c Mississippian domestic economy and formation processes: a response to Prentice. Midcontinental Journal of Archaeology 12(1):77–88.
1989 Monitoring Mississippian homestead occupation span and economy using ceramic refuse. American Antiquity 54:288–310.
1990 Ceramics. The Archaeology of the Cahokia Palisade: The East Palisade Investigations, by W.R. Iseminger et al. Illinois Cultural Resources Study 14. Springfield: Illinois Historic Preservation Agency.
1991 The Dynamics of Pre-State Political Centralization in the North American Midcontinent. Ph.D. dissertation, Department of Anthropology, University of Michigan, Ann Arbor.

1992 The reign and ruin of the lords of Cahokia: a dialectic of dominance. In: Lords of the Southeast: Social Inequality and the Native Elites of Southeastern North America, edited by A.W. Barker and T.R. Pauketat, pp. 31–52. American Anthropological Association, Archeological Papers 3. Washington, D.C.
n.d. The archaeology of Downtown Cahokia: The Tract 15A and Dunham Tract Excavations. Ms. in preparation.

Pauketat, Timothy R., and Thomas E. Emerson
1991 The ideology of authority and the power of the pot. American Anthropologist 93: 919–41.

Pauketat, Timothy R., and William I. Woods
1986 Middle Mississippian structure analysis: the Lawrence Primas site (11-Ms-895) in the American Bottom. Wisconsin Archeologist 67(2):104–27.

Perino, Gregory
1947 Cahokia notes. Journal of the Illinois State Archaeological Society 5(2):57–60.
1960 The micro-drill industry at Cahokia. Central States Archaeological Journal 7:116–20.
1971a The Mississippian component at the Schild site (No. 4), Greene County, Illinois. In: Mississippian Site Archaeology in Illinois: I. Illinois Archaeological Survey, Bulletin 8. Urbana.
1971b Sandstone reamers. Central States Archaeological Journal 18:108–10.
1980 Cahokia notes. In: Cahokia Brought to Life, edited by R.E. Grimm, pp. 61–67. St. Louis: The Greater St. Louis Archaeological Society.

Perry, Louise M., and Jeanne S. Schwengel
1955 Marine Shells of the Western Coast of Florida. Ithaca, NY: Paleontological Research Institution.

Pool, Kelly J.
1989 A History of Amateur Archaeology in the St. Louis Area. The Missouri Archaeologist, 50 (published in 1992).

Porter, James W.
1974 Cahokia Archaeology as Viewed from the Mitchell Site: A Satellite Community at A.D. 1150–1200. Ph.D. Dissertation, Department of Anthropology, University of Wisconsin at Madison. Ann Arbor: University Microfilms.
1977 The Mitchell site and prehistoric exchange systems at Cahokia: A.D. 1000±300. In: Explorations into Cahokia Archaeology (second revised edition), edited by M. Fowler, pp. 137–64. Illinois Archaeological Survey, Bulletin 7. Urbana.

Prentice, Guy
1983 Cottage industries: concepts and implications. Midcontinental Journal of Archaeology 8:17–48.
1985 Economic differentiation among Mississippian farmsteads. Midcontinental Journal of Archaeology 10:77–122.
1987 Marine shells as wealth items in Mississippian societies. Midcontinental Journal of Archaeology 12:193–223.

Prentice, Guy, and Mark Mehrer
1981 The Lab Woofie site (11-S-346): an unplowed Mississippian site in the American Bottom region of Illinois. Midcontinental Journal of Archaeology 6:33–53.

Quimby, George I., Jr.
1957 The Bayou Goula site, Iberville Parish, Louisiana. Fieldiana 47(2). Chicago Museum of Natural History Museum.

Record, Samuel J.
1934 Identification of the Timbers of Temperate North America. New York: John Wiley and Sons.

Reed, Nelson A.
1977 Monks and other Mississippian mounds. In: Explorations in Cahokia Archaeology (second revised edition), edited by M.L. Fowler, pp. 31–42. Illinois Archaeological Survey, Bulletin 7. Urbana.

Reed, Nelson A., James W. Bennett, and James W. Porter
1968 Solid core drilling of Monks Mound: technique and findings. American Antiquity 33:137–48.

Riley, Thomas J., and Karl Lorenz
1989 Stringers and thatch: analysis of the structural members of a lower Mississippian building from the Big Black River, Holmes County, Mississippi. Paper presented at the Southeastern Archaeological Conference, Tampa.

Rogers, J. Daniel, Don G. Wyckoff, and Dennis A. Peterson (editors)
1989 Contributions to Spiro Archaeology: Mound Excavation and Regional Perspectives. Oklahoma Archeological Survey, Studies in Oklahoma's Past, 16. Norman.

Rudolph, James L.
1984 Earthlodges and platform mounds: changing public architecture in the Southeastern United States. Southeastern Archaeology 3:33–45.

Schiffer, Michael B.
1976 Behavioral Archaeology. New York: Academic Press.

Schnell, Frank T., Vernon J. Knight, Jr., and Gail S. Schnell
1981 Cemochechobee: Archaeology of a Mississippian Ceremonial Center on the Chattahoochee River. Gainesville: University of Florida Press.

Shepard, Anna O.
1980 Ceramics for the Archaeologist (Reprint). Washington, D.C.: Carnegie Institution of Washington.

Smith, Bruce D.
1975 Middle Mississippi Exploitation of Animal Populations. Museum of Anthropology, University of Michigan, Anthropological Papers 57. Ann Arbor.
1978 Prehistoric Patterns of Human Behavior: A Case Study in the Mississippi Valley. New York: Academic Press.
1986 The archaeology of the Southeastern United States: from Dalton to de Soto, 10,500–500 B.P. In: Advances in World Archaeology, edited by F. Wendorf and A.E. Close, pp. 1–92. New York: Academic Press.
1992 Mississippian elites and solar alignments: a reflection of managerial necessity, or levers of social inequality? In: Lords of the Southeast: Social Inequality and the Native Elites of Southeastern North America, edited by A.W. Barker and T.R. Pauketat, pp. 11–30. American Anthropological Association, Archeological Paper 3. Washington, D.C.

Smith, Harriet M.
1942 Excavation of the Murdock Mound of the Cahokia group. Journal of the Illinois State Archaeological Society, May:13–18.
1977 The Murdock Mound: Cahokia site. In: Explorations into Cahokia Archaeology (second revised edition), edited by M.L. Fowler, pp. 49–88. Illinois Archaeological Survey, Bulletin 7. Urbana.

Smith, P.W.
1979 The Fishes of Illinois. Urbana: University of Illinois Press.

Snyder, John Francis
1909 Prehistoric Illinois: Certain Indian Mounds Technically Considered; Part Three: Temple or Domiciliary Mounds. Journal of the Illinois State Historical Society 2(2):71–92.

Stahl, Ann B.
1985 The Dohack Site. American Bottom Archaeology, FAI-270 Site Reports 12. Urbana: University of Illinois Press.

Steponaitis, Vincas P.
1986 Prehistoric archaeology in the southeastern United States, 1970–1985. Annual Review of Anthropology 15:363–404.

Swanton, John R.
1911 Indian Tribes of the Lower Mississippi Valley and Adjacent Coast of the Gulf of Mexico. Bureau of American Ethnology, Bulletin 43. Washington, D.C.
1979 The Indians of the Southeastern United States. Washington, D.C.: Smithsonian Institution Press. Originally published in 1946 as BAE Bulletin 137.

Tarr, John, S.
1955 The Archaeological Importance of the Cahokia Mounds and Village Sites. Unpublished M.A. thesis, Department of Sociology and Anthropology, Washington University, St. Louis.

Taylor, Walter W.
1968 A Study of Archeology. Carbondale: Southern Illinois University Press.

Titterington, Paul F.
1938 The Cahokia Mound Group and Its Village Site Materials. St. Louis: Privately published.

University of Michigan Museum of Anthropology (UMMA)
1953 The Dreckshage Site, St. Charles County, Missouri. Unpublished ms. on file at the Museum of Anthropology. Author unknown.

Vander Leest, Barbara J.
1980 The Ramey Field, Cahokia Surface Collection: A Functional Analysis of Spatial Structure. Unpublished Ph.D. dissertation, Department of Anthropology, University of Wisconsin at Milwaukee.

Varner, John G., and Jeannette J. Varner
1988 The Florida of the Inca. Austin: University of Texas Press.

Vincent, Joan
1990 Anthropology and Politics: Visions, Traditions, Trends. Tucson: The University of Arizona Press.

Vogel, Joseph O.
1975 Trends in Cahokia ceramics: preliminary study of the collections from Tracts 15A and 15B. In: Perspectives in Cahokia Archaeology, pp. 32–125. Illinois Archaeological Survey, Bulletin 10. Urbana.

Wagner, Gail E.
1987 Uses of Plants by the Fort Ancient Indians. Unpublished Ph.D. dissertation, Washington University, St. Louis.

Wagner, Robert W.
1957 An Analysis of the Material Culture of the James Ramey Mound. Unpublished M.A. thesis, University of Illinois, Urbana.

Waring, Antonio J., Jr.
1968 The Southern Cult and Muskhogean ceremonial. In: The Waring Papers: The Collected Works of Antonio J. Waring, Jr., edited by S. Williams, pp. 30–69. Papers of the Peabody Museum of Archaeology and Ethnology 58. Harvard University.

Waring, Antonio J., Jr., and Preston Holder
1945 A prehistoric ceremonial complex in the southeastern United States. American Anthropologist 47(1):1–34.

Webb, William S., and David L. DeJarnette
1942 An Archaeological Survey of Pickwick Basin in the Adjacent Portions of the States of Alabama, Mississippi, and Tennessee. Bureau of American Ethnology, Bulletin 129. Washington, D.C.

Welch, Paul D.
1991 Moundville's Economy. Tuscaloosa: University of Alabama Press.

Wesler, Kit W.
1986 Salt-boiling and the Wickliffe funnel in West Africa. Paper presented at the annual meeting of the Southeastern Archaeological Conference, Nashville, Tennessee.

Williams, Kenneth
1975 Preliminary summation of excavations at the east lobes of Monks Mound. In: Cahokia Archaeology: Field Reports, edited by M.L. Fowler, pp. 21–24. Illinois State Museum, Papers in Anthropology 3. Springfield.

Williams, Stephen (editor)
1968 The Waring Papers: The Collected Works of Antonio J. Waring, Jr. Papers of the Peabody Museum of Archaeology and Ethnology 58. Harvard University.

Williams, Stephen, and Jeffrey P. Brain
1983 Excavations at the Lake George Site, Yazoo County, Mississippi, 1958–1960. Papers of the Peabody Museum of Archaeology and Ethnology 74. Harvard University.

Willoughby, Charles C.
1932 Notes on the history and symbolism of the Muskhogeans and the people of Etowah. In: Etowah Papers, by W.K. Moorehead, pp. 7–67. New Haven: Yale University Press.

Winston, Jon H.
1963 Lithic analysis II. In: Second Annual Report: American Bottoms Archaeology, July 1, 1962–June 30, 1963, pp. 12–13. Illinois Archaeological Survey. Urbana.

Winters, Howard D., and Stuart Streuver
1962 The Emerald Mound group and village. Living Museum 23(11):86–87.

Wittry, Warren L.
1977 The American woodhenge. In: Explorations into Cahokia Archaeology (second revised edition), edited by M. Fowler, pp. 43–48. Illinois Archaeological Survey, Bulletin 7. Urbana.

Woods, William I., and George R. Holley
1989 Current research at the Cahokia site (1984–1989). In: A Cahokia Atlas: A Historical Atlas of Cahokia Archaeology, by M.L. Fowler, Appendix 5. Studies in Illinois Archaeology 6. Springfield: Illinois Historic Preservation Agency.

Wright, Henry T.
1984 Prestate political formations. In: On the Evolution of Complex Societies: Essays in Honor of Harry Hoijer 1982, edited by T.K. Earle, pp. 41–77. Malibu: Undena Publications.

Yerkes, Richard W.
1983 Microwear, microdrills, and Mississippian craft specialization. American Antiquity 48:499–518.
1986 Licks, pans, and chiefs: a comment on "Mississippian Specialization and Salt." American Antiquity 48:499–518.
1987 Prehistoric Life on the Mississippian Floodplain: Stone Tool

Use, Settlement Organization and Subsistence Practices at the Labras Lake Site, Illinois. University of Chicago Press.

1989 Mississippian craft specialization on the American Bottom. Southeastern Archaeology 8:93–106.

1991 Specialization in shell artifact production at Cahokia. In: New Perspectives on Cahokia: Views from the Periphery, edited by J.B. Stoltman, pp. 49–64. Madison, WI: Prehistory Press.

APPENDIX I
FEATURE INVENTORY

FEATURE	AREA	DESCRIPTION
1	BP	postmolds(?) at A0 B22 (3 by 6 meters) and 14-18 cm deep
2	BP	?
3	BP	sandy basin fill and floor directly above and sometimes including F5
4	BP	a sandy floor of submound structure
5	BP	floor, roof and wall fall, burned debris of submound structure
6	BP	"Clay trench of some sort, seemingly having no significance" (?)
7	BP	interior hearth associated with F3-5, cleaned and repuddled three times
8	BP	small pit associated with F3-5, charcoal inside, no artifacts
9-10	BP	north and west wall trenches of the F72 structure
11	BP	eastern-most wall trench of the submound F3-5 structure
12	BP	two superimposed hearths at F73 level, el. 101 m a.d.
13	BP	hearth associated with F72 structure, el. 101 m a.d.; lip overlaps F72 clay plate; two sequential stages: upper stage has sand, white ash, and hardened base layers (8 cm deep) and lower stage has white ash, red sand, and gray clay base layers (25 cm deep)
14	BP	hearth, el. 100.85 m a.d.
15	BP	hearth, el. 101 m a.d., orange sand fill, puddled bottom
16	BP	hearth, el. 101.2 m a.d.
17	MP/BP	thick sandy basket-loaded mound fill (with some gumbo mottles) consisting of horizontal and slightly dipping zones and wash laminations
18	MP	cap/occupation surface ("with gumbo buckshot") over lower mound fill at 102.6-102.7 m a.d.; no match in BP area
19-20	MP	basket-loaded zones within lower mound fill below F18
21	MP	pit?/mound fill zone; white sand
22-23	MP	dark brown "greasy" fill zone/prepared floors with charcoal flecks
24	MP	dark brown "greasy" prepared surface/early mound fill
25	MP	black and yellow basket-loaded gumbo mound ("clay base") laminated horizontally into at least 3 layers, distinguished by consistency, the middle being crumblier and yellower
26	MP	dark brown stain--"occupation zone"; no notes, uncertain characteristics (probably=F40)
27	MP	dark brown basket-loaded sand
28	MP	brown sand fill with gumbo "clots" within lower mound fill
29	MP	fill zone within lower mound fill; upper zone of pit F21?
30	MP	fill zones within lower mound fill
31	MP	gumbo-clay mound fill at top of Mound 11
32	MP	a series of 5 or more sand and clay varves atop F34 mound
33	MP	sand and clay cap/occupation surface to F34 mound top
34	MP	sandy mound fill between F31 and F35
35	MP	cap/occupation surface above F17 (4 thin cap zones alternating with laminated wash zones immediately below F35)
36	MP/BP	wall trench associated with F35, visible in profile
37	MP	fill zone above F29 in lower mound fill

38-39	unassigned?	-
40	BP, EA1	pre-mound occupation zone (midden?)
41	EA1	homogeneous light brown sand mound fill above F40; charcoal, artifacts
42	EA1	humus/dark brown sand with charcoal above F41-prepared surface/floor
43	EA1	light brown sand occupation surface above F42-prepared surface/floor
44	EA1	thin, light brown clayey sand fill/occupation(?) zone above F43
45	EA1	wall trench(?) possibly same as F48 (not illustrated)
46	EA1	post pit in F40; dark brown sand fill with sherds, shell, and charcoal flecks
47	EA1	burned basin/surface sand lens in F40 about 8 cm thick
48	EA1	large, complex wall trench(?) including sandy fill with gumbo inclusions
49	EA1	thin sand lens occupation/wash surface(?) atop F51 mound; no humus
50	EA1	ill-defined gumbo fill zone above F53 below F49
51	EA1	occupation surface/mound fill below F49; mottled fill with charcoal and gumbo buckshot
52	EA1	mound fill/wash/humus lens within and/or above F53
53	EA1	light brown sand mound fill/wash immediately above F40(?)
54	EA1	wall trenches below F51 and on F41/42/43 mound
55	EA1	"dark, heavy cultural layer"(?) above F53 without wash or basket-loaded appearance
56	EA1	thin yellowish sand fill zone; occupation/structure surface (not illustrated)
57	EA1	thin clay zone below F56; occupation/structure surface (not illustrated)
58	EA1	pit on F41 mound and superimposed by F59; dark sand fill with flecks of charcoal
59	EA1	two wall trenches on F41 mound filled with "buckshotted gray sand" and containing sherds and shell within fill
60	EA1	post pit with multiple zones
61	EA1	lens associated with occupation surface above F41 and F48
62-63	EA1	one pit(?) partially exposed in plan and profile in EA1, Trench 1
64	EA1	fill lens/fired area/wall trench below F61 and above F48
65	EA1	postmold of F60 post pit, measures about 60 cm in diameter
66	EA1	undefined feature
67-69	unassigned?	undefined features in EA1?
70	BP	south wall trench to F72 structure; brown sandy clay fill
71	BP	circular burned area on F72 structure floor
72	BP	clay to sandy clay cap/structure floor over pre-mound surface
73	BP	four or more prepared clayey surfaces to mound fill F75
74	BP	prepared surfaces over mound fill F79
75	BP	mound fill over F72, basket-loaded brown sand
76	BP	water-laid zone derived from F73 on flank of F75 mound
77	BP	white, basket-loaded sand fill linking north and south F75 mound terraces
78	BP	south mound fill
79	BP	mound fill over F73, grey sand with clay mottles
80	BP	sandy fill underlaid by wash; probably post-dates F79, capped by F74 (not illustrated)
81	BP	mound fill, basket-loaded sand, over F74 and F79
82	BP	dipping clay zone north of and slightly above F74 thought to be collapsed wall of rotunda (not labeled on figures)
83	BP	submound pit/fill zone containing human remains
84	BP	wall trenches, 10-12 cm wide, related to F74 surface and superimposes rotunda
85	BP	hearth in F72 structure; puddled inner walls are black, thin, and delicate (š1 mm thick)
86	BP	pit/midden below F72 consisting of alternating layers of carbonized material and yellow sand; burning was intense near the center "pile" of fill and debris
87	BP	basket-loaded mound fill over F74 and F81
88	BP	burned area on F74 black clay surface (uncertain location, not illustrated)
89	BP	submound amorphous pit containing "conc. of broken conch shell", charcoal, tiny bones, deer bone, chert and pottery; lumps of gray clay included in fill
90	BP	two connected 12 cm-diameter postmolds in center of F72 structure floor

91	BP	red-plastered structure floor below F73, el. 100.95 m a.d.
92	BP	wall trenches associated with F73A
93	BP	"floor" lens or prepared surface(?) on summit of a F81 mound(?)
94	BP	wall trench post-dating F74; filled with F81 fill
95	BP	north wall trench of structure on F78 south mound (F73 surface)
96	BP	west wall trench of structure on F78 south mound (F73 surface)
97	BP	hearth associated with F73C at A6 B24.5; 11 cm deep including top to bottom 3 cm sand mound fill, 3 cm yellowish sandy clay (F73D?), 1 cm charcoal, 3 cm white ash, and 1 cm charcoal
98	BP	intermediate mound fill between F87 terraces or longitudinal profile of wall trench(?)
99	BP	modern(?) disturbance superimposed upon F87 fill (seen in profile)
100	BP	modern disturbance(?) in F87 fill, mottled brown sand fill with chunks of dark "daub"--no basket loading visible
101	BP	modern disturbance in F87 fill
102	BP	red-plastered area of F74 surface
103	BP	hearth on F74 surface--structure F84
104	BP	wide NW-SE trench, sandy fill on F78 surface (post pit ramp?)
105	BP	north wall trench of structure on F131 mound, brown-yellow clay mottled with gumbo
106-107	BP	wall trench pair, east-west orientation, partially excavated, el. of top is 100.40 m a.d., associated with south mound(?) or below the mound
108	BP	rectangular pit in sub-F78 superimposed by F95
109	BP	early south mound fill; brown-yellow clay with gumbo mottles
110	BP	hearth on F74 rotunda black clay near red-plastered area
111	BP	pit(?), 35 cm dia., on F74
112-113	BP	E-W wall trenches associated with F74
114	BP	mound fill over F74 edge, under F87; capped by blue clay
115	BP	laminated surface wash above F73 level
116	BP	hearth in F74 rotunda
117	BP	hearth in F74 rotunda
118	BP	hearth in F74 rotunda
119	BP	east wall trench under and associated with F73C
120	BP	east wall trench under and associated with F73C
121	BP	wall trench in F73C
122	BP	wall trench under 73C
123	BP	hearth under 73A and associated with F92 structure
123A	BP	earlier version of F123, 10 cm deep consisting of clear sand sealing about 3 cm of grey grainy ash with some charcoal
124	BP	ill-defined wall trench in profile at A9 B20
125	BP	east wall trench of F72 structure
126	BP	wall trench associated with F73
127	BP	small pit or postmold(?) at A5 B23.5 on submound surface
128	BP	burned lens/pit(?) under F78, associated with F40 at A3 B35
129	BP	mound fill or floor(?) associated with/above structure, superimposed over F114
130	BP	mound fill, basket-loads of black clay in tan sand matrix, below F114 and above F115
131	BP	mottled grey sand fill flanking south toe of F79-131; may include the unidentified wall trench around F74 circular structure
132	BP	mound fill related to F130, light brown sand with some mottling
133	BP	mound fill below F78, light grey sand with clay mottles (see F109)
134	BP	east wall trench of structure on F133 mound, north wall trench is F105
135	BP	hearth on south mound superimposed by F104 trench, el. 100.35 m a.d.
136	BP	postmold or pit, 44 cm dia., 50 cm deep, in F40 related to F70(?)
137	BP	pit?, partially exposed, on F78 mound; light grey mottled sand fill
138	BP	wall trench associated with F95 "first seen" at A5.2 B35.2

Appendix II
Ceramic Jar Attributes

Area	Fea.	Vessel#	Temper	Ext	Int	Orif.Dia.	% Orif.	Wt(g)	Soot/Wear*	Comments
BE	-	1	SH	PL	PL	40±6	4±2	36.5	-	IRREGULAR ORIFICE
BE	-	2	SH	PL	PL	18	9.5	9.6	-	SLIGHT LIP LUG?
BE	-	3	GG	PL	PL	18	9	18.5	SOOT INT & EXT	-
BE	-	4	SH	PL?	PL	42±4	3	18.5	-	SLIPPED LIP
BP	3	1	SH	S	E	14	5	2.4	-	-
BP	3	2	SH	PS	S	16	5	3.4	-	-
BP	3	3	SH	PL	PL	26	6	14.9	-	-
BP	3	4	SH	S	PL	25±5	3±1	2.4	-	-
BP	3	5	SH	S	PL	20±2	5	5	-	-
BP	3	6	SH	S	PL	-	<5	4.6	-	-
BP	3	7	SH	S	PL	30	6.5	24.3	-	RAMEY
BP	3	18	SH	PL	RS	14	8	10	-	-
BP	3	19	SH	PS	PL	16	5	4.8	-	RAMEY: WEEPING EYE; ELEV. OF FIND=100M
BP	3	20	SH	PL	PL	18	10	25	-	ELEVATION OF FIND=100M
BP	4	1	SH	PL	RS	14	8	14.7	-	-
BP	4	2	SH	RS	RS	-	<5	11.4	-	-
BP	4	3	SH	E	RS	-	<5	3.8	-	-
BP	4	4	SH	S	S	-	<5	4.6	-	-
BP	4	5	SH	PS	PL	14	22.5	58.4	*	BI-KNOBBED LOOP HANDLE
BP	5	1	SH	S	PL	4	30	22.5	SOOT, SPALLS*	MINI-JAR
BP	5	2	SH	PL	PL	15±1	4.5	1.5	-	-
BP	5	3	SH	PS	PL	-	<5	6.3	*	-
BP	5	4	SH	PS	PS	10±2	5	2.8	-	-
BP	5	5	SH	PS	PL	12±2	5	3.1	-	-
BP	5	6	SH	RS	RS	-	<5	24	-	-
BP	5	7	SH	PL	PL	34	12	93.4	-	RS LIP, ALSO FROM F3
BP	5	8	SH	S	PL	32	5.5	36.6	-	-
BP	5	9	SH	PL	PL	8	7	8	*	MINI-JAR
BP	5	10	SH	S	PL	-	<5	11.2	-	-
BP	5	11	SH	PL	PL	36	6	43.5	-	-
BP	5	12	SH	PL	PL	19±1	5	8.3	-	-
BP	5	13	SH	PS	PL	36	15	90.7	-	F3 ALSO
BP	5	25	SH	S?	PL	21	40?	889.8	*	SQUARISH ORIFICE WITH TABS AT CORNERS; 16 BODIES
BP	9	1	SH	S?	PL	18	3.5	2.6	-	-
BP	40	2	SH	PL	RS	28	5	30.9	SOOT	-
BP	40	3	SH	PL	PL	30	6	35.1	SOOT UNDER LIP	RS LIP
BP	40	5	SH	PS	PL	-	<5	18.8	-	-
BP	40	6	SH	E	E	-	<5	9.3	-	RS LIP
BP	40	7	SH	S	PL	-	<5	14.3	-	-
BP	40	8	SH	S	PL	24	5	9.6	-	-
BP	40	9	SH	PL?	RS	35±1	5	23.3	SOOT UNDER LIP	-
BP	40	10	SH	S	PL	-	<5	13.4	-	-
BP	40	13	SH	PL	PL	26	10	58.3	SOOTY LIP, EXT	RS LIP
BP	73	1	SH	E	E	-	<5	10.6	-	-
BP	73	2	SH	S?	PL	-	<5	3.6	-	-
BP	73	3	SH	PL	RS	20	5	4.5	-	RS LIP
BP	73	4	SH	PL	PL	36	4	31.7	-	ZONE=73A
BP	73	5	SH	S?	PL	11	6	4.8	-	ZONE=73A
BP	73	6	SH	S	PL	-	<5	11.8	-	
BP	73	7	GT	S	PL	10	9	4.7	SOOT	-
BP	73	8	SH	PL?	PL	42	6	84.1	SOOT UNDER LIP	EXT SLIP SOOTED OVER/BURNED OFF?
BP	73	9	SH	PL	PL	-	<5	5.7	-	-
BP	73	10	SH	S	S	-	<5	2.4	-	-
BP	73	11	SH	PL	PL	44	4	8.3	SOOT	ALSO FROM F74
BP	73/74	12	SH	RS	RS	-	<5	16.4	*	LOOP HANDLE, ALSO F74
BP	75	1	SH	PL	RS	28	6	20.6	-	-
BP	75	2	SH	PL	PL	30±2	4.5	19	-	SLIPPED LIP
BP	75	3	SH	PL	PL	10	6.5	21.8	SOOT, SPALLS	-
BP	75	4	SH	S	PL	24	6.5	15.2	-	-
BP	75	5	SH	PL	RS	>30	<5	20.4	-	-
BP	75	6	SH	RS	RS	-	<5	2.5	-	-
BP	75	7	SH	PS	PL	10	11	11.5	*	RS LIP
BP	75	8	SH	PL	RS	18	9	12.7	-	ORIFICE MEASUREMENT FROM NECK
BP	75	9	SH	PS	PL	20	7	22.4	-	RS LIP
BP	75	10	SH	PL	PL	14	10	14.2	*	-
BP	75	11	SH	PS	PS	-	<5	3.6	-	RAMEY?: POSSIBLE TRAILED LINE EXT
BP	75	12	SH	PL	RS	32	5	28.3	-	RS LIP
BP	75	13	SH	PS	P	16	5	3.8	-	-
BP	75	14	SH	PL	PL	-	<5	12.2	SOOT	-
BP	75	15	SH	PL	RS	24	8	35.4	-	-
BP	77	1	SH	S	PL	38	4	20.9	-	-
BP	77	2	SH	S	PL	12	9	3.5	-	-
BP	78	1	SH	PL	PL	-	<5	8.4	SOOT	RS LIP
BP	78	2	SH	S	PL	-	*	11.9	SOOT	BI-KNOBBED LOOP HANDLE DISTORTS ORIFICE
BP	78	3	SH	S	PL	18	4	16.5	-	RAMEY: SCROLL AND LINES?
BP	78	4	SH	PL	PL	26	4.5	28.9	-	SLIPPED LIP
BP	78	5	SH	S	PL	28	10	66	SOOT, SPALLS	-

BP	78	6	SH	PL	PL	18±2	4	5.1	-	-
BP	78	7	SH	RS	PL	20	4.5	10	SPALLED EXT	-
BP	79	1	SH	S	PL	-	<5	7	-	RS LIP
BP	79	2	SH	PL	RS	26	6.5	15.3	-	-
BP	79	3	SH	PL	PL	>30?	*	50.4	-	*IRREGULAR ORIFICE
BP	79	4	SH	PL?	PL	16	7	5.7	-	SLIPPED LIP
BP	79	5	SH	PL	PL	-	<5	4.7	-	-
BP	79	6	SH	RS	PL	42±2	3	36.4	-	-
BP	79	7	SH	PL	PL	16	10	26.7	-	-
BP	81	1	SH	PL	PL	30±4	5	21.2	-	-
BP	86	1	SH	PL?	S	14	8	6.2	-	-
BP	86	2	SH	S?	S?	-	<5	2	-	-
BP	86	3	SH	PL	PL	>30	<5	13.6	-	-
BP	87	1	SH	PL?	PL?	34	4	42.3	-	-
BP	87	2	SH	PL	PL	18	5	5.6	SOOT	-
BP	87	3	SH	S	S	32	4	13.4	SOOT	LIP DAMAGED
BP	87	4	SH	S	S	44±4	3	33.4	-	-
BP	87	5	SH	PL	RS	31±1	4.5	17.6	-	-
BP	87	6	SH	PL	PL	-	<5	9.4	-	RS LIP
BP	87	7	SH	PL	RS	-	<5	8.9	-	-
BP	87	8	SH	S	PL	-	<5	13	-	-
BP	87	9	SH	PS	PL	18±2	4	4.5	-	-
BP	87	10	SH	S	PL	28	5.5	22.6	-	RAMEY
BP	87	11	SH	PL	PL	38	4	10.2	-	RS LIP
BP	87	12	SH	PL	RS	-	*	4.2	SOOT	*LIP DAMAGED
BP	87	13	SH	PS	PL	28±2	5	17.2	-	-
BP	87	14	SH	S	PL	20	6	13	-	RAMEY: LADDER
BP	87	15	SH	P (S?)	PL	-	<5	7.2	-	RAMEY
BP	87	16	SH	PL	PL	16±2	10	28.7	SOOT*	LOOP HANDLE
BP	87	17	SH	PS	PL	24	10	39	*	RAMEY: SCROLL
BP	89	1	SH	S	S	50±4	5	85.8	-	-
BP	89	2	SH	PL	PL	38±4	4	12.8	SOOT	S LIP, EXT SLIP COULD BE SOOTED OVER OR BURNED OFF
BP	89	3	SH	PS	PS	24	12	15.8	*	RAMEY: SCROLL, THIN (2.8MM) BODY SHERDS PROBABLY FROM THIS POT
BP	89	4	SH	E	E	-	<5	8.3	-	RS LIP
BP	89	5	SH	PL?	PL	-	<5	12.8	SOOT & SPALLS	RS LIP
BP	89	6	SH	S	PL	38	8	91.9	-	-
BP	89	7	SH	S	PL	26±2	5	9	SOOT	-
BP	89	8	GG-SH	S	PL?	16±2	4	1	-	-
BP	89	9	SH	S	PL	8±2	6	1.7	-	MINI-JAR
BP	89	10	SH	S	?	>40	<5	27.4	-	-
BP	89	11	SH	PL	PL	8	7	2	-	MINI-JAR
BP	89	12	SH	E	PS	-	<5	10.3	-	-
BP	89	13	SH	PS	S	16	7	5.2	-	RAMEY, RS LIP
BP	89	14	SH	PS	PL	20	10	14.9	-	-
BP	89	15	SH	PS	PL	18	15	36.4	*	-
BP	89	16	SH	PL	PL	-	<15*	8.2	*	*LOOP HANDLE DISTORTS ORIFICE
BP	89	17	SH	PS	PL	-	*	78.4	*	*BI-KNOBBED LOOP HANDLE DISTORTS ORIFICE
BP	89	18	SH	PS	PL	-	<5	18.5	-	-
BP	89	19	SH	PS	PL	20	16	55.4	*	-
BP	89	20	SH	PS	P	16	13	37.9	*	RAMEY: ARCHES
BP	89	21	SH	PS	PL	22	10	21.2	-	-
BP	89	22	SH	PS	PS	-	<5	7.6	-	RAMEY
BP	89	23	SH	S	PL	38	6	169.8	SOOT, SPALLS*	-
BP	95	1	SH	PL	PL	-	*	5.3	-	*DAMAGED LIP
BP	100	1	SH	E	E	-	<5	9.7	-	SLIPPED LIP?
BP	133	1	SH	S	PL	14	7	18.2	-	-
BP	-	1	SH	S	S?	34	5	8.3	-	-
EA1	40	1	SH	S	E	20	10	6	-	-
EA1	40	14	SH	PL	PL	26	10	32.5	SOOTY LIP, EXT	RS LIP
EA1	41	1	GG-SH	S?	PL	18	5	5.1	-	-
EA1	41	2	SH	S	PL	-	<5	4.3	-	-
EA1	41	3	SH	E	RS	-	*	9.7	-	*ERODED
EA1	41	4	SH	PL	PL	-	<5	3.6	-	RS LIP
EA1	41	5	SH	PL	PL	45±5	3.5	27.1	-	RS LIP
EA1	46	1	SH	S	PL	28	7	80.3	*	-
EA1	48	1	SH	PL	PL	-	<5	4.6	-	-
EA1	48	2	SH	S	PL	16	5	1.5	-	-
EA1	48	3	SH	PL	PL	-	<5	3.3	-	ERODED
EA1	48	4	SH	PL	S	26	7	20.4	-	-
EA1	48	5	SH	PL	PL	-	<5	13.2	-	-
EA1	48	6	SH	PS	PL	26	6	16.7	-	RAMEY: SCROLL/LINE, TRAILED LIP
EA1	48	7	SH	PS	PL	-	<5	3.4	-	RAMEY: LADDER
EA1	48	8	SH	PS	P	-	<5	2.7	*	-
EA1	48	9	SH	PS	PL	22	33	148.7	*	RAMEY: SCROLL, TRAILED LIP
EA1	48	10	SH	PS	PS	26	19	216.2	*	RAMEY: SCROLL
EA1	50	1	SH	PS	PL	-	<5	6.4	-	-
EA1	58	1	SH	S	PL	16	5.5	7.6	-	-
EA1	60	1	SH	S	PL	-	<5	3.2	-	-
EA1	-	1	SH	E	RS	-	<5	5.3	-	PROBABLY FROM F49 OR F51
EA1	-	2	SH	PL	PL	28±2	8	24	*	FROM TRENCH 2
EA1	-	3	SH	PS	PL	14	10	24.8	-	FROM TRENCH 2
EA1	-	4	SH	PS	PL	36	10	91.7	-	-
EA2	-	1	SH	PL	PL	-	<5	8.8	-	SLIPPED LIP
EA2	-	2	SH	PL	PL	22	10	86	-	2 RIMS, 2 VESSELS?; LOOP HANDLE
MP1	-	1	SH	E	RS	-	<5	15	-	-
TOTAL	-	-	-	-	-	-	-	4458.8	-	-

NOTE: ASTERISK IN SOOT/WEAR COLUMN DENOTES THAT VESSEL SHOULDER IS REPRESENTED

Appendix III
Ceramic Beaker and Bowl Attributes

Area	Fea.	Vessel	Vessel Form	Temper	Ext.	Int.	Orif. Dia.	% Orifice	Wt.(g)	Comments
BE	-	5	BEAKER	GG	PBRS	PBRS	10	11	16.1	ENGRAVED AND EXCISED LINES/BANDS EXT, FINE TEMPER
BE	-	6	BOWL?	SH	PS	PL	-	<5?	5.3	*RECTANGULAR ORIFICE?
BP	3	8	BOWL	SH	PS	PS	34	52	373.1	LARGE VESSEL SECTION ON STRUCTURE FLOOR
BP	3	9	BOWL-BEAKER	SH	S	S	12	14	11.3	OUTSLANTED RIM
BP	3	10	C-BOWL	SH	PL	PL	20	10	38.3	POLISHED EXT, INCURVED CONSTRICTED RIM
BP	3	11	BOWL	SH	S	S	-	<5	4.3	-
BP	3	12	PAN	SH	PL	RS	42	5	37	-
BP	3	13	BOWL	SH	PS	PS	22	7.5	25.6	TRAILED CIRCUMFERENTIAL LINES EXT
BP	3	16	BOWL	SH	PS	PS	-	<5	8.6	TRAILED CIRCUMFERENTIAL LINES, DRILLED HOLE
BP	3	17	BOWL	SH	PS	PS	38±6	3±1	13.3	-
BP	3	21	MINI-BOWL	SH	PL	PL	5	20	16	-
BP	5	14	C-BOWL	SH	PL	PL	18	8	9.4	INCURVED CONSTRICTED RIM
BP	5	15	PAN	SH	PL	RS	-	<5	37.5	SOOTY EXT, SAME VESSEL AS PAN IN FEATURE 3?
BP	5	16	BOWL	SH	PS	PS?	-	<5	6.3	-
BP	5	17	BEAKER	SH	S	S	14	4.5	6.6	TRAILED CIRCUMFERENTIAL LINES EXT, THICKENED LIP
BP	5	18	BOWL-BEAKER	SH	PS	PS	14	5	6.8	OUTSLANTED WALLS
BP	5	19	BOWL	SH	PS	PS	22±2	4.5	7.1	-
BP	40	16	BOWL-BEAKER	GG	BRS	BRS	14	7	4.9	OUTSLANTED RIM, FINE TEMPER, FINE ENGRAVED CIRCUMFERENTIAL LINES
BP	40	17	C-BOWL	SH	S	S	20	5	6.2	INCURVED CONSTRICTED RIM
BP	72	1	BOWL-BEAKER	GG -SH?	PBRS	PBRS	12	7.5	18.1	OUTSLANTED RIM, 15 SHERDS, FINE INCISED CIRCUMFERENTIAL LINES
BP	72	2	BEAKER	SH	PS	PS	10	4	2.8	INSLANTED RIM, FINE TEMPER
BP	72	3	BOWL	SH	RS	RS	-	<5	3.5	-
BP	73	13	MINI-BOWL	SH	PL	PL	6	50	8.3	PINCH POT
BP	73	14	BOWL-BEAKER	SH	PS	PS	-	<5	3	-
BP	73	15	BOWL	SH	RS	RS	-	<5	6	-
BP	74	1	BOWL	SH	PL	PL	8	9	2.8	MINI-BOWL
BP	75	16	BEAKER	SH	PS	PS	10	17	31.8	LIP TAB
BP	75	17	BEAKER	SH	P (S?		8	8	2.7	PERHAPS A BOTTLE RIM?
BP	75	18	BOWL	SH	PS	S	16	17	30	BROKEN AND REWORKED TAB HANDLE SCAR
BP	78	8	BEAKER	GG-SH	PBRS	BRS	-	<5	13	INCURVED RIM, TRAILED/INCISED EXT; ANOTHER EXCISED SHERD FROM SAME POT?
BP	78	9	BOWL	SH	PS	PS	20	5.5	8.1	-
BP	78/133	2	PAN	SH	PL	PL	47±3	4.5±.5	56.2	-
BP	79	8	BOWL	SH	RS	RS	26	5	19.1	LIP LUG/TAB
BP	79	9	BOWL-BEAKER	SH	PS	PS	-	<5	3.4	-
BP	83	1	BEAKER	SH	PS	PS	10	13	5.2	INCISED CIRCUMFERENTIAL LINES
BP	86	4	BOWL-BEAKER	GG	PBRS	PBRS	14	11	4.3	OUTSLANTED RIM, POLISHED CIRCUMFERENTIAL LINE(S)
BP	86	5	BOWL	SH	PRS	PRS	-	*	9.6	*RECTANGULAR ORIFICE?, INCISED INT & LIP, INCISED AND EXCISED EXT
BP	87	18	BEAKER	SH	PS	PS	12	8	6.1	-
BP	87	19	BOWL-BEAKER	GG -SH?	RS	RS	-	<5	4.7	OUTSLANTED RIM, INCISED CIRCUMFERENTIAL LINES
BP	87	20	PAN	SH	PL	RS	58±2	3.5	112.9	-
BP	87	21	BOWL	SH	S	S	-	<5	11.6	-
BP	87	22	C-BOWL	LS	RS	RS	34±2	3	10.8	CONSTRICTED ORIFICE
BP	89	24	BOWL-BEAKER	GG -SH?	PS	PS	-	<5	7.5	OUTSLANTED RIM
BP	89	25	BEAKER	SH	PS	PS	10	9	3.5	-
BP	89	26	BOWL	SH	RS	RS	35±5	≤5	18.2	DISTINCTIVE THICKENED BEVELED LIP, SAME VESSEL APPEARS REPRESENTED IN EU1 FEA. 66 (!)
BP	89	27	DOWL	SH	S	S	-	IRREG*	5.2	ORIFICE IRREGULAR: RIM SPOUT OR INDENTATION
BP	89	28	C-BOWL	SH	RS	RS	10	6	2.4	INCURVED CONSTRICTED RIM
BP	89	29	BOWL-BEAKER	SH	PS	PS	-	<5	8.8	OUTSLANTED LIP
BP	89	30	BOWL	SH	PRS	P*	8	10	4.5	*UNSLIPPED, LIP LUG
BP	89	31	BOWL	SH	PS	PS	-	<5	10.8	-
BP	93	1	PAN	SH	PL	RS	≥50	≤3	30	-
BP	-	2	BEAKER	SH	PS	PS	12	11	7.4	-
EA1	40	18	BOWL-BEAKER	SH	PS	PS	14	10	9.8	-
EA1	41	6	BOWL-BEAKER	SH	PS	PS	16	5	5.7	OUTSLANTED RIM
EA1	46	2	BOWL*	SH	PS	PL	7	11	5.3	*CONSTRICTED RIM, COMPLEX SHAPE
EA1	48	11	BOWL	SH	S	S	16	11	27.3	-
EA1	48	12	BOWL	LS	RS	RS	-	<5	8.8	"MONKS MOUND RED"
EA1	48	13	BOWL	SH	S	S	-	<5	3.2	-
EA1	48	19	BOWL	SH	S	S	20	5	6.5	-
EA1	48	20	BOWL	SH	PS	PS	24	4	2.8	FINE TEMPER
EA1	60	2	BOWL	SH	S	S	-	<5	3.5	-
EA1	63	1	BOWL	SH	PS	PS	16	7	9.2	LIP TAB
EA1	-	5	BEAKER	SH	PS	PS	16	4	3.6	FINE TEMPER
EA1	-	6	BEAKER	GG-SH	PBRS	BRS	12	7	6.8	FINE INCISED CIRCUMFERENTIAL LINES, FINE TEMPER
EA3	-	1	BEAKER	GG	BRS	BRS	14	6	2.7	EXCISED CIRCUMFERENTIAL BANDS, FINE TEMPER
TOTAL	-	-	-	-	-	-		-	1201.2	

Appendix IV
Other Ceramic Vessel Attributes

Area	Fea.	Vessel	Temper	Ext	Int	Orif.Dia.	% Orif.	Wt(g)	Comments
SEED JARS									
BP	5	20	GG-SH	P (S?)	P	12±2	5?	4.8	-
BP	5	21	SH	RS	PL	9±1	6	3.1	-
BP	7	1	SH	RS	PL	22	6	19.9	-
BP	40	4	SH	RS	RS	-	<5	9.6	3 ROWS PUNCTATES, LARGER DESIGN?
BP	40	23	SH	RS	PL	16±2	5	4.3	REED-LIKE PUNCTATES
BP	40	24	SH	RS	RS	16	10	26.6	-
BP	77	3	SH	S	PL	7	15	22	-
BP	79	10	SH	S	PL	-	<5	14.5	-
BP	79	11	SH	RS	PL	-	<5	5.6	-
BP	87	23	LS	RS	PL	12	8	15.8	-
BP	87	24	SH	RS	RS	14	6	3	-
EA1	40	21	LS	RS	-	-	<2	1.1	-
EA1	40	22	SH	S	PL	9	10	5.4	-
EA1	48	14	LS	RS	PL	-	<5	8.9	-
EA1	48	15	SH	RS	PL	-	<5	15	-
MP1	-	2	SH	S	PL	-	<5	9.3	-
TOTAL		-	-	-	-	-	-	168.9	-
JUGS									
BP	3	14	SH	PS	S	>20	<5	8.3	POSSIBLY A BOWL
BP	4	6	SH	RS	PL	10	8	10.2	-
BP	4	7	SH	PL	PL	8	13	3.5	FLARED RIM
BP	5	22	SH	S	PL	12	6.5	3.3	-
BP	5	23	SH	S	PL	10	18	27.6	-
BP	73	16	SH	RS	PL	16	6.5	6	-
BP	75	19	SH	RS	PL	10	9	11.3	-
BP	75	20	SH	RS	PL	8	10	4	-
BP	86	6	SH	RS	PL	10	8	9.1	-
BP	86	7	SH	RS	RS	18	10	17.7	2 RIMS
BP	87	25	SH	RS	PL	18	6	13.9	DAMAGED LIP
BP	87	26	SH	RS	PL	16	10	35.1	% ORIFICE IS TAKEN FROM NECK
BP	89	32	SH	RS	PL	10	10	33.6	-
BP	89	33	SH	PS	PL	8	15	16.3	-
BP	89	34	SH	P (S?)	PL	10	30	61.4	-
EA1	40	11	SH	PS	PL	14±2	5	5	-
EA1	40	12	SH	S	PL	20±2	4.5	14.3	-
EA1	40	15	SH	RS	E	10	11	8.3	FLARED WITH A ROLLED LIP
EA1	46	2	SH	RS	PL?	16	4.5	2.4	POSSIBLY A BOWL? UPPER INT. RIM RS
TOTAL		-	-	-	-	-	-	291.3	-
FUNNELS									
BP	3	15	SH	PL	PL	12	10	22	-
BP	5	24	GG-SH	PL	PL	10	12	27.1	-
BP*	83	-	SH	PL	PL	-	*	18.1	*BASAL SHERD, VERTICAL INCISED EXT.
BP	87	27	GG	PL	PL	16	7.5	29.1	-
BP	89	35	GG-SH	PL	PL	15±1	6	29.4	WHITE RESIDUE ON EXTERIOR
EA1	48	17	SH	PL	PL	-	<5	15.5	-
EA1	48	18	SH	PL	PL	22	40	736.7	2 RIMS, 1 BASAL FRAG, RED "WASH" EXT.
EA1	60	3	SH	PL	PL	10	12	21.1	VERTICAL INCISED LINES EXT.
STUMPWARE									
EA1	41	7	GG	CM	PL	10	50	290.9	Z-TWIST CM
EA1	48	16	GG	CM	MISSING	-	FRAG.	17.3	NO INT. LIP SURFACE PRESENT
TOTAL		-	-	-	-	-	-	1207.2	-

Appendix V
Vessel Body Sherds

Feature	N	Wt. (g)	Notes
SHELL-TEMPERED BODY SHERDS			
3	12	84	Find 1
3	8	17	Find 3
3	5	20	Find 4
3	237	1882	
3, 4	60	605	Find 10
3, 5	9	27	
4	82	631	Find 15
4	1	2	Find 22
4	1	2	Find 24
4	53	459	
5	16	67	Find 20
5	1	7	Find 25
5	248	2368	
9	41	356	
17	2	19	MP1
17	13	175	lower levels MP2
17	24	301	upper levels MP2
17	38	378	
17, 34-36	4	51	
21, 29-30	13	76	
26?	1	5	
26	1	2	
31-34	2	3	
40	265	2387	
41	122	610	
44	20	86	
46	72	352	
46?	1	16	Find 41?
48	40	165	Find 46
48	702	5687	
50	9	14	
51	1	9	
58	8	48	
59	23	45	
60	2	8	
64	1	6	
66	50	131	
70	14	111	
72	28	92	
73A	37	208	
73	67	575	
73/74	16	197	
74	22	48	Find 35
74	16	73	
75	293	2208	
77	9	79	
78/133	1	16	
78	129	948	
79	138	1069	
80	7	41	
81	41	308	
81/87	7	27	
83	24	369	
83/84	20	79	
85	47	250	
86	210	1281	
87	240	2429	
89	430	2744	
91	1	5	
92	2	15	
94	2	36	
95	3	18	
100	1	2	
101	14	88	
103	2	6	
104	7	93	
108	10	56	
109	2	15	
114	30	264	
114/115	5	38	
118	2	18	
133	11	74	
BE	83	1231	
BP	2	23	A2 B37 postmold
BP	14	92	C1 B20 pre-mound
BP	1	3	sub-109
BP	10	61	sub-72
EA1	1	7	gumbo
EA1	1	4	T2
EA3	2	2	T1
EA3	14	44	T1, Sq.A "floor"
EA3	2	5	T1, Sq.B
EA3	7	55	T1, Sq.C
EA3	18	116	T2
EA3	1	4	T2, Sq.B
EA3	19	103	T2, Sq.C
-	9	51	pot hole trench
-	2	14	cat. no. 55248, 55254
TOTAL	4262	32791	

Feature	N	Wt. (g)	Notes
NON-SHELL TEMPERED BODY SHERDS			
3	3	5	gg; at least 1 funnel sherd
3	1	6	gg
40	1	6	fine gg-sh temper
40	1	5	limestone temper; slip ext
48	3	5	gg stumpware
73/74	1	4	gg
78	1	27	gg
87	1	3	fine gg
87	2	10	limestone temper; rs int/ext
95	1	2	fine gg
EA1, T3	1	10	gg, cm Woodland sherd
TOTAL	16	82	

Appendix VI
Decorated Vessel Body Sherds and Miscellaneous Ceramic Artifacts

Area	Fea.	Vessel Form	Temper	Ext	Int	Wt(g)	Comments
*	-	BEAKER	SH	PS	PS	15.1	*FROM TOP OF MOUND; INCISED LINES EXTERIOR, DIA. OF WALL=14CM (10%)
BE	-	JAR	SH	P	PL	8.8	ENGRAVED "RAMEY"-LIKE DESIGN; SMOOTHED UNSLIPPED EXTERIOR
BP	3	-	SH	S	PL	12.8	SHERD WITH GROUND REWORKED EDGES
BP	3	BEAKER	SH	PS	-	33.4	ELONGATE HANDLE
BP	3	JAR	GT-LS	CM	PL	12.8	HAVANA MIDDLE WOODLAND SHERD WITH NODES
BP	3	JAR	SH	PS	PL	2.6	RAMEY INCISED FRAG.
BP	3	JAR	SH	S	PL	1.4	RAMEY INCISED FRAG.
BP	3	JAR	SH	S	PL	4.2	RAMEY INCISED FRAG.
BP	3	-	SH	-	-	10.3	BODY SHERD WITH GROUND REWORKED EDGE
BP	3	-	SH	-	-	22.2	BODY SHERD WITH APPARENT "SAWED" EDGE
BP	4	BEAKER-BOWL	SH	P (S?)	P (S?)	6.2	HIGHLY POLISHED SURFACES, ENGRAVED LINES AND DOTS EXTERIOR
BP	5	SHERD DISK	SH	S	PL	5.6	DRILLED
BP	5	-	SH	-	-	1.8	SHERD WITH GROUND REWORKED EDGE
BP	5	?	SH	PS	PL	1.8	CURVED RIM SHERD
BP	5	?	SH	PS	PS	5.4	REWORKED SHERD EDGE?
BP	5	BEAKER	GG-SH	BRS	-	2	FRAG. OF TRIANGULOIDAL HANDLE
BP	5	BOWL	SH	PS	PS	3.4	BODY SHERD WITH TRAILED LINES
BP	5	BOWL	SH	PS	PS	0.7	BODY SHERD WITH A TRAILED LINE
BP	9	BOWL	SH	PS	PS	1.6	SHERD WITH 3 TRAILED LINES
BP	40	-	SH	S	-	6.6	FIRED COIL OR LOOP HANDLE FRAG.?
BP	40	-	SH	PS	PL	6.8	BODY SHERD WITH EXTERIOR ENGRAVED/SCRATCHED LINES
BP	40	BEAKER?	GG -SH?	BRS	BRS	1.2	FINE GG, ≥4 FINE INCISED LINES EXTERIOR
BP	40	BOWL	GG -SH?	PS	PL	18.3	FINE GG, CONSTRICTED NECK=15CM DIA. (13%)
BP	40	BOWL	SG	PS	-	4.9	TAB HANDLE (EFFIGY TAIL?)
BP	40	JAR	SH	PL	-	10	LOOP HANDLE
BP	72	BEAKER	SH	BRS	BRS	0.7	SHERD WITH ≥3 FINE INCISED LINES, FINE TEMPER
BP	73	?	SH	S	PL	1.6	JAR? SHERD WITH EXTERIOR INCISED LINE
BP	73/74	-	SH	S?	S	20.3	SHERD WITH 3 IRREGULAR TRAILED LINES (MADE WHEN PASTE STILL WET)
BP	75	?	SH	S	RS	8.5	SHERD WITH ≥3 TRAILED LINES
BP	75	JAR	SH	CM	PL	4	PERFORATED RIM
BP	75	JAR	SH	S	S	3	SHOULDER SHERD WITH EXTERIOR DOTS; 4.8MM THICK
BP	75	JAR	LS	PL	-	15	LOOP HANDLE
BP	77	JAR	GT	PL	PL	2.1	RIM WITH EXTERIOR CORDWRAPPED DOWEL IMPRESSIONS ON LIP
BP	77	JAR	SH	S	PL	8	RAMEY INCISED BODY SHERD
BP	78	JAR	SH	S	-	10.2	FRAG. OF BI-KNOBBED LOOP HANDLE
BP	79	JAR	SH	S	PL	6.2	RAMEY INCISED BODY WITH 3 TRAILED LINES
BP	81	BEAKER?	SH	PS	PRS	3.7	EXCISED AND ENGRAVED EXTERIOR
BP	83	JAR	SH	S	E	4.9	RAMEY INCISED SHERD
BP	83	JAR	SH	S	PL	0.9	RAMEY INCISED SHOULDER OF SMALL JAR
BP	84	BEAKER	SH	PS	-	38.5	TRIANGULOIDAL HANDLE
BP	86	-	SH	S	PL	53.9	SHERD WITH TWO REWORKED SMOOTHED EDGES
BP	86	BEAKER	SH	RS	RS	4.2	RED-BROWN SLIP, FINE SHELL, ≥3 FINE CIRCUMFERENTIAL INCISED LINES
BP	86	JAR	SH	PS	PL	17.5	RAMEY INCISED SHOULDER
BP	87	?	SH	RS	RS	3.7	ENGRAVED CURVILINEAR LINES EXTERIOR
BP	87	?	SH	BRS	BRS	2.2	EXCISED AND ENGRAVED LINES EXTERIOR, FINE TEMPER
BP	87	BEAKER	SH	PS	-	21.4	TRIANGULOIDAL/U-SHAPED X-SECTION HANDLE
BP	87	JAR	SH	P (S?)	PL	5	"RAMEY" IMITATION, INCISED MOTIF WHEN PASTE WET
BP	87	JAR	SH	S	PL	11.9	3 PARALLEL UNUSUAL TRAILED OR "BROAD SCRATCHED" LINES
BP	87	JAR	SH	PS	PL	3.7	RAMEY INCISED BODY SHERD
BP	89	-	SH	S	PL	43.8	LINEAR EXTERIOR CARBONACEOUS? STAINS AS IF WRAPPED IN TWINE
BP	89	-	SH	S	PL	1.9	"DOTS" DRILLED THRU SLIP POST-FIRING, 2 PERFORATIONS
BP	89	BEAKER	SH	S	-	13.5	TRIANGULOIDAL HANDLE, U-SHAPED X-SECTION, FRAG.
BP	89	BEAKER/BOWL	SH	PS	-	5.6	TAB HANDLE
BP	89	CERAMIC DISK	SH	-	-	3	UNPERFORATED, FRAGMENTARY
BP	89	JAR	SH	PS	E	5	FRAG. OF RAMEY INCISED WEEPING EYE WITH GROUND EDGES
BP	89	JAR	SH	PS	PL	5.3	RAMEY INCISED FRAG.
BP	89	JAR	SH	S	-	4.9	LOOP HANDLE FRAG.
BP	-	BEAKER-BOWL	SH (GG?)	PRS	PRS	39.9	ENGRAVED LINES/EXCISED BANDS & TRIANGLES EXT.; DIA. OF BASE=14CM (17%)
EA1	41	SHERD DISK	SH	S	PL	16	DRILLED CERAMIC DISK FRAG.
EA1	48	-	GG-SH	RS	?	44	CRUD WARE FRAG., LARGE CIRCULAR APPENDAGE SCAR
EA1	48	?	SH	RS	PL	6.1	BOWL OR JAR? WITH 3 CIRCUMFERENTIAL ENGRAVED LINES, UNMODIFIED, ROUNDED LIP
EA1	48	JAR	SH	S	PL	1	RAMEY INCISED BODY SHERD
EA1	48	JAR	SH	S	PL	3.7	RAMEY INCISED BODY SHERD
EA1	48	JAR	SH	S	PL	0.8	RAMEY INCISED BODY SHERD
EA1	66	-	SH	PL	-	52	2 FRAGS. OF POTTERY TROWEL
EA1	66	BEAKER?	GG	BRS	BRS	2.7	FINE GG WARE, EXCISED AND INCISED EXTERIOR
EA1	✓	JAR	SH	PS	PL	7.3	✓PROVENIENCE=SUB-GUMBO; RAMEY INCISED BODY SHERD
TOTAL	-	-	-	-	-	707.5	-